COOLIE WOMAN

GAIUTRA BAHADUR

Coolie Woman

The Odyssey of Indenture

THE UNIVERSITY OF CHICAGO PRESS | *Chicago and London*

GAIUTRA BAHADUR is a journalist and book critic whose work has appeared in the *New York Times Book Review*, the *Washington Post*, *Ms.*, and the *Nation*, among other publications.

The University of Chicago Press, Chicago 60637
Published by arrangement with C. Hurst & Co. (Publishers) London
© 2014 by Gaiutra Bahadur
All rights reserved. Published 2014.
Printed in the United States of America

23 22 21 20 19 18 17 16 15 14   1 2 3 4 5

ISBN-13: 978-0-226-03442-3 (CLOTH)
ISBN-13: 978-0-226-04338-8 (E-BOOK)
DOI: 10.7208/chicago/9780226043388.001.0001

LIBRARY OF CONGRESS CATALOGING-IN-PUBLICATION DATA
Bahadur, Gaiutra, 1975– author.
  Coolie woman : the odyssey of indenture / Gaiutra Bahadur.
    pages cm
  "Published by arrangement with C. Hurst & Co. (Publishers) London"—Title page verso.
  Includes bibliographical references.
  ISBN 978-0-226-03442-3 (cloth : alkaline paper) — ISBN 978-0-226-04338-8 (e-book) 1. Indentured servants—
Guyana—History—20th century. 2. Women slaves—Guyana—History—20th century. 3. Women, East
Indian—Guyana—Social conditions—20th century. I. Title.
  HD4875.G95B34 2014
  331.4'117—dc23
                                   2013008860

♾ This paper meets the requirements of ANSI/NISO z39.48-1992 (Permanence of Paper).

To my parents Kamla and Mahen
For their sacrifices and their support

To my sisters Kash and Reena
For indulging and understanding

And in memory of my grandfather
Harry Persaud Ramcharan (1933–2009)

CONTENTS

EPIGRAPH

Silence can be a plan
rigorously executed
the blueprint of a life
It is a presence
it has a history a form
Do not confuse it
with any kind of absence

"Cartographies of Silence,"
Adrienne Rich*

* Epigraph from *The Dream of a Common Language*, by Adrienne Rich, ©1978. Used by permission of W.W. Norton & Company, Inc.

ACKNOWLEDGEMENTS

I am grateful to my parents and my sisters first; without them, I could never have written this book. There aren't acknowledgements enough for all the supporting, listening, reading, remembering, feeding, housing and indulging that they did. I thank them for allowing me to abdicate responsibility for almost everything but this book, during four years that saw a death, a birth and the accelerated ageing of us all. I thank them for understanding when I couldn't be there.

My gratitude also to my extended family, who shared memories of Sujaria and of growing up in Cumberland Village in the decades after indenture—my grandmother Maturani Persaud in New Jersey, my great-aunt Maharanee Persaud in Toronto, my great-uncle Bishnodat Persaud in London and Sujaria's granddaughters: my aunt Somewati Persaud in New Jersey and my father's cousins Edna and Sarojini Baisakhu and Bhagmanti "Baby" Ramanan in Florida. What they remembered helped me reconstruct a life and conjure a place.

For knowing from the start the value of this project, and reminding me when needed, I am indebted to my dear friend Sujani Reddy. For their encouragement and company while I pursued a project that was lonely and difficult on many fronts, I thank old friends and many new ones made along the way: my brother-in-law Matthew Lang, Dahlia Lahmy, Guy Shoham, Allan MacWilliam, James Long, Salil Tripathi, Omar McDoom, Rachel Gisselquist, Esther Sabetpour, Ben Markovits, Natasha Warikoo, Ramesh Kumar, Niraj Warikoo, Annetta Seecharan, Rex Jackson, Vidyaratha Kissoon, Juan Carlos Rodriguez, Katherine Tai, Madhu Bora, Saurav Pathak, Jas Knight, Rachel Natelson, Adam Shatz, Manan Ahmed, Elisa Ung, Vicash Dindwall, Mukul and Seema Sukhwal and Indraneel Sur.

For giving me the confidence and funds to begin, I thank the Nieman Foundation for Journalism at Harvard University, former curator Bob Giles and all my community there, especially—for taking an active, sheltering interest in me and this project—Melanie Gosling, Holly Williams, Josh Benton, Carline Watson, Kate Galbraith and Simon and Ulrike Wilson.

Many friends and colleagues provided feedback that improved the manuscript. Especially helpful was Neel Mukherjee, whose appreciative but critical eyes proved

ACKNOWLEDGEMENTS

invaluable in paring it into a tighter, more elegant book. Many thanks also to Alissa Trotz, Sherlina Nageer, Patricia Mohammed, David Alston, Ashwini Tambe, Vidyaratha Kissoon, Natasha Warikoo, Sujani Reddy, Annetta Seecharan, Ethan MacAdam, Sean Westmoreland, Andrea Pitzer and Dan Vergano for the generous gift of their time and observations. At an all-important embryonic stage, Josh Benton, Sadanand Dhume, Amitava Kumar, Tess Taylor, Diana Finch, Adam Hochschild, Marina Budhos, Kevin Dale, Leela Jacinto and Naresh Fernandes all read the proposal and provided advice or moral support.

For vouching for my work, I am grateful to Naresh Fernandes, Amitava Kumar, Bruce Shapiro, Samuel G. Freedman, Carl Bromley, Adam Hochschild, David Dabydeen and Melissa Ludtke. For their insights and collaborative spirit, I thank Alissa Trotz and Nalini Mohabir, scholars in the best, most altruistic sense.

For their great hospitality, in providing places to stay while I researched and reported, I thank Yesu Persaud and Ayesha and Doodnauth Singh in Georgetown, my great-aunt and great-uncle Daro and Dhan Rhambarose in Cumberland, Patricia Mohammed and Rex Dixon in Trinidad, and Frank and Dolly MacWilliam in Scotland. Thanks to Auntie Babsin, my caretaker in Cumberland, who cooked and washed for me, kept me company, brought me Bottom House gossip truer than the newspapers and kept delighting me with the poetry of everyday speech. It's true what she said: "Some people does really tek yuh shadow."

Stabroek News reporter Shabna Ullah and editor Anand Persaud shared sources and knowledge. Kamal Ramkarran opened up to me his law office's rare collection of nineteenth-century *British Guiana Law Reports*. I owe endless thanks to Rex Jackson and Vidyaratha Kissoon for their remarkable kindness in chasing down stray documents in Guyana and for much else that was beyond the call of duty. Sree Sreenivasan made key connections in India. Painter Bernadette Persaud, linguist John Rickford and artists Pritha and Karna Singh, cultural custodians all, shared their families' stories. William Dalrymple and Kathy Fraser helped me navigate archives in Scotland. Brinsley Samaroo took me to tea and guided me to monographs in Trinidad. Manu Vimalassery's footnotes gave me a compass. Moses Seenarine led me to the unpublished autobiography of Alice Bhagwandai Singh.

For guiding me in my travels, I thank Highlands historian David Alston in Scotland; Merle Persaud, the managers of the Rose Hall and Enmore Sugar Estates and the Guyana Agricultural Workers Union in Guyana; and Ishwar Chandra Kumar, Lakshmi Nidhi Singh and Pranav Chaudhury in Bihar.

Visual artist Sarah Cawkwell and her husband, the writer and anti-apartheid activist Sylvester Stein, remembered what it was like to be penniless in a creative cause and cut me major breaks on rent in their London garret as a result.

For helping me to translate *Damra Phag Bahar*, the only known literary text by an indentured laborer in the Anglophone Caribbean, I am grateful to Shashwata Sinha in the US, Ashutosh Kranti in India and Visham Bhimull and Rohit Dass in Trinidad.

ACKNOWLEDGEMENTS

I would like to thank the resourceful staff of the Asian and African Studies Reading Room at the British Library, the Public Record Office at the UK National Archives, The National Archives of Scotland, the Alma Jordan Library at the University of the West Indies and the Walter Rodney Archives in Georgetown, Guyana.

I owe intellectual debts to Verene Shepherd, Patricia Mohammed, Peggy Mohan, Ramabai Espinet, Prabhu Mohapatra, Clem Seecharan and Tejaswini Niranjana, who have all excavated the story of Indian women in indenture and told it with sensitivity and intelligence, in various genres.

For affordable space in which to write, I thank The Writers Room in New York City. For recognizing the importance of telling the forgotten stories of indentured women, through financial awards that helped me complete the book, I am grateful to the Barbara Deming Memorial Fund and the New Jersey State Council on the Arts in the United States. For their steady generosity as mentors, and for the example they set as journalists, I thank Bruce Shapiro and Samuel G. Freedman. David Godwin and his assistant Charlotte Knight helped me navigate the practical and the pecuniary in the contract. Ted Genoways at *VQR* and Jonathan Shainin at India's *The Caravan* previewed *Coolie Woman* in their fine literary magazines. I thank them for providing a raft as I tried to cross what seemed, for a time, like impossibly rough seas to the dry, firm ground of print.

And last but most certainly not least, for believing in this challenging book and guiding it to the dock of publication, I am profoundly grateful to my editors: Michael Dwyer at Hurst, David Brent at the University of Chicago Press and Nandita Aggarwal at Hachette India.

LIST OF ILLUSTRATIONS

A sketch map of New Amsterdam and its outskirts, showing Rose Hall Plantation and Cumberland Village (© *The British Library Board, MOD GSGS 2545, Map Collection*).　　　　　　　　　　　　　　　　　　　　xviii

(Between pages 74–75)

1. Bahadur family in Cumberland on the day we emigrated to America, 7 November 1981 (*Author's Family Collection*).
2. Portrait of Lal Bahadur in New Amsterdam, Guyana, 1950s (*Author's Family Collection*).
3. Indian girl in Trinidad, c. 1890 (*MS AM 2211, Houghton Library, Harvard University*).
4. Postcard image of "Coolie Type, Trinidad, BWI," c. 1900 (*Michael Goldberg Collection, The Alma Jordan Library, University of the West Indies, St. Augustine, Trinidad and Tobago*).
5. Postcard image of "Coolie Types, Trinidad," c. 1900 (*Michael Goldberg Collection, The Alma Jordan Library, University of the West Indies, St. Augustine, Trinidad and Tobago*).
6. Postcard image of "Coolie Woman," c. 1900 (*Michael Goldberg Collection, The Alma Jordan Library, University of the West Indies, St. Augustine, Trinidad and Tobago*).
7. A view of the Hooghly River and Garden Reach, by James Baillie Fraser (slave-era Berbice planter), 1826 (© *The British Library Board, X644 (4), Plate 4 of Views of Calcutta, published by Smith Elder & Co., London, 1824–26, Asia, Pacific and Africa Collections*).
8. Indentured men and crew on the deck of an indenture vessel recently arrived in Georgetown, Demerara, c. 1890 (*MS AM 2211, Houghton Library, Harvard University*).
9. *The Clyde*, the ship on which Sujaria sailed from Calcutta to the Caribbean (© *The British Library Board, 8808.i.30, Basil Lubbock's Coolie Ships and Oil Sailers, General Reference Collection*).

LIST OF ILLUSTRATIONS

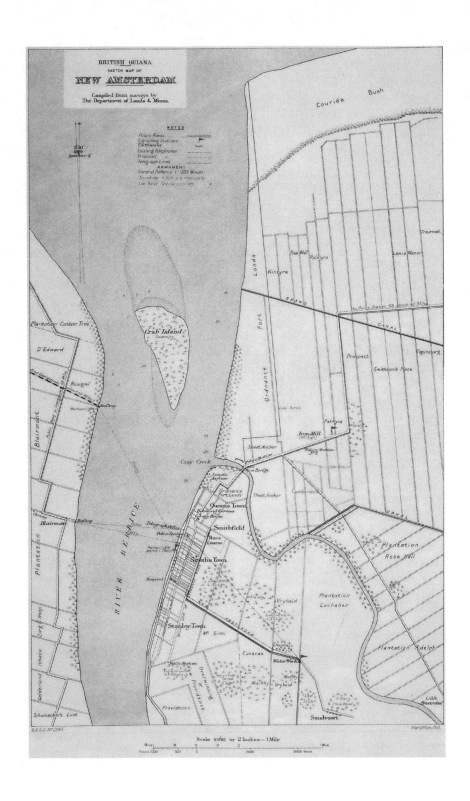

BRITISH GUIANA

SKETCH MAP OF

NEW AMSTERDAM

Compiled from surveys by
The Department of Lands & Mines.

Scale 31686 or 2 Inches = 1 Mile

PREFACE

THE C-WORD

Oh, cooly girl with eyes of wonder!
With thoughtful brow and lips compressed!
I know not where your thoughts do wander;
I know not where your heart doth rest.

Is it far away by rolling Indus?
Or down by Ganges' sacred wave?
Or where the lonesome Indian Ocean
The shores of Malabar doth lave?

Ah no! Those lands you never saw!
This Western world can claim your birth;
Your parents thence their life may draw,
Their thoughts of joy—their themes of mirth.

This land of mud has been your home.
'Twas here you drew your natal breath,
Your home of childhood—doomed to be
The land shall hold your dust at death.

Then why so foreign? Why so strange
In looks and manner, style and dress—
Religion, too, and social ways?
Thy mystery I cannot guess.

From an anonymous poem in a British Guiana newspaper, 1893[1]

I know that the title "Coolie Woman" might be offensive to some. I'd like to explain why, despite knowing this, I've chosen it. I hope this explanation will also provide some context for those who don't know why the title might cause displeasure or pain. Several dictionaries define "coolie" as "an unskilled laborer employed cheaply, especially one brought from Asia." Several also flag it as pejorative. A few go deeper, to qualify it as a term used by Europeans to describe the non-European workers they transported across the globe.

"Coolie" comes from the Tamil word *kuli*, meaning wages or hire. It was first used, beginning in the late sixteenth century, by Portuguese captains and merchants along the Coromandel Coast in India, who passed it on to the other Europeans who vied with them to control the lucrative trade with the subcontinent.[2] They all described the men who worked for them, carrying loads at the docks, as coolies. Gradually, the word took on the broader meaning of someone paid to do menial work.

When, after the enslaved were emancipated in the 1830s, the British began to rustle up replacement workers for plantations worldwide, this was the epithet they used for the indentured laborers they enlisted. Ultimately, over the course of eight decades, they ferried more than a million "coolies" to more than a dozen colonies across the globe, including British Guiana, Trinidad, Jamaica, Suriname, Mauritius and Fiji. These were the first group of Indians abroad in any significant numbers, the vanguard of a larger, broader diaspora that India presently views with pride, courts and cultivates, but who were denigrated at the time.[3] Imperial bureaucrats imposed the coolie label on a wide group of native people, from many castes and occupational backgrounds. Most indentured laborers would not have used the word to describe themselves. They registered their protest in folk songs sung for generations. One, composed in British Guiana, asks: "Why should we be called *coolies!* We who were born in the clans and families of seers and saints."[4] They felt mislabeled and degraded, unable even to name themselves.

Coming from the lips of plantation managers and overseers, the c-word stung, a reminder of lowliness in the hierarchy of a sugar estate, a hierarchy based on race. Indians were at the bottom, below the English, the Scottish and the Irish as well as the African descendants of slaves sometimes assigned as "drivers," or foremen in charge of work gangs. Each group held power over indentured laborers in the field and the factory, and each addressed their underlings as coolies. Magistrates and missionaries, while claiming there were no hierarchies in the realms of justice and the soul, also used the word. It was inescapable and it was permanent, an apparently inheritable marker of ethnicity more than a job description. Even if Indians in the West Indies became milk-sellers, or village shopkeepers, or rice farmers—or, generations later, teachers or lawyers—they were still called coolies.

The anonymous author of the 1893 ode to the "cooly girl" that opens this Preface was addressing someone born in British Guiana—someone, in other words, who had never been indentured. She tended her father's herd of cattle. In any case, it wasn't her labor that inspired the invocation "O cooly girl." It was her strange ways "in looks and manner, style and dress." It was, in the probably British poet's perception, her mystery.[5] By the time the poem was penned, the word "coolie" had evolved a new layer of meaning in the Caribbean vernacular; it signified someone exotic, someone different in his or her very essence, someone fundamentally foreign.

As tensions simmered between Africans and Indians, during the indenture era and beyond, "coolie" became an ethnic slur, a reminder to Indians of menial origins and a subtle challenge to their claim to belong. "Coolie" was so loaded a word that, in 1956, Trinidad's future prime minister urged his countrymen to banish it, along with the n-word, from their vocabularies. This was during the height of the anti-colonial struggle, and Eric Williams was calling on Trinidadians to cast off two varieties of hate inculcated by the colonizers: hate for each other and hate for themselves. Many have internalized the word "coolie" and its abject sense of self—even independence and nationhood have not completely eradicated this.

A movement to reclaim the word coolie, to invest it with pride and subvert the old stigma, is at least a generation old. Before I was born, the Guyanese poet Rajkumari Singh issued a call: "Proclaim the word! Identify with the word! Proudly say to the world: *I am a COOLIE.*" Insisting that there was no shame in origins as indentured laborers, she said:

the word must not be left to die out, buried and forgotten in the past. It must be given a new lease on life. All that they (the indentured) did and we are doing and our progeny will do, must be stamped with the name COOLIE, lest posterity accuse us of not venerating the ancestors.[6]

She conjured the image of "our great Coolie-grandmother squatting on her haunches," igniting early morning fires to cook humble peasant fare for her family as they headed into the fields. The prominent British writer David Dabydeen, born and raised in Guyana, heeded the call a decade later, with poems bearing such titles as "Coolie Odyssey" and "Coolie Mother." Meanwhile, in the mid-1990s, the Mauritian poet Khal Torabully began to formulate the principles of a movement called Coolitude, a cousin of Negritude, that aims to be the basis of pride for a broad group of people, scattered across the globe, who have roots in Indian indenture.[7]

"Coolie" may bare a jagged edge, like a broken bottle raised in threat. But it also ricochets still down dirt lanes in the Guyanese village where I was born, in far more complicated ways, in greetings that are sometimes menacing but also often affectionate and intimate, signifying a sense of shared beginnings. Much depends on who is using the word and why. I have chosen to employ it because it is true to my subject. My great-grandmother was a high-caste Hindu. That is a fact. But she left India as a "coolie." That is also a fact. She was one individual swept up in a particular mass movement of people, and the perceptions of those who controlled that process determined her identity at least as much as she did. The power of her colonizers to name and misname her formed a key part of her story. To them, she was a coolie woman, a stock character possessing stereotyped qualities, which shaped who she was by limiting who she could ever be. The word coolie, in keeping with one of its original meanings, carries this baggage of colonialism on its back. It bears the burdens of history.

PART ONE

EMBARKING

1

THE MAGICIAN'S BOX

I don't need no axe
to split/ up yu syntax

John Agard, "Listen Mr Oxford Don"*

On 7 November 1981, my family left our village, which sits along a creek surrounded by sugar cane, which grows in grids cut by canals, which criss-cross the
coastline, which sinks below sea level in a wet and muddy corner of South America.
In the picture we took to mark the moment, we stand in the front yard of the house
my grandfather built, the house I grew up in, a house raised on artificial wooden legs
like all the rest. In the photo, everyone looks annoyed. My mother, in bellbottoms,
holding my baby sister, appears to pout. My father, in sideburns, his arm hanging
over my mother's shoulder, looks cross. His eyebrows are knit. Mine are, too; they
counter the optimism of my kiskadee-colored dress and matching ponytail holders,
blinding balls of yellow. I wonder what was wrong. Why do we look so displeased?
Was the sun in our eyes? Were there packages from neighbors, intended for sons
somewhere in America, waiting to be stuffed, somehow, into our suitcases? My
grandmothers, flanking us, neither headed for America just yet, seemed content
enough. Maybe we weren't looking forward to the long journey ahead, over the
Canje Creek Bridge by car, across the fat, pulsing Berbice River by ferry, through
even more geometric fields of cane to our country's capital and then, finally, across
ear-ringing skies on our first plane ride ever, a Guyana Airways flight to New York
City. Into the house in the picture, electricity had just come, but there was no phone
or indoor toilet.

* Epigraph from *Mangos and Bullets*, Serpents Tail, 1991. Used by permission of Profile
  Books.

COOLIE WOMAN

I was almost seven, old enough to have memories of Guyana and young enough to be severed in two by the act of leaving it. Emigrating was like stepping into a magician's box. The sawing in half was just a trick. In time, limbs and coherence would be restored, and a whole, intact self sent back into the audience. But at my age, unformed and impressionable, I didn't know that. All I knew was that everything seemed to split apart. Time became twofold, divided into the era BA, or before America, and the one after it, after 7 November 1981. Space was also sundered, torn slowly and excruciatingly into two conflicting realms, inside and out.

My memories of Guyana are almost all set outdoors. The houses there stand on stilts, to avoid the flood underfoot. That kicks open, underneath, a concrete terrain known as the Bottom House. There, curries are cooked and eaten, laundry washed and set to dry. There, life unfurls, exposed to the eyes of the lane, open to the comment of neighbors. And there, visits are paid. Hammocks rock back-and-forth, marking the absence of time, as hours pass in *gyaffing*, a West Indian brand of aimless talk, encompassing everything and nothing at once.*

I remember the outside of our house in Cumberland Village much better than the inside. The Bottom House opened into the front yard, where we posed for our photo that last day. To the left stood our *guinep* tree, the scant, sweet pulp of its fruit encased in a green shell. To the right stood our concrete temple, the size of a toolshed. It lay outside the frame of that final picture, but I remember it vividly. The *mandir* was honeycombed for ventilation and painted as blue as the clay gods within. It sat next to my grandmother's garden, where so many times, zinnias tucked into our braids, sheets wrapped like saris around our waists, my cousin and I played at being brides. We staged our weddings in and around a curvaceous blue car parked inside the gate. It belonged to Brudda, a taxi-driving cousin renowned for his ability to squeeze in a dozen passengers in any one go. The car had died and, for some reason, Brudda had laid it to rest under the guinep tree. Three decades later, Brudda is in Canada, and we are in America; but the remains of the car still lie there, an indestructible shard of blue in the weeds choking our abandoned plot of Guyanese earth. The temple, the garden and the car comprise the hazy landscape of my first childhood, like stickers pasted onto a board-game map of the past. Flat, but brightly colored, they represent what was, in the wide-open place we left behind.

In the America we arrived in, it was too cold for all that. Our aunts gave me and my cousin matching grey winter coats. We wore them through our first season of snow. We learned how to speak and shoved indoors the Creole words that vibrated with Bottom House and playmates. There wasn't much extra room for those words in the close spaces of our new life, on the first floor of my uncle's house in New Jersey. We rented three tight rooms and slept five in a row, on two beds pushed together,

---

* In the novel *The Sly Company of People Who Care*, the narrator, an Indian travelling in Guyana, says, tongue-in-cheek: "I was still not versed in gyaffin—the key was to make a joke, preferably obscene, denounce something strongly, share a rumor or at the very least discuss somebody's plight."

for half a decade. My grandmother, who had crossed a border crawling on her belly to join us by then, made the fifth. From the fire escape, we could see the Twin Towers. Despite the panoramic view of Manhattan, our apartment promoted claustrophobia. The door swung into the windowless bathroom to reveal my mother balanced on the edge of the bathtub, attacking clothes in sudsy water, pummeling hand-me-down jeans until they screeched, beating the ugly green corduroys that made me look as awkward as I felt. She nearly fainted once, with the fumes of Clorox bleach concentrated in that tiny room.

The gods were also crowded; they, too, had been forced inside. From the airy temple perfumed by zinnias, they were driven into the closet—the linen closet in the bedroom, to be precise. There was a box of Barbie dolls on the bottom shelf, and nightly, the rats made incisions into the pale plastic of their perfectly formed legs. On the top shelf rested framed prints of the gods: elephant-trunked Ganesh, the remover of obstacles; Hanuman, the monkey with a mountain in his palm; and Sarasvati, the goddess of knowledge.

Every Sunday, the white shutters of the linen closet would open. Fresh flowers were placed on a bronze plate, and incense sticks lit. My mother would sing *bhajans*, Hindu devotional songs. She knows very little Hindi. Yet there was always in her cadence—in that lovely, high voice—a crack of sadness seducing me into false belief. It led me to believe that she had occupied the insides of every last syllable of song. Those early years in America often sent my twenty-something-year-old mother to her shuttered gods. They gave the hymns she did not understand, from an India she had never seen, a tangible quality. You could touch the words. They bent down to your feet, imploring your blessings. *Main ik nanha sa, main ik chota sa, baccha hoon.* I am a tiny child, I am a small child. She stood in front of the makeshift shrine with a white lace scarf over her head, and she prayed with her eyes tightly shut.

Hindi echoed through our apartment, hinting at India, every Sunday—and not only through the soft rustle of my mother's prayers. It blasted with shoulder-shimmying force from our television set, tuned to a station that broadcast Bollywood on the weekends. I remember sitting on the edge of our bed one morning, playing with the Velcro straps on my sneakers. We were about to see off our cousins on a visit to Guyana. The hour was obscenely early, and I was in a sour mood. But that changed when I saw Kumar Gaurav's face fill the screen. It was a scene from *Love Story*, a Bombay musical I had last seen in Guyana, at a cinema hall near our village. The hero, a Romeo repackaged for the subcontinent, was haunting the grounds of his Juliet's home on the day of her wedding to someone else. His chiseled face was long and soulful, and his star-crossed song seduced me all over again through the static of the Zenith.

It's not that I was in love with Kumar Gaurav (although, aged nine, I might incidentally have been). I used to dream then of waking up in our Bottom House from forever-long stays in a Nighttown made up of three small rooms. At that time, Kumar Gaurav had the warm glow of a flashback to Guyana, triggering memory like Cod Liver Oil or Marmite or an overheard snippet of Creolese on the otherwise ordinary street. All belonged to an inner enclave, severed from the external world. Outside, Americans were speaking "Proper English." Inside were all our secrets, good and bad: the cracked English, the hidden gods, the dal and roti on Sunday mornings and the lachrymose lyrics of Lata Mangeshkar, the GOLden VOICE of BOLLYwood, as the men who gave us our cassette culture kept insisting in singsong promos.

Indian movies were part of the landscape of inside, existing in a rarefied private place that had little to do with a specific location on a map. For me, Bollywood did not refer back to India. In fact, I did not know to call it Bombay's Hollywood until college. Nor did I know what most of the Hindi words I had picked up from film songs meant. I had heard them all intoned onscreen so many times, melodramatically cueing violins, that they were part of the airtight space of my complicated ethnicity, having sensibility without sense. Intuitively I knew, without knowing, these words: *Pyar, zindagi, shahdi, mushkil, akela.* Love, life, wedding, troubles, alone. These were words well suited to the play of little Guyanese girls rehearsing futures in Bottom Houses on the edges of rectangles of cane. They were arguably less relevant to futures imagined from claustrophobic apartments on the margins of Manhattan.

Hindi films imparted nothing of the social rifts or other realities in India. After all, Pinky and Bunty weren't star-crossed because one was Muslim and the other Hindu, or one Brahmin and the other from a "backward caste." If India looked anything like the country of Bollywood, then it was a place where lovers ran into each other's arms across flowering fields, while breaking into song—a land where arch-criminals cavorted in underground lairs with scantily-clad dancing girls. For some reason, the arch-criminals always wore beards and dark glasses, and the lovers changed outfits every two minutes, mid-song. Even so, Indian movies *did* impart an odd, foetal sense of identity to me. I received it effortlessly, through the navel string* of culture, becoming as familiar with Rekha, Shashi Kapoor and Amitabh Bachchan as with the Technicolor deities inside the linen closet. The Bollywood megastars were gods, too. Both religion and the cinema gave me the conviction that I was Indian, although I had never stepped foot in India, nor had my parents, nor had my grandparents. Bollywood and the *bhajans* also gave me language.

Frantz Fanon, the Caribbean intellectual who was a freedom fighter in Algeria, once wrote: "A man who has a language consequently possesses the world expressed and implied by that language."[1] It's an apt statement from the frontlines of a struggle against a colonial power. Take away my language, and you also take away access to the stories that my forebears created, in the cadences that they created them. Educate me in a language lacking the rhythms of home, and I am likely to speak as a seg-mented self, to sound surgically snipped and etherized in the official world, shorn of the words that resonate with Bottom House and *gyaffing*, altercation and intimacy, mother and father.

Over the generations, various Indian tongues have been lost as spoken languages in Guyana. The missionary-run schools during British rule taught English—not

* umbilical cord.

Hindi or Tamil. Many Guyanese living in the gravitational pull of sugar plantations got little or no formal schooling, well into the twentieth century. Whether educated or not, they still had to assimilate into a multiethnic society where various versions of Creolese, an English dialect that evolved from plantation pidgin, was the idiom. This is what we spoke inside our immigrant home; this was our cracked, our stained-glass English, made from smashed bits of multicolored glass, a thing of beauty constructed from fragments, including fragments from India.

Shards of Hindi have remained, indestructible, like the scrap of Brudda's fender in our Bottom House. Words for family, for religion, for food, for love have survived, as has something more difficult to define. Colonialism and migration are inextricably joined in my family history. Colonialism caused us to migrate, first to British Guiana, then from an independent Guyana still struggling to emerge from its colonial past. Migration involves resistance, too—resistance against the loss of culture, of memory, of dialect. Those of us engaged in this daily struggle against loss know that it's possible to "have" a language on many levels. We know that it's possible for a language to resonate emotionally even when it has been literally lost. We know that, even when slurring the surmised remains of our once-upon-a-time language or parroting it without understanding it, it's possible to wrap our tongues possessively around the world it expresses and implies. My mother, worshipping her shuttered gods with shuttered eyes, knew that.

There were reasons for her to pray with her eyes tightly shut. In 1987, the same year we moved to our very own house, bigots began terrorizing the neighborhood. We picked up the local newspaper to find their crudely scrawled manifesto. They signed their note "The Dot Busters." It was a few years after the release of *Ghostbusters*, and their nom de guerre was a terrifying play on the movie title and on dothead, an anti-Indian slur mocking the *bindis* that some married Hindu women wear on their foreheads. "We will go to any extreme to get Indians to move out," the note read. "We use the phone books and look up the name Patel. Have you seen how many of them there are?" Soon after this declaration of violence was published, three white men assaulted an Indian doctor with baseball bats. They were prosecuted, but their victim could not remember the details necessary to convict them; such was the severity of his brain damage. Days after the attack, another Indian man was beaten to death less than a mile away, in an adjacent town.

The assaults both occurred a few blocks from my family's house in the Heights, a hub of working-class respectability in Jersey City. This city of a quarter-million people, located directly across the Hudson River from Lower Manhattan, styles itself as a sixth borough of New York. Its brittle row houses lean close together, ogling the backside of the Statue of Liberty like a cluster of lewd old men. Its landscape is squat, huddled, massed with immigrants. At the time, a third of its residents were born outside the United States. Many were recently arrived Indians, mainly from the state of Gujarat. They comprised the largest and the most visibly different group. It wasn't just the color of their skin, which was also the color of our skin. It was their saris, their accents, the bindis enunciating their foreheads. It was their Mahatma Gandhi

Square, its air thick with curry, its lamp posts hung with Indian flags. Most of all, it was their striving, their ambition in a city that had seen better days. The Dot Busters made Indians in Jersey City fear for their lives, and they made us, Indians nearly a century out of India, feel just as menaced.

My parents wouldn't let us play outside that autumn. Once, a man in a car idling next to ours at a red light spat directly into my father's face. Another time, hoodlums brandishing a broken bottle chased him for blocks. Someone scrawled "Hindus Go Home" in black paint across the side of our house, and my mother spent the next day scouring the aluminum siding with paint thinner. The vandals didn't know that their decree was not a straightforward one. They couldn't have cared less that home was not what it seemed—was not, in fact, easy to define. To them, Indian-looking meant Indian. Certainly, there was no command of the cracks that colonialism had created. They didn't imagine that, among their Indian-looking neighbors, there might be strangers eyeing each other from a distance, fascinated and even moved by what linked them and by the limits of what linked them. What makes an Indian? Did our religion, our movies, our shards of Hindi make us Indian? Did the attacks of a racist gang targeting people who looked like us? Did hate crime make us Indian?

We did feel solidarity with Indians in our neighborhood because of the attacks, and many of my school friends were Indian-American. But the embrace offered to Indo-Caribbeans by immigrants directly from the subcontinent often has a subtle edge. Their tenderness can be patronizing. Probably, they are only trying to bond when they point out that the unraveling of our arms, when we dance, is *like* North Indian folk dance but, somehow, off. Indeed, they are eager to tell us our own story—what part of India we probably came from, what dialect of Hindi our ancestors probably spoke, how our singers inevitably garble those dialects when they perform chutney, the hybrid dance music indigenous to the Caribbean but rooted in India. I doubt they mean to offend, or to hold us to the light like an artifact, a fascinating shard of pottery. Often, there is no embrace at all but just a nod, like one given to a poor cousin, barely acknowledging kinship. Sometimes, there isn't even that. Sometimes, they would rather deny us like an "outside child"—which is what West Indians call a child born outside a legal marriage. To some, we are India's outside child. When class isn't their issue, authenticity—some apparent concern over our parentage—seems to be.

My parents did not make any new friends because of the hooligans who terrorized the Indian and the Indian-looking in the Heights. In fact, they had hardly any friends at all, beyond family. They continued to turn inward, and except for the constant intimacy of so many uncles, aunts and cousins, our home became a fortress. Outside, after all, there lurked physical danger. Outside, there were racists armed with spray paint and spittle, baseball bats and broken bottles. But America in all its habits and promise also lay there. Outside defined "normal." For one, everybody there knew girls have boyfriends, go to proms, grow up to move away and own their own lives. Inside, my immigrant parents knew no such thing because an elsewhere continued to exert its influence. Entrenched inside, my mother kept throwing up ramparts against the world outside her home.

THE MAGICIAN'S BOX

We rarely returned to Guyana after emigrating. My parents were too busy work-ing, striving, building new lives for us. They couldn't spare the time or money for sentimental journeys, especially once all of our close relatives had followed us out. The country they fled, the country we fled, was a country without. Ruled by a dicta-tor who had rigged elections for decades, it was a country without legitimate democ-racy. Because it banned foreign goods as neocolonialist, it was a country without the wheat flour needed for staples such as roti and bread. Divided by race, and ruled by the African-dominated party, it was a country without equal opportunities for Indi-ans, who were largely shut out of higher education and the civil service. And for some time, ever since Cold War interference by both the Americans and the British, Guy-ana had been a country without real control over its own destiny.

I was too young to remember ration lines, or empty grocery store shelves, or the black market, but my father did. He remembered having to buy back-lane baby formula, because Enfamil, a foreign import, was what he wanted for me, born two months premature, weighing 4 pounds-3 ounces. He also remembered refugees coming to live in our village when he was a boy of eleven. They were driven out of a town at the mouth of Guyana's forested interior, where gold diggers and miners gathered, a town later renamed Linden, after the election-rigging, flour-banning dictator. The refugees had been ethnically cleansed. Indian homes had been burned down, my father said. Indian women had been raped, Indian people killed. For the record, African people were also killed. Guyana's race riots scorched in both direc-tions, but the intervening First World governments anointed the African-led political party, less socialist at the time, and its constituents as the winners. Despite all this, scarcity and injustice did not loom large in my memories of Guyana. I did not see it as others might have: a Third World basketcase, one of the poorest countries in the Western hemisphere, the nation that had welcomed Jim Jones and his suicidal Kool-Aid cult into the heart of its darkness. For me, the country of my birth and first childhood was an area of mystery and longing, a place of imagined wholeness.

My father probably understood this when, sixteen years after migrating, he took me to Guyana as a graduation gift: my first trip back as an adult, our second return ever. It was the summer of 1997, and as we waited for our flight at Newark Airport, I watched other passengers lug duct-taped bags—bags bulging, I was sure, with Goya Sardines in Tomato Sauce, Betty Crocker Instant Potatoes and Cadbury's Chocolate. These things had made Guyanese mouths water in seasons of shortage, and relatives overseas still kept hefting them back home whenever they visited, as if the regime had not ultimately changed, as if the economy had not eventually liberalized, as if import bans had not finally been lifted. The foreign brands—this kitchen cabinet largesse—had become part of the ritual of homecoming, intended as much for the gift-givers as the gift-receivers. I listened to the other passengers talk about how the country was coming up, how the days of shortage were gone: "Guyana nice baaad, maan. Every-ting you can waaant, you can ge'. Plenty, plenty ting." Everywhere around us, they spoke in a dialect so private, so intimate to my ears, that every time they opened their mouths, there was a tingling fusion of inside and out, an electric union of outside and in, a sparks-flying soldering together of the soul.

This trip home led me to ask about another, more epic journey. As we sat, poised to board our flight, I asked my father what he knew about our family's roots in India. My father—my responsible, caretaking, in-charge father—keeps the records in our family. If anyone had a paper trail to our past, he would. And he did. My father lost his father when still a child. The old man died of chronic bronchitis the year before the refugees came to our village. His Will contained the place and year of his birth: *The Clyde*, 1903. My father grew up knowing that his father was born on a ship from India, and he knew which ship, in which year. He also knew that his grandmother, Sujaria, had climbed aboard that ship as an indentured servant. "She was a pregnant woman travelling alone," my father told me, matter-of-factly. Any more than that, he could not say. He had no insights into this earth-shaking revelation. All he knew was that Sujaria had given birth to my grandfather at some point during the passage from India, and she had given him the name "Lalbahadur." This name, the short version of which my father and I both carry in the world, was not her own. Like most Indians who migrated, she did not have a last name.

I never knew Lalbahadur, of course. A black-and-white studio portrait of him, probably taken in his late fifties, hangs in our house in New Jersey. In the photograph, he stands straight and tall, his hands hanging stiffly at his sides. His nose is my father's nose, once narrow but in later years slightly swollen, like a snail in the middle of his face. He wears patent leather shoes, a long-sleeved button-down shirt, properly-creased pinstriped trousers. He has the bearing of a dignified man. My grandfather was a peasant farmer, growing rice and raising cows and chickens, which is what most Indians with ambition did in rural Guyana at the time. He also worked on sugar plantations for most of his life. He belonged to the gang of muscular men who dug drains, disciplining the cane fields, imposing straight lines and right angles with his shovel. Long before I was even born, he laid out the landscape of my childhood in the same orderly way. He built the first house I called home, and he built the tiny temple, the honeycombed shed to house the gods, in its front yard. Lalbahadur was a strict Hindu. His legacy to his eight children—aside from the house he made of greenheart wood—was a traditional morality as tough as that impervious timber. By all accounts, he had a strong hand, unafraid to make its raw force felt when needed.

The story of his birth, possibly out of wedlock, intrigued me. I used to think that we inherited our conservatism about sex and relationships—that the generations had handed it down to us as who they were and who we ought, also, to be. Hadn't my own shut-in immigrant upbringing provided ample proof of that? But at the departure gate in Newark, I was learning things about our family history that, rather than answering my questions about identity, only raised more. Even if I didn't know precisely where I belonged, or how Guyanese I was or could ever be, I did believe that I knew, at the very least, what it meant to be Guyanese. Even before we had stepped onto the plane, this homeland journey had started to shake that belief.

We were visiting Guyana at a historic time, a few months after the death of its president, Cheddi Jagan, the independence leader who was a hero and father figure to Indians in the country, as well as a symbol of how they had been wronged. He had spent more than three decades in the political wilderness because the CIA, paranoid at the thought of yet another Caribbean Marxist right in Castro's geopolitical neighborhood, pushed him out and paved the way for Linden Forbes Burnham, the dictator who banned flour. Listening to grown-ups in my world, I had formed an image of Burnham as bogeyman. He seemed spectral, superhuman. When he died, his body was embalmed and displayed in a purple glass coffin in the Botanical Gardens. This was according to his instructions and on the model of Lenin's tomb. He was not, as it turned out, the curb against Soviet-style socialism that the United States had hoped. Seven years after Burnham died, Jagan finally ascended to the presidency. And in his own death, he ascended to a status approaching sainthood. His wife, Janet, would be elected to succeed him before the year was out.

During our visit, the air was still charged with mourning. I bought a children's book called "When Grandpa Cheddi Was a Boy" and a tape of folk songs canonizing him. The country—or at least half of it—was engaged in a months-long eulogy that by its nature reopened racial wounds. For these Indians long out of India, the sense of being Indian was fierce and instinctual, born in great part out of a century-and-a-half old competition with the half of the country that wasn't Indian. But I did not see myself in this fight. I did not want to find myself there. I was the product of a multicultural education in post-Civil Rights Act America. I had grown up a minority in a city of minorities, subject to racism that connected me to black skins, rather than pitting me against them. How then could I locate myself in my homeland's history of hate? For answers to my questions about identity, I had to look elsewhere, in the personal rather than the political.

* * *

When we reached the house where we would be staying, deep in the countryside, our host showed my father and me to our room. Twisted into a tight knot, mosquito netting hung from square frames above two tiny beds. Against the wall was a shelf with garlanded pictures of a plump Indian man, wearing what looked like an Afro and decked out in saffron Hare Krishna robes. I asked who he was. Our host fixed me with disbelieving eyes. "That's Sai Baba," she said. "You don't know who Sai Baba is?" I didn't, but I did know the look she was giving me. I'd seen it on more than one face since arriving in Guyana. It was a look that took me in slowly—first, the short skirts and the boy's haircut; then my careful English, calibrated to books with many clauses and precise pauses; and finally the endless questions about things I should have known. It was a look reserved for clueless foreigners.

Kavita was in her early twenties, like me. She had a warm, pretty face. One perfectly plaited braid reached all the way down to her waist. She was married to my Bhauji's* brother. They ran a rice mill, and their Bottom House was stacked with

* This is a term of respect for elder brother's wife; but literally, she is my cousin's wife.

burlap sacks containing paddy. Her husband had lived in the United States for a while. An accident in a factory had cut that stay short, but he seemed to be doing much better in Guyana anyway. He was polite and hard-working, and I liked him. They had two little girls.

"How did the two of you meet?" I asked. Kavita smiled. She gave me the look again, gently, forgivingly, almost as though she knew that not so very long ago, in a Bottom House in Cumberland, I used to rehearse my own sari-clad wedding. Kavita's marriage had been arranged. I should have known not to ask. I met many women my age—and younger—in Guyana whose lives were already settled, by forces or people outside themselves. The circumstances varied, of course; and the happiness or the hope for it also varied.

I met an eighteen-year-old, recently married to a Guyanese man from the Bronx. He was over thirty, and they didn't know each other before the wedding. The groom had returned to New York after their honeymoon; she was waiting for her visa to join him. Her family was struggling, even by Guyanese standards, and I wondered what exigencies might have driven the match. What were those words provided by Hindi films, like a mantra for our futures? *Pyar, zindagi, shahdi, mushkil, akela.* Which progression, exactly, suited reality in Guyana's sugar belt? Was it love, then life, then a wedding? Or did love come after marriage? Did trouble and loneliness also follow? Or was it more common for troubles to come before and, indeed, pre-cipitate a wedding?

It wasn't only economics or the lust for a First World passport that led to marriages arranged across the continents. In the week I stayed near my childhood home, I also got to know a twenty-four-year old woman named Mala, the daughter of a timber mill owner in a village which sits on Canje Creek, next to ours. Mala watched *Seinfeld* on the television set in her grandparents' house. The house, near their mill, was framed by heaps of sawdust. Her grandparents spent the winters in Guyana and the summers in a suburb of Toronto. When we went for a ride along the river in one of their speedboats, Mala wore a T-shirt with "Waiting for Mr Right" emblazoned across the front. She showed me pictures of a beaming Canadian fiancée, posing in front of a shiny silver Toyota Avalon. They had exchanged letters and spoken on the phone. Although they were, in a sense, courting long-distance, this too was an arranged match. When my mother married at eighteen, it was a "love" marriage. This meant that my parents had liked each other when they spoke in the hallways of Corentyne High School, where they both taught. They did not date. My mother's family had been approached, inquiries into suitability made, a collective decision arrived at. That was in 1974. Mores had not stood completely still in a quarter of a century. After all, there was the shock of *Seinfeld* in a house along the Berbice River. Yet, for most Indians in Guyana, arranged marriages were not only a social fact; they were still the norm at the time of our visit.

My trip to Guyana, from the minute I saw its criss-cross of canals from the plane, was profoundly strange. The deepest alienation came from the unspoken rules about what women should not and could not do. I kept making impolite demands to be let into the circle of men talking politics over El Dorado Rum. I wanted to go with my father and Kavita's husband to see his rice mill. When that was denied, I sulked like someone left behind, although I knew it was rude, although Kavita was a kind host, although her baby daughter had made me her *Pua*, or aunt. While I enjoyed the intimate places set aside for women in Guyana, the kitchens where stories were told, I also wanted access to the places reserved for men. I could never be content segregated and confined, just tending to children and a home.

Although I knew I couldn't be Kavita, I didn't know it righteously, the way you might expect an American feminist to know it. Her life had a seductive order to it that I was nowhere near achieving in my own. Concretely, she knew what her impact was. She was a mother and a wife. She hadn't fallen in love with her husband, but hadn't she also avoided the vagaries of falling in love? If I had a right to judge her, then she had a right to judge me. She had already started with the look, and I wondered what she would find, if she turned her full gaze on me. Would she ever see me as more than a foreigner? Could she guess how like a pilgrimage it was for me to return to the Bottom House of my childhood, where a grandfather I never knew had raised pillars of greenheart wood? Could she sense the primal, raw, sacred places inside this opened up? Could she tell how thrilling it was to be in a place where, outside and inside, Creolese lived, Hindi film music scorched the air and Kumar Gaurav didn't have to be explained? How would she make sense of the fact that this ecstasy of union, of wholeness, existed side by side with an unnerving feeling of dislocation? Would she realize that, mostly, this had to do with being a woman?

I had a similar experience when, five years later, I went to India for the first time. I wasn't there to track down any ancestors. At the time, I wouldn't even have known where to begin. Officially, I was there to visit a university friend who lived in Bombay, but I knew—and he knew—that the objective was far deeper than that. This was more than a vacation in an ancient, clamoring, multitudinous country where I happened to know someone who could serve as local informant. I wanted to experience what it felt like to be in the matrix of the culture that had shaped me from a distance, through Hindu gods and Hindi love songs. When my plane landed, I almost couldn't get out of my seat. I was frozen on the threshold, like the tears in my eyes, which were suspended on the very edge of becoming.

I did manage to disembark, however, and spent the weeks ahead roaming Bombay and Goa and Kerala, following a travel agent's itinerary. My friend was working, and I was by myself, which seemed to send the wrong signal entirely to hotel busboys and restaurant waiters and one very forward hill station guide. I was travelling alone through the country my great-grandmother had left, also travelling alone, and the circumstance seemed to raise questions about my character much as it did about hers. Perhaps this preset my vision so that I saw, everywhere, evidence of the separate and restricted lives of women. I noticed the "Ladies Compartments" on Bombay's trains, set aside as a barrier against the aggressive gazes of men. I was struck by the fat concrete benches along its most romantic promenade; custom-made for chastity by the city's conservative ruling party, they seated only one. Atop a hill with a wrap-around view of tea gardens, what made an impression was the mosque whose threshold adult women cannot cross. I knew that India was still a place burdened with many rules for women, despite changes in social attitudes that had come at high speed in the 1990s, especially to big cities, but I wasn't prepared for the alienating force of those rules once I had to abide by them. I wasn't prepared for how I would feel when travelling solo sparked gossip and encouraged advances. I wasn't prepared to be told not to go to the cinema by myself at night if I didn't want to be groped. And I wasn't ready to check my American-bred sense that I could do what I wanted, when I wanted—within reason, and with respect, of course. I didn't wander around in short skirts or tight clothes. I dressed conservatively, trying to pass, in kurtas with loose jeans or in salwar-kamizes.

Indeed, my ability to pass seemed to be part of the problem. Because I looked Indian, I was expected to act Indian. I was held to a different standard than other Americans. In Kerala, where I spent most of my time on that first trip to India, I sat alone on the beach for hours, reading and staring at the Viking-like fishing boats skimming the Arabian Sea. For some reason, this attracted an audience: a group of men who gathered around me, standing and staring. I wasn't wearing a swimsuit. I was dressed in an orange paisley churidar: pants tapered at the ankles, a loose tunic that flowed down to my shins and a long scarf pulled over my head. At that point, my rickshaw driver Ashok emerged from the wings to shoo the men. He had stayed close while I was reading on the beach, although I had arranged with him to return for me in three hours. Ashok had appointed himself my protector because, he later explained, "You look just like a regular Kerala girl." Regular Kerala girls, he said, do not sit by themselves on the beach, just staring into the sea, unless they've had problems at home and are perhaps contemplating suicide.

I wanted to pass as an Indian, to transcend the role of tourist, to connect in meaningful ways with the people around me. India was more than a commodity to me, and I wanted to be more to it than just another American consumer, but I also wanted to be seen as an American when it suited me—when, for instance, I thought it might explain my behavior or make me seem less odd to others. I felt this from my first hour in India, when the immigration officer reviewing my visa demanded to know why I had been talking so warmly to the man in line ahead of me, a tabla player from New York. The official's rebuke was as crisp as his khaki. He upbraided me for being open and informal with a strange man. In reply, I didn't ask the immigration agent what business it was of his. I didn't assert my right to speak to whomever I pleased, as warmly as I pleased. Instead, I just said: "I am an American."

I admit there may have been some bristle, indeed some swagger in the declaration, given his accusing tone. And I know that it was gratuitous, given the fact that he had proof of my US citizenship in his tight grip. My response was, nonetheless, mostly just an explanation. I felt the need to put my brown skin in context for him. In the process, I seem to have affirmed my identity more simply, and with greater confidence, than I had ever done in America itself—and I did this at the very gates of the country that I thought had made me, from a distance of generations and thousands of miles. Was it possible that the magician's box of emigration had set me free as well as cut me in half? Had leaving Guyana liberated me, because I am a woman? And was it possible that leaving India had done the same for my great-grandmother a century earlier?

2

ANCESTRAL MEMORY

The ancestors curl and dry to scrolls of parchment.
They lie like texts
Waiting to be written by the children
For whom they hacked and ploughed and saved
To send to faraway schools.

David Dabydeen, "Coolie Odyssey"*

Our journey took us past endless fields of flowering yellow along the northern banks of the Ganges. When we pulled into towns, we asked for directions, from children balancing loads three times their size on their heads, from crouching women tending baskets of cauliflower and eggplant by the roadside, from men in the stores that stared open-faced onto the street, framing a tailor at his sewing machine, a man pumping air into bicycle tyres, a camera-wallah behind his counter. We sought the guidance of random people on the route, turning to them as to a massive human compass. And they obliged. They pointed us along bumpy roads bracketed by tiny pastel altars made to worship the sun, until one man finally indicated a rocky path. "That way," he said.

We had travelled five hours over shell-shocked roads and narrow dirt lanes to arrive here, at the threshold of a place I wasn't even sure still existed. It did a century ago. That's what a document that I had discovered two years earlier, in Guyana's national archives, indicated. It was the emigration pass issued to my great-grandmother on 29 July 1903, the day she sailed from Calcutta for the Caribbean.

Catalogued on this brittle artifact, sepia and crumbling with age, was everything about Immigrant #96153 that the imperial bureaucracy had considered worth

* Epigraph from *Coolie Odyssey*, Hansib, 1988. Used by courtesy of David Dabydeen.

recording: "Name: Sheojari." "Age: 27." "Height: five-feet, four-and-a-half inches." "Caste: Brahman." Here was colonial officialdom's cold summary of an indentured laborer's life. Yet, it included strokes of unsettling intimacy. The emigration pass told me that my great-grandmother had a scar on her left foot, a burn mark. Someone had scribbled "Pregnant 4 mos" in pencil at the document's edge. On the line for husband's name, there was only a dash.

Though my great-grandmother claimed no husband, she did list coordinates for home. The pass pointed to it precisely, almost like a map to some mythic location with hidden riches. X marks the spot: the state of Bihar, the province of Chhapra, the police district of Majhi and the village of Bhurahupur. There the past rested, buried. And here we were, just a few miles away, more than a century later, hoping to excavate lost history. Bihar isn't a place where people typically go in search of buried treasure. Outsiders typically don't go there at all, although it's the second most populous state in India. The few foreign tourists it attracts are on Buddha's trail, making pilgrimage to the place where he attained enlightenment. Bihar was once the seat of a vast and ancient empire stretching to Iran, but few people see it now as anything but a corrupt and dangerous backwater. Its per capita income is among the lowest and its illiteracy rate among the highest nationwide. One historian has branded the state "a stinking skeleton in India's democratic cupboard."[1]

It was November 2005, four days before provincial elections—a bad time to be travelling in Bihar. Ballot boxes had been stolen at gunpoint in the past. And Marxist rebels had just broken out of a jail south of the capital, Patna, when we set out. The military had been ordered to keep civilian vehicles off the roads until the votes had been cast. One of my guides decided we would pose as journalists to get past the roadblocks. He taped a phony "PRESS" sign onto the windshield of our white Ambassador. This voluptuous vintage car is a relic from the pre-globalized era when Indians drank Thums Up instead of Coca-Cola, and its presence everywhere on Bihar's potholed highways was another sign that the sleek, new India of nanos and glimmering shopping malls has not reached all corners of the subcontinent. Surprisingly, our Scotch-taped stratagem worked. Soldiers in khaki fatigues stopped us, but they did not ask for credentials. They took us at our word.

My guide Abhijit eyed the rocky little lane that stood between me and my great-grandmother's village. It seemed impossible that the massive Ambassador could force its way through. He chuckled. "That's a great scene, just like *Veer Zara*," he said, with a sudden, sarcastic edge. "Preethi Zintha is searching for her forefathers." He was referring to a Bollywood movie that had cast its dimpled starlet along village backroads in search of a lost love—not lost forefathers. But the imprecision of the analogy seemed somehow appropriate to my journey. Ancestral memory had told my family the story of who we are: brown-skinned people with many gods and peculiar, stubborn habits. It had told it imperfectly. Memory, after all, fails us. That we expect, especially over generations and across oceans. Details get smudged, and dialogue garbled. The will to remember the past is undermined by an equally formidable will to forget. Given how facts had fared with the passage of time, how could I do anything but fumble my way inaccurately through India? I had to rely on Abhijit to name things like the yellow fields, and the comedy was unavoidable. "Is it saffron?" I asked. Yes, he said—though saffron does not grow anywhere near this corner of the subcontinent, and those stalks were mustard.

We arrived at the village in the late afternoon, an hour before the winter sunset, and we had to be back in Patna by bedtime. Our time was limited. My second guide, Jitendra—a man with a face so straight and correct it could have been drawn with a protractor—took charge. He did not ask anyone about Sujaria. There would have been no point, he assured me. "Women," he explained, "were not known persons at the time." Instead, he dropped the name of Sujaria's father: Mukhlal. It was listed on her emigration pass, along with a next-of-kin, a female cousin. Armed with this information, Jitendra approached a group of men loitering near the entrance to the village, off a gravel lane, along a tributary of the Ganges. He asked if anyone knew of a Mukhlal who had lived in Bhurahupur a century ago. No one did.

The villagers took us to a toothless man with a helmet of white hair, sitting on a bench outside his house, a mustard shawl draped over his bony body. He was a schoolteacher and an elder, the kind of man you might expect to be the keeper of local memory. He had, however, no information. My heart sank a little, although I wasn't expecting anything concrete from this trip. I hadn't even known whether or not the village would still be standing. I couldn't really believe I was here. In Bhurahupur. X marks the spot. The precise point where an umbilical cord connected me to India. And here I was, being sized up by a curious crowd of real-life men who called it home.

"Alright," I told Jitendra. "I just want to ask some general questions about the village. Can we do that?"

The schoolteacher called for three chairs, and we sat.

"Go ahead," Abhijit snapped. "Ask your questions."

It was my turn to speak, and I didn't know where to start.

"My great-grandmother left this village," I ventured, throat tight, conscious that our entire impromptu entourage was looking and listening. I turned to Abhijit, waiting for him to interpret my words into Bhojpuri, the dialect spoken in the district, but he was mute. Jitendra, thankfully, stepped into the breach. Though he spoke less English than Abhijit, he understood much better what I was after and how to help me get it.

The schoolteacher listened, his eyes on me, on the long white kurta I wore over red tapered leggings and on my hair, loose and tangled from the bumpy ride and contradicting my traditional dress. He fixed me in one penetrating gaze and pronounced: "You should be living here." It was delivered like a reproach. India's diaspora, now at 17 million worldwide, has quit India's borders despite a prejudice with the force of religion behind it. To leave was to cross the *kala pani*, "the dark waters,"* of the Indian Ocean and therefore to lose caste, according to the strictures of Hinduism.

* Literally, it means "black water."

No good Indian girl in 1903 would have done that, much less a good Brahmin girl. The schoolteacher, from his perch along the Ganges, was channeling the stern judgment of generations past on a prodigal: "YOU should be living here."

I continued with my questions, however flaccid they felt in the face of his reproach.

"Have many villagers left over the years?"

"No, not many. From time to time, someone would go to Fiji or Mauritius, but mostly people stay close to home."

"How many people live here?"

"About 8,000."

"How do people in the village make a living?"

"There isn't much to make a living at; people get by farming."

By now, more onlookers had encircled us, and another question, this one full-bodied and potent, pushed itself forward with the force of its beseeching: "Does no one here know of a Mukhlal, a Brahmin, who lived here around 1900?"

Someone, suddenly, did. He scurried off and, moments later, returned with a man named Bijender Dubey. Round in the middle, with close-cropped grey hair and front teeth that stuck out like a chipmunk's, he looked to be about fifty. He wore an ankle-length white *dhoti* and a black-and-white shawl around his otherwise bare shoulders. According to my guides, he claimed his great-grandfather was a soldier named Mukhlal Dubey, who died fighting for the British in Burma. Jitendra questioned him: Did Mukhlal have any children? "Yes, a son and a daughter." What was his daughter's name? "Ramjaro," Bijender ventured.

Ramjaro is a Bhojpuri name that means "follower of the god Ram." My great-grandmother's name was probably badly mistransliterated by the British. The "Sheo-jari" catalogued as a passenger on *The Clyde* was called Sujaria in Guiana. In Bihar, she would have been known as Shivajaro (pronounced Sheewa-jar-o), or "follower of the god Shiva." British officials registering her for the West Indies could have mis-heard her name, or she could simply have lied about it, just like she could have lied or been misunderstood when she told them she was from Bhurahupur, in which case the X might have marked the wrong spot entirely.

"Are you sure?" Jitendra asked. "Was it Ramjaro or Shivajaro?"

Bijender revised his answer: "Oh, yes, you're right. It was Shivajaro. She died in this village." Then he declared to the throng, with a nod in my direction: "This girl belongs to our family."

I was wary. Sujaria obviously did not die in that village. There was physical evidence to contradict the claim: a tombstone, shaded by jamoon trees in a swampy graveyard in Cumberland Village, half a world away. Carved into the stone in shaky letters, letters a child first learning to write might have scratched out, is an Om sign, preceded by the epitaph: "In Loving Memory of My Beloved Mother Sewjharia." Sujaria died in Guiana in 1962, at the age of 89, according to the tombstone. It might be desirable for all sorts of reasons, I thought, to have an American in the family. Or, maybe the Dubeys just wanted to give me an ending to justify my journey to their village. After all, I had come a long way. I doubted them, but allowed myself to be claimed and swept along to the family compound: a one-story brick house with six rooms, each opening onto a square courtyard.

Women, some of them crying, surrounded me. Abhijit and I were offered throne-like wooden chairs in the courtyard. We sat, awkwardly, and drank tea. I was made to recite the story of my great-grandmother, to the extent that I knew it: "Her name was Sujaria, and this was her village. The British took her away in 1903 to work their sugar plantations in a place now known as Guyana. She sailed on a ship called The Clyde. My grandfather was born on that ship." Abhijit interpreted some of this—how much, I was never really sure—and there were more tears by the women. It all seemed to come as a revelation. None of them had known anything about her.

I barely do either. I have little to go by to unravel her story, except for the minimal clues on the emigration pass and one elevating act of transatlantic naming. She called her child Lalbahadur. *Lal* means son. It can also be an endearment, a prefix or suffix that, when added to a name, adds the affectionate connotation of "beloved little one." And *Bahadur* used to be a title like "sir," often earned by men who had proven their mettle in the military. In Hindi and Sanskrit, the word means "brave." The last Mughal emperor, for instance, won the title: Bahadur Shah Zafar rallied the first rebels against the British in 1857. Bahadur was the *nom de guerre* of a popular 1980s comic book hero, a battler of dacoits in the subcontinent. In my own family, the name seems to have come into being, along with my grandfather, on *The Clyde*. As far as I can tell, Sujaria made it up. It wasn't her name. It wasn't the name of the man she ultimately married in Guiana. And, if the archives are to be believed, she had no husband on leaving India. She conferred a high title on the child of her middle passage, possibly born out of wedlock.

Much later, when Sujaria was in her eighties and blind, and razzed by boys in our village because of her milky eyes, she would summon her son in Hindi: "Bahadur," she would cry, invoking the name and the role she had invented for him, "they're troubling me."[2] Her son born at sea, inheritor of her fair skin and good looks, out-lived her by a year. He conducted the traditional Hindu rites for her, at the end of the customary year of mourning. He had promised her that he would, and he lived just long enough to keep his word. He also managed to erect the tombstone twice declaring his love: "In Loving Memory of My Beloved Mother." Had Sujaria christened this son, destined to memorialize her, "beloved little hero" at birth? Or was the brave one cued in the name his father, as in "son *of* a hero"?

It is pleasing to think the *Bahadur*—the hero—of this story could have been Sujaria herself. She did, after all, leave a village in the most conservative corner of India. At the time, she was twenty-seven, middle-aged by the standards of the day and the dateline. As a member of Hinduism's highest caste, Sujaria had the most to lose by crossing the Indian Ocean. This was a forbidden passage, especially for a woman, especially for a Brahmin, and most especially for a Brahmin woman travelling without a male relative. I like to think she claimed the decidedly masculine title

21

of *Bahadur* for women, too—and for acts of valour that have more to do with crossing boundaries than with killing anyone in battle.

Sujaria was a passenger on *The Clyde* and also part of its cargo. The iron sailing ship, owned by the Welshman James Nourse, ran a regular route between the West Indies and India, exchanging salt and railway iron for "coolies." The British traffic in indentured servants was a third the size of its trade in African slaves, whom the Indian laborers succeeded on plantations across the globe. From 1838 to 1917, the British transported a million Indians, half of them to the Caribbean, to grow and cut sugar cane. That migration had put thousands of miles and an even greater psychological distance between me and the village women of Bhurahupur. Yet, their tears seemed to implicate me. The women were trying to twist me into the hem of their saris and their suffering, to knit me into their family tree and their fate. Their tears made me as uncomfortable as the brass cup of water that the family had extended. I couldn't offend them by declining. Nor could I drink with ease, knowing how my North American stomach might later react. I accepted their offering of emotion, awkwardly, the only way I knew how to handle the tears of strangers who could be kin.

I remember slipping Bijender a few thousand rupees as I was hustled into the Ambassador to drive off, with the sun sinking behind us and a bunch of boys from the village running after us.

PART TWO

EXPLORING

3

THE WOMEN'S QUARTERS

The girl reveals her arms,
Her long legs, innocently bold;
The woman wraps her shawl modestly about her,
Her open glance a little veiled.

"In Praise of Krishna: Songs from the Bengali"
Trans. By Edward C. Dimock and Denise Levertov*

The elder in Bhurahupur had reproached me for not living there, as though I could answer for my great-grandmother's actions. He seemed to feel that she had violated some ancient, unspoken pact never to leave the ancestral village. In his imagination, Bhurahupur was as proud, as immemorial as the banyan tree, which displays the glory of its roots for all to see, never dreaming anyone would want or need to sever them. But the truth is that rural India in the nineteenth and early twentieth centuries was the scene of epic uprooting.

A wide array of social and economic deprivations drove villagers from home. The practice of imperial capitalism destroyed traditional livelihoods, plunging weavers into unemployment by flooding India with factory-made textiles from England. At the same time, colonialism created new routes for moving across the subcontinent: by the mid-1800s, the British had recruited 10,000 sepoys for their army from the district that included Bhurahupur alone.[1] In times of famine, peasants tramped the roads in search of work, sometimes all the way to growing metropolises such as Calcutta in the Bengal presidency. India suffered twenty-four famines in the last quarter of the nineteenth century,[2] more than enough to cause sustained, large-scale displace-

* Epigraph from *In Praise of Krishna*, Doubleday, 1967. Used by permission of The Asia Society.

25

ment. Nor were women sheltered from this. Indeed, as women, they had more reasons to flee, greater oppression to escape. In 1901, they made up more than half the migrants into Bengal from the neighboring region, the eastern United Provinces.[3]

The simple fact is: my great-grandmother had already quit her village before she quit India. She was 160 miles away, in the town of Faizabad, when she was registered to emigrate. Faizabad sat just across a guava orchard from the bigger, more densely populated town of Ayodhya, a place of pilgrimage for Hindus, who believe the god Ram was born there. In the late nineteenth century, the area was known as a magnet for wanderers. Temples and holy sites, then as now, were natural places for runaways to seek refuge and alms. Labor recruiters looking for people desperate enough to cross the Indian Ocean found them in exactly such places. In 1882, a colonial administrator noted that Ayodhya "furnishes many recruits [for indenture] from among its pilgrims."[4] This may have been where my great-grandmother met her recruiter. That she was registered near there raises questions: Why was she so far from home? Had the crops failed in Bhurahupur? Was she looking for work? Had she run from mistreatment, or was she thrown out for transgressing? In short, was she a victim—or had she taken charge of her own destiny?

My search for the answers shifted from potholed roads and mustard fields in Bihar to archives in England. What I found there was a revelation. I once thought that my great-grandmother must have been an exception. As it turns out, mystery darkened the lives of many women who left India as coolies. The hint of scandal was communal. Some historians have called indenture "a new form of slavery."* In many ways, it was; once in the sugar colonies, coolies suffered under a repressive legal system that regularly convicted more than a fifth of them as criminals, subject to prison for mere labor violations, which were often the unjust allegations of exploitative overseers.[5] The story, however, is more nuanced than that, especially for women. From the beginning, in all the colonies that turned to indenture to rescue their plantations from ruin after slaves were freed, men enormously outnumbered women. This gave women some sexual leverage. They could take new partners, and frequently, they did. Theirs was often a tale of leaving their country, then leaving their men. Even before leaving their country, many had left their men. I don't know whether my great-grandmother had intentionally left hers. If she was recruited with a husband, she lost him somewhere along the way.

The very summer she crossed the Atlantic, a debate was raging over a law intended to keep married women from deserting their homes for the colonies. No woman could emigrate without her husband's permission. If she claimed to be single, and officials thought she was lying, she could be detained for up to ten days as constables checked her story. Robert Mitchell, the man in Calcutta who had been in charge of securing immigrants for British Guiana for two decades, complained that the law was being applied too religiously. He blamed overzealous magistrates in rural areas, which

---

* It is the title of Hugh Tinker's comprehensive book about indenture. He borrowed the phrase from Lord John Russell, a British parliamentarian and an early critic of indenture.

furnished the most recruits, for his trouble collecting women for the colonies. In a 1903 letter to Guianese officials, he chastised the magistrates for holding single women for at least ten days, not *up to* ten days, before registering them; recruiters needed to gather several dozen women to travel together from the countryside to Calcutta, but before enough women could be cleared of suspicion, a month would often pass, pause enough for second thoughts and desertions by the women.

Mitchell was furious. Because of the way the law was being applied, he couldn't muster enough women to meet his quota. No ship could sail unless there were forty women for every 100 men among the coolies it carried. Mitchell's ships were grounded while, as he saw it, white men protected the interests of Indian men. His own frustrations seemed to coincide with those of the women denied a chance to go. Mitchell had been the government-appointed protector of immigrants in Guiana for three years, and he had once worked as an overseer in the Caribbean.[6] As such, he felt he knew enough about coolie women to express outrage on their behalf: "The Magistrate … has advanced as his reason for these detentions that the female emigrants are so immoral that they would desert their husbands for a 'sari' … worth a shilling," he wrote. "The fact probably is that the unfortunate women of the peasant class in this country are hardly removed in some districts from ordinary beasts of burden."[7]

From his office along the Hooghly River, Mitchell pleaded his case to officials in London, Guiana and India's hinterlands. It had rained that season in the district embracing Faizabad: the United Provinces of Agra and Oudh, which sent the greatest number of coolies to the colonies. This was a gift to wheat growers—and to wheat consumers, because it led to a fall in the price of grain. There seemed to be bountiful harvests all across India that year. "A gentleman who arrived lately from Bombay informed me that the whole country looked like a garden on the journey across India," Mitchell reported to the Colonial Office.[8] It was drought and famine that made his depot hum with recruits. Mitchell knew that, and he knew that if men were going to be tough to recruit, women would be even tougher. There were slightly fewer women in India to begin with. Migrating overseas to work had always been a mostly male enterprise the world over. And then there were the cultural barriers against Indian women crossing the threshold of home, into the world. It proved so hard to get enough of them to dispatch the season's first ship that, when *The Erne* finally sailed, some of the women aboard had been in the depot for almost a year. Meanwhile, Mitchell fretted that the season's second ship would probably leave late—and even then, with well fewer than the 649 adults it could hold. That ship, as it turned out, was *The Clyde*, and it sailed with 560 adults. My great-grandmother was one of its last-minute catches, registered in Faizabad on the very day the ship was originally scheduled to sail.

The law that aggravated the shortage of indentured women, the 1883 Indian Emigration Act, was intended to stop wives from passing as widows or single women to escape their husbands. In the rural backwaters that supplied the most recruits for indenture, it was customary for girls to be married as children. The 1891 census of the United Provinces reported that 90 percent of girls between ten and fourteen were already married.[9] There were widows there, of course—some 3.6 million—but it was rare to find adult women who had never been married. As one emigration agent put it, "there are no spinsters to draw upon."[10] Still, Mitchell charged that women who were genuinely unattached were detained, too. He reminded a magistrate in Raipur that the 1883 law as written "contemplates special cases only and not ordinary."[11] Instead, he scolded, it seemed to be applied in almost every case.

This extra scrutiny of women—which Mitchell argued amounted to sexist harassment—resulted from the travels of two English civil servants in the remoter parts of northern India in the early 1880s. They were sent to investigate claims of all kinds of chicanery in the recruitment of coolies for the West Indies, Fiji and Mauritius. The reports they filed and the diaries they kept provide fleeting glimpses of the women targeted as potential emigrants. At times, it almost feels like these elusive figures are peeking through the pages, from behind a curtain separating the women's quarters from the rest of the house of official history.

That's exactly the way Major D.G. Pitcher encountered a handful of women at a depot for recruits. It was just someone's house, a hive of tiny, dirty rooms that competing recruiters had denounced as "a disgrace to emigration." Allegedly, there was no licensed recruiter in sight, and women were falsely "kept there under promise of marriage." Pitcher, a minor judge in Lucknow, had been assigned to scrutinize recruitment in the northwestern provinces. When he visited the discredited depot, he found several rakish-looking men loafing around but only three recruits—two men and a woman. As soon as Pitcher left, recruiters from other depots pounced on him, claiming that the house was actually bursting with women who had been concealed from him. Pitcher returned immediately to check it out.

"I took the people by surprise," he wrote, "and found about half a dozen more women who rushed into an inner room, and were said to be *purdah*. Of course, I could not on this insist on their coming out."[12] Confronted with a tradition that had kept women from the prying eyes of outsiders for centuries, Pitcher had no choice. He had to interview them from outside a closed door. The women told him, through an interpreter, that they were not coolies bound for the sugar colonies. They were concubines, they said, in relationships with various men living in the house. The men were later convicted of illegal recruiting.

Had the women disappeared behind closed doors because the specter of a white man with authority terrified them? Were they really in *purdah*? Or did they have something to hide? They might have concealed their true identities, using false names and invented pasts to sign up for indenture. Or, they might have been recruiting for the colonies. Officially, women were not allowed to recruit, but many of them did so regardless. Delegated by male recruiters, they convinced other women to board ships bound for British plantations abroad.

Mainpuri, the district where Pitcher encountered the women hiding behind the door, had a reputation as a good place to find women for the colonies. The number of its recruits was so high that Pitcher wondered aloud in his diary if it had "anything to do with the existence of canals, and the (as frequently asserted) impotence of men in canal districts?"[13] Women seemed to outnumber men drastically in the streets.

Mainpuri was on the road to Vrindaban, the site of a major temple to the god Krishna, born in the town nearby according to lore. In Hindu scriptures, Vrindaban was the scene of Krishna's mischievous childhood exploits. It was there, in ancient forests where peacocks strutted, that he cavorted with the cowherd maidens known as *gopis*, multiplying himself in order to dance and play with each of them. Chief among the *gopis* was Radha, the consort worshipped as a deity in her own right, but the god had multiple lovers, each of them someone else's wife. The faithful read the *gopis'* ecstatic and erotic love for Krishna as an allegory for the soul's longing for God, a pining sweet with the anguish of the unattainable.[14]

In the sixteenth century, the Bengali saint Chaitanya inspired a branch of Hinduism that departed drastically from those dominant at the time. It contended that the soul would be released from the endless cycle of birth and death through a *gopi*-like devotion to the divine, rather than dutiful conduct or knowledge in Sanskrit of the religious texts. This doctrine created much broader spiritual access. It also made Brahmins less important as middlemen to the gods. Chaitanya believed that birth and bloodlines should not determine caste; instead, devotion should. The sect he developed is known as Vaishnavism, after the god Vishnu, who is its centre of worship and who, Hindus believe, took human form as the carousing lord Krishna. In the early sixteenth century, Chaitanya dispatched his disciples to Vrindaban to make it the sect's base, by laying down physical and theological foundations, in temples and texts.[15] By the time of indenture, Vaishnavism was the predominant form of Hinduism in the areas where most coolies were recruited, especially among the peasants who were its main recruits.

By the nineteenth century, Vrindaban had developed a reputation as a shelter for fallen women, where—it was also widely believed—an infrastructure existed for those women to fall further.[16] Widows and outcast women flocked to the temples and ashrams there. Chaitanya's inclusive brand of Hinduism made room for them and gave them hope, the hope that with a depth of emotion in their *bhajans* and chants, their souls too could transcend. But Vaishnavism also carved out a special and unsettling role for women in its more heterodox offshoots, such as the Sahajiya movement. To much controversy, even within its own ranks, this movement maintained that ritual sex outside of marriage, a kind of extramarital yoga, was the way to spiritual union with Krishna for a disciplined elite.[17] These select few could either seduce the wives of other men, or they could turn to the only unattached women there were— the very same ones targeted by coolie recruiters. Widows and outcasts were perhaps as close to *gopis* as the pilgrims, gurus and ashram managers engaged in this esoteric practice could come. In many ways, they were ideal. According to the Tantric-like principles involved, the women chosen as partners had to be special—because the sex itself was supposed to be ethereal, not carnal. They also had to be unmarriageable, because initiates saw unions that could lead to marriage, one of the householder's everyday duties in society, as merely earth-bound love. To lead to god, they believed, love had to be illicit and elusive; to pursue the divine, pangs were required. Their female partners also had to be discreet, because the men maintained dual identities, keeping up appearances to the outside world—which disapproved—while cultivating an underground, transgressive self. Secrecy was not just desirable or crucial strategically; it became part of the Sahajiya ethos.[18] The degree to which this clandestine sexual ritual amounted to the exploitation of marginalized women—versus a form of religious service by genuine devotees—is murky.

This ambiguity continues still in Vrindaban, popularly known as the city of widows. A feminist academic who once served in India's parliament cites the high number of abortion clinics in nearby Mathura as one sign of ongoing sexual servitude within or through religious institutions in the area.[19] A 1996 report by the National Commission for Women in New Delhi found that young widows chanting for charity in the homes of priests and ashram managers in Vrindaban were often sexually abused and exploited.[20] Filmmaker Deepa Mehta dramatized the plight of such women in *Water*, with its emblematic, elegiac screen shot of a beautiful young widow being ferried nightly across the Ganges, from a home for widows to the bedroom of an ageing landowner. When she meets a tragic fate, a prepubescent widow takes her place. The film was set not in Vrindaban, but in Varanasi, another holy city in the state of Uttar Pradesh, whose boundaries more or less coincide with those of the United Provinces of Agra and Oudh under British rule.

Mainpuri's prolific supply of women for indenture, the mystery that led Pitcher to theorize about canal districts and impotence, might be explained by its place on a well-established pilgrim circuit for widows that began in Chaitanya's birthplace in West Bengal, wound its way to Mehta's Varanasi and then the Ayodhya of my great-grandmother's probable passage, past Mainpuri to where their souls could attain their final release, in the ashrams of Vrindaban.[21] Indeed, Pitcher later discovered that many of the women in Mainpuri had begged their way there en route to the holy site. It's safe to say that the women who found themselves in the town's emigrant depots, suddenly on their way to sugar cane fields at the other end of the globe, were probably not refugees from erectile dysfunction. Most likely, they had been siphoned from the pilgrims on their way to Vrindaban in search of food, shelter and god.

Widows historically led a precarious existence in northeast India. After their husbands died, they were supposed to negate themselves in mourning, forever. For the rest of their lives, they could wear no long tresses, no colorful saris, no vermilion in their hair, no rouge on their lips, no kohl decorating their eyes, no bangles tinkling on their wrists. Enshrouded in white, almost erased, they were viewed as inauspicious and shunned by many. They could not remarry, especially if upper-caste. They could not inherit property. If they had no sons to support them, they were subject to hunger and poverty. And they could be forced to sit on their husbands' funeral pyre, a practice known as *sati*. In the dozen years before the ritual was banned, in 1829, at least 8,000 widows in Bengal committed *sati*.[22]

A series of progressive laws to improve the chances of women in India followed, as a result of pressure from both Indian and British reformers. By mid-century, legislation allowing widows to remarry and banning child marriages went into effect, on paper if not in practice. Later, laws to uncover and penalize clans practicing female infanticide were implemented, and changes to land tenancy rules under British administration granted women succession rights to their husbands' property. But this last measure seemed merely to shift the course of persecution for widows, like a river of oppression redirected, often along a path that led directly to places of pilgrimage. Relatives of the dead would dispatch his widow on a holy tour, in order to get her out of the way and claim property that should have been hers. Sometimes, family members took widows to pilgrimage sites and abandoned them there.[23] At other times, widows found their own way there, as they fled mistreatment and sexual advances in their in-laws' homes. A complex mix of victimization and Vaishnavite devotion brought them—and other ostracized women—to holy sites where recruiters for indenture often found them. Many British government agents viewed emigration as yet another way that they could free Indian women from the most barbaric elements of a heathen culture. As they saw it, they had banned *sati* and child marriage. They had given widows the right to remarry and inherit property. And indenture, too, would liberate India's most oppressed women and thereby demonstrate empire's civilizing influence.

It's difficult to divine what the women targeted to be saved thought of this rhetoric. In the records of the India Office in London they are mostly hidden, or hiding. But occasionally, for brief moments, some flit into view. There's Manharni, who left a village near my great-grandmother's in 1872. Sir George Grierson, the civil servant and Orientalist chosen to do in Bihar what Pitcher was doing in the northwest, tried vainly to find her relatives. He could "gain no intelligence," he wrote. "Nor did any one in the place know even the name of either herself or her father."[24] And there's Rojha, an 1873 emigrant from the same area, whose father "denied having any such relative, and probably she had gone wrong and been disowned by him."[25]

There are glimpses of headstrong women, determined to go or determined not to. One—an untouchable "turned out of home by her husband, who had taken up with another woman"—then signed up as a coolie.[26] Her father offered her food and shelter, but she refused to abandon the idea of leaving India. Further east, in the village of Jagdispur, in what is now Bihar, a starving and almost naked woman succumbed to the offerings of a recruiter named Ram Phal.[27] He fed her for a month and gave her his mother's clothes. When he took her to a magistrate to be registered for the colonies, she refused to go and walked off with the clothes. Not far from there, police raided the house of a recruiter for Mauritius in search of a woman, at her husband's insistence.[28] She had just been released from jail, but didn't go home to him. No one was ever able to find her, and she seems to have eluded both her husband and the authorities.

There are glimpses, too, of conflicted women, who seem barely to know themselves or their intentions. Consider the strange story of the woman who accused a "procuress" of enticing her to a coolie depot. She said that a female recruiter for Trinidad's plantations approached her at a well one day: "She told me that she would get me work at Patna, where I should earn much money," the woman later swore, in a deposition. "She told me this every day for three days. I had never met her before that. On the morning of the fourth day, I met her again, and she told me I should get much money, and told me to go with her."[29] The woman did as instructed. She took her children at night to a grove where two men waited. She did not know them. Nor did she ask their names. Yet, she let them take her, with her children, to the coolie depot, where they locked the door behind her. "I had no quarrel with my husband," this woman later insisted. "I did not tell my husband while the woman was trying to persuade me to go, because she told me not to do so." Once her husband tracked her to the depot, a criminal case ensued; warrants were issued for the arrest of the recruiters, who fast hightailed it out; and no recruiter dared venture into the area for four years. Either the woman was incredibly malleable and naive—or she may have been open to enticement, no matter what she told the authorities. Hers is a story divided against itself.

And it came to posterity filtered: translated into English, guided perhaps by the magistrate or her husband, characterized by Grierson. For the most part, it was colonial officials like him who described the progress of coolie women from India to elsewhere. The archives leave gaps. Missing, with few exceptions, are the voices of the women themselves. They did not leave behind diaries or letters. The vast majority wasn't literate, in English or in any Indian language. They did not tell their own stories, except indirectly, through the often-biased prism of government investigators and court officials who occasionally took their testimonies. The relative silence of coolie women in the sum total of history reflects their lack of power. But could it also reflect a strategy by women who had secrets to keep? Is it possible that, on some level, each individual silence was a plan? Could they have harbored ambivalence in their hearts, an ambivalence to account for their actions, much like the woman who willingly shepherded her children into the wooded dark to meet strange men but then blamed it all on a procuress? Is it possible that my great-grandmother would not want me to know why and how she left? Would she deliberately disappear behind a curtain to escape questions about her past?

Recruiters for indenture assumed that decent women would not go without their husbands and that decent men would not take their wives. Pitcher was told: "It is out of the question to expect respectable men, however ready themselves to venture on the unknown, to expose their wives to they know not what set of risks."[30] Knowing the customs of the Indian countryside, recruiters looked for women who had no one—no one to provide for them and no one to prevent them from going. They targeted the most desperate. Pitcher witnessed many who entered the depots in "a garment of filthy rags, which can hardly be said to clothe them."[31] He took the unpopular position that women should be allowed to serve as recruiters because, he reasoned, "it is only women at their last resource who would bargain with strange men."[32] One emigration register he examined revealed who such women were. The handwritten notes next to their names read: "The enquiry now ended, resulting in the fact that she has been forsaken by her husband on account of her unchastity, now allowed to go." "A married woman forsaken by her husband on account of her bad conduct." "A widow under enquiry."[33]

Grierson concluded that the female emigrants consisted of four groups: the wives of men who had already been to the colonies and had returned to fetch them, destitute widows with no one to take pity on them, prostitutes and "married women who have made a slip, and who have either absconded from their husband's house with or without a lover, or who have been turned out of doors by their husbands." The widows were blameless, he said. The colonies would gladly take them. Grierson objected only that they were "seldom comely." The wives of re-migrants were few. And there could, of course, be no official sanction for prostitutes going—certainly not from colonial administrators expected to be model servants of Victorian and Edwardian England.

And yet, under British influence, prostitution in India thrived like never before. Foreign soldiers and sailors provided a reliable, never-ending demand for commercial sex. Colonialism also created a vast new breed of clients in lonely Indian men uprooted from their families. They included both educated middlemen—upper- and middle-class traders, clerks and professionals who had moved into jobs in administrative settlements newly created by the British—and poor migrant laborers pushed from home partly by British policies. Meanwhile, some of those same policies expanded the supply of female sex workers. They grew from 3 percent to more than 7 percent of Calcutta's population between 1853 and 1867.[34] Prostitution provided a means for uprooted women to earn money, either as a supplement to their meager incomes as factory workers and domestic servants, or as a full-time trade.

But even as opportunities for sex work exploded, and the profession flourished, its character was negatively transformed by British rule. Prostitutes had long held a place in Indian society, as artists who sang and danced, auspicious participants in certain Hindu religious festivals and performers at wedding and funeral ceremonies. Some had even enjoyed the material support of the state, as devadasis (prostitutes dedicated to temples or, literally, "servants of god") or courtesans (whose refinements in northern Indian classical music made them the darlings of Mughal rulers and princely states). Sex workers had a certain status, however grudgingly bestowed. During the colonial period, this faded. Both society and the state increasingly penalized them, making them the targets of coercive legal measures as well as moral outrage. "They were," in the words of one cultural historian, "driven away from society as outcasts and branded by the state as criminals."[35] Victorian attitudes to sex, the colonizer's official prudery, drove this radical change in the standing and fortunes of prostitutes. Paradoxically, so did the colonizer's unofficial acknowledgement that its soldiers in India, infected with venereal disease to an alarming degree, needed access to safer sex.

Colonial administrators sought, through legislation, to create a contained market of disease-free prostitutes, specially certified to operate in regimental bazaars within the boundaries of British cantonments. They were reserved exclusively for soldiers, in a segregated order: one set just for officers, another for white enlisted men and a third for Indian sepoys. A madam on the government's payroll selected the women. In 1864, the Cantonment Act required the chosen ones to register with the authorities as sex workers. They also had to submit twice a month to painful and humiliating physical exams denounced by feminists in London as "instrumental rape by a

33

steel penis" and "medical lust."[36] If infected, the women were incarcerated in lock hospitals for treatment, rendering them unable to work and support any dependents. Four years later, a copycat of existing British law, the Contagious Diseases Act (CDA), extended those rules to prostitutes serving the wider population in major towns and cities across India. Under the law, every prostitute in those jurisdictions had to carry a pass bearing her name, caste and address and confine herself to certain neighborhoods. Every sex worker also had to declare herself to be one, an official avowal that removed, irrevocably, all grey areas in her life. Kept women, moonlighting factory workers, flower-sellers and milkmaids who did it on the side, high-class *baijis* who were divas of classical dance all had to embrace an identity that—even as it was being regulated as a necessary social evil—was becoming black-and-white and stigmatized.

Police conducted frequent raids and harassed women, who faced the prospect of jail, with hard labor, if they failed to register as prostitutes or be examined regularly for venereal disease. The CDA was a law to be resisted and fled, and many women did resist and flee. They resisted by bribing police, in some cases. In others, they produced false marriage certificates or presented evidence before magistrates that they were mistresses rather than professional prostitutes.[37] Many fled to a French settlement north of Calcutta or to areas in the outlying countryside where the act wasn't in effect. Others snuck into central neighborhoods to work at night, commuting home to suburban safe zones during the day. As one feminist historian has put it, "women in prostitution played a hide-and-seek of sorts with policemen."[38]

But did they take the game as far as escaping to the other end of the globe as menial field workers? Even if recruiters had sugar-coated the jobs waiting, how would those jobs have compared to an occupation that, driven by a growing demand, was profitable and had given some women freedoms that housewives lacked? Where was the economic incentive to leave? The CDA largely failed, both in its end (curbing venereal disease among British soldiers) and in its means (getting prostitutes to register and submit to examinations). It was, as a result, repealed in 1888. Given how widely flouted and ineffective it was, and given that there were hiding places nearby, did any women find it necessary to board ship to evade the act? By defying its provisions, they became criminals; but when the majority was defiant, what was the need to run? Or was the new stigma attached to prostitutes enough to make them quit India? To a great extent, the answer is unknown and unknowable. Sailors, who were such reliable clients and who worked as crew on coolie ships, might have made sex workers aware of the option of indenture.[39] In any case, recruiters certainly worked the prostitute bazaars.

British officials at the time and historians since have disagreed about the extent to which indentured women were drawn from among sex workers. The year after the CDA was passed, the chief emigration agent in Madras claimed that, in all emigrant ships from that port:

Nearly one half the emigrant women are of doubtful character or about one-third confirmed prostitutes, and since the Contagious Diseases Act has come into force the supply of emigrant women from this class of the population has diminished, as a good many of these have run away into the interior to avoid the restrictions imposed upon them by the act, and no small number are confined in the lock hospitals of Madras.[40]

The agent may have felt the need to please his superiors by documenting how well the act was working. It may also have been in his interest to burnish the reputations of the women he was sending, since neither planters nor the Colonial Office officially approved of prostitutes among the indentured. The act may actually have reduced the proportion of prostitutes on indenture ships, but it's worth noting that the majority of the indentured were recruited from the interior—and that in other parts of the world, the CDA had spurred migration, not checked it.[41]

In indenture's final years, two British envoys sent to investigate alleged abuses against coolies in the West Indies and Fiji concluded that only a small percentage of the women were professional prostitutes: "[T]he great majority are not, as they are frequently represented to be, shamelessly immoral," they reported in 1914. "They are women who have got into trouble and apparently emigrate to escape from the life of promiscuous prostitution which seems to be the alternative."[42] The following year, a district medical officer in Fiji drew the same conclusion, attributing venereal disease among the indentured there to "perhaps a very few professional prostitutes" but, more broadly, to women who had lost their honor in India.[43] This man of science managed, somehow, to quantify the dishonor: 20 percent of indentured women were fallen women, but not necessarily prostitutes, he ventured.

Despite the colonial zeal for rigid classification, backed up by data, there was massive overlap between the various categories of women seen as the pool for indenture. And there was also massive overlap between the categories of women targeted for indenture and those driven or attracted to sex work in India. In 1851, a Bengali newspaper interviewed twenty-seven prostitutes. Sixteen were widows of all castes set adrift after rejecting the austere rituals of widowhood, being mistreated by their families or, in two cases, being lured by "paramours."[44] There is a reason the word *randi* or *ranri* can mean both young widow and prostitute in both the Bhojpuri and Bengali languages.[45] Two other sex workers had fled daily beatings by their husbands. Two could no longer stand husbands who cheated on them.[46] The remaining seven were single women whose families followed *kulinism*, a Brahminic system with such precise rules governing the marriage of daughters, by caste, sub-caste and clan, that many found no husbands or had to share one, polygamously.

Circumstances outside their control often led them to dishonor, as the story of one *kulin* Brahmin woman demonstrates. At three, she was married to a man with other wives, but continued to live with her parents. When she was sixteen, this husband more than three decades her senior turned up at her doorstep. "I was shocked by his uncouth appearance, his decrepit limbs and gnarled white hair," she wrote, in a letter to a Bengali journal in 1842. "I had never knowingly accepted him, never met him ever since I had come of age. There had never been any harmony of minds or love between the two of us, and yet he was my husband."[47] The next morning, having claimed his conjugal rights and some money from her father, he left—never to return. Traumatized by the sudden appearance of this ancient husband, to deflower then disappear, she realized what lay ahead: a wasted youth, "denied the happiness of a life with a husband." She may as well have been widowed. In a deeply patriarchal society, with a growing body of laws restricting the ability of women to work outside the home,[48] she had few options. "I genuinely tried to remain chaste and maintain the honour of my family and religion," she explained, but "finally, out of sheer torment, I chose to go astray, and I came to Calcutta and I am living independently now."[49] She signed her letter, "A Prostitute Living in Calcutta."

Might she have signed it, instead, "A Coolie Woman Living in Guiana"? Had she known about indenture, would she have chosen it over her independence in Calcutta, in a settlement of prostitutes who shared her predicament as a *kulin* Brahmin daughter? Prostitutes, especially the first generation of the early nineteenth century, included many women from high castes or middle- and upper-class upbringings. Indeed, the heterogenous world of sex workers in India had many hierarchies, with regimental prostitutes near the top in the era of the Contagious Diseases Act, and still others lit up in the afterglow of the Mughal courts, displaying proudly their accomplishments in classical dance and music. But as the nineteenth century ended, prostitutes were increasingly drawn from squalor. They included girls sold by famine-stricken parents, girls born into the profession ("hereditary prostitutes") and displaced migrants forced to supplement paltry wages. To these women, toiling in sugar cane fields may not have seemed downwardly mobile. And widows and seduced-then-abandoned women, still the profession's stalwarts whatever their socioeconomic background, were the very women Grierson recommended recruiting.

By going after them, he believed, the British would not so much recruit prostitutes as save women from prostitution. He considered the hapless victims of seduction to be the best hope for the colonies to attract more women. As he wrote:

They are generally comely, and comparatively pure. I do not think that anyone can say that the recruiting of these poor creatures is anything but good, both for themselves and the country. Once they leave their home, whether they abscond or are turned out, their husbands will never receive them back again, and if they do not emigrate, they will have only two alternatives: suicide or prostitution.[50]

Agents for indenture pitched a third alternative to them. They circulated notices in the Bihari countryside promising women that, if they migrated to the sugar colonies, they would "find husbands at once among the wealthier of their countrymen."[51] Perhaps what the agents had in mind, with this advertising strategy, were the motivations of their own women of the "Fishing Fleet," who had sailed out to India in force to catch husbands, preferably upper-echelon, as soon as steam travel and the Suez Canal had allowed them to do it relatively quickly, in the mid-nineteenth century. The problem that coolie men faced, stranded far from home without enough women of their own kind, was not at all alien to the civil servants whose job it was to recruit and dispatch them.

Anxiety over how to handle this last group of women—who had left husbands, willingly or unwillingly—is what had prompted the expeditions by Grierson and Pitcher in the first place. The confusion had started in 1878 in a region bordering Bihar, when a man banished his wife.[52] She wandered to another district seeking help from relatives. When rebuffed there, she signed up for Guiana. Three months after she sailed, her husband found out and filed a complaint against emigration authorities. As a result, the British government in India issued instructions for registering officers to find out, in the cases of married women, whether their husbands minded if they left. Grierson and Pitcher thought the directive absurd. "A man who has turned his wife out of doors, if asked whether his wife might emigrate would probably say—no," Pitcher averred.[53] In Faizabad, a magistrate sent a would-be migrant home because her husband objected to her going, only to have him refuse to support her. She landed right back in the coolie depot after she was found starving in the streets.[54]

Many magistrates interpreted the government's memo to mean they had to refuse all women unaccompanied by husbands. They put the burden on the woman to prove that she was a widow. Pitcher railed against "the ludicrous travesty of justice involved in expecting a woman who had tramped the country for months hundreds of miles from her home to produce 'evidence'."[55] Magistrates sent police to hunt down husbands and secure permission. The process could take so long that the women and the recruiters, who meanwhile had to feed and house them, gave up the bid. In one district, Pitcher found that even women accompanied by men were investigated, in case they were eloping. If police brought back the reply that a woman wasn't known at the address she had given, she was rejected for providing false information.

Grierson, reacting to the way the whole legal apparatus was put to work nullifying women's wishes, sounded almost like a feminist. "There seems to me," he wrote:

to be everywhere too great a tendency to treat a native woman as an ignorant child. She is not an unreasoning brute, if she may be a little dull of comprehension. ... A wife will not leave her husband in this country without extreme pressure of some kind or another, and if she insists on going, ... I do not think that any government official has any right to stop her.[56]

Grierson may have been a forward-thinking man, but it's more likely that his passionate defense of women's rights was calculated to meet his government's interests. Coolie women were in demand in the sugar colonies, and if it helped to solve the problems his government was having attracting them, surely they ought to be allowed to make their own choices.

But the popular perception was that no one, male or female, whatever his or her ability to make rational decisions, would willingly choose indenture. The prejudices against overseas emigration were profound. In the countryside, people believed recruiters were actually gathering coolies to hang them by the heels and extract oil from their heads. The oil, or *mimiai-ka-tel*, was supposedly sold to thieves who rubbed it all over their bodies to elude capture. Grierson found that the sugar colonies had gotten "a bad name" as "a kind of Limbo" into which people disappeared, never to be heard from again:

It is stated everywhere that it is a hard thing to leave one's motherland. This is everywhere admitted, and several persons told me that they would have emigrated long ago but for the fear they had of breaking the tie which had bound their families to the same spot for generations.[57]

Recruiters lived in the local imagination as schemers, liars, even kidnappers. According to widespread belief, they did not inform. They misinformed. They gave recruits the false impression that they could return home from their jobs for the weekend; they promised work as easy as sifting sugar; and they exaggerated the gains to be had, inflating wages and conjuring lands of milk, honey and gold. In coolie folk songs, the recruiter is a cursed and vilified figure. The cry of one song is: "Oh recruiter, your heart is deceitful./ Your speech is full of lies!/ Tender may be your voice, articulate and seemingly/ logical,/ But it is used to defame and destroy/ The good names of people."[58] A pamphlet by a descendant of indentured laborers, published in Guiana in 1930, claimed that female recruiters eavesdropped on secrets and gossip exchanged at wells and other places women gathered and used the tidbits they gleaned to trap women into indenture.[59]

In the tales of leaving India handed down to the generations, chance encounters with recruiters who exploited misfortune feature regularly. A widow trying to find her way back to her parents' village after a quarrel with her in-laws met a recruiter on the road. Her five-year old son was in tow, and all her wealth—in the form of her jewellery—was bundled in her headscarf. The stranger promised to guide her back to her childhood home, but instead stole her jewellery and put her on a train to the coolie depot in Calcutta.[60] A man who left India as a boy around 1905 remembered how his mother became beholden to a recruiter after the death of his father, an army bookkeeper. As a widow, she had become so friendless and destitute that she ventured out into the market one day to beg. A recruiter approached, asking how a high-caste woman like her had been so debased. She told him her troubles. The recruiter bought figs for her and her hungry son, thereby making her obliged to him. "That was the way he said, 'Well, look, come let me carry you all to the table'," where emigrants were registered, the son recalled.[61] The great-grandmother of the Guyanese poet Rajkumari Singh was on a pilgrimage with relatives when she and her son became separated from the group. Phuljharee was a woman of high status, the widow of a wealthy landowner and the daughter of a Brahmin priest. A recruiter promised to help her locate her relatives. Days later, she found herself in an emigration depot in Calcutta.[62]

Colonial records also document cases of dishonest recruiters, giving credence to the lore and the stories that descendants tell. The year my great-grandmother sailed, among the thirty recruiters who had their licenses revoked were: two for "carelessness in the recruitment and registration of a female emigrant," one for "attempting to cheat and abduct a woman," one for "attempting to recruit a woman against her wishes," one for "fraudulent character, inasmuch as he was found conveying two females to his sub-depot under false pretences" and one for "making a false statement in respect of the registration of two persons reported to be husband and wife."[63]

There was particular incentive for recruiters to ensnare women, because the emigration agencies paid higher bounties for female recruits.

Suspicions that the intentions of recruiters were evil ran understandably deeper when it came to women. One Indian man told Grierson that recruiters regularly seduced away wives and daughters, without ever disclosing the real reason they wanted them. The women discovered it too late; once they had spent a night outside the home of a father or husband, they could no longer return. They were irreparably dishonored. In one remarkable account, being recruited for the sugar colonies struck one woman as more disgraceful than serving as a concubine. She was discovered one morning by men who followed her cries to a sandy waste near their village.[64] They found her in the company of an *arkati*, one of the unlicensed subcontractors who rounded up coolies for recruiters. He had lured her from Lucknow with her small children and set up camp overnight near the village. But he didn't go near her all night. That's why she cried out for help. She seemed to want a protector and provider and expected to be asked for sexual favors in return. But the *arkati* was looking for a coolie woman, not a kept woman. That's what alarmed her; it was generally held that coolie recruiters abducted Indian women into prostitution overseas.

What, then, was the truth? Into which category of recruit did my great-grandmother fall? Who was she? Displaced peasant, runaway wife, kidnap victim, Vaishnavite pilgrim or widow? Was the burn mark on her left leg a scar from escaping a husband's funeral pyre? Was she a prostitute, or did indenture save her from sex work? Did she see herself as part of the subcontinent's own version of the "Fishing Fleet"? Did the system liberate women, or con them into a new kind of bondage? Did it save them from a life of shame, or ship them directly to it? Were coolie women caught in the clutches of unscrupulous recruiters who tricked them? Were they, quite to the contrary, choosing to flee? Were these two possibilities mutually exclusive, or could both things be true?

The two British envoys who assessed indenture near its end looked back on all the women who had taken part, in more than a dozen colonies worldwide. They estimated that, whether willingly or unwillingly, two-thirds of indentured women left India unaccompanied by men.[65] It's true that many found partners on the way, while awaiting ships in the depots or during their sea journeys. But, whatever else remains enigmatic about who they were, this much isn't: on leaving India, most coolie women were on their own, like my great-grandmother. The year Sujaria sailed, 76 percent of female recruits were somehow allowed to go alone, despite all the drama over background checks and detentions in the rural recruiting grounds that year and for decades before.[66] The debate that took place in the summer of 1903, when she left India pregnant and alone, does not make what happened to her any clearer. If anything, it throws shafts of darkness on the circumstances leading to her departure. So desperate were British administrators for female recruits, they may have bent rules to get them. There may have been lies told about the women's identities and origins, both by recruiters and the women themselves. The possibility only made my goal, to dig up my great-grandmother's true story, more elusive.

4

INTO DARK WATERS

Half-torn by the wind
Their words reach
The shore, demanding
I memorize their
Ancient and recent
Journeys

Agha Shahid Ali, "A Footnote to History"*

As he sailed upriver towards Calcutta for the first time, the doctor Theophilus Richmond paused to admire a stretch of imposing neoclassical mansions a few miles south of the city. With fat porches fortified by gleaming white columns and tree-lined lawns sloping down to the banks of the Hooghly River, they spread their weight expansively across the landscape. The British mercantile and governing elite lived there, directly across the river from the Botanical Gardens. "The last few miles of the approach from the river is a succession of beautiful villas...," Richmond wrote in his diary on 8 December 1837. "It is named Garden Reach, and both in appearance and situation reminded me strongly of English scenery."[1]

He didn't know that this graceful spot, so reminiscent of home, would one day be linked—as he himself already was—to the traffic that succeeded the slave trade. Richmond was sailing to Calcutta to fulfill an appointment aboard *The Hesperus*, which, along with a second vessel travelling by its side, *The Whitby*, was the first to transport indentured laborers to the West Indies. The British politician John Gladstone, who wanted them for his sugar plantations in British Guiana, had chartered

* Epigraph from *The Country Without a Post Office* by Agha Shahid Ali, ©1997. Used by permission of W.W. Norton & Company, Inc.

41

the ship. It would leave India two months later, and Richmond's job would be to oversee the health and well-being of the emigrants aboard.

He was a recent graduate of the prestigious medical school at Edinburgh University, a young man barely out of his teens whose Byronic bent compelled him constantly to seek out the company of pretty women. The day before, he had hidden behind a tree to steal his first glimpse of women from the subcontinent, whose elusiveness intrigued him. As he wrote:

The women, who are not permitted to see or be seen by an European, covered their faces with the long veil that they all wear and ran away still faster till they had bolted themselves in as firm and secure as though I had been Dr Faustus or the Devil himself.[2]

Of the 170 emigrants aboard *The Hesperus*, only seven were women. By the time the vessel sailed, Richmond had discovered that he wasn't attracted to Indian women, except perhaps the biracial daughters of Europeans, who struck him as "bright angels come down from heaven, only slightly discolored by their aerial journey through the grosser atmosphere of this lesser universe." But even if he had found the women on the ship desirable, Richmond had little time to indulge any romantic inclinations. Soon, he had to contend with a cholera outbreak that claimed the lives of ten emigrants, who died in feverish fits, their tongues blackened, lips desperately dry, bowels contorted. Soon, the only woman he was noticing was a patient, a mother:

lying nearly in a state of insensibility with sunken cheeks and lustreless eyes, shewing no sign of life, except as she occasionally opened her parched and burning mouth for a little water, and yet clasping her infant to that chill and almost pulseless bosom, that was no longer able to give the nourishment it was crying for, on each side of her two other children, one in the same condition as herself and the other already stiffening in the embrace of death, whilst to complete the picture the affectionate and wretched husband, whom neither threats nor endeavours could keep away from those he loved so well, watched over them unceasingly…[3]

Richmond gave milk with tapioca-like pearls of sago to the woman's baby and a teacup of rum, administered in sips over sixteen hours, to her four-year-old. Except for the remaining child, who was five, the family survived both cholera and the crossing.

Richmond was the first to perform the role of "surgeon superintendent" on a vessel carrying Indians to plantations in the West Indies. In the eight decades to come, as indenture ship after indenture ship departed India, no single figure would matter more to emigrants during this other middle passage than the surgeon. He could be their caretaker and protector, or he could be the very devil, to the women aboard in particular.

The fashionable address that Richmond noticed on his approach to Calcutta would also come to hold great significance for indentured emigrants. From the late 1880s, the neighborhood housed depots for recruits awaiting ships to the sugar colonies. Garden Reach became the point of departure for the emigrants, the place where they said goodbye—forever, for most—to the land their families had called home for centuries. It was also the place their metamorphoses began.

The suburb had changed character well before it started warehousing the emigrants. An ousted Indian king had set up his court-in-exile at Garden Reach after the British removed him from power in 1857. For three decades, poets and courtesans thrived there under the aegis of the Nawab of Awadh, host of many decadent parties. When the king died in 1887, however, the landscape was transformed. Jute factories and dockyards took the place of pleasure gardens. During the monsoon season, water stagnated on tracts of undrained land, breeding mosquitoes and malaria. The king's palace was razed, and the mansions of his ministers were sold to clear his debts. The house once used by his prime minister became headquarters for the government agency sending workers to British Guiana. Operations for four other colonies—Trinidad, Fiji, Mauritius and Jamaica—shifted to a nearby villa, with its own private river jetty.

One scholar of indenture has remarked that the British didn't recruit "coolies" for their sugar cane fields.[4] Rather, they *made* "coolies." By this logic, the system took gardeners, palanquin-bearers, goldsmiths, cow-minders, leather-makers, boatmen, soldiers and priests with centuries-old identities based on religion, kin and occupation and turned them all into an indistinguishable, degraded mass of plantation laborers without caste or family. This reverse alchemy began at Garden Reach, as the emigrants ate and slept side by side, violating the taboos and rules that had so far governed their lives.

This apparent undoing happened in a setting eerie with remembered decadence. Emigrants for British Guiana were treated for humiliating diseases in the prime minister's old "Bear Pit." A balcony that once offered a view of wild animals fighting opened instead onto patients suffering from cholera and dysentery. The stone wall that once marked the boundary of the nawab's court still stood, its mile of terraces and the curve of its arches intact. By the time it enclosed the indentured, it was overgrown with bushes and infested with cobras, which regularly slithered into the depot.[5] For weeks, sometimes months, the emigrants stayed behind the nawab's wall, sleeping in sheds with palm-leaf roofs, ant-eaten walls and mud floors near marble-paved agency headquarters.[6] Police searching for wanted men regularly combed the depot, as did people looking for missing wives, husbands, brothers or sisters.[7]

When they first arrived, the emigrants were stripped of their own clothes and given soap to wash in the Hooghly—again, side by side, the concerns of caste seemingly disappearing down the river, like the sacred thread that one migrant saw some high-caste Hindus discard as they bathed, in 1898.[8] There was good reason for those men to let slip downriver the thread, called the *janew*. Brahmin boys receive it as part of their ritual initiation into manhood at the age of thirteen. Today, in a filigreed ring box kept with the family jewellery, my father's own *janew* lies cushioned, tinted with turmeric used during his initiation rite in Guyana and countless other religious ceremonies since. Hidden away like that, a century after Sujaria may have watched men of her caste release their *janews*, it testifies to the secrets and stratagems of Brahmin emigrants. They may have hidden their identities, but they did not disavow them. The *janew* persisted across continents and generations. Brahmins probably knew they were unwanted. The word had gotten out: planters saw them as unfit for hard labor in the fields and, moreover, as a potential threat to their authority. Those who abandoned the *janew* must have known it would betray them to government doctors, instructed to check for the soft, disqualifying hands of Brahmins.*[9]

Those bound for the West Indies were given new and unfamiliar clothes for the cold, rough weather they would encounter around Africa's southern tip. The regulations allotted women two flannel jackets, a woollen petticoat and worsted stockings, as well as a sari, while men received wool trousers, a red woollen cap and a jacket. Sometimes, the jacket was the hand-me-down scarlet tunic of a British soldier.[10] Sometimes, there were no trousers but a *dhoti*, the loose cloth with which men in village India typically girded their loins. Whether traditional in style or Western, and whether of good quality or literally rotten,[11] the clothes issued to any particular group of migrants were identical. They were a uniform. One emigrant—who spent his final years back in India, in an ashram with Mahatma Gandhi, campaigning against indenture—remembered it this way: "We were given prisoners' shirts, caps and pants to wear."[12]

A folk song sung in British Guiana for generations captures the emigrants' sense that they were denuded of their identities, disrobed and degraded at the depot. It goes:

> When we reached Calcutta, our miseries increased.
> We were stripped of all our beautiful clothes,
> Rosary beads and sacred threads.
> Bengali rags decorated us now.
> The sadhu's hair was shaved.
> And sadhu, Dom, Chamar and Bhangi,
> All were thrown together in a room.[13]

The oral tradition speaks of meals violating caste and religious rules and depot staff assaulting emigrants who refused to eat. One song testifies:

> They beat us with a cane. Lifting us over their heads,
> They threw us on the floor;
> In abusive language, they called us *sala* and other names.[14]

Depot doctors were supposed to ensure that recruits were free of diseases, including sexually transmitted ones. A civil surgeon who inspected emigrants for Guiana from the 1870s to the 1890s described his method, in the case of men: "A thorough examination of the genital organs is made. Hernia, hydrocele, varicocele, enlarged or

---

* In 1891, Jamaica's emigration agent described the criteria to be used by civil surgeons when selecting emigrants: "The hands should be hard, showing that the emigrant is accustomed to manual labor. Temple Brahmans, Kayaths, Banias, shop-keepers, weavers, dyers, Panjabis, priests, beggars, jogis, etc. should be rejected... Men bearing on their bodies the marks of branding from the various places of pilgrimage should be specially examined and should be unhesitatingly rejected if of high-caste...."

pendulous testicles, syphilis, gonorrhoea, enlarged glands are all looked for and if found are causes of rejection. ... The man is then turned round, the anal region is examined for piles, fistula, fissures or other diseases."[15] Women did not have to undergo the same degree of clinical ogling before departing. The shame would have made them even harder to recruit than they already were. Indeed, the reports filed when indenture ships reached their destinations routinely mention women who, upon landing, were found to have venereal disease. Some men were later found to have it too, despite the intense peering at their privates. While it's true that recruits could have contracted the diseases aboard ship, after being chosen, it's also true that doctors examined them under tacit pressure to fill ships swiftly with coolies, whatever their condition, especially in the cases of women.

Depot officials, seeking to dispel the belief that indenture dishonored women, segregated them from men, even when in line for food. One man who migrated in the early 1900s described the sleeping arrangements at the depot this way:

> Bachelor man sleeping one side
> 'oman sleeping one side
> Separate
> Separate[16]

But another who stayed in the same depot for a month in 1906 said efforts to keep the sexes apart failed. "In the depot, all ate together, and people slept with each other's wives," he told a historian seven decades later. "I did not like such behavior. ... There was no caste or religion there."[17] The same memory troubled Munshi Rahman Khan, the indentured emigrant who witnessed the *janews* being discarded in 1898. He denounced the depot as a place where higher-caste Hindus began to lose their religion. Though he was Muslim, this seemed to violate his own sense of the universe's order. Many decades later, he wrote:

These people resorted to infidelity. They did not hesitate to have other women from different castes and creed to keep them company. They also were very close and intimate with the untouchables, and ate, drank and had fun with them, and started relations with their womenfolk. Their company was, therefore, those very people who ate pigs, cows, etc., and they even impregnated their seeds in these women.[18]

Most men had left their own wives behind in their villages, as migrant laborers all over have done for centuries, and most women had left their husbands behind—if they had not already lost them to famine, migration or other women. The history books tell us that the uncoupled regularly became coupled in the depots, out of convenience or necessity. Women perhaps calculated it would help to have a protector on the journey ahead, and men may have seen the benefits of having someone to cook and care for them where they were going. New husbands and wives were regularly taken, without ceremony or priestly sanction, across caste and religion.

I try to imagine my great-grandmother in this setting, preparing to board *The Clyde* in 1903. Had she found a protector, too? Was he of her caste? In her week in the depot, did she see any men cede their sacred threads to the river and, if so, did that disturb her? What did she make of the worsted stockings? Did the presence of cobras, venomous but venerated among Hindus, strike her as auspicious—or ominous? Who had certified her as fit to sail, and disease-free, and "Pregnant 4 mos," if the depot doctors didn't really examine women?

Was Sujaria anxious about the 10,500 nautical miles ahead? Was she aware that the distance would be so great, or that it would take three-and-a-half months to sail from Calcutta to Georgetown? Had she ever been on a *jahaj*?* Or heard about the *Pagal Samundar*, the point where two oceans meet at the Cape of Good Hope and where the waves rage against this meeting, churning up a "mad sea"? Did she view sea voyages as Hinduism's ancient books of right conduct, the *dharma-shastras*, did? Presumably because conditions on board thwarted ritual purity, *The Laws of Manu* declared seafarers spiritually unfit. Judged polluted—along with thieves, perjurers, physicians, one-eyed men, black-toothed men and inexplicable others—they were barred from eating with their kin, making offerings to their dead or the gods, and receiving offerings once dead.[19] Did it unnerve my great-grandmother to contemplate excommunication so complete, it reached into the afterlife? Coming from the world she did, where community was life itself, she must have feared that the dark waters would swallow her very self and soul.

Or could she see that the seven sins that led to the forfeiture of caste** all challenged the primacy of Brahmins in some way and were therefore in their self-interest to sanction? Was she cowed, or baffled, by the atonement required to reclaim caste: every day for three years, eat only one small meal, stand all day, sit all night, bathe thrice? If Sujaria doubted the punishment and the penance, she wasn't alone. In Bengal, in the 1890s, peaked the Sea Voyages Movement. Upper-caste Hindus wanting to study in England argued that religious tradition allowed travel for merit—for education, progress, pilgrimage—as long as no polluting contact occurred.[20] Did my great-grandmother also reject the notion that seafarers automatically lost caste? Or could she not care less? Was the female "caste," so to speak, the only one with concrete meaning for her existence?

And if caste didn't define her, did place? In rural India, navel strings are buried where babies are born, signifying a sacral attachment to that land. Did it grieve Sujaria that she might never return to the earth that held her navel string? Her descendants would continue to bury the umbilical cords of their children, wherever born. They would retain that folk custom, but lose any sense that sacred texts declared the seas would erase their identities. Did my great-grandmother realize that this would really only matter for the returned—and that she wouldn't be among them?

* Hindi for ship.
** The seven sins, according to the *Baudhayana-Dharma-Sutra*, are: (1) voyaging by sea, (2) trading in any kind of merchandise, (3), stealing a Brahmin's property, (4) giving false testimony about land, (5) serving the lower castes, (6) getting a lower-caste woman pregnant with a son and (7) being the son of such a union.

46

Was she thinking of Deodhar, the man later identified as the father of the child she was carrying? Why—according to that child's "infant born on board" certificate—was Deodhar left behind in India? Was he her husband? Did she leave him, or had he left her? Or was it some third party who had separated them, perhaps a recruiter who had deceived or even outright kidnapped her? Was she telling the truth when, four decades later in a Guiana Bottom House, she talked about leaving India?[21] As she smoked a tobacco pipe, encircled by women who had been her shipmates, did she really say that she had been on a pilgrimage when white men in boats came, promising to ferry her to the next stop on her holy tour? Did the eavesdropping grandchild who shared this redolent detail with me understand Hindi well enough to get the story right? It's unlikely that white men were doing the lowly work of sub-recruiter in the hinterlands. Would Sujaria, in any case, have trusted them? But why would she lie? Why would she embroider a tale for her *jahaji behen*, her "ship sisters," given the bond among emigrants who crossed on the same ship, a bond so strong, so intimate, it replaced family ties for many?

Could she possibly have foreseen me someday asking such impertinent questions? What would she have made of my poring over *The Clyde*'s passenger manifest with gloved hands, examining the emigration passes of 207 of the 225 females aboard, afterwards brushing away the ash from the quiet cataclysm of turning century-old pages?[22] Did she get to know the sixteen other pregnant women I found in those pages? Did she envy the five among them who had husbands by their side? Did she bond instinctively with the eleven who didn't? Would it have comforted her to know that 71 percent of the women whose passes I studied left Garden Reach without a husband, as she did; or that 11 percent were pregnant, as she was; or that 8 percent were both pregnant and travelling husbandless, exactly like her? Did my grandfather kick?

In the depot, did my great-grandmother talk to Rukmini, a nineteen-year old who was a hermaphrodite? Was that secret discovered in Calcutta, or did it have to wait, like the venereal diseases, to be uncovered by Guiana's medical inspector? How would Rukmini, both man and woman, fare in the depot and on the ship—places simultaneously segregated by sex and fraught with sex? Did my great-grandmother notice Rahsi, an Untouchable woman travelling with her husband, who was disfigured, her left nostril cut? Had the woman's husband inflicted the cut? On seeing it, did Sujaria feel pity? Did she know Tirnal, the farmer from Mirzapur travelling with five girls, the youngest three, the eldest fourteen? What had happened to the mother of those girls? Wasn't the eldest too grown, by the marriage conventions of the day, to still be in a father's care? Could that man possibly have been trafficking those girls? Single fathers were few, while at least twenty-eight single mothers sailed on *The Clyde*, accounting for 20 percent of women aboard. Did Sujaria find the motherless family at all suspicious?

Did the children remind her of ones she had left behind? Had she left any behind? How did she ever get to this point of departure, surrounded by so many fragmented families and outcasts, bearing secrets and unstated loss? Did she look back over her shoulder, as she boarded the ship? Was there regret in her glance?

I don't know, because she didn't say. Except for one fragment of overheard Bottom House talk, her story was not handed down to the generations. Sometimes, I think the women who left India as coolies kept quiet on purpose. It may be that the circumstances were too traumatic to remember, much less proclaim. It may be that their emotions were too conflicted to convey. Perhaps language limited them; they may have lacked the words in English to express the deep dividedness of departure to their children and grandchildren. The stories that did descend often reveal as much about how families choose to see their histories as they do about the actual histories. There are two main narratives: one of escape, the other of kidnap.

In another family, the image that survives of its matriarch is as a baby on a ship, cradled in the arms of her parents, who fled a tradition of female infanticide in their clan. According to the tale, they bribed a midwife into saying their newborn was a boy, and then they ran. If Mahadai had not sailed to Guiana on *The Ganges* in 1871, the clan would have killed her by putting salt under her tongue. So the story of her exit from India goes.[23] Her great-granddaughter frames it as a flight to safety and freedom, not only for Mahadai but for the generations to come: "We are fortunate," she says, "that no one was able to put salt under our tongues—because of our heroic great-great-grandparents, who preferred to cross the *kala pani*."

In yet another family, two versions of leaving India have survived to contradict each other. One goes this way: It is 1895, in a village near Ghazipur in the United Provinces. It is midday, and the men of the village are away, working. White men descend in force and, in a single sweep, they unwife and unchild the village. A nine-year old girl named Manakia is, along with her mother and brother, among the boatload kidnapped into indenture that day. She never says goodbye to her father. Ever after, she imagines the moment he returns to find his home empty and bereft. In this version, recounted by Manakia's granddaughters, her father was robbed of his family.[24] In the alternative version, recounted by her great-granddaughter, he left them, and Manakia's mother was on the brink of suicide when she met a recruiter for the colonies. I don't know which version is true, whether the mother wanted to leave India or regretted it always.

But I do know the story of one woman who had no regrets when she left Garden Reach in 1916. Maharani could not remember her parents' names by the time she told her story, in a voice frail with age.[25] She was a child when they died. It was her uncle who provided a lap for her to sit on during her wedding to a much older man, whose name she couldn't remember either. Providing a lap to a bride, during the era of child marriages in India, seems to have been comparable to walking one down the aisle. Maharani was five when she got married. And she was still just a child, only twelve, when widowed. Soon after, her brother-in-law took her to a magistrate's office where, too young to know better, she ceded the rights to her inheritance from her husband. For eight years after his death, she cooked and cleaned for her in-laws, bearing their beatings for minor mishaps much like the one that ultimately triggered her journey to Trinidad.

She left, literally, over spilled milk. Maharani had just boiled milk for her in-laws, when a cat crept up to lick the pot. She pelted the cat, the cat fell over and the pot capsized. Anticipating another thrashing, and suddenly unwilling to accept one, she slipped out while her in-laws were eating. In 1987, Maharani explained why she fled:

> I say dem go beat me.
> Because I getting too much licks.
> I say dem go beat me.
> Well, I run.
> I no tell nobody I leaving.[26]

On the road, later that night, she met a man with one foot at a well. When he heard her predicament, he offered to help: Did she want a job on an island where she could make 25 cents a day? All she would have to do, he claimed, is sift sugar. Did she want to go? Maharani said yes. She did want to go. She *would* go. "Me nah had nothing," she said, recalling how, at twenty, she calculated the costs and benefits of leaving India. "I come way. Me nah have nothing."[27]

As her boat, *The Chenab*, was anchored in the Hooghly, another ship pulled in, bringing home Indians who had finished their indentures. They clamored to portholes to warn the emigrants staring back out of their own portholes. From a distance, the repatriates shook their hands, gesturing for the emigrants not to go.[28] But it was too late for anyone to heed that message.

This was the point when the umbilical cord connecting the emigrants to India was, presumably, cut. Several survivors of indenture, in the rare accounts that describe the severing, mention weeping; they conjure a scene of breast-beating and wailing as the ship embarked.[29] This was also the point when, according to some versions, the emigrants decisively lost their freedom. The ex-indentured laborer who was Gandhi's acolyte described a solemn moment: "At that time, many emotions were born in our hearts," he wrote. "In just the way a free bird is imprisoned in a cage, we were all locked in."[30] For generations, the descendants of indentured laborers in Guiana, accompanied by the plaintive notes of harmonium and sarangi, sang of a parting that was woeful:

> Listen, oh Indian, listen to the story of us emigres,
> The emigres who cry constantly, tears flowing from their eyes.
> When we left the ports of Calcutta and Bombay,
> Brother left sister, mother left daughter.
> In deep love of the mother country we cried;
> Water flowed from our eyes…
> Painful is our story, choking is our voice.[31]

But Maharani did not cry. Nor did she remember sounds of sorrow. She remembered drumbeats. Looking back across the span of seven decades, she described how her *jahajis* played drums provided by the crew and how they sang and danced during the journey:

> dem bringing happy
> dem en bringing no trouble

> dem bringing happy
> nobody to study nothing
> that's why dem bringing happy[32]

There was nobody to make her "study" a single thing. Nobody to cause her grief or worry. No brother-in-law to cheat her. No mother-in-law to beat her. Nobody, she thought, to make her tremble in fear any longer. But should Maharani have been so convinced that no one would cause her grief anymore? The warning by the repatriates, as her ship got ready to leave the Hooghly, was ominous. Might they have been warning about the voyage itself, to begin with? Indenture vessels were, after all, crossing in the wake of slavers, with their well-documented horrors, from tragic mortality rates to the rape of women.

5

HER MIDDLE PASSAGE

middle-passaged
passing
beneath the colouring of desire
in the enemy's eye
a scatter of worlds and broken wishes
in Shiva's unending dance

Arnold Itwaru, "We Have Survived"*

What started it all was a chance glimpse of an Indian woman, in an encounter with a sailor. That's what sent *The Main* veering five days off course, flying flags of distress, in 1901. The ship was ferrying indentured laborers to British Guiana, but stopped unexpectedly at the island of Mauritius in the Indian Ocean. As it approached, it signaled: "Crew mutinous, police wanted."[1] There had been a standoff between the captain and much of his crew, which escalated to a scuffle, which could have escalated even further if the surgeon hadn't pulled a gun—and the entire struggle was prompted by that glimpse, of a moment between the sailor and the woman.

She had just come from the toilet when the ship surgeon caught sight of her. Dr Stuart Oliver was finishing his evening rounds when he saw two sailors leaning against the hospital on deck. The location was strategic; women had to pass it to go to the toilet. Latrines on indenture ships served as a bizarre portal to the women aboard, where "puddings" were occasionally left as sad enticements for sexual favors. The gifts—biscuits with sugar and other morsels not rationed to emigrants—were paltry and pathetic, suggesting desperation, confirming deprivation.

The woman emerged from that odd gateway, and Albert Stead, a black able seaman from Guiana, spoke to her. She tried to walk past him, but he caught her by her

* Epigraph from *India in the Caribbean*, Hansib, 1987. Used by courtesy of Arnold Itwaru.

sari and held onto her. The danger did not last long. Stead let go as soon as he real-ized he was being watched. Dr Oliver ordered him to the front of the ship, and the sailor obeyed, grumbling under his breath. Posterity knows nothing about the woman—only that she had probably just narrowly escaped becoming a victim of sexual assault.

At the voyage's outset, a month earlier, Captain H.C. Robinson had mustered his crew on deck to caution them. His duty was clear. It was spelled out in *The Main*'s contract, in a clause standard for charters with indenture ships: "The Master shall prevent by all means in his power any intercourse whatever between the officers and the crew and the female emigrants."[2] The captain warned his men never to go to the back of the ship after dark, unless work required it.

There—"aft"—was where the single women stayed, down the hatches, below deck, in the stuffy hold where the floors, doubling as beds, were often so impregnated with salt from previous cargos, they sweated. The 'tween decks, as it was called, was parti-tioned into three. Single emigrant men stayed in the front of the ship; married cou-ples in the middle; and single women at the back. The partitions were occasionally physical: an iron mesh or horizontal bars.[3] Usually, however, they were invisible lines reinforced only—and then, only at night—by the dim glow of lanterns, extinguished everywhere but where the single women slept.[4]

Despite the vigil kept by the lanterns, and the captain's orders, there had been many attempts to get at the women on *The Main*. Stead, in particular, had defied the rules. He had won a reputation for arrogance on this and previous journeys. He acted as if he could do whatever he wanted. Several times, he was caught in the women's toilets, smoking or simply lingering. He and a few mates had been repeatedly seen talking to the *topazes*—the sweepers, male emigrants who were assigned to clean the toilets and who, along with the *sirdars* serving as night watchmen, could act as go-betweens to the women. Stead had given one *topaz* biscuits and sugar to offer to a woman the sailor liked, and the captain had pulled him aside to admonish him.

But Stead had ignored the message. He'd got away with worse in the past. Eight years earlier, he was caught having sex with an emigrant on another ship to Guiana.[5] He confessed to bribing a *sirdar* with rum to fetch that woman. By then, Stead had already made several overtures to female emigrants on that earlier ship, *The Brenda*, even lifting the screen on a woman while she was in the toilet. He was so incorrigible that the surgeon had tried to have Stead rusticated when the ship stopped to refuel. "I consider him an unprincipled ruffian," the surgeon had written in his diary, "and it is necessary for the safety of the emigrants that he be removed."[6] No crime had been committed, however, and the surgeon failed. Even when Stead literally broke the rule against intercourse with female emigrants, he still got off unpunished. The ship's charter agreement did not stipulate any penalties. Contracts with some ships did, but *The Brenda* wasn't among them.

The night after Dr Oliver saw Stead corner the woman on *The Main*, Capt. Rob-inson mustered his crew on deck yet again. He reminded his men of the agreements they had signed not to molest the emigrants. On *his* ship, as they should have known, there *were* penalties for violating the rule—a fine of 10 shillings for the first offence and a month's wages for each subsequent one. Do not, he told his men, "loll about the main hatches or the latrines." The captain warned that the next report of misconduct he received would, in fact, lead to punishment. Did Stead believe him? Or had his escape on *The Brenda* led him to doubt the resolve of the men in power? Is that what gave him the nerve to challenge his captain?

Stead did not shrink back in guilt or fear. Instead, he exclaimed: "What, fine us for talking to a coolie? You can't do it!" He declared that he would talk to the Indians if he pleased. What, he taunted, was the captain going to do about it?

"I should have to place you in irons if you disobey my orders," Capt. Robinson said.

"You couldn't put me in irons for shite," Stead shot back.

The captain ordered that handcuffs be brought immediately, and a group of men sprang to Stead's defense, cursing, laughing and shouting loud enough to be heard in the engine room. Half the crew was black. These twenty-one sailors took Stead's side, superior airs or not. They told the captain they wouldn't *allow* Stead to be handcuffed.

The officer who fetched the handcuffs, Harry Darling Cloughton, was the third mate, in charge of issuing rations on the ship, a job with power over the pantry and, so, perversely, also over the emigrants. Later, just days before the ship arrived in Guiana, two emigrant women from the same district would quarrel over Cloughton. One, named Tulshia, was seventeen. The other, in her late twenties, would claim that she saw Tulshia "eating biscuits and things which emigrants do not get." The older woman would report that she saw the girl talking to Cloughton. She would accuse Tulshia of going to the third mate at night. Confronted with the charge, Cloughton would confess that Tulshia slept with him in exchange for a present. He would call his gift *kajatie*, mangling the word so that it's difficult to tell if he meant date palm jaggery or a cashew confection or something else entirely. Cloughton would admit to enlisting a return migrant who spoke English well enough to act as middleman. This emigrant would swear that Cloughton promised to buy him his freedom in return. Tulshia would be promised no more than something to eat. Even so, she would wake the procurer one midnight, and he would take her up to the deck, where the third mate would be waiting.

During the standoff on deck, however, handcuffs dangled from Cloughton's grip, highlighting his authority, calling attention to his righteous stance. Cloughton stood ready to enforce a rule against sex with emigrant women. Meanwhile, Capt. Robinson, seeming more schoolmarm than ship master, sent for a piece of paper to record the names of insubordinate sailors. "Which of you," he asked, "resists my authority to put this man in irons?"

He heard someone holler: "You can put my name down." It was Thomas Roberts, the seaman most guilty of molesting the women, aside from Stead. These two men, who both called Guiana home, were mates. They had sailed together from the sugar colony to Calcutta on a ship transporting ex-indentured laborers back to India.

Allegedly, Stead and Roberts had misbehaved on that ship too. Some of its repatriates happened also to be on *The Main*, returning to Demerara as "coolies" once again. These return migrants, English-speakers, knew Stead and Roberts. When the pair wanted women, they turned to this group, just as Cloughton would two months later.

Or, had Cloughton been doing it from the start? If he had, did Stead and Roberts know about it? Were the black seamen sensitive to a double standard? At this particular moment, were they asserting an equal opportunity to exploit? And was there, perhaps, some inherited memory of shackling on ships with human cargoes that made the idea of being put in irons so unacceptable? As slave descendants, did they feel any kinship with the bonded laborers aboard—as *jahajis*, brothers and sisters of the boat?* Or was there, rather, disbelief that anyone would even begin to compare this middle passage to the one in their history? Did they resent the coolies as imported scabs? One by one, the black seamen told the captain to write them down as defiant. They closed in on him, while the white seamen hung back, watching the confrontation unfold.

The second mate, Francis Crompton, snatched the handcuffs from the third mate. It was Crompton's first voyage on an indenture ship, and he contracted venereal disease during it. The third mate alleged that he did, at any rate. Infected or not, Crompton made as curious an enforcer of the rules as the friend who volunteered such damaging information about him.

The night before *The Main* pulled into Georgetown, Crompton would descend into the hold of the ship. In the twilight of the lanterns, meant to expose exactly this kind of trespass, the *sirdar* on watch would see him browsing the women's section. Crompton would search, without success, for someone. A short while later, he would repeat the foray and, again, fail. On the third try, his eyes would alight on Habibulla, a tiny Muslim woman about twenty years old, curled beside two women. Habibulla, apparently the someone he was seeking, would have just returned from the toilet. Crompton would reach down and take her by the hand, eliciting the cry: "Don't hold my hand. Or I will complain." According to two eyewitnesses, Crompton would then fondle her breast. But Habibulla would contradict that testimony before a magistrate in Guiana. Perhaps too ashamed to admit that she was groped, she would insist that he only grabbed her by the hand. In his own turn as witness, Crompton would deny any and all wrongdoing. He would claim he went to the 'tween decks because he heard a row: "I only tapped one of the women on the head and told her to be quiet," he would say. He would also claim ignorance about a woman in his cabin the day the ship landed, as well as a third woman charging that he propositioned her.

This was the man who rushed to handcuff Stead as the showdown on deck reached a crisis, with the captain encircled. Stead, of course, resisted. Facing off, did the two men see any irony in their struggle? At the point when they clashed, had the officer

---

* The 1995 calypso "Jahaji Bhai" would urge a brotherhood of the boat between Caribbean blacks and Indians.

already been making nocturnal visits to the 'tween decks? And did the seaman suspect?

Cloughton sprang to Crompton's aid, and chaos broke out. Stead's sidekick, Roberts, clutched at Cloughton's throat. A sailor grabbed Crompton by the scruff of the neck. Another shoved the captain. One reached for a knife. And then, Dr Oliver stepped into the climax: "Stop this, or I will shoot," he said. He waved his revolver around. Everything went quiet. Everyone froze. Then Stead pushed out of the crowd. "All right," he said, opening his coat, calling the bluff. "Shoot me."

In the end, no one was shot, and no one handcuffed. The captain knocked Stead off duty and confined him to the forecastle until the ship reached Mauritius. The magistrate there refused to try the seven sailors pulled off the ship on charges of mutiny, because there was no proof of a conspiracy. Ultimately, three were sentenced, lightly, for lesser crimes, and the ship quickly moved on to its destination, without them. Stead and Roberts each spent twelve days in jail.

The committee in Guiana set up to investigate the mutiny on *The Main* could not ignore the condition of the immigrants the ship landed. The colony's medical inspector reported that there were "many weedy, and of poor physique, and a large proportion of sickly ones."[7] One-third had suffered from a flu epidemic so severe, it claimed lives during the crossing. Dr Oliver's assistant said many of the immigrants looked starved when they arrived in Georgetown, as well as when they left Calcutta. The government, fearing planters wouldn't pay their two-thirds of the passage money for such substandard coolies, kept their arrival secret for a week and a half. Meanwhile, it put the immigrants on a regimen of cod liver oil and iron. One hundred ultimately had to be kept back in Georgetown for treatment or observation. And 200 of those who were sent on to their estates were later discovered to have dangerously enlarged spleens. Given the shocking state of the immigrants, the committee was compelled to ask if they had received their rations.

But then, it did not ask too searchingly. It heard a woman, Jainab, testify that she accepted extra food from a crew member who made sexual advances to her. But it did not probe too deeply what might make her consider trading her body for a bit to eat. Nor did it consider that women, according to published ration lists, received fewer chapatis than men did. In the end, the committee found no neglect of the immigrants' bellies. Nor did it perceive a connection between flaws in the system, on a level as primal as hunger, and the opportunity for sexual exploitation.

Instead, it scapegoated blacks.* The committee blamed the troubles aboard the ship on an inferior crew, particularly noting "the large proportion of colored men shipped." Curiously, it did so while acknowledging that it was two white officers who had undisputedly and most brazenly violated the rule against molesting women: "The captain," the committee concluded, "very properly endeavored to prevent any inter-

---

* Verene Shepherd provides another example of black sailors being blamed for the sexual exploitation of indentured women in her groundbreaking *Maharani's Misery*, an account of a fatal rape aboard *The Allanshaw* in 1885.

ference with the immigrants. It seems amazing that this did not serve as a warning and that the second and third officers should have been the worst offenders." To its credit, the committee suggested that Cloughton and Crompton as well as Stead and Roberts be barred from indenture ships in the future.

But it also suggested that *all* black sailors be barred, briefly reviving a debate from the previous decade. There had been several reports of black sailors molesting women on indenture ships to the West Indies in the early 1890s. There was even an incident much like the one on *The Main*. On another ship—*The Bann* in 1894—another surgeon saw another set of black sailors hanging around another female toilet; and another captain tried to stop them, leading ultimately to handcuffs brandished and resisted, blows exchanged and cries of mutiny.[8] The attitude to seamen of African origin at the time was best captured by Jamaica's protector of immigrants, who wrote in 1891: "On account of their generally incorrigible addictedness to sexual inter-course, Negroes, if employed, should be in a minority in a coolie emigrant ship."[9] Twice at annual conferences ship surgeons passed resolutions declaring that "the employment of Negroes and Mulattos in any capacity on board coolie ships is most undesirable."[10] The surgeons pushed for a ban.

This effort failed, largely for practical reasons. Excluding black sailors would have delayed the departure of indenture ships; there weren't enough white sailors to keep the vessels moving as briskly as planters wanted. Indian sailors—*lascars*—were disparaged as no good in cold weather and likely to have their own intrigues with the women aboard. Also, many ships arrived in Calcutta with black crews; in the night-mare scenario of Calcutta's port officer, if indenture ships didn't take them back to the West Indies, they would "roam about the city," "swell the ranks of its disorderly population" and "be a source of trouble to the inhabitants in certain parts of town."[11] Combined with pragmatic business interests, these racist anxieties worked to defeat the proposed ban.

Both the pragmatism and the racism still existed when the committee on *The Main* made its recommendations. On 6 February 1903, a government spokesman in Bengal wrote to the Colonial Office about the most recent sally against black sailors: "It would … be unjust to stigmatize the whole Negro seafaring community for the unfortunate occurrence on board *The Main*, which was due to a very lax state of affairs brought about by incompetent and tactless officers."[12] As for the lascars, suggested as alternatives, there was a long-established consensus on them too. The captain of *The Hereford* had summed it up two decades earlier: "They get on better with the coolies than Europeans, merely because they understand them better," he wrote, "but as for morality, I never expect it in the lascar, nor indeed in the European sailor."[13]

And indeed, examples abounded of white seamen sleeping with women on indenture ships. In 1894, a Colonial Office official scribbled in the margins of a report on several errant sailors:

It is not stated that the offenders in this case were Negro sailors. If not, it tends to confirm my view that all crews are much alike in these respects. And that what is wanted is not so much the prohibition of Negro crews as the power to deal with the offenders.[14]

He was referring to the absence of penalties in the rules against sex with female emigrants—or, for that matter, in the rules against any form of abuse of any indentured emigrants. Some offenders faced consequences; others did not. But more seemed to be lacking than the power to punish. So, often, was the will to punish. Some of those entrusted with protecting emigrants—whose very reason for being was to embody the state's new posture as caretaker, rather than slaver—were themselves offenders.

* * *

In his *Handbook for Surgeons Superintendent in the Coolie Emigration Service*, the reclusive Scotsman James M. Laing, a veteran surgeon, instructed novices in the trade to look to the rule against molesting women. "By far the most important and, in some cases, fatal cause of trouble is jealousy from women being interfered with," he warned. "Some may feel inclined to smile at this, but I assure him he will find it no laughing matter, as most of the serious trouble and all suicides, or attempted suicides, can be traced to this one cause."[15]

The surgeon's duty was delicate. In effect, he had to police the nocturnal activities of a crew he technically had no authority over. He was marooned outside the chain of command, able to discipline no one but the emigrants. Laing explained the protocol in the case of violations: Insist in writing that the captain punish any offences by officers or the crew, and punish any by the emigrants yourself. "It surely should," he added, "be quite unnecessary to say that the surgeon superintendent himself ought to show a good example."[16]

The job of surgeon on an indenture ship—isolating, demanding, sometimes life-threatening—did not always attract the best and the brightest. It was paid by commission—a set number of shillings for each emigrant landed alive, depending on the surgeon's experience. This didn't necessarily lead to conscientious or humane treatment. The indenture scholar Hugh Tinker described the surgeons as loners and misfits drawn to the "coolie" voyage by a paternalistic sense of responsibility.[17] This could manifest in odd ways, as with the surgeon who punished a man who admitted having gay sex in the 'tween decks by blistering his penis.[18] Or, it could manifest as heroics, as with the surgeon on *The Main* who brandished a revolver in 1901. Dr Oliver caused a near mutiny among the crew because he was trying to safeguard the women aboard.

It is, however, difficult to ignore the example of another surgeon. Dr William Holman caused a near mutiny among the emigrants in his charge because they believed he was preying on their women. Instead of a hero's gun, he wielded a leather strap—thick as a ruler, but longer and wider. The crew said he always carried it in his pocket, as an "emblem of authority," and used it freely to discipline the emigrants, both men and women.[19]

Holman came from a family of professional adventurers, his father a Royal Navy commander and his uncle the famous "Blind Traveler" who published volumes about his sightless exploits across the globe.[20] A river in Equatorial Guinea was named Holman, according to that uncle, in recognition of his contributions to the fight against the slave trade. The surgeon superintendent, who spent four decades in the successor trade in coolies, left rather a different legacy. At the outset of his career, during the voyage of *The Merchantman* to British Guiana in 1857, 31 percent of the emigrants in his care died.[21] That was one of the highest mortality rates ever for an indenture ship, anywhere in the world. An additional ninety-three of the emigrants had to be sent to hospital on arrival, "all pale and emaciated and listless, some but crawling skeletons, many unable to articulate and others moribund." Despite this, Holman kept his job. He survived to make another shameful mark, midway through his career.

On 23 November 1875, the protector of emigrants on Saint Helena, the South Atlantic island where indenture ships often stopped to refuel, boarded *The Ailsa* for routine checks. He soon found himself surrounded by the women aboard, who fell at his feet to complain about Dr Holman. Later, as the protector and the surgeon were in the captain's cabin, hundreds of emigrants stormed up from the 'tween decks to demand Holman's ouster. They threatened to jump overboard if he was allowed to sail on with the ship. And they made slashing gestures at their throats, indicating Holman's fate if he stayed. The emigrants claimed that the doctor did not give them enough to eat. They said he pinched and slapped women on the bottom. And they charged that he forced several women to sleep with him.

Four spoke up against Holman. Their testimonies, preserved in transcripts of a Guiana inquiry into the disquiet on the ship, provide a rare example of "coolie women" speaking for themselves in the historical record. The words are not entirely their own. Government interpreters paraphrased them, perhaps even misreporting details. The questions put to the women have been cut out of the record. The answers—rolled out flat in long, uninterrupted strips—lack the right rhythm, and colonial officials ultimately discounted them as "improbable," "almost impossible to credit." Still, however mediated, flattened and discredited, their testimonies survive.

The first woman said: "The doctor came down one night between decks, took me by the arm and dragged me upstairs into his cabin. ... He is a great scamp. ... The doctor used to offer me biscuit and sugar, and did so as I was going to the [water] closet, taking that opportunity. ... I did complain to the commander but he is as bad as the doctor."

The second woman said: "On one occasion, the surgeon asked me to go into his cabin, but I refused. ... The surgeon was in the habit of pinching us and slapping us on the bottom; we did not like it."

The third woman said: "One night, the surgeon came down between decks, took me by the arm, and dragged me up into his cabin, and had connexion with me. ... He put his hand on my mouth when I was between decks. ... The surgeon was in the habit of taking liberties with the women. ... The surgeon used to ill-treat the immigrants by beating them with his hand and putting some of them in irons."

Then three weeks later, the same woman, in a group recalled from their sugar estates to be cross-examined by Holman, suddenly took ill with fever. Rojeah—that was her name—had to be hospitalized. On recovering, she found that her compatriots had all been cross-examined and sent back to their plantations. Facing Holman alone, in the colony's immigration office, she said: "The surgeon of the ship never seduced me, or did anything to me, nor did I ever go into his room, nor did he ever ill-treat or abuse me."

The fourth woman stood by her story. She said: "The surgeon frightened me.... I was afraid to refuse. ... He used to slap me hard on my bottom and hurt me. ... The surgeon came after me, and made me go by force. ... Inside his room, the surgeon had connexion with me near the door, on the floor; the door was shut. ... It is true that on three nights the surgeon took me into his room and had connexion with me. ... I was not a prostitute in India."

It's not difficult to guess what the questions, edited out of the transcript, were. The commission probably asked Ramjharee—that was her name—if she had invented the charges so the immigrants wouldn't be tried on charges of mutiny. It no doubt tried to cast aspersions on her character by suggesting she had been a prostitute. But Ramjharee would not recant. She said she had denied the surgeon once, fifteen days after the ship departed India. He had cornered her on her way to the toilet, promising, "I will give you biscuit. Come at 12 o'clock." Ramjharee testified that she refused—and was, as a result, handcuffed for ten hours. Other emigrants also claimed that Holman handcuffed them when they resisted or informed on him.

The emigrants did succeed in forcing Holman off the ship at Saint Helena. Another surgeon finished the voyage for him, receiving part of his pay. But the committee in Guiana ultimately cleared him of taking any "indecent or licentious liberty" with the women aboard. It allowed that he "acted very injudiciously by carrying about with him a leather strap" and that his use of it was "indiscreet." But it concluded that Holman was the victim of a vengeful plot by the third mate, who had been reprimanded by the surgeon for having a woman in his room. Several crew members testified that the third mate nightly took emigrant women to bed, and several heard him say, as the doctor left the ship at Saint Helena: "Ah Mr Bloody Doctor, you tried to catch me, but I have caught you. If you can stop my money, by Jesus Christ, I can stop yours."

In a letter to London, Guiana's governor reported the committee's findings and acknowledged that their "view of the case necessarily involves the assumption that the coolies who have sworn that the doctor took women into his cabin for improper purposes have conspired to swear falsely." He also admitted that he wished "the charge had been more completely disproved." But in the end, the governor and the Colonial Office backed Holman. After calling attention to some inconsistencies in the statements against him, the surgeon had sown some blatantly racist doubts to defend himself. "I confess that I feel not only anxious but pained that these charges should have been made," he wrote, "but knowing as I do the faculty of the coolie for favourication (sic) and his tendency to exaggeration, I am hardly surprised."

Holman survived two more decades in the coolie trade. He was even consulted as an expert on maintaining morality on the ships. In 1883, after a woman on the Trinidad-bound *Hesperides* accused a boatswain of raping her, the surgeon aboard called on colonial officials in India to insist that single women occupy a compartment separate and distinct from married couples and single men.[22] That was, in fact, already the law. But in practice, like many regulations aimed at partitioning indenture in the public mind from slavery, it was a figment of bureaucratic imagination. As one official noted: "In Bengal, ... a compartment seems to have as much real substance as the Equator or the North Pole."[23] The protector of emigrants in Calcutta enlisted a few surgeons to defend the repeated breach of the rules. Holman was one of them. The doctor matter-of-factly related how he broke down the bulkheads in one ship before it sailed.[24]

There were valid arguments to be made against physical partitions. They obstructed the flow of air in the already suffocating 'tween decks. And, in a way, confining the single women to a specific section of the ship—whether sealed off in their own compartment, or not—was like pointing a blinking neon arrow directly at them, advertising their vulnerability. The hatchway to the single women's section was guarded at night, but the *sirdars* could be bribed, bullied or evaded. On *The Hesperides*, a sailor who slipped down the hatch threatened to stab a female guard with a knife when she tried to stop him from molesting the women.[25] On *The Ailsa*, Holman entirely bypassed the guarded main hatchways. A special ladder had been set up to lead directly from his cabin to the 'tween decks. He claimed that it was a convenience in bad weather and that initially he had resisted it, given its strong appearance of impropriety.

Partitions would have prevented Holman from moving freely in and out of the women's section, after he had gone to the trouble of building his own private steps into the 'tween decks. Asked his opinion of partitions—after being accused of doing the very things they were meant to prevent—he dismissed them as unnecessary. "I cannot say," he asserted, "that I have seen any gross immorality on board any vessel to which I have been appointed."[26] He wouldn't concede that a problem existed, and the system, by turning to him as judge, showed itself to be as richly capable of denial. Holman continued to serve as a surgeon superintendent until he died in an apoplectic fit, breathless and foaming at the mouth, on an indenture ship in 1895.[27]

* * *

On Holman's mutinous vessel, the first mate charged that the women, "very often ... very cheerful themselves," would "meddle" with him on deck, and the captain testified that they "would take liberties and laugh and joke with the men." Women who accused, found themselves accused. Throughout the archives, repeatedly they face the classic insinuation against victims of sexual assault. The boatswain charged with rape on *The Hesperides* swore that it was the woman who came after *him*—and not the other way around.[28] A surgeon consulted during the debate on partitions insisted the indentured women would not "take kindly to such a separation from the men at starting."[29] Another argued that partitions were besides the point, because "it would be no more easy to prevent the women going down the ladder to the men's quarters than it is now to prevent them going from their own end of the well-lighted decks to the men's end."[30]

Mincingly, they characterized the women aboard indenture ships as sluts, while others depicted them as victims. But was that the full range of their possibility, or was there some disconcerting middle ground? Did they ever exercise choice? And what choice could they truly have in a landscape of want and coercion, of biscuits with sugar and a leather strap? Looking for answers, I analyzed the records available on seventy-seven indenture ships, most of which landed in Guiana in the dozen years before my great-grandmother did. Whenever a ship docked, the chief immigration agent at its destination had to report to the Colonial Office on its passage from India. Some of these dispatches, including the one detailing my great-grandmother's voyage, have been destroyed. Those that survive pull back the screen, if only for brief moments and partial views, on the lives of the women aboard. It is hard, in these glimpses, to escape the angle of sexual exploitation by figures of all ranks and races. In these archives of misconduct, the women appear resisting advances. Or, giving in to them. Or—in the eyes of many ship officials—courting them. But the records also provide other views of the women: on deathbeds, giving birth, losing children, going mad, being driven to suicide, engaged in infanticide, rejecting or being rejected by shipboard husbands, demanding that husbands prove themselves, stowing away, crying, cursing, possibly in love and clearly in anguish. Admittedly, the reports present psyches aboard ship at their most awry, since they typically only mentioned a migrant when something had gone wrong.

Still, I cannot imagine that the journey was anything but a saga, even for emigrants whose lives passed relatively without incident. Seasickness afflicted most. A majority aboard fell ill with mumps, measles, dysentery, hookworm or fever. The ache for home was so sharp that Laing the handbook writer declared: "I know that many die from nostalgia pure and simple… The excitement of the newness of everything keeps them up for a time, but soon dies away, and is followed by depression when they realize what they have done."[31] The realization must have dawned slowly, as the sea lengthened and the conditions aboard affected them one by one: as blankets rough as jute, sometimes rotten and foul-smelling, caused pus to form on children;*[32] as the fans for circulating air were shut down at night, when most needed; as the condenser to make the water potable broke, which it routinely did; and as the floor beneath them sweated. For decades, surgeons urged that vessels transporting coolies be barred from transporting salt, which made the 'tween decks damp and unhealthy,

---

* The medical inspector who boarded the *EMS*, arriving in British Guiana in 1895, retched after putting his face in a blanket. He remembered an instance on another ship, where the blankets were "very rough and irritating, especially to the skins of very young children, many of whom have developed pustular eruptions."

but the practice persisted and emigrants continued to succumb to fever. And their stomachs often churned from unfamiliar, religiously forbidden or spoiled food. The ship reports refer to putrefying pumpkins, potatoes past their prime, milk that had curdled, tins of mutton gone bad, dal infiltrated by dirt and drinking water laced with rust and cement. In the few first-person accounts by survivors of the crossing, the theme of being reduced to animals recurs: they slept like cattle, and they were fed biscuits fit for dogs.[33]

All the while, surgeons prepared their balance sheets of births and deaths, recording "Shiva's unending dance" without realizing it. The Hindu god who destroys in order to create, who dances in an aureole of flames to maintain the universe's ceaseless cycle of creation and destruction, did not forget the 'tween decks. Four percent of emigrant women arriving in Georgetown in the dozen years before Sujaria did gave birth aboard ship, but I'm referring to something far more metaphysical than that birthrate, roughly equal to India's at the time.[34] Just listen to a woman born on a ship to the West Indies in 1888: "On that mad ocean, when all was tossing, people's heads were spinning, and then labor pains started for her to have her child, on that mad ocean I was born, on that mad ocean I came to life."[35] She was describing her own origins but, with her incantatory words, she could have been telling the creation story of our people, mine and hers. She could have continued, in her voice of myth: In our beginning, there was a boat. On that mad ocean, we came to life. We passed the red sea to reach the black. The water was blue before it was green, and then it was mud. We crossed seven seas: seven shades of water, shades of darkness and light, light that died and darkness that was born, darkness somehow extinguished and light rekindled. The captain's wheel became Shiva's fiery circle, turning and turning in its cosmic spiral. And in the gyrating of the gales, and the churning of the waves, as one steered and the other danced, we became new. The moorings of caste had loosened, and people who had left behind uncles, sisters, husbands and mothers substituted shipmates, their *jahajis*, for kin. Unraveled, they began, ever so slowly, to spin the threads of a novel identity.

Indenture ships were not slave ships, of course. Coolie vessels were four to five times larger than slavers. In indenture's early years, the emigrants aboard occupied about 5.5 square feet per person, twice what each slave had; later, the space grew to 10 square feet, or a human-sized chunk about 6 feet long and slightly over 1.5 feet wide.[36] Covering three times the distance as slavers, indenture ships to the West Indies took two to three times longer, more for sailing ships, less for steamers. Indentured emigrants had to contend with the conditions aboard for far longer. But they could break the monotony by playing cards and drums, by singing and wrestling. The surgeons encouraged these pastimes, as well as exercise, to avert the melancholy of the emigrants. On indenture vessels, it often seemed like regulations existed simply to be violated, often with impunity, but at least they existed. During the most catastrophic years of the coolie trade, between 1854 and 1864, the death rate on ships to Guiana was 8.54 percent, equal to that on slave ships in the final decades of the eighteenth century.[37] But by the time my great-grandmother sailed, the mortality rate on most indenture ships had fallen to between 1 and 2 percent.

Despite these colossal distinctions, there can be no denying a few ties that should have bound the three million Africans trafficked by the British as slaves and the million Indians transported as coolies. The people in the hold, in both cases, were cut from the same demographic, mainly young and overwhelmingly male. Women were in short supply and subject to sexual exploitation during both crossings. And both journeys were transformative, signaling a break with the past, making whatever came before it seem almost as unimaginable to later generations as time and space before the Big Bang. In the beginning, there was a boat. Having emerged from its belly, as survivors, the indentured Indians could no longer be who they had been. Like the slaves before them, they were an entirely new people, forged by suffering, created through destruction. In this sense above all else, theirs was a middle passage.

How do I even begin to situate my great-grandmother in this odyssey? If I draw an imaginary line from moment to moment on the ships, from glimpse to glimpse of women aboard, will her shape emerge, constellation-like? Could the wrong shape emerge, if I connect the wrong moments to each other? How do I know which are right? Will her constellation give off light?

Because the Colonial Office destroyed the report on *The Clyde*'s 1903 crossing, I can only read between the lines of the threadbare statistics that have survived to imagine the textures of her journey. Aboard ship were 171 women and 389 men, just barely meeting the quota of women mandated to sail. My grandfather wasn't the only child born during the crossing; twelve babies entered the world, and four of them left it soon after.[38] Five men also died at sea, one from cerebrospinal meningitis, a brain inflammation accompanied by high fevers, severe headaches, frequent vomiting and delirium. Victims often got a "wild frightened look on all (their) faces as if seized with some sudden terror" and cried out for their mothers and fathers, according to a ship surgeon who witnessed many die from it.[39] A common affliction on the ships, the disease indicated cramped and badly ventilated 'tween decks.

Sujaria spent three months and a week in that iron belly. That may have been what induced premature labor. My grandfather came two months early, and he was born legs first, a dangerous debut even under normal conditions. Without the official chronicle of Sujara's journey, I had to seek proxies for her in the records. Fortunately, I found a few. I even found a namesake. Soujharia, an emigrant on *The Jura* in 1892, disappeared one morning from the hospital bunk she had been sharing with her son Parbu. For weeks, the boy had been ill. At about sunrise on 19 October, the ship's senior compounder—the dispenser assisting the surgeon—went into the hospital to give the patients their medicine. He noticed that Soujharia was gone. The boy, still warm to the touch, was dead under a blanket.[40]

Infants and children lost their lives to a disproportionate degree during the crossings. Occasionally, heartbreakingly, babies were "overlaid," suffocated while cradled beside a sleeping mother. On a disquietingly regular basis, surgeons listed "neglected by mother" as a cause of death. They didn't connect the many babies who died from malnourishment with insufficient or bad milk. For indenture's first two decades, ships weren't even required to carry milk. And once they had to, as a result of a few seasons of double-digit mortality rates, it wasn't always of good quality. During *The*

Jura's 1898 crossing, tins of lumpy milk held over from old stock had to be condemned, and three of the five babies born on board died of malnourishment.[41]

In a case in 1883, a newborn died two days after his mother switched from breast to bottle.[42] His mother Churaiya insisted that "the child was a full time strong one." But at noon on his third day of life, he developed a fever. The surgeon descended to the 'tween decks to examine him. He declared "This child will not live," and promptly left. At 8 p.m., the baby, named Rohilla, after the ship, gave a short, last gasp. His body was thrown overboard the same day. No cause of death was ever given, because the surgeon recorded neither the boy's birth nor his death in his books. Had it not been for the immigration agent general's close perusal of the chief officer's logbooks, the baby Rohilla would have been less than a blip. Officially, he would not even have existed. A premature baby born on *The Jura* in 1891 was luckier, in one respect. The surgeon aboard did capture her first, and final, days in his journal:

Sept 4: Laria, No. 326, prematurely confined of a weak, puny female infant at 2:30 a.m.
Sept 5: The infant born yesterday is very weak and takes but little nourishment. I fear she will not live.
Sept 7: The infant born on 4th instant becomes weaker and scarcely swallows.
Sept 8: The infant born on 4th instant died during the night.[43]

How was it that my grandfather, also premature, escaped this oblivion? Fully a third of the infants born on his ship died before it docked. What saved him? And what if he hadn't survived? Would my Sujaria have shared a fate, as well as a name, with this other Soujharia?

The records don't say what caused her son to die. After discovering his corpse, the compounder searched for Soujharia in the 'tween decks and latrine, to no avail. In his journal, the surgeon wrote, "I considered that after the death of her child, remorse had caused her to commit suicide. She was last seen at 4 a.m. ... beside her boy." He assumed that remorse—not grief, but its wrongdoing-wracked twin—had motivated her. And he assumed that Soujharia had jumped overboard. This was the way that indentured emigrants killed themselves, with alarming frequency, during the sea voyages.

Many were presumed to have met this end after vanishing. This was the fate of Mathuri on *The Main* in 1893[44] and Manjharia and her toddler Jamni on *The Jura* in 1891.[45] Ramratia, who was four months pregnant, disappeared during *The Avoca's* 1894 voyage.[46] As the ship was towed down the Hooghly, she complained of a pain in her belly. She was afraid of miscarrying. A few days later, she was nowhere to be found. Did my great-grandmother—also four months pregnant at the outset—feel a foreboding in her womb too? *The Clyde* sailed in July, the worst month to leave India; any ship departing then faced the full force of the southwest monsoons. Did Sujaria, tempest-tossed, perhaps seasick, also have the urge to abort it all—the voyage, the pregnancy, the seas of uncertainty ahead? What kept her from suicide? Or did she try but fail?

There *were* some who failed. Lachminia, a woman prevented from suicide after a fight with her husband on *The Avon* in 1893,[47] had to face him afterwards. What had they argued about? And did her attempt to throw herself into the sea make him angry, or solicitous? Did Mussibun, saved by a *sirdar* who jumped in after her on *The Rohilla* in 1875, feel grateful to the man, or resent him for preserving her in a state of chaos? According to the governor, Mussibun had tried to kill herself after "quarreling with two men who, it appeared, shared her affections."[48] Others who failed were physically restrained, to keep them from trying again, but also as punishment. In 1899, a woman berated by others because she "took a fancy to a man who was married" was kept overnight in the hospital, with her ankle shackled to a stanchion, because she had threatened to jump overboard. Five days later, the object of her affections, the *sirdar* Dookhiran, lost his position on *The Foyle* "for being too intimate" with her.[49]

Was there a special stigma attached to women who stole husbands on the ships, or was it understood that, under the circumstances, such things would happen? For Sujaria, the answer mattered concretely. Her granddaughters, my aunts, say that she befriended a couple aboard *The Clyde* and later came between husband and wife. What, precisely, passed between Sujaria and the married man during the crossing? Was there a spark? Did he admire her fair skin, her cat's eyes, her long, straight nose, her forceful personality? What did she see in him? Did she see a protector? Was it wrong to want someone already spoken for? What was it like for my great-grandmother when her son was born, three weeks before landing? Did she deliver in the 'tween decks, or in the hospital on deck? How ever did she survive a legs-first baby? Might she have felt the full weight of her aloneness at the very moment he arrived? Did her milk come easily, or did the premature birth interfere, as it often does? And her affections for the baby—did they come easily, or was there an unsettling flatness of feeling? Had the breach birth exhausted her both physically and emotionally? How would she survive without support? Might a husband help?

How about Furchee, the woman on whose account the *sirdar* was dismissed? What did she want? Did she really "take a fancy" to him, as the immigration agent general put it? Would he have been dismissed for a consensual affair, or was abuse of power involved? What did the surgeon mean by saying that Dookhiran had been "too intimate" with Furchee? Was some sexual expression on the ships permissible, some grounds for dismissal? Did it depend on who was doing the expressing? But really, why did she threaten to harm herself? Was it out of shame? Might there have been another, more basic reason?

An underlying motive could, perhaps, be teased from the circumstances surrounding another woman's suicide. The surgeon noticed her on *The Bann*'s first day at sea. He noted in his diary on 24 December 1893: "Discovered an idiot woman on board, Radhia No. 237."[50] Radhia had spent three weeks hospitalized at Garden Reach. She was sick, her hands and feet swollen. Two other female patients saw attendants put "a liquid medicine on her eyes and head" twice a day, but the women didn't know exactly what ailed her. At the last minute, on the very day *The Bann* sailed, the depot doctor handed Radhia, thus far rejected by three ships, an emigration pass.

"I will not go on board," she wept. "If I go on the ship, I will die."

"You must go on board and not sit here wasting the money of the government," the doctor insisted. "You must go. The food on board will make you well, and you will earn much money in Demerara."

He told another woman to carry Radhia's bundle for her and made her board the ship. Shortly after sunrise, six weeks later, Radhia was reported missing. "There was only one conclusion to be arrived at," the surgeon wrote. Was Radhia's prophecy a self-fulfilling one? Could her story suggest a reason other women took or tried to take their own lives? Was it simply that they didn't want to be there in the first place? Perhaps suicide, for the women who attempted it, was a desperate form of asserting control over their own lives.[51] Perhaps that was why they were chained when they failed—to reinforce that their lives were, actually, not theirs to take. Did they know that each death cost an experienced surgeon superintendent a pound sterling in pay and that shipowners also lost money whenever an emigrant died? Is it wrong of me to speculate like this? But isn't my conjecture as valid as any arrived at by colonial and ship officials, through lenses tinted by racism, sexism and self-interest?

How about the carbon-copy conclusion of Immigration Agent General James Crosby, seen as one of the more aggressive protectors of indentured servants in British Guiana's history? Was he in earnest when he reported to London, with the docking of every single ship in 1875, that he had never before seen "a more contented, happy or cheerful body of immigrants"? How could he have sandpapered such turbulent odysseys to a conclusion so smooth to the touch? Was his self-congratulation like the promo for the soap issued to immigrants on *The Brenda* in 1894, a crude heap of potash and grease, about which the surgeon aboard acidly remarked: "'Superfine Marine Soap', the manufacturers have the arrogance to call it: it would be interesting to learn from the Metropolitan Soap Manufactory what their second class soap is like if this is SUPERFINE"?[52]

Despite Crosby's conclusion, and similar assertions by agents after him, there are many hints of mental trauma in the official records. Despite themselves, the reports point to icebergs of discontent, to say the least. It wasn't just the suicides. Consider the diary of William Kenny, the surgeon on *The Volga* in 1892, who documented the case of an emigrant detained at Garden Reach for more than two months before embarking:

Aug. 10: In consequence of the very peculiar conduct of Phooljhari, F, No. 129, age 22, it has been found necessary to place her under constant observation. She appears to be suffering from a form of melancholia.

Aug. 13: The woman Phooljhari, No. 129, is daily becoming more and more peculiar and today assaulted the chief compounder and will I fear have to be placed under constant restraint.[53]

When the ship reached British Guiana, she was certified as mad and sent to the colony's lunatic asylum. The 1875 report on *The Atalanta* gives a glimpse of a woman, Rutnee, who apparently committed infanticide. "This woman," Crosby reported to London, "had been seen to treat [her] child cruelly at various times, and on the 11th of March was overheard threatening to throw it overboard, shortly after which the child either fell or was thrown overboard."[54] Later that year, on *The Linguist*, a husbandless woman gave birth to a son in the latrine. Crosby reported that she "cruelly endeavored to get rid of [her child] by thrusting it as far back into the shoot as possible. He was fortunately heard to cry, however, and was rescued." The baby, reportedly neglected by his mother, died three weeks later.[55] What lay below the surface of such apparent cold-bloodedness? Were the women suffering from post-partum depression? Did they fear that their children's birthright might be a perverse one, not worth having? Was ending a child's life another tragic way of exercising choice? Was it a mercy? Could the women have suspected that the children of indentured servants, although not indentured themselves, would end up as the system's collateral damage? Did they know that the damage could begin on the voyage itself?

In 1907, on an indenture ship to Suriname, a sailor defiled a little girl.[56] Several seamen who shared Arnold Balmer's cabin saw the girl in his bed one night. They witnessed statutory rape through the half-open curtain of his bunk. One sailor saw Balmer unbutton his fly and lift the girl on top of himself. "I could hear by the child's breathing and the working of his muscles that he was having intercourse with her," the sailor said. Another sailor saw Balmer descend from his bunk with the girl at 11:10 p.m., take her to a biscuit box and then send her back out on deck.

This sailor, Charles Philip Meredith, was the one who had brought the child into the cabin in the first place. He had found her standing outside, he said. Meredith described her as "the prettiest girl on board." She was seven or eight years old. Saroda—that was her name—wasn't travelling with a mother. She was supposed to stay with the "single" women at night, but often slipped through the mid-section reserved for married couples to the front of the 'tween decks, where her father slept. The front of the ship was also where the sailors berthed, up on deck, in the forecastle. With *sirdars* supposedly on guard at the hatchways, it isn't clear how she could have clambered up unnoticed into such a prohibited place. And it isn't clear why she was there, apparently waiting to be brought inside. Meredith not only let her in. He lifted her into the bunk where she was outraged. It isn't clear what his motives were in reporting Balmer, since the two had fallen out earlier that day. And it isn't clear what accessory role Meredith may have played in the child's rape; a few sailors claimed that he put the girl in more than one bunk that night.

It is clear, however, that she *was* raped. In the captain's cabin, Saroda identified Balmer as the sailor who had indecently assaulted her. She also told the Indian compounder, in her own language, precisely what the sailor had done to her. The surgeon examined her. He later gave a statement to the British consul in Suriname, explaining what he found: "She had been tampered with, the parts being inflamed and swollen." Confronted with indisputable medical evidence, Balmer confessed while the vessel was still at sea—but he retracted this when brought before the British consul for an official hearing in Paramaribo, the Surinamese capital. The notes on the hearing reflect a shift in the testimony of the motherless girl, too. They read: "*Saroda Emigrant child, No. 451*: 'I know the accused. I was in his bunk some days ago. I have often been in his bunk.' (The child, being frightened, is unable or unwilling to give any definite statement as to what occured.)" Her father, meanwhile, claimed ignorance. He knew only that she was, he said, "in the habit of going to the forecastle and getting biscuits and cigarettes."

Who were the cigarettes for? Why did her father allow her anywhere near the cabins of grown men, alone, at night? Is it possible that he sent her there? Who, ultimately, was responsible? And why was no one punished after the consul took evidence in Suriname, or at least after the ship reached Guiana, its final destination and a British colony—unlike Suriname, a Dutch possession that imported laborers from British India under a special treaty, but where British magistrates did not sit? Why was no one punished when the Colonial Office in London became aware of what had happened? Did British justice not sit in London?*

And yet, alongside the glimpses of tragedy and injustice, there is at least one of a woman determined to be aboard. Shortly after *The Lena* sailed in 1899, its surgeon superintendent discovered a stowaway.[57] Munia was a single mother in her late twenties, possibly a widow. The records say that her seven-year old was in tow and that his father had died in India. But they do not say whether the man who died was her husband. The doctor at Garden Reach turned Munia down because she had venereal disease, but she ignored the rejection, nonchalantly boarding the ship with everyone else. And just as nonchalantly, a fortnight into the journey, she lined up when the surgeon mustered the emigrants for inspection. She presented a ticket borrowed from one legitimately registered laborer and an emigration pass belonging to another, an epileptic woman who may have lost it during a seizure. Caught with not one assumed identity, but two, Munia had to give a statement to British Guiana's immigration chief when *The Lena* landed. She said: "I went with the others on board because I wanted to accompany my cousin Ramdaia. I was not asked by anyone to go on board, nor was I forced to do so. I went of my own free will, because I wished to be with Ramdaia." Munia had exercised a choice—one other than ending her life or her child's. The immigration agent, saying simply that she "appeared likely to prove a good worker," assigned her to a sugar estate near the capital.

It could, of course, be argued that Munia's choice was not an informed one. She didn't know what she was getting into. But there were significant numbers on indenture ships who, by definition, did. About 7 percent of emigrants arriving in Guiana in the dozen years before my great-grandmother did—2,075 people—had been indentured before, either there or somewhere else.[58] These return migrants had served out their time on sugar estates in various colonies, exercised their right to a passage back to India and then decided to leave again, usually indentured, but from time to time as free passengers paying their own way.

One such passenger, "a fine looking woman about forty years of age," captivated the captain of *The Sheila*, W.H. Angel.[59] She makes an appearance, namelessly, in the

---

* The Colonial Office concluded that the public prosecutor was unlikely to take the case; all witnesses would have to be in England for the proceedings, and that would be hard.

sections of his autobiography describing his ship's maiden voyage to British Guiana in 1877. The book includes a photograph of her dressed like a bride, although she wasn't one. She wears the bells of *jhumkas* in her earlobes, a diadem-like *matha patti* along the part in her hair and concentric circles of heavy, elaborate necklaces, a widening gyre of gold florins and enchantment. And she stares confidently back at the camera, nose and mouth sculpted like a Greek statue's, eyes pretty and direct.

Angel does not record her name. He may not have taken the trouble to know it. Instead, he calls her the Queen of Sheba. Not her name, no name in fact, but a title, it's also a perfect Orientalist projection, evocative of wealth, sensuality and the exotic. The Queen of Sheba, in the Bible and according to legend, travels from a distant kingdom to meet King Solomon in Jerusalem. She comes bearing riches—and questions to test the king's wisdom. In some versions, she also seduces him and bears him a son.

The return migrant in Angel's autobiography had worked on Trinidad plantations. Even in that less than stately setting, according to his account, she managed to expand her wealth through strategic romantic alliances, the way a monarch might. Angel writes: "She had made quite a considerable fortune in the island, partly by judicious marriages, and partly in her widowhoods, and as a trader, for as such she had a natural inclination." She then returned to India, longing to see it again, but had balked at the price that Hindu priests demanded to restore her to caste. And so, she boarded another ship to the West Indies, declaring to the captain and anyone who would hear her truth: "India only fit place for coolie." Had she gone back bearing, like her imagined namesake, questions as well as riches? Had she tested the wisdom of the Brahminical elite and found it lacking? And how, in fact, did she raise herself up from coolie to Angel's "Queen of Sheba"? Did she know the captain was projecting fantasies of sexualized female power onto her? What questions did she have for him? And what nicknames? Were they complimentary?

Angel wasn't the only one smitten. Returnees, as a group, seemed to seduce colonial officials. Twice-migrant, they could be held up as paragons of free will and educated choice, excellent PR for indenture. The Methodist missionary H.V.P. Bronkhurst, a government-subsidized minister, underscored this point when he wrote in 1883: "If it is slavery, it is strange that they should deliberately choose it, and bring their friends into it."[60] In the ship reports, colonial officials take pains to point out returnees on board, especially if they had brought back with them gold and silver jewellery or large sums of cash. In 1883, for example, Guiana's immigration chief eagerly announced the arrival of a woman carrying 900 rupees: "It says much for Rubussia's satisfaction with her former lot as an indentured servant that she should be willing to engage for another five years, with ample means at her disposal."[61]

Despite such gloss, most migrants did not return bearing riches. One woman, Mathura, had been shipped back to India as a pauper.[62] Her indenture was cancelled because she became permanently disabled while working on a plantation. But Mathura didn't seem to get the message that she was no longer wanted in Guiana. She turned up again two years later, on *The Elbe* in 1893. Was hers a stubborn will to be in a new world, or did she have no other choice but to return? Was there any-one to receive her in India? Could she find her way back to them? Did she remember the way? How did they receive her, handicapped as she was by the cane? Did they acknowledge that she was theirs, or cast her out? Choice is sometimes a frail, unre-sounding thing.

It can be as slender as the choice made by a woman groped by a sailor on the deck of *The Foyle* in 1899. A disinterested bystander saw the sailor squeeze Rohimon's breast as she stood near the hen coop. Her husband saw it, too, from where he was lying near the wheel. She didn't shrink away or passively accept the sailor's disrespect. Rohimon swore at him. The sailor told her never to call him a "damned son of a bitch" again. And when her husband rose to defend her honor, the sailor cuffed him above the ear, then raised his shoe as another weapon, another insult. Rohimon decided to complain to the surgeon aboard, Henry Cecil. There was, however, little satisfaction to be had from that authority. Cecil wrote in his diary: "The accusation appeared to be doubtful, and the sailor was warned by the captain and myself to be more careful."[63]

But how could Rohimon have known that the surgeon would be so dismissive? How could she have known that, seven years earlier, he had boxed the ears of a woman on *The Erne* who charged its captain with sexual misconduct?[64] Or that Cecil, too, had allegedly slept with women on that ship of ex-indentured laborers returning to India in 1892? If she had been aware that the ship's compounder called it "a float-ing hell in which Dr Cecil was Raja,"[65] or that he had accused Cecil of condoning "cruelty and immorality" on every ship that he had ever overseen, would she have chosen to complain? What if she had known that the Colonial Office punished not Cecil but the compounder: Francis Mewa, a self-made descendant of coolies with testimonials to his integrity from the Canadian missionary who raised him and from his old boss, the head of Trinidad's immigration office, where he had worked his way up from messenger to interpreter, while studying pharmacy by night to qualify as a compounder?[66] Mewa was thereafter banned from the steady, gainful work aboard indenture ships, although he had a wife, four children and a disabled sister to sup-port. Would Rohimon have hurled expletives at that situation, too?

Her encounters with white men onboard—the one who wronged her and the one who failed to punish that wrong—doubtless made Rohimon feel impotent. I imagine that feeling took root in many a coolie woman's soul, as stoutly as the paragrass that they would have to weed in cane fields to come. Was that what it would mean to be a "coolie woman": to be disgraced—and powerless to do anything about it? To not only *be* powerless, but made to *feel* just how powerless she was? Was "coolitude" not just an economic circumstance, not just a social condition, but also an emotional state? And was that emotion best expressed by a curse?

One Indian woman had a more advantageous encounter with a white man aboard a ship to Guiana, in 1883. Janky was a widow in her mid-twenties who listed no next-of-kin on her emigration pass. She belonged to the landowning *thakur* caste, and her father had been—or was, if still alive—a clerk. At 5-foot-7, Janky towered above most of the women aboard *The Silhet*.[67] On meeting her in Calcutta, a relatively high-status Muslim cast his wife aside for her. But then, during the voyage, he cast Janky aside too. "He saw," authorities in Guiana reported, "that the surgeon was fond of her."[68] As a *sirdar* on the ship, and a man who had been indentured before, Deemohamed could offer Janky the concrete benefits of his experience—he probably knew some English and understood the system—as well as the protection of his slight authority on the ship. But how could he possibly measure up to *The Silhet*'s surgeon superintendent?

Thomas Dealtry Atkins, LRCP, MRCS, was a bachelor in his late-thirties.[69] As the initials impressively following his name indicated, he was licensed by Edinburgh's prestigious Royal College of Physicians and was a member of London's Royal College of Surgeons.[70] His connection to India was generations-deep. Atkins was born in Calcutta, as was his mother, a headmaster's daughter in the British governmental enclave in Bengal.[71] Atkins' late father, the Reverend Thomas Atkins, was an anti-slavery pamphleteer and restless wanderer, chaplain to convicts in Australia before he was to sailors in Calcutta.[72] In a memoir about his travels, Reverend Atkins described himself as "a clerical Ulysses" but made no reference to the wife and sons acquired during his five-year sojourn in Calcutta. It seems he left them behind there when he moved on.[73] It may have been this background that led the surgeon, raised more in India than in Britain, with unorthodoxy in his family tree, to do what he did when *The Silhet* landed.

Like ship surgeons accused of impropriety before him, and after him, Atkins denied that anything had happened. But unlike most of them, he saved the woman involved from indenture. Atkins paid the colony and the planters the cost of importing Janky and applied to have her contract cancelled.[74] He said he intended to marry her and take her to England. The authorities, failing to find anyone who saw her visit his room during the voyage, granted his wish. Three weeks later, on 15 February 1883, Atkins and Janky were married at St. Andrew's Kirk, a Scottish Presbyterian church in the Guianese capital. And there, shortly after making her extraordinary appearance in history, Janky disappears from the records. By the late 1880s, Atkins was practicing medicine—and appearing in bankruptcy court—in Australia. But there is no sign that Janky accompanied him, and there is no indication that they had any children in Australia, England or India. Atkins died on 3 July 1896 in Calcutta and was buried there the next day, in the same spot where he had been baptized.

Did Janky attend his funeral? Had Atkins lived with her as man and wife? Did he take her to Australia, or leave her in his mother's care in Calcutta while he was away? Or did he install her in a house by the sea in Torquay, where the English census had found him with his mother, a widowed cousin and a servant in 1881? What did his mother make of this wife who would, without Atkins, probably have been fertilizing sugar cane stumps on a remote West Indian plantation? Had Atkins fallen in love with her? Had he seen in her his mother: another widow and, also, another woman abandoned? Or had he rescued Janky out of guilt, as an abolitionist preacher's son employed in transporting Indians to a life that publications in England were calling a "new form of slavery"? Was theirs a paper-marriage to secure her freedom? What-ever happened to Janky? Did she end up right back in India, and was that what she wanted? However rare her example, if Janky did manage to get what she wanted, she wasn't alone. During the passage from India, power was being renegotiated between men and women in the 'tween decks. What had seemed unthinkable in India was becoming conceivable as the seas were crossed. In some cases, women discovered a whole new ability to set terms and boundaries.

Consider the story of the prostitute Sukhia and her *jahaji* Roocha, emigrants on the same ship as Rohimon.[75] Although they weren't travelling as a married couple, they were discovered having sex together within their first month at sea. Roocha had given Sukhia $10 in India in order to sleep with her. She didn't dispute this, telling the surgeon that the man had "lived for some time with her and on her prostitution in India." At first, Sukhia didn't complain about it. She seemed content enough with him. Earlier in the voyage, the two of them had landed in trouble together. On the same day she was handcuffed for trying to steal water and "using threatening lan-guage," he was chained to an iron stanchion for trying to steal biscuits with sugar and threatening to cut the third mate's throat. It sounds as if they, allies in misad-venture, had conducted a raid on the ship's pantry. But a shadow had already fallen over Roocha by the time they were caught having sex. He accused a *sirdar* of giving Sukhia biscuits and sugar. (He had clearly grasped the less than innocent connota-tions of that gesture.) By the end of October, something had definitely come between the pair. One night, Sukhia woke to find Roocha lying next to her, with his arms wrapped around her. He had broken the wire screen separating the men's section from the rest of the 'tween decks to get to her. This time, Sukhia raised a cry. The next evening, as she was sifting rice on deck with some women, Roocha stole up behind her and whacked her in the back three times. He then accused another *sirdar* of fondling her breasts.

Was Roocha jealous? How could he be, when he wasn't even her husband? Did he think he had bought Sukhia's exclusive and permanent affections for $10? What did the surgeon mean by saying Roocha had lived "on her prostitution" in India? Did Roocha imagine himself her pimp? Was he? Had she grown tired of him? Had he reached his $10 limit? Was she trying to assert control over her own body? If so, was her daring born onboard? Did the shortage of women explain it? Or was it due to the existence of regulations to protect the women, even if those regulations were honored more in the breach? And was Sukhia the only woman to use her sexuality for gain? Might others have occupied that strategic but unsettling terrain, in more subtle ways?

When *The Rohilla* landed in British Guiana in 1883, the immigration agent-gen-eral reported that "the Nipalese [sic] woman Morti refused to acknowledge Amirbun as her husband."[76] If in fact they had been married, it was probably a hastily-struck depot or shipboard marriage. I say this because they weren't from the same part of India, not remotely. The colony's immigration authorities registered couples as mar-ried if they said they were, no further questions really asked. A sample of five dozen ships landing in Guiana between 1883 and 1908 indicates that 28 percent of women did what Morti could not bring herself to do—they acknowledged husbands on landing, husbands who had accompanied them from home or husbands acquired along the way, either at Garden Reach or on the transfiguring seas.[77] Sometimes, captains performed marriages for the emigrants. The master of a ship that sailed to the Caribbean the year my great-grandmother did instructed everyone to find partners, according to an Indian aboard. "He told them couple up, and he made a wedding right there," the man recalled a lifetime later. "He told them: 'Who would cook for all of you, all of you going to Trinidad to work? You need a woman.' So they made a pair. ... They say that they 'take this woman' and the woman say that they 'take this man'."[78] I wonder if Morti had pledged onboard to 'take' Amirbun and why ultimately she refused him. Had he failed to protect her during the crossing? Had he mistreated her? Or, had he already served his purpose? Did it even occur to him that she could change her mind? Was such a prerogative within the country of his experience and understanding? Did he see in it a sign that the world he had sailed to would be new in unexpected senses? Would this newness be his undoing?

One husband felt the need to promise his wife jewellery if she agreed to stay with him once in Guiana.[79] He deposited a gold nose ring, silver bangles and silver armlets with the surgeon for safekeeping on *The Foyle* in 1899. How had this woman, Mariam, gained the power to choose: to stay with him, or not? Was theirs a shipboard or depot marriage, or one of longer standing, secured by the ties of village, caste and religion? Or, had they eloped together? If their emigrant registration numbers are any guide, they were recruited together, suggesting a firmer bond. Nonetheless, the voyage seems to have caused a sea change in their relationship. The surgeon found Mariam, who was helping out as a nurse, crying in the hospital one day. Her husband, the *sirdar* Ilahikhan, had been beating her regularly. He believed that she had developed "an improper intimacy" with the Indian junior compounder aboard. Ilahikhan said he found them in the hospital together thrice. To punish him for hitting Mariam, the surgeon dismissed him from his post as *sirdar*. But he reinstated him the next day, when he promised not to err again.

The surgeon never tried to determine if there were real grounds for the man's fears. It was Cecil, who saw no evil when coolies alleged it. He later wrote to Guiana's immigration director: "These charges amongst coolies are always or nearly always brought to annoy each other, and there is no foundation for them whatever." Was Ilahikhan's jealousy founded? Could Mariam have been in the hospital with the junior compounder simply to do her job as nurse? Was that enough to explain the tête-à-têtes? Were there, in fact, tête-à-têtes? What exactly had Ilahikhan seen to set his insecurities ablaze? When the ship landed, he handed Mariam the nose ring and bracelets. She, forgetting or forgiving the beatings and possessiveness, promised to accompany him to the same sugar estate. But how emphatic was her choice? And how permanent?

1. Bahadur family in Cumberland Village on the day we emigrated to America, 7 November 1981 (*Author's Family Collection*).

2. Portrait of Lal Bahadur in New Amsterdam, Guyana, 1950s (*Author's Family Collection*).

3. Indian girl in Trinidad, c. 1890 (*MS AM 2211, Houghton Library, Harvard University*).

Coolie Type, Trinidad, B.W.I.

Stephens Ltd., Trinidad.

4. Postcard image of "Coolie Type, Trinidad, BWI," c. 1900 (*Michael Goldberg Collection, The Alma Jordan Library, University of the West Indies, St. Augustine, Trinidad and Tobago*).

Stephens Ltd.: Trinidad.   Coolie Types.   Trinidad.

5. Postcard image of "Coolie Types, Trinidad," c. 1900 (*Michael Goldberg Collection, The Alma Jordan Library, University of the West Indies, St. Augustine, Trinidad and Tobago*).

Coolie Woman.

6. Postcard image of "Coolie Woman" (*Michael Goldberg Collection, The Alma Jordan Library, University of the West Indies, St. Augustine, Trinidad and Tobago*).

7. A view of the Hooghly River and Garden Reach, by James Baillie Fraser (slave-era Berbice planter), 1826 (© *The British Library Board, X644 (4), Plate 4 of Views of Calcutta, published by Smith Elder & Co., London, 1824–26, Asia, Pacific and Africa Collections*).

8. Indentured men and crew on the deck of an indenture vessel recently arrived in Georgetown, Demerara, c. 1890 (*MS AM 2211, Houghton Library, Harvard University*).

"CLYDE."

9. *The Clyde,* the ship on which Sujaria sailed from Calcutta to the Caribbean (© *The British Library Board, 8808.i.30, Basil Lubbock's Coolie Ships and Oil Sailers, General Reference Collection*).

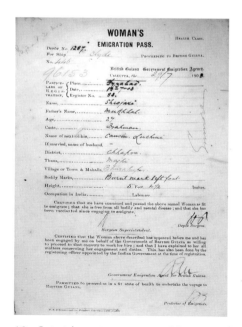

10. Sujaria's emigration pass (*Courtesy of the Walter Rodney Archives in Georgetown, Guyana*).

11. Mahadai Singh, who sailed on *The Ganges* in 1871, rescued from infanticide by her parents (*Courtesy of Bernadette Persaud*).

COOLIE PASSENGER ON BOARD.

12. Return migrant aboard *The Sheila* (© *The British Library Board, 08806. bb.53, Capt. W.H. Angel's The Clipper Ship Sheila, General Reference Collection*).

13. The immigration depot in Georgetown, where newly arrived immigrants were processed, c. 1900 (*MS AM 2211, Houghton Library, Harvard University*).

14. Architectural flourish in downtown Georgetown, c. 1880 (*Reproduced by Permission of the Essex Record Office, England*).

15. Camp Street, Georgetown, c. 1900 (*The Schomburg Center for Black Research, New York Public Library*).

16. Water Street, Georgetown, c. 1900 (*MS AM 2211, Houghton Library, Harvard University*).

17. "Idea of a Gentleman's House, Guiana," c. 1870 (*Reproduced by Permission of the Essex Record Office, England*).

18. Enmore Great House, c. 1875 (*Courtesy of John Platt*).

19. Rangali Singh with her family, posed in front of a logie at Plantation Leonora in British Guiana, early 1900s (*Courtesy of Jung Bahadur Collection, The Rajkumari Cultural Center, New York City*).

Coolie Dwelling, Essequibo.   10/8/96

20. Postcard image of "Coolie Dwelling," c. 1900 (*Courtesy of Charles Kennard*).

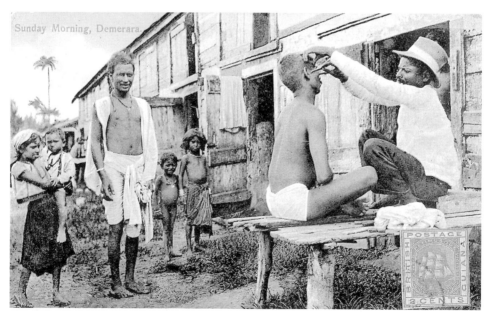

Sunday Morning, Demerara.

21. Postcard image, "Sunday Morning in Demerara," showing a barber at work in the logies, c. 1900 (*Courtesy of Charles Kennard*).

22. Portrait of George Maximilian Bethune, c. 1900 (*Courtesy of Charles Bethune*).

23. Postcard image of "Coolie Man," c. 1900 (*Michael Goldberg Collection, The Alma Jordan Library, University of the West Indies, St. Augustine, Trinidad and Tobago*).

24. "Coolies, Demerara," c. 1890 (*MS AM 2211, Houghton Library, Harvard University*).

25. Postcard image of the Strand, New Amsterdam, c. 1900 (*Courtesy of Charles Kennard*).

26. Overseers, Demerara (*Courtesy of Dennis Driscoll*).

Coolio Bello
Waterman, 15 Frederick Street, Trinidad

27. Postcard image of "Coolie Belle" in Trinidad, c. 1890 (*Michael Goldberg Collection, The Alma Jordan Library, University of the West Indies, St. Augustine, Trinidad and Tobago*).

28. Postcard image of "Coolio Bello" in Trinidad, c. 1890 (*Michael Goldberg Collection, The Alma Jordan Library, University of the West Indies, St. Augustine, Trinidad and Tobago*).

29. Overseers lodge, Demerara (*Courtesy of Dennis Driscoll*).

30. Postcard image of "Coolie Children, Trinidad, BWI," c. 1890 (*Michael Goldberg Collection, The Alma Jordan Library, University of the West Indies, St. Augustine, Trinidad and Tobago*).

31. Postcard image "Group of Coolies, Trinidad, BWI," c. 1890 (*Michael Goldberg Collection, The Alma Jordan Library, University of the West Indies, St. Augustine, Trinidad and Tobago*).

32. Donald Howell Rickford, the son of an overseer and an Indian woman from Albion Plantation in British Guiana (*Courtesy of John Rickford*).

Indian Woman and Child, Trinidad.

33. Postcard image of Indian woman with baby (*Michael Goldberg Collection, The Alma Jordan Library, University of the West Indies, St. Augustine, Trinidad and Tobago*).

34. Chhablal Ramcharan—repatriation officer on *The Resurgent*, the last ship to sail back to India from British Guiana—as a boy with his mother, who left India indentured in 1898 (*Courtesy of Nalini Mohabir*).

35. Portrait of my great-grandmother Sujaria with her son Lal Bahadur and daughter Belle and two grandchildren, Cumberland, British Guiana, c. 1930 (*Author's Family Collection*).

36. Matabikh Maharaj and his wife Dasoda, who arrived in British Guiana as a married couple on a coolie vessel in 1905. My great-great-grandparents (*Author's Family Collection*).

37. Raghubansia, their daughter, my great-grandmother, born on a ship to British Guiana in 1905 (*Author's Family Collection*).

38. My great-grandmother Bechetra, born in plantation barracks during indenture, with her daughters, also born in plantation barracks during indenture (*Author's Family Collection*).

39. My great-grandmother Dukhni, daughter of indentured immigrants, born in British Guiana, in Cumberland Village with her children, c. 1950 (*Author's Family Collection*).

6

A NEW WORLD

Remember one-third quota, coolie woman.
Was your blood spilled that I might reject my history

Mahadai Das, "They Came in Ships"*

For the indentured immigrants who landed there, Guiana would be a new world. But it had long been identified, more broadly, with *the* New World. In the European imagination, this was where the risk and reward of the swashbuckling unknown were located. This, indeed, was where Sir Walter Raleigh had gone in search of El Dorado, the mythic city of gold. Three centuries before my great-grandmother reached this shore, Elizabeth I's own court explorer had peered at it from a ship and wondered what fate—and what riches—it might hold. To the Dutch, French, Spanish, Portuguese and British colonizers who staked and swapped claims there over the next 200 years, the entire northeastern fringe of South America, stretching from the Atlantic to what is now Venezuela, was known as Guiana—after the Guayano Indians who lived along the Orinoco River,[1] but eventually acquiring the meaning "wild coast." To colonial eyes, it was a *terra incognita*, a mystery complete, waiting to be mapped, peopled—and taken.

Demerara was the shorthand the British used for the part of Guiana that they took, early in the nineteenth century, from the Dutch, who had turned the low-lying coastal strip into prime plantation ground through an elaborate system of drainage canals, dams and dykes. In the end, it wasn't gold that enriched Raleigh's countrymen. It was sugar, the main harvest of that drained land, rich with the alluvium of

* Epigraph from *India in the Caribbean*, Hansib, 1987. Used by courtesy of Peepal Tree Press Ltd.

rivers beginning deep in the colony's interior. Long after Raleigh, Demerara continued to have the aura of the ends of the earth where adventurers went to make their fortunes. A parlor song popular in Victorian England captured the feeling. The chorus went: "So here we sit like birds in the wilderness/ Birds in the wilderness!/ Down in Demerara."[2] That name still survives on the packaging for brown sugar the world over. Most of it doesn't actually come from Demerara anymore, but in 1903, when my great-grandmother landed there, the plantations studding its marshy coast still had a monopoly on the name.

Not only was the colony still supplying the world with Demerara sugar, it was supplying more sugar than any other territory in the British West Indies. British Guiana was one of the top ten producers of cane sugar globally, but the world was increasingly buying cheaper, subsidized beet sugar from France and Germany. The cane that once was planter's gold was in crisis. Its selling price had plummeted by half in the two decades before Sujaria arrived.

And yet, in order to produce it, the British continued to people Guiana. Just as they had after the abolition of slavery, planters pleaded they would be ruined and the nation's pride wrecked if they did not get what they wanted: a continual supply of new indentured laborers from India. Guiana had been the first colony in the West Indies to receive coolies, and it received far more in total than any other colony in the region. These were the workers who bore the brunt of the cane sugar depression. As revenues fell, the only way for planters to maintain profits was to lower costs; they did this by squeezing more work, for less pay, out of the indentured.[3] The laborers already in the colony—ex-indentured and their children as well as slave descendants—had more leverage to insist on higher wages and better working conditions. They were less exploitable because officially free. The cry, therefore, was to import ever more "bound coolies," as the indentured were known in Demerara: "Give me my heart's desire in coolies, and I will make you a million hogsheads* of sugar ...," a planter once told the visiting novelist Anthony Trollope.

So it was that, despite hard times for cane sugar, *The Clyde* arrived in British Guiana on 4 November 1903. I can't say if Sujaria was on deck or if it was light enough for her to see the flat coast of her new world, with its monotonous line of black mangrove, broken occasionally by cabbage palms or a plantation smokestack. The ship pulled in beside a floating lightship at the mouth of the Demerara River, its waters muddy with silt carried from the interior, a territory almost as undeveloped and lightly populated as when Raleigh explored.

Despite the colony's reputation in Britain as a "white man's grave" of malarial swamps, yellow fever and hard drink, the capital was a graceful, modern city. Georgetown's boulevards were broad—and down their middles ran grassy medians or freshwater canals with Victoria Regia lilies. Everywhere there were luxuriant trees providing shade and beauty: the *samaan* with its umbrella of foliage; the Flambouyant, with its scarlet bloom; and a peculiar palm with its leaves splayed flat like a lady's

---

* A hogshead is a cask capable of holding 100 to 140 gallons.

fan. Fruit trees enfolded elegant wooden houses with verandahs for taking the air and jalousies for letting it flow. The architecture had fanciful flourishes: cupolas or towers rising from roofs, fretwork crawling like vines from verandah posts. The city boasted botanical gardens, a philharmonic hall and a gothic cathedral that is still among the world's tallest wooden buildings. Along the Demerara River ran a bustling commercial road with electric tram service. Nearby, dock workers loaded casks of sugar, rum and molasses and unloaded endless ice from America for coping with the heat. Schooners continuously returned from the interior with Raleigh's fortune-seeking heirs; during the 1890s, these miners began exporting more than 100,000 ounces of gold every year,[4] somewhat vindicating his vision of El Dorado. It was in the briskness of all this shipping in and shipping out that *The Clyde* landed its human cargo.

It dispatched them, escorted by immigration agents, into a diverse city of 50,000 people. A tenth of Georgetown's population was British, but the rest were mainly the black, Chinese, Portuguese and mixed-race descendants of plantation workers imported over several centuries. Few of the city's residents belonged to the group most recently imported. Although Indians made up 40 percent of the colony's population, more than any other ethnicity, the vast majority lived in the far countryside—on or near plantations. With the exception of domestic servants, a handful of interpreters, a few policemen and a single doctor,[5] Indians in the capital were mostly "jobbers" who hustled for work daily. They carried loads at the railway station or harbor as porters, "coolies" in the original sense of the word.

The authorities saw the jobbers as public nuisances. Some, half-starved, rifled through rubbish for food. Others, with no way to defecate but publicly, were made objects of cruel fun by street children. Many slept and—in a few cases—died on the streets. Some of the day laborers had chosen to leave the countryside after serving out their indentures. But a significant number, finding the tasks or the treatment on plantations too harsh, had deserted and drifted to Georgetown. Planters insisted that the city council find and return them, and the council passed an ordinance requiring porters to be licensed. The crackdown applied only to Indians. To get a license, they had to pay a fee few could afford and present "free papers"—an official certificate, requiring a separate fee, proving that an immigrant was no longer indentured. The jobbers became the frequent target of harassment and nighttime raids by police demanding documents.

Discriminated against, and in dire need, this tiny community found an unlikely champion: an overseer from a far-flung sugar estate. While on home leave in Scotland, Alex Alexander had heard someone from the Salvation Army preach, and he had an awakening of conscience. Alexander came to believe that his mission in life was to help the shipload's worth of Indians barely scraping by on the streets of Georgetown. He quit the plantation, changed his name to Ghurib Das ("servant of the poor") and adopted Indian dress and customs. "Coolie Alexander," as the planters called him, ate no meat, went barefoot and wore a turban along with a scarlet Salvation Army jacket. In 1897, Alexander opened a home and soup kitchen where Indians could get cheap lodgings and three inexpensive meals a day.

His coolie shelter was in the same neighborhood as the immigration depot, which sat squat and boxy as a warehouse in the lonely border ground where the Atlantic met the Demerara River, and both met land. On their short walk from the wharves to this depot, where they were processed and assigned to plantations, the immigrants disembarking from *The Clyde* probably passed Alexander's shelter. Did these most recent recruits to Guianese plantation society encounter those despised as its rejects? Were there women at the shelter? Did they notice Sujaria walk by, carrying her three-week old baby? Did she notice them? Who felt more pity for whom? Whether they crossed paths, and how they reacted if they did, can't be known. Like so much else that's important, it can only be imagined.

This frightful disparity

Over the next few weeks, *The Clyde* appeared in fine print in the pages of the colony's *Daily Chronicle*. The details presented were bare and mercantile: The ship had brought 300 bales of gunnysacks from India and a box of cigars. When it left four days later, it took 15,958 bags of linseed to the English port of Falmouth.[6] Of the immigrants aboard, all that survives is a census, a mean tally of births and deaths, and a ship's manifest of everyone who had made it to Guiana.

Slightly more had been made of the arrival of the first immigrant ship of the season, *The Erne*, two weeks earlier. *The Daily Chronicle* reported on its "exceptionally healthy-looking lot" of indentured laborers, including the striking presence of "a giant among the coolies: a great, big, stalwart fellow standing six feet three on his natural heels." But their correspondent dedicated most of his copy to what he called, in the white-gloved idiom of the parlor room, the fairer sex. "The women, moreover, were pretty and youthful," he wrote. "Coolie women are in demand here, as … a large number of vacancies for coolie wives exist; but the difficulty about the shipment is that all the ladies seem to be very much engaged already to their fellow passengers of the male 'persuasion'. There were very many more men than women on board."[7]

It was like that in the colony, too, and it wasn't getting any better with the arrival of new recruits. The ship that followed *The Clyde* to Guiana arrived with a note from the emigration agent in Calcutta. "The collection of emigrants for this vessel," he wrote, "has been attended with exceptional difficulty, owing to the phenomenal scarcity of women."[8] It had been a bad year for recruiting women in India. The British government was so hard up that it even tried its hand at matchmaking. Two months before Sujaria's arrival, the managers of plantations across Guiana had received a memo from the colony's immigration agent-general, A.H. Alexander.[9] It was a plea to spread the word among their coolies that the government would help if they wanted to import brides from their villages. But only six laborers across the entire colony applied, and three were rejected because they already had wives.[10]

Men had also outnumbered women in slave cargoes to the British Caribbean, in keeping with the demand of planters for field muscle. Women made up 35 to 40 percent of slaves transported in the final years of the British slave trade.[11] The gender ratio among slaves tended to even out in the colonies over time, as more slaves were born than imported. Also, when the slave trade was banned, sugar barons had to improve the way they treated their female chattel. If planters could not import the next generation of field workers, enslaved women had to live to reproduce. Their mortality rate declined. At emancipation, the number of enslaved women was roughly equal to the number of enslaved men in most of the Anglophone Caribbean.[12]

The evils of a sexual imbalance—and the mistreatment of slave women—had figured in campaigns against the slave trade in Britain. The details of those campaigns must have been branded in the brain of Sir John Gladstone, the man who introduced Indian indentured laborers into the Caribbean. A chairman of the West India Association and a member of parliament, he was both politician and planter. He owned more than 2,000 slaves in the Caribbean; at emancipation, the British government compensated him roughly $10 million in current dollars for his losses in Guiana alone.[13] When Parliament debated the abolition of slavery in 1833, his son William Gladstone—the future prime minister, who succeeded him in those chambers— argued against it. In the rhetorical thrust and parry, his opponents had only to turn to the family's Demerara holdings for vivid examples of slavery's horrors. They cited the high mortality rate on one particular plantation, Vreed-en-Hoop. John Gladstone had to be savvy to the comparisons that might be drawn between indenture and the system it replaced, because he was one of the most influential lobbyists for that system as well as a high-profile target of those who condemned it. He had to know that any shortage of indentured women could create an outcry.

Still, Gladstone seemed relatively blithe about the issue. He did instruct the firm he hired to recruit Indian workers to include women in the shipment. He wrote to Messrs. Gillanders, Arbuthnot & Company in 1837 that "in Demerara, the females are employed in the field as well as the men; and if the female coolies will engage to work there, a larger proportion may be sent, say two women to three men, or, if desired, equal numbers." He allowed that if the firm couldn't manage it, one woman to every nine or ten men "for cooking and washing, is enough!"[14] That was the gender ratio in Mauritius, the colony off the African coast where coolies had already been imported as workers, and Gladstone thought that it might do in Guiana as well. A Quaker investigator for the British Anti-Slavery Society would later disagree stridently, saying: "It is easy to conceive that, from this frightful disparity of the sexes, the most horrible and revolting depravity and demoralization must necessarily ensue."[15]

The first group of coolies to arrive in the West Indies didn't even meet that "frightful" ratio of one to ten. Even Guiana's *Royal Gazette*, a government organ, could foresee the problems. The newspaper editorialized: "We protest the barbarous and flagitous system of bringing into a strange country hundreds of men without an adequate proportion of women."[16] In May 1838, three months before slaves in the British Empire would be finally and fully free, the ships that Gladstone had privately commissioned, *The Whitby* and *The Hesperus*, landed in Guiana with about 400 men—and just fourteen women and eleven girls. Less than a year later, one of the girls was dead. Her name was Nunneedy, and she was eight years old. The coroner concluded that she had "died in consequence of her person being violated by some man unknown."[17] Guiana's governor promised a £100 reward for the rapist, but no one was ever turned in.

A magistrate visited Plantation Belle Vue, the scene of Nunneedy's rape, to investigate conditions there in 1839. Through an interpreter, he spoke with the only two women among the coolies there. Like all women in this first batch, they were not actually indentured. That would soon change. For the time being the women received rations, but did not work in field or factory. Their unpaid job was to serve the needs of the men, needs that likely extended beyond cooking and cleaning. A census of coolies recorded their height, complexion, religion and age. Sudney and Luckeah were short, "copper-colored," Muslim and, respectively, thirty and twenty-two. That's all the records say about them, except that one—it's unclear who—shared a room in the plantation's sick-house with an indentured man. The other lived with the rest— sixty-three men—in communal quarters with a dirt-floor. The day the magistrate visited, he discussed privacy with the women. He later said, as if they had a choice in accommodations: "They do not seem to be sensible of the indecency of sleeping with their husbands in a public room."[18]

The situation was as grim at nearby Vreed-en-Hoop, the Gladstone plantation infamously invoked during the abolition debate in Parliament. Three women and two girls lived among sixty-three men and two boys. The mortality and suffering were high among this first group (known as The Gladstone Coolies, though many worked on plantations that were not his). One hundred died.[19] Some were flogged with cat-o-nine-tails and had salty pork pickle rubbed into the wounds. Others were afflicted with chigoes, sand fleas that burrow in the feet, causing lesions that literally ate away at their toes. Still others tried to escape, thinking they could cut an overland path through the jungle to Calcutta.[20] When their contracts were up in 1843, only sixty stayed in Guiana.[21] All twelve remaining women took the free passage back to India.

The outcry over the treatment of the Gladstone Coolies led to a five-year moratorium on new workers from India. When the traffic resumed in 1845, it was with a mandatory quota for women. No ship could leave port until it had recruited fourteen women for every 100 men. That gender ratio fluctuated over the remaining seven decades of indenture, as colonial policymakers responded to planters complaining that it was nearly impossible to meet the quota, despite the higher bounties eventually paid to recruiters for female coolies. The quota peaked at fifty women for every 100 men before dropping to twenty-five for every 100, as concerns took hold that the wrong kind of woman was being dispatched.[22] Rumors had spread that recruiters were kidnapping women into indenture or combing red-light districts when they fell short. An official in Guiana once described the female arrivals as "the sweepings of the bazaars of Calcutta."[23] By the time Sujaria arrived, the quota had settled at forty per 100.[24] Twenty-nine percent of every shipment had to be female. That was a smaller percentage than on British slavers, and that was where the quota stood until indenture ended.

A NEW WORLD

Parallel worlds

The moon was full the first night Sujaria spent in Georgetown. The next afternoon, the Demerara Agricultural Show opened at the Promenade Gardens, with a performance by the Band of the British Guiana Militia. On display was the colony's harvested wealth: varieties of sugar cane, coffee, rice, plantains. If the newspaper advertisements were accurate, there were electric lights, refreshments and al fresco suppers, all for the price of one shilling.[25] But that genteel world would not be my great-grandmother's. In her world, one shilling was the value of a human life. It was the amount the government docked from the pay of ship surgeons whenever a coolie died during the crossing. One shilling was also the wage contractually promised to indentured men for a day's work, though planters habitually broke the promise through a sleight of hand, measuring a day's work not in hours but in tasks—"daily" tasks that could rarely be done in just one day. Women were promised less, two-thirds a shilling for a day's work.

This was to be Sujaria's world. Like the larger world, it did not treat women equally, and it often did not treat immigrants, whatever their gender, justly. But it was also a world where women were the scarcer sex. There were sixty-four women per 100 men on Guiana's plantations. For the indentured, the problem was more acute, with forty-one women per 100 men.*[26] To a woman alone, with a newborn to support, what must this world have looked like? What possibilities—and what terror—did it hold? Did Sujaria sense that the shortage of women could have dark implications? How did she weigh her options for survival? Was there hope of freedom, or power, and what would be the source? Exactly what kind of a new world would this be?

If she had turned to the landscape for answers, it might have raised her expectations. The planters had given fanciful names to the sugar estates along the coast, investing them perhaps with their own desires. The train that transported Sujaria to her plantation chugged through Industry, Triumph, Success and Liberty's Delight.** I wonder what she made of Bachelor's Adventure as it came into view? Did anyone tell her that was the name of the village of slave descendants, or translate its meaning for her? What ideas might such a name have given the British overseers, mainly single young men, who had worked there when it was a plantation? Against the usual expectations, Sujaria reached Paradise before she reached Hope along the coastal railway line. And then, finally, she arrived at a plantation with a less whimsical name. Enmore was christened after the parish in England where its first owner had been born, 150 years earlier. The plantation was among the colony's largest, as well as one of its most stable and successful. When slavery was abolished, estates across Guiana were abandoned or auctioned, claimed by wild bush or new owners. But Enmore

---

* Only 20 percent of the population on plantations was indentured. The rest were immigrants who had served out their time but still lived and worked on the sugar estates.
** Rendered in Dutch as "Vryheid's Lust."

survived for more than a century as the property of one family.[27] With Sujaria, as she descended at its railway station, fifteen miles east of the capital, seven decades after slavery's end, was the couple she had befriended on *The Clyde*.

By then, Enmore's owners had become absentee. The plantation was run by the owner's nephew, George Maximilian Bethune. He had spent three decades working on the family's Guiana plantations, beginning as overseer but quickly rising to manager. At fifty, Bethune cut a stern, remote figure. A portrait of him in late middle age shows an angular man with a hawk's nose, an imposing moustache that hid his mouth, close-set eyes and hair precisely parted at the side. Bethune came from a long line of Anglican ministers; his grandson remembers him as a "man of strict Christian principles," who joined an evangelical group when he retired to England.[28]

As Enmore's manager, Bethune lived in the plantation's Great House. A photograph taken outside it in 1876 suggests grandeur in scale and style. Brick pillars with ivy crawling up their sides hold the house aloft, some twenty feet off the ground. Posed in front are a dozen white men defying the tropical weather with full suits—waistcoats, pocket watches, cravats, top hats politely off their heads. One is a manager who preceded Bethune, and another looks like a younger Bethune—although softer around the edges and dashing enough for his grandson to see "quite a touch of Clark Gable in *Gone With the Wind*."[29] Mostly, the men are overseers. One—stretched out on a blanket, his face full and fleshy, his eyes alight, his hair wavy and slightly tousled—has some color in his cheeks. Is his pose entitled and cocky, or just at ease? Is he sunburnt? Or is his face red with Liberty's Delight?

In the photograph, there are wives, but not enough. Puffed out in high-collared, frilly regalia, four women sit. They include the manager's mother-in-law Sarah,[30] her bronze skin the sign of an earlier era, when black or colored mistresses often "looked after … the comfort of her master generally,"[31] as a Guiana sheriff once put it. At the time, people would have said that Sarah had "the negro taint, the touch of the tar-brush."[32] They may also have looked askance at her apparent marriage to plantation engineer James Cooke. Starting in the 1850s, steamships had made travel between England and Demerara faster, bringing in more British wives and would-be wives and making their relationship much less accepted. But there James stands, behind Sarah, in the photograph. Huddled in the shadows of the Great House, receding into the background, are two Indian men. A black man stands off to the side, separate. Oddly, a third Indian man stands with the main group. He wears simple clothes and appears to be holding something indistinct and furry, held out in front of him, as if for the camera. Is it a miniature pet dog, that indispensable accessory for fashionable Victorian ladies? Is it a poodle being presented for posterity by its own personal attendant, but blurred by its own wriggling? Even photographs leave questions.

Bethune was married, with children. Living with his family, in the Great House, was a governess. She had got the job through the official charged with overseeing the welfare of indentured immigrants—her father, the district immigration agent. Also living on the plantation was the district magistrate, whose job it was to judge the guilt of immigrants accused of labor violations, such as leaving the plantation without a pass or insulting an overseer. Colonists believed that decades of reform had brought indenture "to perfection... as an example to all the world of British fairness, honesty and organization in the beneficial control of a humble and dependent race."[33] For an immigrant to break the laws governing this perfection was to commit a crime, punishable by jail. The system was penal, and it incarcerated widely. The court house, the police station and the jail recur as images in the folk songs the immigrants bequeathed.[34] When Sujaria arrived, in the system's final and presumably most flawless decades, two in five coolies were prosecuted yearly for breaches of indenture rules in Guiana; one in five were convicted and fined or imprisoned, sometimes with hard labor.[35] As further punishment, their indenture was extended by the amount of time lost in jail. And the magistrate who decided whether and what Enmore's coolies would suffer lived right next to its luxurious Great House.

This map of Enmore's tangled relationships was provided by an extraordinary immigrant indentured there: Bechu. Deemed frail and unfit for field labor, he was put to work as a house servant, like the figures in the margins of the 1876 photograph. Bechu, however, did not recede into the backdrop. Orphaned young, he had been raised and educated by a missionary in Calcutta.[36] He could read English—and write it, with formal elegance, biting sarcasm and moral force. Enmore's deputy manager had given Bechu the run of the Overseers Reading Room, where he found the colony's newspapers. He used them to expose inappropriate intimacies and conflicts of interest at Enmore in the decade before Sujaria got there. In regular letters to the editor in *The Chronicle*, and testimony before a Royal Commission, Bechu posed tough questions. Of the immigration agent whose daughter worked for Bethune, he asked: "How is it possible, under the circumstance, to receive justice at his hands?"[37] Of the magistrate, he asked: "When [he] can live on a plantation and be on friendly terms with the manager and exchange his hospitalities, who, permit me to ask, is to protect the indentured man?"[38] Bechu's targets dismissed him as a ridiculous ingrate, but they did not dispute his facts.

This was the world that ran alongside and occasionally met Sujaria's world. Hers was the "nigger yard," where 2,600 immigrants, including 800 children,[39] lived in "logies" previously occupied by slaves. The single-story barracks, barely raised from the ground on short stumps, were partitioned into small rooms. In each room lived one family, however large, or a group of single men. Because the partitions didn't reach the roof, every sound was communal. Typically, the floors were of mud or clay, and there was no furniture, except perhaps a charpoy, the simple Indian bed of ropes that Gandhi famously and ascetically used. Metal roofs under an almost equatorial sun made the rooms murderously hot. One planter in nearby Trinidad defended his iron roofs as a check on laziness: "The people," he said, "ought to be in the field all day long. I do not build cottages for idlers." Asked about people forced to stay at home, such as pregnant and nursing women, he replied: "What do you talk to me about lying in and nursing women; I only want working hands."[40] The roof usually extended a bit to provide shelter for cooking, using clay stoves called *chulhas*, built on the blunt verandahs wrapped around the logies. Throughout the colony, the immigrant quarters on sugar estates lacked latrines as well as privacy. Nor was there typically a source of clean drinking water. In the songs they improvised, gathered on the verandahs at night, the indentured frequently compared their lodgings to stables.[41] In other colonies, they used the words *narak* (hell) and *kasbi ghar* (brothel). Gandhi's comrade in the fight to abolish indenture, visiting Guiana a decade after the system ended, described the logies there as "death-traps," "filthy slum property" that should be condemned as unfit for human habitation. "It was high time," wrote the Reverend C.F. Andrews, "that these relics of the past, with all their evil associations, were swept clean away."[42]

There were few exits from this squalor, and the way out was occasionally shadowed with shame, as at Enmore in 1899. An overseer there, J.F. Jackson, rented a house in a neighboring village for an Indian woman and visited her there at night. She was the daughter of indentured immigrants who had arrived in the colony forty years earlier. In all that time, although their indentures had long ended, they hadn't managed to escape the "nigger yard." But their daughter had, as the local planter's rag reported: "A young coolie girl from Enmore is said to be hidden from her parents in a house at 'Two Friends'. I hope this may catch the eye of the immigration agent general. There is much talk about it in the district."[43] Bechu threatened to inform authorities in India. This prompted the immigration department to investigate, Jackson to confess and Bethune to fire him, saying he had "justly earned his dismissal."[44] In government dispatches about the matter, the overseer's mistress was identified as Parivadee, most likely a British mangling of the common Indian name Parvati. The girl had been named after the Indian goddess of power.

Did my great-grandmother have any power when she arrived at the logies? Did she and her infant have their own room? And if not, did Sujaria choose her roommates, or did an overseer choose for her? Accounts by the indentured* suggest that plantation officials allotted unattached women to men, just as the government allotted immigrants to plantations—as part of standard operating procedure.[45] The immigrants arrived, each was assigned a room, and each man was assigned a woman. The government took care not to separate married couples or parents from children. But beyond that consideration for families, one not shown during slavery, there was significant meddling in the private lives of immigrants. One widow, hospitalized on landing after a sea voyage passed in illness, arrived late at her estate barracks to find that a Muslim shipmate was asking to keep her. But she wasn't the one he asked. He asked a driver, typically a black or Indian sub-overseer. As the woman's son explained a lifetime later, the driver was "the only man who could fix up this business." Her Muslim suitor had fed her boys while she was hospitalized. When she was released, the driver urged: "This is a different kind of country. You can't live by yourself. You

---

* An indentured immigrant in Suriname described the procedure thus: "You were allotted a room. Everybody also received a woman to share the room with. If there were no women left, you got a man. I got a woman, but didn't want her. A week later a man came who wanted a woman but hadn't received one. I gave her away. I didn't ask anything for her."

have to pick somebody, and look, that man minding your children...."[46] The degree of fixing up by management may have depended on the overseer, the plantation and the colony. But if a woman arrived manless, she likely had little control over her living arrangements.

Remember Maharani, the child widow who ran away after spilling milk, the woman who sounded so thrilled to be alone? When she arrived at her plantation, every unattached woman went off with a man—but not Maharani. She managed to resist until her indenture was almost over. Then, a light-eyed, handsome Indian who was no longer "bound" lay claim to her.[47] As a driver, Ramgolam held authority, and he lived off the plantation. Despite these advantages, Maharani didn't want him. She thought he was wicked and knew he was a womanizer. Perhaps she had seen a touch of cruelty in him as a driver in the cane fields. Ultimately, her preferences didn't matter. Ramgolam asked a white overseer to arrange the match. The overseer summoned Maharani to his house, and he pleaded Ramgolam's case as she stood outside, below the house.

"Maharani, you want de man?" the overseer asked.

She said no. She told the overseer, perhaps as an excuse, perhaps in truth, that she wanted to return to India when her indenture was done. Taking a man would make that harder.

"When you fall sick an' ting, you have nobody," the overseer persisted. "You have to take somebody. You alone cyan [can't] stop."

Maharani begged to differ. She could take care of herself if she got sick. She insisted that she didn't want anyone: "I stop alone," she said.

Ignoring every intention and wish that she had expressed, the overseer instructed Ramgolam to take her by the hand, which he did. Ramgolam took Maharani away from the logies. Seven decades later, recounting her life's arc for a sociologist, Maharani raised her frail voice only once, almost fiercely, to set the record straight on their relationship: "Me nah like 'im, but 'e tek me just so." She didn't like him, but he took her just like that. She insisted to her dying days that Ramgolam had drugged her into accepting him. In time, she gave him nine children. Five died. He continued to sleep with other men's wives. He had a violent temper and beat her often, and he closely policed her movements, not allowing her to talk to other men or leave the house much.

It is remarkable that Maharani got to stop alone, as she put it, for as long as she did. At another scene of arrival, at a Suriname plantation in 1898, the batch of new coolies consisted of five men and one woman. The manager asked the woman, a low-caste Hindu, who her husband was, and she pointed to Munshi Rahman Khan, the Muslim man who had been so distressed by the sight of high-caste Hindus ceding their sacred threads in Calcutta. His horror at being marked out as the woman's spouse was just as great. "I do not know what happened to this bitch," he wrote in his autobiography half a century later. "Maybe she found me more youthful and handsome than the others."[48] He denied that he was her husband, but the manager threatened to lock him up in a dark cell if he refused her. Each room in the coolie barracks there was for at least two people. "I could not," Khan discovered, "be given a separate, single room."[49] Khan was planning to return to India and the wife he left there. Other men had taken women earlier in the journey but he, purposefully, had not. He deeply regretted that decision when the manager forced the lower-caste woman on him: "Had I known," he later wrote, "I would have brought with me a beautiful young Brahmin or *Kshatriya* [warrior caste] girl … of my choice, because there would have been so many girls who had wished to accept Islam and stay with me."[50]

A month later, Khan thought he had bought his way out of the situation, but the woman raised a cry, as he gathered his belongings to leave. According to Khan, she screamed: 'What will I eat now? How will I survive?"[51] He tried to appease her by giving her his food allowance, but she still complained to the manager. She claimed that she was pregnant and that Khan had deserted her. "Who," she asked, "will look after me and bear my expenses?"[52] The manager ordered Khan to give her one-fifth of his wages every week until the baby was six months old, but no baby ever materialized. The woman didn't get to tell her side of the story, and she emerges as a grasping liar in Khan's account. But this much is clear: briefly, she had her pick of men, trading up to an educated man who regarded himself as high caste. This much is also clear, and equally significant: she didn't think she could support herself and her possibly imaginary child, although indentured women worked and earned wages in every colony that imported them, except Mauritius.

So how did my great-grandmother fare with her very real infant, when she first reached Enmore? Did she worry that she, alone, might not be able to support him? Did Sujaria somehow manage a room for just herself and her son? Or did she live with Shewratan Singh, the tallish *thakur* in his late twenties who had also come on *The Clyde*? Did she live with this man from the prestigious landowning caste *and* his wife, Munrai? Did an overseer ask Sujaria what she wanted, or consult Munrai about sharing? Wouldn't Bethune, the strict Christian manager, have disapproved? Perhaps there was no room for morality in the cramped immigrant quarters. Perhaps the overcrowded logies conspired to bring Sujaria and Shewratan together. Did he want another woman, because Munrai was barren, as the generations have whispered? How did he feel about my grandfather, the *bahadur* born on the seas; did Shewratan very much like the idea of an adopted son? And how was it fair for one man, *thakur* or not, son-envious or not, to have two women, when there were just forty-four for every 100 men among Enmore's indentured?

A new view of women's rights

Their threesome was remarkable—but only because it was usually a woman shared between men, not the other way around. The institution of indenture didn't promote traditional, stable families. It's true that planters didn't separate couples or children from parents, as they had with enslaved Africans. It must also be remembered that the family bonds of coolies had already been broken; most landed without their original wives and husbands and often without siblings or parents. Still, the realities of plantation life played even further havoc with their personal lives.

It wasn't just the competition for scarce women that destabilized relationships and the family. It was the paper-thin partitions in the military-style housing and the subsistence pay, which was frozen at the same rate for indenture's entire span: eight decades of spiraling costs of living. These factors all contributed to the extraordinarily low rate of births among Indian women.[53] There weren't enough women to bear children at a rate considered natural for the size of the population. The high incidence of venereal diseases, which can cause infertility, may have contributed to the problem.[54] The prospect of intimacy without any real privacy might also have proved inhibiting.[55] And the long hours that women had to work, for unequal and meager pay, must have convinced them that they couldn't afford to raise children. Most women had to go right back to work after childbirth, since they weren't paid for time off to nurse babies.[56] In many cases, they earned nothing for months and even years as they repaid planters for rations provided while they were pregnant.[57] Many indentured women, probably finding those costs too high, used natural methods of contraception and herbal concoctions to induce abortions.[58] Enslaved women had adopted the same strategies against their own fertility. Although progeny was property when children were born enslaved, planters were still relatively uninterested in encouraging families. They calculated that it was cheaper to import slaves than to have women reproduce and raise them, and the same held for coolies.[59] No doubt indentured women realized that planters wanted them not for their wombs, but their backs—to raise and bend them, whacking at weeds in indentured service, and to lie flat on them, in sexual service.

That second desire seems to be one that many women fulfilled. The households that Indians typically formed are telling. Six patterns took hold: (1) a woman living alone except, perhaps, for children; (2) several men succeeding each other in a woman's home; (3) a woman passing from the home of one man to another; (4) traditionally monogamous; (5) much less frequently, polygamous; and (6) some combination of three or more men and women living together, without marriage.[60] The colony's chief justice crudely characterized one example of the last arrangement in 1919. A dispute had arisen when a man gave a woman title to half his land west of the Demerara River, where they lived with a second man. Chabuye, the woman, had landed in the colony at fourteen. At that time, her shipboard alliance with the second man had been registered as a bona fide marriage. On that basis, he claimed title to half the land, too. He maintained that all three had pooled their wages to buy the property after their indentures were done, and he argued that the legal principle of community of property between husband and wife entitled him. But the colony's highest court concluded that he had not legally married Chabuye in India and rejected his claim. "The only relation between them," ruled the chief justice, "was that of fornication, a relation carried, in fact, into the only community of property I have been able to discover in the lives of [the trio], namely that of Chabuye by the other two for the purposes of sexual intercourse."[61] Such polyandry was a widespread strategy, adopted by indentured Indians across the globe to cope with the shortage of women. Three women once indentured in Fiji, asked how the excess of men had affected their lives, couldn't bring themselves to confront it. One wept, explaining: "What can we say? It was very bad."[62] Many, she said, kept two or more men.

The shortage of women had other effects that made the Victorian mind reel. A Scottish minister posted to Guiana identified "illicit intercourse between the sexes" as the colony's "most prevalent vice—and besetting sin."[63] But, he reported in 1866, even greater offences against morality were being committed by the indentured: "Uncleanliness in its most revolting forms is now exhibited amongst them, by the coolies and Chinese, under the names of bestiality and Sodomy."[64] The highest court heard at least one case involving "unnatural crime" amongst indentured men, in 1892.[65] Apparently, some immigrants did what men in cramped quarters, including British soldiers in India during the same era, have historically done without women.[66] They turned to each other for satisfaction.

But Indian indentured men, lacking enough women of their own kind, departed from similarly deprived British men in one significant way. Colonialists in India often took local mistresses or wives, called "bibis," until white women ventured there in force in the mid-nineteenth century to hunt for husbands.[67] Colonial officials expected that indentured Indians would become involved with local women, too. In 1839, Governor Henry Light reported to the Colonial Secretary that the Gladstone coolies were starting to do just that. Sounding like a dirty old man, he wrote: "The magnificent features of the men, their well-shaped, though slender limbs, promise well for the mixture of the negress with the Indian."[68] One Gladstone coolie did cite a wife of African descent to explain his intention to settle permanently in Guiana. Ultimately, however, he returned to India without her.[69] Despite the governor's rhapsody, few relationships developed between former slaves and the Indians who replaced them—or between their descendants. Three generations into indenture, the colony's sheriff observed: "[I]t is the rarest thing in the world for an Indian to take up with a black woman. There is a mutual antipathy between the races."[70]

Soon after Sujaria's arrival, a gruesome murder in cane fields near her own cast a spotlight on one exception to that rule. One August evening in 1905, a pregnant Indian was hacked to death on Plantation Melville, and her unborn child cut out of her and carted away.[71] Hours later, on the same estate, a black woman in her mid-forties apparently gave birth, bloodlessly, to a stillborn baby with fair skin and straight hair. She had refused the help of a midwife, just as she had refused to be examined while pregnant. Her name was Eliza Jones, and her child's father was said to be Joe Sukul, the Indian in charge of the estate's child workers. The pair had lived together, on and off, for seven years but had no children. Jones was charged with the murder, convicted and sentenced to be executed. According to prosecutors, she was afraid that Sukul would leave her if she didn't present him with a child and, so, had faked her own pregnancy and killed the Indian woman Kishuny in order to steal her baby.

Jones was pardoned and released when irregularities in the case came to light, including the suppression of testimony by another estate worker, who had overhead Kishuny and her husband fighting with another couple. Along with curses and blows, a threat had been lobbed: a threat, in Hindi, to "take out the child." Meanwhile,

Jones implicated a healer on the estate, the same man who had quarreled with Kishuny. Jones went to him, according to her sworn statement, because: "I was fourteen months with big belly but found no life inside me… So I said, 'I have been wanting to see you for a long time.' He replied, 'I know you are with child for a long time.' So I begged him very hard and told him that if he makes me bring forth the child, I will pay him." She promised him $10 for his help. The day of the murder, she said, he brought her a dead child in a bag.

The transcripts of the trial provide an example of an interracial relationship and evidence of contact between blacks and Indians that most contemporary observers and historians since have argued didn't much exist on the plantations. Jones lived with Sukul in the logies, crammed into the same shoddy barracks lacking privacy where the immigrants lived. It was through the holes in a logie wall that one witness spied her undressed, wrapping layers of cloth around her belly. The midwife she refused to see was summoned to attend to pregnant Indians on the plantation. She was a black woman who regularly delivered Indian babies. And Jones seemed to have assimilated Indian ways. Another black woman, who also lived in the logies, recalled asking her a question in Hindi: "I spoke in Coolie," the woman explained, "because she speaks mostly Coolie, and all her actions are Coolie." An Indian man passing the deserted rows of cane where Kishuny was later found dead saw Jones squatting there, with her friend, an Indian girl, posted nearby on lookout. Recounting rumors that "bush Negroes" had been seen wandering the fields, he warned the girl to be careful. Then Jones shouted, in Hindi: "Go away. I'm easing myself." (Since planters did not provide toilets, estate workers had to relieve themselves in the open.) The Indian man had invoked the immigrants' bogeyman: blacks living in the forests who occasionally raided the plantations. And he was answered, in Hindi, by a black woman who lived with them and claimed to be carrying a half-Indian child. Fear and intimacy walked side by side, in tension.

Although the case of Eliza Jones shows a more intertwined history than blacks and Indians in the Caribbean, through generations of political conflict, economic rivalry and racial violence, have wanted to admit, her story is probably an exception that proves the rule. In Trinidad in 1911, only 1,514 people—less than 0.5 percent of the population—were mixed Indian and black; two-thirds had Indian fathers and black mothers.[72] Contemporary observers blamed caste and race prejudices, concluding that Indian men viewed black women as Untouchables.[73] But equally prohibitive were the attitudes of blacks, who resented Indians as unfair competition in the labor market. As a missionary in nineteenth-century Guiana put it, "The Negro hates the coolie as a hard-working interloper and despises him as a heathen."[74] One historian has pointed out that black women did not need to look for mates outside their own community, where ultimately there were equal numbers of men and women;[75] and black women spurned Indian men as inferior for the alien languages they spoke, the strange gods they worshipped and the unfamiliar food they ate, usually with their hands.[76] Many women of African descent had internalized and aspired to British notions of civilization, and the coolie was not it.[77] But the strongest curb on interaction between the two groups was the ironclad control that planters exercised over the movements of the indentured. The pass system, enforced by constables, kept them largely confined to plantations where, Eliza Jones notwithstanding, few black women lived.[78] Residential segregation and mutual distrust kept blacks and Indians, for the most part, sexually separate.

Had Indian men in the Caribbean turned more often to black women for partners, the arc of history might have bent in a far different direction for Indian women. As it was, it seemed to bend towards the exercise of a sexuality so willful, betrayal was anticipated by contract. At Enmore in 1870, for example, two laborers signed an agreement to live together as man and wife that included the proviso: "The woman Nelliama agrees in case she leaves the man Ermeinin to pay the sum of forty dollars …, which she agrees to pay in case she leaves him for another man."[79] The fear of cuckolding was so pervasive that hedges against it regularly featured in betrothal contracts. So profound was the fear that an indentured man jailed for a month reportedly instructed that his wife be sent, for safe keeping, to the sheriff who sentenced him. The sheriff described the spangled beauty who appeared on his verandah as coy. She gave him "a raking look out of her large eyes, and then turned them modestly to the floor," he said; and she pouted when rebuffed. The episode, aside from stroking the sheriff's self-image, led him to conclude: "Young handsome women, whose husbands are sent to gaol, run great risks on sugar estates, where there are scores of young men unprovided with wives; so I presume that Ramdass preferred that the sheriff alone should look after his wife."[80]

Colonial observers, gazing on Indian women, saw an unsettling liberation. One Guiana governor declared that women there possessed "a value and an influence they would not otherwise have."[81] Writing for a planter's journal in 1913, the archdeacon of Georgetown's Anglican cathedral declared: "[A]s women are so scarce in this colony, they feel their power. They are also sure they can exchange one lord and master for another with the greatest ease."[82] A similar confidence in Trinidad distressed the wife of a Canadian Presbyterian missionary. Sarah Morton trained Indian girls to become proper wives for teachers hired by the island's mission schools. But as she touted the housewifely ideal—fidelity in the curriculum as much as ironing, sewing, the Bible and basic math—she witnessed the constant capsizing of that ideal. In an account of her years in Trinidad, Morton wrote:

The loose actions and prevailing practices in respect of marriage here are quite shocking to the newcomer. I said to an East Indian woman I knew to be the widow of a Brahmin, 'You have no relations in Trinidad, I believe?' 'No, Madame,' she replied, 'only myself and two children; when the last immigrant ship came I took a 'papa'. I will keep him as long as he treats me well. If he does not treat me well, I shall send him off at once; that's the right way, is it not?' This will be to some a new view of women's rights.[83]

On another occasion, in the early 1890s, Morton met a group of women returning from the fields. One, a recent Christian convert, had just left one man for another. The women singled her out for Morton's attention: "Your disciple is going to church now," they said. The missionary's wife answered, "That will do her no good unless she changes her living." One of the women then shot back, capturing pitch-perfectly the paradox that many Indian women found themselves living out: "What can she do? This husband takes better care of her than the other did."[84] It was true that the scarcity of women had empowered the convert to leave her husband—but the implication was that she *had* to leave him. What, her defender asked, *could* she do? Where Morton saw a woman emancipated enough to sin, might there instead have been a woman pressured into pragmatism? And what precisely were the pressures: what made her husband an inadequate caretaker, and just what was it that made her require any husband at all?

To justify indenture, planters and government officials made much of the fact that women earned their own money in the fields. When the system came under attack in Guiana, from blacks arguing that falling global demand for cane made it unnecessary to import more Indian laborers, *The Chronicle* pointed to the enhanced position of "the East Indian woman in Guiana" as one reason why immigration should continue. "The fact that she receives her wages in her own hands at the pay table gives her a feeling of independence, and renders her husband less domineering than he would be in India,"[85] the editorial writer maintained. The rhetoric of empire cast the white man as the brown woman's savior, but in fact white men paid brown women one-half to two-thirds what they paid brown men in every colony that received indentured laborers.[86] Coolie women were assigned tasks requiring less strength, such as weeding and fertilizing. But even when they did what men did—cutting cane, loading it or digging irrigation trenches—they were paid less, on the assumption that their wages merely supplemented the incomes of male breadwinners.[87] A partner was required in order to survive on the female wage rate.[88]

Still, it was better than nothing. In Mauritius, the only sugar colony that explicitly imported women as wives not workers,[89] women were more vulnerable to exploitation because they lacked contracts guaranteeing them plantation work, even if for discriminatory pay.[90] And emigrating women showed a definite interest in paid work. Because they knew they wouldn't be indentured in Mauritius, they preferred other destinations—so said a British emigration agent who had trouble recruiting them for the colony.[91] A tiny fraction of Indian women in Mauritius had independent incomes as *ayahs* or domestic servants, but the overwhelming majority did unwaged work at home. They cooked, they cleaned, they washed. They raised children. And they tended cows and gardens, to sell the milk and produce. They also provided casual labor for the plantations; but in this erratic incarnation, they were "easily dismissed and poorly paid."[92]

So, wages earned under indenture *did* matter. They should not be underestimated as a regular, reliable source of income. Nor should they be overestimated as a source of independence. Indeed, it begs asking if the widespread infidelity ascribed to Indian women indicated their power, because they were scarce—or if it actually indicated their lack of power, because they earned less. Did they change partners frequently because they could—or because they had to? The evidence suggests a subtle alchemy between the two. It suggests that Indian women continued to be economically dependent on men after leaving India, but had their pick of which men to depend on. Even if overseers initially arranged matches, the women didn't have to stay. Many could and did leave partners, sometimes more than once. Wasn't this what made the world they had landed in so exhilaratingly new? Colonialists emphasized that women could do what had been unthinkable in the motherland. The Georgetown archdeacon remarked that in India, women were known for meekness and chastity: "Such a thing as a woman leaving her husband is unknown," he wrote. "Here in Demerara quite the reverse prevails."[93]

Coolie women could leave their husbands, and they could partner across caste. Relationships taboo in India became necessary and practical in indenture, because women were few. They could marry up in caste, but at least some had to marry down. After all, many—perhaps most—of the immigrants who declared themselves high-caste were women. In 1898, for example, more than two-thirds of upper-caste migrants who landed in Guiana were women.[94] Among the middle and lower castes that year, men far outnumbered women. The opposite was true for the upper-castes because the sugar colonies attracted many Brahmin widows, who had greater incentive to migrate than their lower-caste counterparts. The stigma against remarriage was more profound for upper-caste widows in India.[95] The shortage of indentured women, more than enabling them to ascend in caste, whittled the importance of caste. It still carried ceremonial meaning as well as some status. But women gravitated to men who could help them endure and even escape the rigors of the plantation, regardless of caste.

New hierarchies emerged across the dark waters. In the plantation's ranks, the *sirdars* or drivers in charge of work gangs—who came from all castes, including Untouchables—had privileges that made them attractive to immigrant women. Men who had been in the colony the longest were also favored, according to government officials, because they were more secure financially.[96] In some cases, they were even able to pay off a woman's indenture and set her free. A register of births in Demerara, covering three months in 1878, lends credence to this official claim. Of thirty-two immigrant women who gave birth during that time, only five had arrived in the colony before their partners.[97] Among the rest, more partnered with men who had come before them—often, well before them—than with men who came at the same time. Coolie women weren't exactly like Jane Austen heroines, practicing love as a form of social mobility; but they seem to have used their scarcity to survive as best they could in an exploitative environment.

Crossing the seas overturned another tradition fundamental to marriage in the villages of northeastern India. Dowries gave way to bride price as girls, once considered an economic burden, gained economic value in the sugar colonies. The old-country practice of offering the groom and his family gifts and money to accept a bride collapsed, and instead the groom had to pay out.[98] If the bride received the gifts, as sometimes she did, she clearly benefited financially. But if her parents did, of what use to her was her increased value? Was she simply a commodity to be sold off, for $50 and a cow?[99] Despite this and other complicating questions, colonial observers continued to trumpet the emancipated state of Indian women in the West Indies. The archdeacon went so far as to say: "We have known some Indian women to keep their husbands in proper subjection as their sisters do, or try to, in the West. Just imagine a woman daring to 'summons' her lord and master in India! Here on the other hand, it is frequently done."[100]

Fathers and father figures

One gutsy young woman, nicknamed Baby, dared to "summons" more than one master.[101] She asserted her rights in legal claims against overlords political as well as personal.

In 1896, she took the man she had recently left to court for assault. The charge stemmed from a scuffle one summer morning when the ex, Talloo, barged into a Georgetown lodging house where she was living with another man.

Born in Guiana, on a plantation neighboring Enmore, Baby had been married typically young by her parents. At twelve, she became a wife, not legally, but by Hindu rites. Just six months later, Talloo stole her. Raised like Baby, in plantation barracks by indentured parents, he had pulled off a feat of mobility: he had escaped the sugar estate. Talloo tended to the horses of the district police inspector, and when Inspector Claude Francis became the colony's police chief, the groom accompanied him to Georgetown. By then, Baby was in her late teens, a decade younger than Talloo. The couple lived under the officers' quarters at the central police station. That's where fate engineered an arguably just reversal in Talloo's fortunes. Once the seducer, he became the cuckold, as Baby at last succumbed to Lieutenant George Hamilton Alexander, a British sub-inspector who had already tried and failed once to steal her away to his god-forsaken, malaria-infested post along the Venezuelan border.

At first, Baby had denied that anything was happening with the lieutenant. Then she warned Talloo not to abuse her. She could leave, she said—the lieutenant wanted her. That, at least, was Talloo's version of how things began to fall apart. Afterwards, even with Alexander back at his remote post, Talloo decided that Baby wasn't safe at police headquarters. He sequestered her in a hut on the capital's outskirts. "She promised to behave good," Talloo later stated. Every evening, Baby brought him dinner; and every night, she slept with him at Central Station. According to Talloo, all was well until Alexander returned to the capital. On 29 July 1896, two days before assuming his duties at a new post in Berbice, along the border with Suriname, Alexander apparently sent Baby ahead by steamer, with his servant and his luggage. As soon as Talloo found out, he went straight to his boss, Inspector Francis, who ordered everyone's immediate return and revoked Alexander's promotion. The misadventure had ended with Baby right back in Georgetown—and right back in Alexander's room at the Eve Leary Barracks, according to officers and servants who saw her there.

But when Talloo tracked Baby down, she was at the boarding house where she lived with another Indian man. It was 8 August, months after she claimed to have left

Talloo, but just a week after she attempted to elope with Alexander. That escapade had aggravated Talloo's wounds. He shoved his way into Baby's room, and she pushed him back out: "What do you want here?" she demanded. "You don't live here."

"I came for what belongs to me," Talloo said. He wanted her jewellery. He claimed that he had given her the bangles and foot rings that she was wearing, and he demanded their return. Talloo disavowed any lingering feelings for Baby, but wouldn't concede the silver ornaments as the sunk cost of his affections. Recovering them might be petty consolation for the loss of a woman, but it was some recompense. As long as he got the jewellery back, Talloo professed not to care what Baby did or with whom she did it. But Baby insisted that the trinkets were presents from her mother. Later, provocatively, she testified that Inspector Francis had given her the only bauble that didn't belong to her mother, a pair of silver earrings, as well as some gold coins. She refused to surrender the jewellery to Talloo.

A policeman waiting outside then stepped in. He was Talloo's enforcer. The constable had been walking his beat that morning, when Talloo approached with orders that he claimed came from Inspector Francis. According to Talloo, the police chief had instructed him to fetch a constable if he saw Baby—and to seize the jewellery and deliver it to the inspector. Baby was perplexed by the constable's sudden appearance. Was he charging her with a crime? She had the self-possession and the savvy to ask if he had a warrant. The constable did not, but he said he was there on Inspector Francis's authority. Talloo grabbed Baby by one foot, and the constable took the other, nearly exposing her. They removed her toe and ankle rings, and then they took her bracelets. During the roughhousing, Baby's foot was hurt, and her skirt torn. Her new man, Dabydeal, tried to help, but the constable grabbed him by the collar and threatened arrest.

Ultimately, they all went to the nearest police station to resolve the dispute. But the trouble was not over for Baby—or for her gentleman lover. While on patrol, he happened to stop by the same police station where Talloo and Baby were contending for the jewellery. Alexander took instant charge. He sent the pair under police escort to the Immigration Department, which usually handled disputes between Indian husbands and wives, indentured or not. He also forwarded the jewellery, by private buggy, in his own servant's care, along with a message for the colony's immigration agent general. Arthur Harvey Alexander, a Scotsman who had started his career as a policeman in Jamaica, served for more than two decades as head of Guiana's Immigration Department. A figure of influence in the colony, he was a retired colonel in its militia and a member of its ruling Executive Council. From 1883 until his death in 1905, he was the official protector of the indentured and their descendants, the man whose job it was to act *in loco parentis* to them. According to the rhetoric of empire, he was like a father to the colony's 130,000 Indian residents. More to the point for Baby, he was also Lieutenant Alexander's father. A.H. Alexander had pulled strings to get the job in the British Guiana constabulary for his son, a soldier in the Royal East Surrey Regiment. The younger Alexander was twenty-one and at the start of his military career. This was his first overseas assignment.

Halfway to the immigration department, Talloo broke away from Baby and the constable escorting them. Perhaps he didn't trust that Immigration Agent General A.H. Alexander would view his role as father figure, arbitrating between two Indians over anklets, as more important than his role as biological father. Talloo did not want to see the old man. He headed, instead, to work. On the way, he ran into Lieutenant Alexander, who threatened to blow Talloo's brains out if he bothered Baby again. Meanwhile, at police headquarters, Talloo's boss was looking for him. Inspector Francis asked if anyone had seen his groom. Lieutenant Alexander, back at headquarters by then, said nothing. This silence did not serve him well. He had failed to note his encounter that morning with Baby and Talloo in the police station's incident book. To Inspector Francis, it looked like the lieutenant was trying to hide his interference in the case.

Just as Talloo feared that the immigration chief might not be an impartial judge, Lieutenant Alexander doubted Inspector Francis. That's what the lieutenant indicated to the Colonial Office when he had to plead for clemency. Inspector Francis *was* Talloo's employer, after all. The inspector was the one who had told the groom to seize the jewellery in the first place. Lieutenant Alexander may also have been smarting from the collapse of his Berbice plans and the humiliating way that Inspector Francis had handled Talloo's charges. On 29 July the groom had sent a letter to his boss. It had read:

Sir,

I beg most respectfully to state that my wife Baby has gone off to Berbice by this morning steamer with Mr Alexander servant Charlie and has taken away all my jewels and $12 in cash money, and Sir I made to understand that it is Mr Alexander who has enticed her away, as it was never my intention to take her back from the last time how she behaved, but as her mother come and beg me, and she promised to behave herself, that's why I take her back. I kindly beg you Sir that on her arrival to Berbice you can send a telegram and let the police stop her and take away my jewels and money from her as I don't mind what she do. Talloo your truly servant humbly beg to grant me this favour as Baby put me in so much distress for if I know she was going to do so I would never buy a house and put she in, for I lost too much money. Do Sir, I beg you kindly send and let the police take away my jewel and money and so she can do what she like then. [Sic]

The police chief had confronted the lieutenant in front of Talloo. The lieutenant had denied knowing anything about Baby's whereabouts. The inspector had asked for that in writing, and Lieutenant Alexander had complied: "I beg to state," he had written, "that the woman is not going to live under my protection or in my employ. I have no improper intention towards her."

By the following afternoon, a sergeant at Lieutenant Alexander's suddenly imperiled new post, near Suriname, had received a telegram from him: "send servant Charles back New Amsterdam tomorrow Mail with luggage &c …." Minutes later, Charles had showed up with Baby at the police station. He had received the same message. When Charles wired to Lieutenant Alexander for money for return fares, it was the elder Alexander who had replied. He had instructed the servant to ask Berbice's sheriff for a loan, on his guarantee, and to return to Georgetown. There had been no mention of Baby, the "&c" in Lieutenant Alexander's telegram. No doubt intrigued, the sergeant in Berbice had asked Charles who the coolie woman was. The servant had hesitated, then whispered that Lieutenant Alexander had enticed her away from Inspector Francis' groom. The inspector would not learn of these revelations at the Berbice police station until much later. For her part, Baby had refused to return by steamer to Georgetown. Her husband would be at the landing waiting to deliver a beating, she had said; she planned instead to travel by train to her mother's plantation.

On the day of the scuffle, once Lieutenant Alexander finally got around to reporting that he dispatched the immigrants and the jewellery to his father's office, Inspector Francis was furious: "I have a good mind to put you under arrest," he threatened. He said that he no longer took Lieutenant Alexander's word about Baby and the whole Berbice affair.

"Then, sir," Lieutenant Alexander replied, "you call me a liar."

Inspector Francis was doing just that, and in fact, Lieutenant Alexander had lied. When later he begged the Colonial Office to be allowed to resign, in lieu of dismissal, he wrote: "I acknowledge with deep regret and shame that I have had immoral intercourse with the woman mentioned." He excused his dishonesty by saying that he didn't want to expose Baby to any retaliatory violence by her husband. "My only aim was to shield a woman whose reputed husband had charged her with misconduct," he insisted. "Could I have disgraced the woman?"

He wanted someone other than Inspector Francis to judge his sins. The case was laid before the governor, who privately urged A.H. Alexander to convince his son to resign. The governor promised to use his influence to get the boy another posting, outside Guiana, if he quietly gave up his position. But the immigration chief decided that it was in his son's best interests to have the Executive Council—of which he was a member—hear the entire case publicly, even at risk of suspension. The council met, with A.H. Alexander recusing himself, a month after the scuffle in the boarding house. Baby appeared, wearing borrowed jewellery, since her own had been confiscated. There was nothing between them, she said, her denials more sweeping than Lieutenant Alexander's. He no longer repudiated their relationship, but argued that Charles had taken her to Berbice on his own enterprise, anticipating his master's desires, without explicit orders. Baby backed this up: "I went to Berbice. You did not ask me to go," she told Alexander before the Executive Council. "After I came from Berbice, you had nothing to do with me in the way of living with me." Then she added: "I never came to your room after I came from Berbice. I don't know your room." When a council member pointed out that Lieutenant Alexander had admitted their intimacy, she replied: "If Mr Alexander says he had anything to do with me, he lied." Was she shielding him the way he said he had tried to shield her? Whatever her intent, she hurt rather than helped his case.

The hearing was a disaster. The lieutenant implied that other officers also kept coolie women, and this alienated his judges. Five days later, in a postcard to a Colonial Office undersecretary, A.H. Alexander reported: "I am very sorry to have to tell you that my son in the police here has got into trouble and has been suspended by the governor." The bet on the Executive Council had been a losing one, and he asked that the colonial secretary offer his son the original option of resignation. Soon after, on 17 September, Lieutenant Alexander sailed home on medical leave.

The Colonial Office granted his father's request, allowing him to resign. The scribbles in the margins of his case file shed light on the Colonial Office's view of the whole affair. One reads: "On the whole, considering the general level of morality in our ill-paid colonial service, I think that dismissal would be too severe a penalty." Another telegraphs empathy: "Feeling what I fear is the case, that Mr Francis was not impartial in the matter, he declined to answer further until the matter had been referred to the governor. He was wrong, but not inexcusably wrong." Within six months, Lieutenant Alexander was posted to West Africa, where he died on active duty. His father petitioned the British government, in 1898, to erect a cross on his grave in Lagos. It declined.

Baby was left to fight her own battles, which she did aggressively. Two days after testifying for Lieutenant Alexander, she took the stand against Talloo and the constable who helped him seize the jewellery. The magistrate found both guilty of assault and sentenced them to serve five and twenty-one days in jail, respectively, or to pay fines of $2.40 and $10, respectively. On the stand, Baby also offered an explanation for the police's bizarre intrusion into a petty domestic squabble: she had been sleeping with Inspector Francis for years, with Talloo's knowledge, she said.

Here was the dangerously emancipated coolie woman of colonial travelogues and official correspondence. Five men figured in her story as lovers or alleged lovers. She also apparently had assets: two houses a mile from police headquarters. Baby contradicted Talloo's story that he bought the hut in the country to keep her chaste. She bought that house for $16, she said. She insisted that the second house was hers as well—her property and her deal. "I made the bargain," she said. Baby had an income from selling milk. She and her sister had delivered it to the garrison for months, earning profits enough to deposit savings in the bank—and reimburse Lieutenant Alexander's servant for her fare to and from Berbice. Indeed, Baby swore that the fights that made her leave Talloo erupted over her money as a milk seller, not over Lieutenant Alexander or any other rival. Her version of events provides a striking portrait of female financial wherewithal, and not just her own. She bought the country hut from another coolie woman. And Dabydeal—a casual laborer in the interior, where the work, usually in gold-digging, was irregular and risky—wasn't a breadwinner. "His mother supports him," Baby said. "She has plenty money."

Her sexual activity and financial prowess notwithstanding, Baby's greatest expression of independence may have been the several ways in which she pressed for justice. Three weeks after winning the assault case against Talloo, she was back in magistrate's court testifying in another suit—this time a complaint by Dabydeal, alleging trespass. It arose from a visit paid to the lodging house on the day of the scuffle, after the brouhaha had died down. A plainclothes policeman went to Dabydeal's room to question Baby. He wanted to know: Who paid the rent? Who bought the furniture? Why did she leave Talloo? Three times, Baby asked the policeman to go, and eventually he did—a fact that led the magistrate to throw out the trespass suit.

For six weeks after the scuffle, the police watched Baby and restricted her movements. That is what led to her most audacious legal petition: a claim for compensation for the violation of her rights, addressed to the British Secretary of State for the Colonies. In the petition, Baby alleged that the police had persecuted her on the orders of their chief, Inspector Francis, "because she has left his employ, and no longer wishes to continue the immoral relations she has had with him for years past." She was repeating an explosive accusation already made in court a month earlier. But then it had been ignored, struck from the formal notes of evidence. With such an attack on his character in a document bound for London, the inspector was compelled to respond. He sent his own missive to London. The inspector, a married man with a wife and son living with him in Georgetown, flatly denied the charge. He blamed "a vile conspiracy ... in revenge on me for having performed fearlessly a very trying and painful duty in connection with the recent trial of sub-Inspector Alexander whose paramour the petitioner was." He had never employed Baby, he said, never had sex with her, never punished her for leaving.

But Inspector Francis didn't deny that his detectives were tailing her. He claimed it was for her own protection, in case Talloo tried to harm her. Baby insisted that she didn't ask for or need protection. She appealed to A.H. Alexander, who involved the governor, who soon said that "the police supervision which it was considered necessary to exercise in the interests of the woman has ceased." Her circumstances had changed in only one significant way: the immigration chief's son had just sailed for England. Talloo, the excuse for the surveillance, was still in the colony.

Although the police ultimately backed off, Baby still pushed for reparations. To elevated government officials, she declared: "Your petitioner has been guilty of no offence against the laws of the colony, yet she has been subjected ... to the same police supervision as is meted out to confirmed criminals." She didn't just put forward a personal grievance, but criticized an entire system. Baby, whose formal name was Sumarea, boldly marked her X on a document that leveled a politically savvy charge. It read:

Your petitioner as well as other East Indian immigrants have latterly been subjected to great annoyances and indignities by the police, and such treatment can only have a deterrent tendency to the East Indians remaining in the colony and making their homes in it, as is the wish and offer of the government.

Her extraordinary petition—alleging a pattern of police harassment and racial profiling to which many jobbers could testify—was all the braver because she wasn't literate enough to sign her name. She had the courage to demand accountability not only from her commandeering ex, but also from the very state of British Guiana.

Of these two adversaries in the lives of coolie women, their men and the government, the colonial state may have been the more controlling figure. The Guiana police was not the only British authority that curtailed their freedom. Just across the Corentyne River, in the Dutch colony of Suriname, the British consulate and the immigration agency interfered with one woman's attempt to leave her partner and her plantation. They arrested her when she travelled from the sugar estate to the capital, although she had an official pass for a week's leave, and sent her back to her plantation, with orders that she never be allowed to leave again. The woman, Sukhdai, had apparently raised some money to buy back her liberty. That was her purpose in the capital.

She was already known to the authorities, owing to what had unfolded when her ship landed three months earlier, in December 1893. The man registered as her husband, Luchmun, had tried to hang himself and was put on suicide watch at the immigration depot. During the crossing, he had tried to cut her throat. Luchmun accused her of flirting with the compounder aboard, an Anglo-Indian named Solomon. "It was reported," the colony's immigration chief told the Foreign Office, "that Solomon's attitude towards Sukhdai and hers toward him in the depot caused Luchmun to try to put an end to his life."[102] At the depot, Sukhdai refused to be sent to the same plantation as Luchmun. The British consul and immigration chief both ordered her to accompany him. It was her duty as his wife, they said. But Sukhdai wouldn't yield. The authorities reluctantly separated them, but insisted that this be temporary. If they thought that Sukhdai was a woman afraid for her life, clearly they didn't think that her fear would or should last. And yet the consul ultimately justified her arrest as necessary for her own protection, "to prevent Luchmun from murdering her." No doubt, he ventured, she had gone to the capital to join Solomon.

The consul offered that explanation for her arrest after Solomon petitioned the Foreign Office on her behalf. The compounder had stayed in the colony as an overseer—coincidentally, on the plantation where Luchmun worked. In his missive for Sukhdai, Solomon asked that she be freed from her contract. She had raised the money to pay off her indenture from relatives and friends, he said; and her master, finding her unfit for the field, was willing to release her. Solomon pointed to the case of another indentured woman who had bought off her indenture. The consul, however, strongly objected. The woman freed from her contract was unmarried, he said: "It speaks for itself that, Sukhdai being married, there could be no question at all of cancelling, at her request, her contract independently from the contract of her husband." Doing so would sanction the illicit relationship between Solomon and Sukhdai, the consul declared.

Solomon denied that any illicit relationship existed. He claimed that he met Sukhdai in his official capacity as compounder. While he was treating the wounds that Luchmun had inflicted, he said, Sukhdai divulged that Luchmun had lured her to emigrate under false pretenses. They weren't married. Nor did she want to be with him. He attacked her because she was resisting his advances. That was Sukhdai's side of the story, according to Solomon. "Luchmun's allegation of any intimacy," he charged, "was made only to cloak his guilt and lighten his punishment." The consul had accused Solomon of having an affair with Sukhdai. The immigration agency had blacklisted him from coolie vessels, costing him a job on a ship to India. Solomon did his best to defend himself against the rumors. "That I stayed in the colony for the sake of the woman Sukhdai is not true," he insisted. He was not her lover, he said, but her disinterested advocate. And indeed, he continued to plead her case as a lawyer might, citing precedent, offering specific examples of other indentured women who had been allowed to leave fraudulent husbands.

A year later, Luchmun was revealed to be just that, and Sukhdai was finally given permission to cancel her indenture. Witnesses in India had sworn to a deputy magistrate that Sukhdai was Luchmun's sister in-law and that they had eloped together. When the consul called Sukhdai to his office to inform her that she could at last end her indenture, she replied:

that she had no wish to be freed from her indenture, as she had contracted an attachment for a British Indian immigrant, named Bahalu Sing, indentured on the same estate, and she prayed for nothing but that she might be allowed to remain with him.

Bahalu Sing's indenture terminates one year before that of Sukdai, and he intends—if the attachment at present existing between them extends beyond the period of his indenture—to purchase her release from her engagement from the moment when he attains his own freedom.

Colonial officials had held out hope, even in the face of attempted murder and attempted suicide, that husband and wife would be reconciled. Only when her marriage was proved conclusively to be a lie did they relent. With their permission, she could have her liberty. For reasons of love or pragmatism, she no longer wanted it.

But she had once wanted to be free. Sukhdai had tried to assert her independence, but the colonial state had handcuffed her and put her back in her place, just as they did with the woman wrestled by a constable for her toe rings. Baby had wanted justice, but the Colonial Office rebuffed her claims for compensation. The Brahmin widow who shocked Morton with her "new view of women's rights" had wanted to be treated well. Whether her "papa" fulfilled this longing or not is unknowable. They had all wanted to shape their own lives in ways that preserved their dignity, but their strivings played out against the backdrop of plantation societies. In this coercive setting, however much coolie women were in demand, they faced obstacles in getting what they wanted. Their own men got in their way, but so did the white men in charge, who made decisions and enforced laws that curbed their freedom as laborers and as women.

In a travelogue about Guiana, the missionary H.V.P. Bronkhurst offered a parable. It was meant to capture the absurdity of marriage in the colony, but it also illustrates the forces that constrained Indian women during the indenture era. While riding along the Demerara River one day, Bronkhurst met an Indian woman on the road. She was on her way from her plantation to the capital, and she was crying. Bronkhurst, who was half-Indian and could speak several Indian languages, asked her what was wrong. What she told him moved him to pity. The young woman had refused a drink to her father, who had recently been robbed while in an alcoholic daze. Infuriated by her attempt to curtail him, he had her married off for $10. But she had refused to go to the man who paid the bride price. Her father then beat her without mercy, and she fled. When Bronkhurst asked where she intended to go, she replied: "Sir, I am going to town, to see if I can find a man of my own caste, who would make me his wife, and support me, and deliver me from my cruel and drunken father."[103] Bronkhurst stopped her from going any further. He explained the laws controlling the movements of Indian immigrants: since she didn't have a pass to be on the road, she was risking arrest. The young woman had rejected the rule of her father. She had literally rejected patriarchy—only to be confronted with the higher paternalism of the state, which had long argued that it kept immigrants confined to their plantations as any father figure would, for their own protection. She returned to the plantation that day but, in the long run, married a man of her own choice.

7

BEAUTIFUL WOMAN WITHOUT A NOSE

Said the king of Lanka:
"Tell me what has happened to you.
Who has struck off your nose and ears?"

Tulsi Das, "The Ramcharitmanas"*

When she arrived at the hospital, in a mule cart, her left foot hung by a strip of flesh, just above the ankle. The doctor amputated the leg—and her left arm. They were beyond saving. Though still alive, Laungee looked beyond saving, too. More than thirty-five wounds covered her body. Later, at the coroner's inquest, the doctor provided a precise inventory of them. One cut, 2.5 inches long, pierced her skull. Another, 1.5 inches long, bit into the bone on the left side of her face. The gash above her left elbow was so deep, there was no choice but to amputate. On that one arm alone, Laungee had been cut in eighteen places.[1] Her wounds were the work of a cutlass, the long, curved blade used to cut cane. It had been deployed against her with force enough to sever metal; the bangle on her wrist was chopped in two. Bruises covered Laungee's entire body. While being hacked to death, she had been beaten.

Her attacker was a man with whom she had lived for a year. Badal, like Laungee, was indentured to Vriesland, a Demerara River plantation. The newspapers sometimes called him her "paramour," sometimes her "reputed husband"[2]—language reflecting the ruling elite's low opinion of Indian unions, which were seen as fitful and rarely recognized as official marriages.[3] Muslims and Hindus had to undergo a costly, cumbersome process to legitimize their marriages in the eyes of the state.[4] Most didn't bother.[5] For many, it was enough to be legitimate in the eyes of their

---

* Epigraph from Tulsi Das, *Sri Ramacaritmanasa: The Manasa Lake Brimming Over With the Exploits of Sri Rama* (Gorakhpur, India: Gita Press, 2004), p. 680.

103

God, or gods. It's unknown whether either law or religion had sanctioned Laungee and Badal's alliance. They didn't leave India together.[6] Since both arrived in Guiana in their twenties, the odds are great that they had already been married—to other people—in India. Their relationship, whatever its status, was volatile. For six weeks, Laungee had lived with another man. She had deserted Badal. And when she returned, he treated her as if polluted.

The morning of the crime, a neighbor saw the couple outside their room in the coolie barracks, on the verandah. Badal was refusing to eat the food that Laungee had cooked.

"Why don't you eat," Ogeerun, the neighbor, asked him.

"I cannot eat with a woman whose hands are not clean," Badal said.[7]

Then Laungee cursed him. She called him a *dougla*. The word means mixed breed. In North India, it described the children of intercaste marriages—flesh-and-blood evidence of pollution, to orthodox minds. In the Caribbean, the word had evolved into a slur for people of mixed African and Indian blood, with the added suggestion of illegitimacy. *The Daily Chronicle* translated it as "mongrel."[8] Laungee had hit him with the worst insult imaginable.

Their fight escalated, and they took it into their room. Still, it wasn't private. From her room four doors down, Ogeerun heard Laungee cry: "Why you throw me down?"[9] Then came the sound of blows and Laungee's screams. Ogeerun ran to their door, but found it barred. Through a chink, she saw Laungee bleeding on the floor, and Badal standing over her with a cutlass. Then the door flew open, and Laungee ran out, with Badal in pursuit. She collapsed at Ogeerun's door, where witnesses saw Badal cut off her toes. Four hours later, she was dead. At the police station, a constable asked him why he had killed her. He answered, in Hindi: "She was a bad woman."[10]

During his trial for murder, Badal said little. The plantation manager described him as a "quiet man who had never given trouble before."[11] Reporters depicted him as a brooding savage, while his attorney portrayed him as a victim. "It is easy to understand," the lawyer said, "that with a man of his nation, uneducated but wrapped up in tradition, that his passion blinded him, and he was not responsible for his action."[12] The attorney argued that Badal should not be blamed: his reputed wife had been unfaithful and his country's traditions dictated that he should punish her. In his closing remarks, the attorney told the jury that:

It had always been the law in the East that an unfaithful woman should receive a very severe punishment, and in fact it had become so much a part of the life of the people that to punish an unfaithful woman was an instinct. East Indians were an intensely jealous people, whose anger was easily roused, and when their wives were unfaithful, fury overcame them, and these spontaneous acts of violence were the result.[13]

His strategy was bold. It deflected the responsibility for Badal's crime to the woman who left him and the culture which, the attorney said, called for her dismemberment.

But the strategy failed. On 31 October 1903, a few days before my great-grandmother landed in Georgetown, the city jail raised a black flag, its signal that an execution had taken place. That Saturday morning, Badal was hanged for murdering his wife. During that year in British Guiana, three other women were killed in the same way, hacked to pieces by partners punishing them for perceived infidelity.[14] On the scaffold, Badal moaned: "Oh, Lord. Oh, Lord. Lord, this is my last day."[15] That is how *The Chronicle* translated his last words, spoken in Hindi. What he probably said was: "*Hai, Ram. Hai, Ram.*" For generations, that has been the traditional cry for divine help among Hindus in the West Indies. It's a lament and an invocation, and it's also a concrete bid for salvation. Even sinners who, on dying, utter the name of the god Ram are supposed to be liberated, their souls freed from Hinduism's cycles of death and rebirth.

* * *

I imagine evening on Plantation Enmore: The drunken, sticky scent of scorched cane spikes the air. The fields have been set on fire, and ash from the singed leaves settles on everything. The flames are consuming the danger of the cane leaves, which wound like razors, their tapered edges elegant but sharp. The flames are chasing the rats and snakes slithering through the purple-green stalks of flowering cane. The fires are easing the way for coolies to weave in and out with their cutlasses. Once the sun rises, the men will deliver blow after blow, leaving behind only stumps of amputated cane. But now they sit cross-legged on the floor outside their barracks. The women share their anticipation. Crickets call out in the coming dark. Crappo* answer. The immigrants add their voices to the encircling racket.

They sing, with rough soul. They sing the story of *The Ramcharitmanas*—"The Holy Lake of the Exploits of Ram." It is a version of *The Ramayan*, the ancient Hindu epic about the god Vishnu, who has taken human form as Ram, the eldest son and heir of a king. Through the wiles of his stepmother, who wants the throne for her own son, Ram is banished to the wilderness for fourteen years. With him go his wife Sita and brother Lakshman. Although believers consider *The Ramayan* a sacred text, divinely inspired by the god of creation, it has been retold through the centuries by hundreds of poets, their idioms and interpretations varying. There is a Marxist retelling, even a feminist one** written in the sixteenth century by a Bengali woman.[16] But the version most alive to the indentured is *The Ramcharitmanas*, composed by the sixteenth-century saint-poet Tulsidas, in the Hindi dialect spoken in Ayodhya— where the story of Ram's exile starts, where Sujaria's had started, indeed where so many stories of indentured exile had begun.

As night settles like cane dust around the logies, a group of men chant lines from the epic: "Lust, anger, greed and pride make up the most powerful army of igno-

* Folk word for frog or toad, in Caribbean English.
** The feminist retelling is by the sixteenth-century poet Chandrabati, who "told only the story of Sita and critiqued Ram from a woman's point of view."

rance. But the fiercest and most troublesome among them is that incarnation of Maya called woman."[17] (Maya is illusion.) A second group answers: "All the different virtues are like a bed of lotuses. Like the middle of winter, woman blights them all." With escalating speed, a man slaps both ends of the *dholak* in his lap.[18] The drum sets the tempo for the call-and-response,[19] as it rises to a crescendo of misogyny: "For owls in the shape of sins, woman is a delightful night thick with darkness." I imagine my great-grandmother, squatting on the verandah, puffing on her clay pipe, listening. She knows these verses, has chanted them a million times. She joins the chorus.

There is a quality of raw abandon in their voices—and not only because *The Ramcharitmanas* belongs to the *bhakti* tradition, where what matters most for salvation is intensity of feeling.[20] There is more to their rhapsody than the longing of man for god. For the indentured, British Guiana presents its own owlish night thick with darkness. The coolie men identify with Ram as he wanders demon-infested forests, far from home, barely clothed, his locks matted, subsisting on roots and fruits. In his deprivation, in his fixed term of exile, they see their own; and to survive it, they invoke him. In the moment, perhaps they even imagine that his plot is theirs.*

Still, they know—they must—that he is an incarnated god, and they are merely men. His story does not so much reflect their lived reality as the ideal they should strive toward. Ram models what a man should be: the embodiment of right conduct, what Hindus call *dharma*. And Sita models what a married woman should be, according to Hindu orthodoxy: faithful, obedient, chaste. The tale that the indentured tell by torchlight is the tale of that ideal wife tempted. They sing of Sita's abduction and the attempt on her honor by the demon Ravan, who rules a netherworld empire from his base, on an island. They sing of the suspicion that unsettles her husband and the purity test to which he subjects her after her rescue.

For these displaced Hindus, the *Ramayan* is lifeblood. That it courses with anxiety about adultery only makes it more relevant. The epic, like the diaspora that identifies with it, is preoccupied with women who break the codes of accepted sexual behavior. Their punishment takes the breath away. Through the din and onslaught of insects, the immigrants huddled in the night recount what befell Ravan's sister, Surpanakha, and why it did.

One day, the demoness caught sight of Ram and Lakshman at their forest hermitage and fell instantly in love with both. Besotted, Surpanakha transformed herself from a pot-bellied ogre into a ravishing beauty. She approached the god, smiling. She came on to him, confidently. They were made for each other, she said. Ram glanced at his demure Sita, emerging from their hut, and told Surpanakha to try her luck with Lakshman instead. Indiscriminate in her lust, Surpanakha slinked over to Lakshman.[21] The brothers taunted her, and in her fury, Surpanakha revealed herself as the demoness that she was, terrifying Sita and prompting Ram to cue Lakshman, who cut off Surpanakha's nose and ears with his sword. In one swift stroke, she was mutilated.

---

* The ex-coolie and anti-indenture campaigner Totaram Sanadhya began his autobiography, *My Twenty-One Years in the Fiji Islands*: "From this place begins the story of my own insignificant life, a sorrowful story of Ram."

BEAUTIFUL WOMAN WITHOUT A NOSE

The ancient Hindu law books forbid killing women, even as punishment for serious crimes.[22] But the religious texts do describe—some have said, prescribe—the disfigurement of women who transgress sexually.[23] In Indian mythology and folklore, the nose represents honor. To cut off a woman's nose is thus to tell the world that she has lost her honor.[24] Her mutilation telegraphs that she has crossed boundaries by having or seeking sex before marriage, outside it or after its end. That was Surpanakha's crime.[25] She was a widow who expressed desire, aggressively.

Sita saw what happened to her as a result. The indentured women listening to *The Ramayan*, many also widows, likewise provide an audience for Surpanakha's disfigurement. She serves as a warning to them: a noseless, earless mannequin for the consequences of uncontrolled sexuality. Punished, disfigured, Surpanakha ran to her brother, fueled his avenger's fury against Ram and Lakshman and stoked his lust for Sita. That's why Ravan dispatched a golden deer to tempt her, and that's why Sita sent her husband away: to pursue the glittering animal. Ram left Lakshman behind as protector, but the demon lured him away with sham cries. When Lakshman resisted following them, Sita insinuated, in anger, that her brother-in-law wanted her for himself. So it was that when Ravan abducted the unguarded goddess in his chariot, she moaned: "Ah! Lakshman! The fault is none of yours! I have reaped the fruit of the temper I showed."[26]

The indentured women, sitting on their haunches in the cool Demerara night, hear Sita take the blame. How does her self-reproach strike them, compared to Surpanakha's war-causing fury? My great-grandmother—her infant asleep in the barracks, his biological father left in India and already replaced—hears how Sita, on Ravan's island, rebuffed all the demon wooer's advances, whether offered as sweet nothings or threats. I envision Sujaria, *bound* if not kidnapped, reciting with unease the familiar lines about Sita passing her days in captivity, by repeating Ram's name endlessly. How jarring to the self it must have been for her to hymn Sita's message for Ram, brought back by his spy: "The agony of separation from you is like fire."[27]

The reference to fire was prophetic. After Ram defeated Ravan, his first act was to require that Sita prove her chastity through a trial by literal fire. She sang his praises as she entered the flames. The odd thing was: since Ram possessed divine foreknowledge, he knew that Ravan would abduct his wife. Preemptively, Ram had secreted Sita in a protective fire. He had pulled a switch. As Tulsidas tells it, Ravan hadn't stolen the real Sita but a decoy, a shadow. The real Sita was never in danger—not from Ravan's temptation, nor from Ram's test. The flames incinerated the shadow Sita and the "stigma" of her stay with another man.[28] It satisfied public opinion, which would have pilloried Ram for reclaiming a wife kidnapped by an enemy in war. Burning up the shame and the shadow, the fire released the real Sita, unharmed.

With their own fires burning away the bad in the cane—not shadows but real rodents, actual razor-sharp leaves—the skeptics among the singers secretly wonder why Ram bothered with his fire. Why the show? He knew what was going to happen. Shouldn't he have known that Sita didn't betray him? Was the divine lord acting out a play? And if so, did that mean that existence was a trick, an elaborate performance by the gods? Did it occur to the immigrants that their world—the sting of mosqui-toes, the inebriating aroma of burning cane, the maiming edge of the cutlass—could all be just so much *Maya*. Did the thought comfort them?

Playacting like Ram did, the indentured staged his story often. After Tulsidas died, a devotee started performing the *Ramcharitmanas* in India.[29] The immigrants took this *Ramleela* tradition (*leela* means "play") with them. At their most lavish, *Ramleelas* across the dark waters were ten-day carnivals with spectators from afar and vendors selling sweets, jewellery and musical instruments.[30] On the final day, the immigrants held wrestling and tug-of-war contests to mimic the battle in which Ram slays Ravan. Telling the story, in addition to its religious and allegorical significance, provided a social life for the indentured and their descendants. They sang the *Ramcharitmanas* in small jam sessions called *goles*.[31] They recited it at *kathas* ("storytellings"), where holy men read the Tulsidas text.[32] Invitations sometimes came from boat brothers and boat sisters on distant plantations.[33] But often, Ramayan sessions were more informal, impromptu ways to pass the evening. A famous Trinidadian musician, born on a plantation to indentured immigrants, remembered hearing Ram stories by torchlight, at night, outside their barracks.[34]

Such scenes of storytelling unfolded thousands of times over, from Fiji to British Guiana.[35] Did indentured men act under the influence of the narrative, drinking it in as often, in as many ways, as they did? Did some try to reenact the *Ramcharitma-nas* offstage, in their real lives, without costumes or fairground backdrops? They may have cast themselves as Ram, but perhaps they didn't find many women willing or able to fill the worshipful role of Sita. Perhaps when they looked, they saw only Surpanakha. When their partners sexually betrayed them, and added insults to the injury, perhaps they wrestled with the right way to respond. What was their duty? What would Ram do? With the *Ramayan* as present and tall in their lives as cane, it's likely that they asked those questions.[36] The epic sheds light on how they may have seen themselves and the moral choices that they faced, and it represents one possible influence for the chilling acts of violence against Indian women in sugar colonies across the globe.

* * *

Between 1859 and indenture's end in 1917, more than 167 women were killed by intimate or would-be intimate partners in Guiana.[37] Infidelity—or, the fear of it—motivated the crime in most cases, colonial authorities claimed. The first formal sign of a problem was a proclamation in *The Official Gazette* in 1863.[38] It warned in no uncertain terms that the perpetrators of so-called wife murders would be hung. Coolies should not, it cautioned, believe that "previous provocation … will either excuse or at least palliate any crime."[39] The murders seized the public imagination around the same time. Reports of them crossed the Atlantic on mail ships. In 1864, in the midst of a drought and dysentery epidemic, an overseer on Canje Creek wrote home to England: "The coolies are dying like rotten sheep. The cattle on the coast farms are dying by scores. The canes are being dried up. ... As this letter is full of amusing incidents, I may as well state that two coolies are going to be hung here today for cutting off their wives' heads, two regular Bluebeards."[40] The murders were part of the Englishman's evocation of empire's uncivilized backlands—a surreal landscape of grisly, almost mythological horrors. Both in the colony and the imperial capital, the killings caused disquiet enough to lead the Colonial Office, in 1871, to commission a study. What it found was disturbing: such murders occurred at a rate ninety times greater in Guiana than in India in the previous decade. In the heartland district where most migrants were from, the picture was even darker: Indian men killed their romantic partners at a rate 142 times greater in Guiana than in India's Northwestern Provinces and Oudh.[41]

Guiana wasn't the only scene of the crimes. Throughout the sugar colonies, disputes over women led to horrific and frequently fatal violence. In Suriname, a man who chopped off his wife's arms accused her of adultery. Amazingly, she survived to tell her side of the story: her husband had sent her to live with the other man, in order to clear his debts.[42] Natal, among other colonies, passed special laws in an effort to curb wife murders.[43] In Fiji, the killings were common enough to occasion an appeal to end the death penalty in all such cases. A group of Indians petitioned that: "The majority of those found guilty of such crimes are otherwise quiet and law abiding; and the murders for which they are condemned to death, are not due to any murderous instinct in them but really to sexual jealousy."[44] On the island of Reunion, where the British sent coolies by treaty with the French, the British Consul reported: "It is the custom for four or five men to subsidize among themselves to maintain one woman who acts in the capacity of wife or mistress to each one of them in turn, an arrangement which not infrequently leads to quarrels, violence and sometimes bloodshed."[45] In the 1870s, a Royal Commission noted the same practice and fallout in Mauritius.[46] More murders occurred in Guiana than elsewhere, but Trinidad's statistics were only slightly less grim.[47] Year after year, officials worldwide dutifully recorded the cases, which appeared all across the map of indenture, like pushpins marking casualties in a bloody struggle by Indian men for scant beachheads of power.

The violence against women was greater than the murder statistics suggest. Often, the aim was to disfigure, not kill. Indeed, the cases that didn't end in death outnumber those that did. Between 1886 and 1890, when twenty-five women were murdered in Guiana, thirty-five were wounded, usually with cutlasses.[48] Noses, those representatives of women's honor, seemed to be a particular target. In 1914, an indentured man assaulting his wife aimed for her nose; failing to reach it with either cutlass or knife, he bit the tip off with his teeth. Guiana's immigration chief explained that the man was trying, pointedly, to inflict "the brand of infidelity."[49] Of course, the men did not always act symbolically, carving a woman's body into a statue modeling dishonor. Sometimes, the violence exploded without design, through the weapon nearest at hand, as it did for the indentured woman Doolarie, a widow who remarried in Trinidad. There, her new partner hit her on the head with a hoe, scarring her. "The husband bad," Doolarie confided decades later. "He beat me for talking to a next man."[50] Domestic violence against Indian women was pervasive. As one missionary in Guiana noted: "[T]he rod and blows are freely laid upon them."[51]

In every colony that accepted indentured immigrants, the majority of Indian murder victims were women.[52] Women bore the brunt of the violence; it wasn't typically directed at the men who stole or threatened to steal them away.[53] In both Guiana and Trinidad, it took half a century of indenture for the first male rivals to be murdered.[54] Indentured men did, however, take their own lives on a regular basis. The man who bit his wife's nose did. He surrendered to police and, while in custody, hung himself with his *dhoti*.*[55] Colonial officials concluded that chaos caused by sex motivated almost all violence, including self-inflicted violence, among coolies.[56]

The murders escalated then peaked in the 1880s, during the global depression in cane sugar. In 1888 alone, ten women were killed in Guiana. The statistics were so alarming that, while instructing jurors in an 1882 trial, the colony's chief justice made an oddly political remark: "The cases of murderous revenge by coolies upon their women are so frequent as to justify the allegation that there is here a serious blot on the system of coolie immigration and labor."[57] His message was clear: the murders could have implications beyond the coolies, implications that could endanger the very existence of coolies. If nothing was done, indenture itself could be indicted.

* * *

The woman almost decapitated in a bed of plantain trees on 11 July 1904 can't say what her ex wanted when he followed her to work that morning. A constable saw them together. He saw Lutchminia walking, a knife for cutting grass over her shoulder and the indentured man she used to live with at her heels, a cutlass under his arm. Ramautar seemed to be making advances. In response, Lutchminia pulled her *urni*—the long, loose scarf worn out of modesty—over her head.

"You sir," the constable rebuked. "You make um rascal?"[58]

Ramautar grinned. Less than an hour later, another policeman saw him running along the road and, suspecting he was deserting, stopped him. The policeman noticed blood on Ramautar's jaw and ear. The indentured man said: "*Ek randi hum kathi hai.*" The policeman, who knew some Hindi, heard: "I have cut a woman."[59] The word he understood to mean woman, *randi*, actually means prostitute, or widow. In the West Indies, it probably had come to signify woman, as in Fiji, where overseers in charge of female workers bore the title *randi-wallah*.[60] Ramautar—whose name, by unnerving coincidence, means "avatar of Ram"—may indeed have judged Lutchminia a whore. According to *The Chronicle*, she had left him for another man, and he had followed her to beg for her return. "As usual, jealousy was at the bottom of it," the newspaper proclaimed. "Finding every attempt to regain her affections useless, the desperate man thought his only solace laid in putting an end to her existence, which he did with the usual atrocities."[61]

---

* A *dhoti* is a length of cotton wrapped around the torso by men and worn as pants and loincloth.

BEAUTIFUL WOMAN WITHOUT A NOSE

The usual atrocities meant mutilation. Lutchminia's head, almost severed by two slashes to the neck, hung by a muscle. She was found lying face down in the plantain bed, her knees bent. She must have been crouching, cutting grass, when hit from behind. Her knife lay under her belly, which protruded—Lutchmania was seven months pregnant. It's unclear if Ramautar was the father. She had left him more than once, the first time for an Indian who grew plantains on the farm where she was killed. But that man became too ill to work; he couldn't afford to keep her any longer.[62] So Lutchminia returned to Ramautar, who ranked low in the plantation hierarchy. He worked as a weeder on Nonpareil, eight miles from Enmore. Weeding was the least well-paid job on any plantation, one usually reserved for women. Ramautar was so poor, he owned only one shirt. After the killing, he discarded this, because it was stained with Lutchminia's blood.

Keeping the silence of the grave, Lutchminia can't say why she left him, twice. Was it because, scrawny and pock-marked, he wasn't terribly heroic as far as avatars of Ram go? Or, did he call her *randi* to her face? At his murder trial, one of his roommates testified that Lutchminia had a son and Ramautar couldn't support them with his paltry earnings. "That was why she left," the roommate said. "They had no quarrel."[63] With a son to feed and another child on the way, Lutchminia no doubt worried how they would all survive. Because she was pregnant, the plantation eventually stopped giving her work. The last time it paid her was eighteen days before her death. A month earlier, probably anticipating the day she could no longer earn, Lutchminia moved in with a man who lived in the same barracks. He was in the shovel gang, the best-paid gang. Shovel men were generally the strongest, most muscular men on sugar estates. The weeder who owned only one shirt must have paled by comparison.

Ramautar confessed to police. He said, three times: "I killed my wife Lutchminia, because she left me and went to one Bhika." On 29 October 1904, he was hanged.[64] Between this execution, of a man whose name pointed directly to Ram, and that, almost exactly a year earlier, of the man who called Ram's name on the scaffold, there had been much blood. The weeks and months of my great-grandmother's first year in Guiana had passed in unrelenting violence. All around her, dark dramas had churned, filling the calendar with seemingly real-life enactments of Ram's story of exile and punishment. It had unfolded like this:

31 October 1903:   Badal was hanged. His last words were "*Hai, Ram. Hai, Ram.*"

4 November 1903:   *The Clyde* pulled in at the Demerara lightship, with too few women.

8 November 1903:   *The Clyde* sailed for England. That afternoon, the church at Enmore, St. Mark's, held its annual harvest festival. From a pulpit decorated with cassava and cane, the Reverend Harry Gainer preached to planters.[65] Somewhere in the plantation's barracks, Sujaria was settling in, between the married couple she had met on the ship.

4 December 1903:   On Plantation Melville, a few miles southeast of Enmore, the indentured woman Surjodai quarreled with Jitwa, her shipmate

and—for three weeks—her common-law husband. Later that day, he came home from work to find her gone. He tracked her down, but she refused to return. Jitwa dragged her back to his room, where he attacked her with a piece of wood a foot-and-a-half long. The blows ruptured her spleen. Several witnesses saw him carry her out of the room and lay her on the ground. Surjodai asked for a glass of water. Before she got it, she died.[66] Jitwa ultimately received a light sentence—eighteen months, for manslaughter—because the judge doubted he intended to kill her. "Had he had a more serious object," *The Chronicle* commented, "no doubt he would have done what most East Indians do in such cases and used a cutlass or some other dangerous weapon."[67]

14 December 1903: In New Amsterdam, an Indian named Jugbundhoo pleaded guilty to attacking Surbauhee, the woman with whom he had lived on Canje Creek. She had deserted him for someone else, and a week earlier he had confronted her about it. They fought, and he hit her on the head with a stick, leaving two serious wounds. The magistrate sentenced him to two months in jail, with hard labor.[68]

12 January 1904: The Supreme Court in Georgetown heard the case of Mootie, a laborer on Plantation Uitvlugt, west of the Demerara. He had cut a woman across her nose with his cutlass. The wound was deep, extending from cheek to cheek, a little below her eyes.[69] The accused and his victim, Mahareah, had been intimate. The previous October, she had fled both him and the plantation to renew a relationship with another man, who lived miles away, on an island in the Essequibo River. But plantation officials had prosecuted her for deserting, and she was forced back to Uitvlugt and fined. Mootie had paid her fine, hoping to win her back, but had failed.

13 January 1904: Mootie was sentenced to three years in prison.[70]

22 January 1904: The milk seller Kalyan Singh, accused of hacking his mistress to death, was released from custody after three juries failed to agree on a verdict.[71]

For five years, the "greyheaded, life-worn coolieman," as the press described him, had kept Umrai, a woman young enough to be his daughter. The couple lived together in Kitty Village, at the capital's edge, just a few rooms away from his legitimate wife and children. Neighbors said that Kalyan's love for Umrai was intense. She had left him once, and when she returned, they had loud and frequent fights, incited by accusations of infidelity.[72]

One midnight the previous May, Umrai's cries awoke the gold digger next door. Going out to investigate, he saw Kalyan emerge from his room with blood on his clothes. The case against Kalyan hinged on the words he spoke next—and then repeated to two constables. Either they were a confession, or a lament. Either he said: "My wife. Me no killum? Me no shame. Me give too much jewel, house, me keep um five years, an me no sorry me killum. And me no sorry."[73] Or, he said: "My wife. Me no killum. Me no shame? Me give too much jewel, house, me keep um five years, an me no sorry me killum? And me no sorry?" Either he had asserted his right to take the life of a woman he possessed, because he had spent money on her. Or, he was dismayed that anyone would think him so remorseless as to kill a woman on whom he had lavished material proof of his affection. At his trial, his attorney used the clashing dialects and languages of the witnesses, the police and the accused to raise doubt.[74]

Two constables arrived shortly after the attack and took Kalyan into the room where Umrai lay, dying or dead. He called her name three times then paused, as if expecting a reply. Kalyan stood looking at the wreck of her. Illuminated by a lantern, her body lay in a pool of blood that trickled through the floorboards and soaked into the mud below.[75] Her face was slashed beyond recognition, with six cuts on the right side and five on the left. Her nose was chopped off, her ear almost severed, her lower jaw smashed in, and her brain exposed in four places, where a cutlass had penetrated the skull. Twenty-five wounds covered Umrai's body.[76]

Immediately after the murder, an immigrant named Mathura Singh bolted, running ten miles through the night to the nearest settlement.[77] Prosecutors argued that he ran out of terror that Kalyan would attack him next. Mathura had lived in the same barracks as the couple for three years. He claimed that the milk seller became convinced, shortly before the murder, that Umrai was having an affair with him. Allegedly, Kalyan ended his rows with her dramatically, declaring that she could go live with Mathura, for all he cared. Mathura testified that he was blindsided by the allegation and told Kalyan: "When you see your wife comes to me, you say something. But don't give me a bad name before that."[78] He insisted there was nothing going on between them, that he didn't even want the woman.

Three days before the murder, Mathura moved out. The couple visited him at his new lodgings the night Umrai was killed. They all drank rum and brandy and smoked ganja together.[79] That much is clear. But that's all that is clear. Either Kalyan was jealous of Mathura. Or—Mathura, of Kalyan.

Either: Kalyan and Umrai left Mathura's house that night, fighting as they went, leaving Mathura to fall asleep on his verandah, and the next thing Mathura knew, someone was calling out his name. He said he awoke to the bellicose figure of Kalyan, standing out on the road, confessing to the night: "I kill the little wife, Mathura Singh make."[80]

Or: an inebriated Mathura threatened to kill Umrai if she slept with Kalyan that night, and Kalyan and Umrai walked home together, without quarreling, secure in each other's affections. Kalyan said his head was muddled and his heart hot from the liquor and drugs. He swore that he fell asleep in the cool of the verandah and left Umrai sitting at the door, alive and well.[81] The next thing he knew, he said, there an uproar, and Umrai was dead inside their room.

Either Mathura fled for his life or was guilty of taking one. Either Kalyan killed his wife to assert that he owned her. Or, he didn't kill her, because she was his. Either possession meant control, or love beyond violence's reach. Aside from the men, only Umrai knew which was true.

26 January 1904: An indentured immigrant named Rikhee murdered his thirteen-year old betrothed. The victim, Sahadaya, was born in Guiana and lived with her family at Plantation Herstelling, on the east bank of the Demerara River. She and her family shared two rooms with Rikhee and his. The females slept in one room, the males in the other. Rikhee, who was twenty, had been giving his wages to Sahadaya's parents as a bride price. Then he heard a rumor that the family wanted to change living quarters. He believed her parents were going to break their promise and marry her to someone else. Before that could happen, Rikhee slashed Sahadaya twice on her neck, nearly severing it, while she served him tea. He also cut her on the face and left the fingers on one hand barely hanging.[82] He attacked her in front of her four-year old sister. The child later recounted in court: "He held my sister, and she said, 'Loose me', and then he killed her … with a cutlass. He struck her more than once, and my sissie said, 'Oh my Mama, me gone.'"[83]

30 April 1904: Rikhee was executed.[84]

2 May 1904: At Enmore, the immigrant Etwarri hit his wife Soomcharrie on the head with a sharp-edged hoe.[85] Believing he had killed her, he surrendered at the nearest police station. Soomcharrie suffered

three severe head wounds, but lived. She was treated at the plantation hospital, and Etwarri was jailed for six months for assault.[86]

10 May 1904: A court heard the case against Ashfarally, charged with wounding his wife Bulakan, with the intent to disfigure her.[87] They were married in India and had crossed the seas together, three years earlier. At Plantation Wales, on the Demerara's west bank, Ashfarally had sliced off Bulakan's nose then carved off a piece of her lip. When he went to surrender, his wife followed, blood flowing down her face.

7 June 1904: Ashfarally confessed before the Supreme Court in Georgetown. He explained that Bulakan had left him for another man. *The Chronicle* cast the couple as familiar types: "A Jealous Husband and a Naughty Wife," according to the headline.[88] He claimed that Bulakan had returned to his room to retrieve her clothes and cursed him. That's when he mutilated her. Ashfarally got nine months in prison.

11 July 1904: Ramautar attacked Lutchminia as she knelt in the plantain bed.

22 July 1904: In a rice field on Leguan Island, the woman Juggi was found dead. She was legally married to her shipmate Nirhoo, but was also intimate with another man. It was this lover who murdered her in the desolate backdam, after she refused to loan him four shillings. He was hanged for the crime.[89]

17 August 1904: Yaphoo Khan, bound to Plantation Wales, was charged with inflicting grievous bodily harm on his partner Sardoogeah. He had tied her hands and feet and suspended her from a beam in their room. He had beaten her until he was exhausted, and then he had cut off her nose and part of her upper lip. When done, Khan had left her hanging. In court, he explained that when he confronted her about being unfaithful, she had snapped: "I don't give a damn."[90]

29 October 1904: Ramautar was executed.

* * *

In their attempt to explain the violence, the European elite—planters, government officials, journalists and missionaries—resorted to racist stereotypes. They cast the "wife murders" as morality plays in which place was irrelevant. As one historian has put it: "A radical rupture was effected between the crime and the scene of the crime. It was as if the script for the murders was written beforehand in India and the plantations were a mere stage where it was enacted."[91] As setting shrank in imperial rhetoric, character swelled, outsized. European observers fixated on what they saw as "national" character. Although some located the problem in the plantations themselves, mostly they ascribed the murders to possessiveness and promiscuity, traits they saw as inherently Indian.[92] Thus investigators sent to Guiana in 1871 blamed the murders on "the constitutional jealousy of the Oriental."[93]

In Calcutta, the emigration agent for Guiana argued that the violence was "due rather to the race than the place."[94] In an official dispatch to London, he quoted from newspaper articles detailing cruelty to wives in India to prove his point. Planters had already embraced the race-not-place theory. They cited the low incidence of wife murders among Chinese, who had also come indentured and who confronted the worst woman shortage of any community in Guiana.[95] The colony's *Royal Gazette* editorialized in 1863: "The disproportion being greater in the case of the Chinese … the same sad result might be expected, but experience has shown that while as a rule the Chinese females are chaste, the same cannot be said for the coolie women."[96] Not long after, the same paper reported on a Chinese woman's fatal stabbing, by a man she had sexually betrayed.[97] But such crimes were few, because the Chinese were few.[98] The impression persisted that Indians murdered their women, while Chinese did not.[99]

Some colonial officials were convinced that religion was to blame, even more than race. Trinidad's protector of immigrants ventured:

The cause lies deeper in the breeding and blood of the Hindoo and in his religious creed, where the latter exists at all. In this matter, he contrasts strikingly with the Mohammedan Indian who might be supposed to labor under comparatively greater privation from the limited introduction of women; but if this be the case, the latter does not relieve his feelings by a violent assault on his wife.[100]

In his anatomy of the crimes, Guiana's sheriff asserted that a coolie's response to adultery depended on his religion. "If a Hindoo," wrote Henry Kirke, "he mutilates her by chopping off her nose, breasts or arms, and if in a violent rage hacks her to pieces with his cutlass."[101] He offered an example of a Muslim who cut off his wife's nose only as an exception that proved the rule.[102] Muslim assailants were, in fact, few. But, as with the Chinese example, officials overlooked a simple demographic explanation for this: Hindus accounted for 84 percent of migrants to Guiana and Muslims, only 16 percent.[103]

Indeed, stakeholders in indenture put the blame everywhere but on the system itself. They largely ignored evidence that the killings were tied to indenture—to the institution, rather than the race or the religion. The indentured were implicated to a far greater degree than Indians no longer bound by contract.[104] The shortage of women was most acute among the indentured. And indentured men ranked lowest in the hierarchy of suitable partners. A chief justice in Guiana, describing his typical murder case, captured their vulnerability:

A man and a woman are brought here as immigrants from India in the same ship; they become intimate; on their arrival, they are married by the immigration agent general and are indentured to the same plantation and settle there as man and wife. All goes smoothly at first. After a time, however, the woman who is young, uninstructed and vain is attracted by a coolie who has been longer resident in the colonies and is able to offer her presents of silver or gold ornaments and to make her promises of wealth, which her husband cannot approach. The woman either openly abandons her first husband and goes to live with him, or carries on an intrigue with him, which comes to the knowledge of the husband. ... The injured man is left a mark for the jeers and ridicule of his fellows, and the consciousness that such is the case is often a powerful factor in goading him on to the fatal violence.[105]

Sheriff Kirke, meanwhile, noted that a coolie landing without a wife "has very small chance of getting [one] until he has worked for some years and amassed sufficient money to enable him to purchase the daughter of a fellow-countryman."[106] In the virtual auction for women, men still under indenture could rarely make competitive bids. The statistical correlation between the system, with its scarce women and insecure men, and the murders was strong.

Indenture was also what distinguished Indian from Chinese women. The latter were required to live on plantations, but weren't bound by contract to work on them. Unexposed to the glare of sun and suitors in cane fields, most Chinese women led lives more protected and more restricted than their Indian counterparts did.[107] Although the press charged that Chinese women were "better" than Indian women, their backgrounds were similar. Guiana's chief justice once described the Chinese women imported, at a rate of twenty for every 100 men, as "refuse":

to a very great extent indeed this small proportion has been made up of women in no way related to the male immigrants—mere outcasts, filled into the ships by the Chinese agency from the dregs of Chinese life, and such in respect of age and personal defects and infirmities, that to enumerate them in the proportion of women required for the help and solace of the men seems little better than a mockery.[108]

Most Chinese women who went to the colonies were widows, said the official who dispatched them.[109] The Taiping Rebellion, a civil war, had claimed their husbands and set them adrift, as discarded as Indian widows. And since the depots in Canton and Hong Kong paid married migrants, many married for the bounty money, right before sailing;[110] their relationships were as infirm as those of many Indian indentured.

Still, the question of the "quality" of Indian women dogged the debate on why they were killed. The circle of culpability narrowed, from Indians to Hindus until what remained was gender. Because the women could be blamed, even those who attributed the crimes to the nature of Indian men didn't always hold them responsible. The court of public opinion viewed them with sympathy. Fiji's governor commuted a man's death sentence for fatally stabbing a woman after fellow coolies petitioned on his behalf; he had been a soldier in India and was esteemed.[111] A Guiana jury exonerated one killer because he witnessed his woman making love, on his bed, to someone else.[112] Another killer's lawyer told the jury that "the deceased was a very bad woman," then asked: Would they hang "this poor coolie man for a woman like that?"[113] Many assailants *were* convicted and hanged, but even those not granted legal clemency were pitied. An official in London, regretting that he couldn't halt an execution in 1873, wrote: "There is nothing to be done on this. The case is a very sad one. The woman seems to have been thoroughly depraved."[114]

The women were twice victimized. First, they were physically mutilated; then their reputations were dismembered, by European and Indian men alike. A former coolie in Fiji reflected, from the vantage of old age: "Money, the desire for money and more money and jewels, led to the downfall of our women. ... They changed their men as they changed their *lehengas* [skirts]."[115] An Australian overseer in Fiji, who also disparaged Indian women as unfaithful and mercenary, veered between portraying them as, on one hand, amorally sensual as animals and, on the other, immorally calculating in their conquests. In his memoir, he recounted an exchange between an Indian beauty—"a Hindu with the morals of an alleycat"[116]—and a man she outbid at an auction. When the man stage-whispered, "Ask the little slut where her bank is," the woman retorted: "Tell the fat one that it's where he can't get his hands on it... between my legs."[117]

Even men without a sexual stake in the women cut them to pieces. The Reverend C.F. Andrews, indenture's great critic, rued the women he met in Fiji. "The Hindu woman in this country," he reported, "is like a rudderless vessel with its masts broken being whirled down the rapids of a great river without any controlling hand. She passes from one man to another and has lost even the sense of shame in doing so."[118] A missionary in Guiana declared: "The great majority of women imported from Calcutta are very loose in their habits. They were bad in Calcutta and so they will ... remain in Demerara."[119] A muckraker for the British Anti-Slavery Society repeated the hearsay that many had been prostitutes. "No doubt," he remarked, "the standard of reliance and self-control was lower among them than the average of their fellow countrymen."[120] These were the judgments of watchdogs and sympathizers, who understood that the gender imbalance caused the sexual chaos but still assassinated the character of Indian women.

The formal protectors of immigrants, on the other hand, wouldn't even concede that the imbalance played a key role. Perhaps not surprisingly, it was these officials most vested in indenture who resisted the growing consensus that female scarcity, a flaw built into the system, explained the violence. In the 1880s, while drafting a law to stop the murders by making it easier for Indians to marry legally, British Guiana's attorney general and governor both identified the shortage of women as the real issue.[121] But immigration chief A.H. Alexander's main contribution was to speculate that Indians rarely contracted marriages partly because the women were low-class. "It is not to be wondered at that marriage with such women should be regarded as rather hazardous and objectionable," he ventured.[122] Over the decades, he continued to minimize the impact of the sex ratio. In 1901, he wrote: "Whether women are many or few, the men will always bear animosity to the particular women on whom they have spent their money."[123] Hadn't his own son lost his position over a coolie lover, whose ex publicized the affair to recover presents of jewellery? Blaming the murders on the alleged cupidity of Indians—the men's possessiveness, the women's desire, their mutual lust for money—allowed Alexander to deflect responsibility from indenture itself. Attacking the women's reputations also served another purpose: planters and their proxies could counter any push for more women, perceived as less profitable workers, by contending that increasing numbers would decrease moral caliber.[124]

Rarely do coolie women get to talk back to official history, to challenge its view of them. If they answer the slander, it is indirectly, across time, through the women in their families who told tales across the generations. One story is of two immigrant forefathers, one Chinese, one Indian, adapting to Guiana's shortage of women.[125] The Chinese man was an imperial civil servant who had fled the Taiping Rebellion. The Indian man came from a similar background, unused to hard labor. Displaced, out of their element, they toiled side-by-side, weeders both. The Indian man had a wife and children to carry on his name; the Chinese man did not. And so, in "an act of brotherly love," the Indian loaned his wife to the Chinese man.[126] The swap lasted only until the woman became pregnant. She gave birth to a boy, and the Indian man gave the baby to the Chinese man to be raised. Every Sunday, ever after, they would all meet by the riverside. The two men would *gyaff*, and the child would play with his mother: the generous Hindu woman shared between two men, known to the generations only as Gang-Gang.[127] Her story suggests an alternative way to understand the fluid, unorthodox sexual relationships during indenture. They may indicate accommodation, not immorality. Perhaps they were another improvisation, as when the indentured found ship sisters and ship brothers to replace families left behind.

Of course, not all cases ended as amicably. In Guiana in 1909, a woman who refused to choose between two men was murdered by one of them. But hers wasn't a case of adultery; neither man was her husband.[128] While colonial elites depicted the murders as parables involving "jealous husbands and naughty wives," the victim and assailant were frequently not husband and wife, legal or common-law. The attacks against women in Guiana during indenture's final two decades reveal more complex dynamics.[129] In several cases, women were killed for spurning advances. In 1897, an indentured man who failed to entice an Indian woman from her husband stabbed her. "She resisted his importunities," A.H. Alexander explained.[130] In 1914, near Enmore, a leper chopped a woman who wouldn't leave her husband for him.[131] In 1917, a man wounded his shipmate with a cutlass because she refused him.[132] Infidelity didn't cause these assaults; on the contrary, the victims were trying to be faithful, like Sita. And husbands, when rejected, weren't always rejected for other men. One woman was nearly decapitated by her husband, because she wouldn't return from her mother's.[133] Rather than greed or libido, what the victims had in common was choice. They had all exercised a choice to say yes—or, in more cases than acknowledged, to say no.

* * *

How colonial officials explained the violence naturally determined what they did to stop it—and what they didn't do. They didn't pay women as much as men, although unequal wages arguably created the need to man-hop for economic survival. Nor did officials recruit significantly more women, although the shortage indisputably

119

empowered women to man-hop. At the end of the 1860s, the first decade of alarm over the murders, officials raised the quota of indentured women slightly, from twenty-five for every 100 men to forty for every 100.[134] But that is where officials held the line: recruiting fewer women was better than recruiting more, if those women had loose morals—again, "quality" not quantity. Nonetheless, the colonies continued to attract husbandless outcasts and runaways, rather than families. As officials saw it, if the murders were caused by the immoral character of coolie women—coupled with the misogyny of coolie men following a backward religion—there wasn't much to do; after all, they argued, natures can't be changed.

Officials tried to manage, not solve, the problem.[135] They tinkered with punishments. When hangings proved no deterrent, they proposed flogging.[136] And indeed, men who wounded their wives did receive lashes as well as jail time.[137] H.V.P. Bronkhurst, a half-Indian missionary deemed an expert on Eastern religions, proposed beheadings. Hindus were fatalistic about the death penalty, he said, because they believed they would return to India when executed: "A man must have a head on his shoulders when he goes to India; he can't find himself there minus the head."[138] He also suggested—without irony—that a lifetime sentence of plantation labor might be a more effective deterrent than hanging.[139] To prevent intimate partner violence, the Colonial Office considered inflicting its own punishment for adultery; but it ultimately rejected as unprecedented a proposal to shame women by shaving their heads.[140] Efforts to punish seducers went further. An 1860 ordinance called for a $24 fine or three months in jail the first time a man stole another's wife and a $100 fine or a year in jail for each subsequent offence. The law instructed deserted men to "make no quarrel or disturbance," but to alert the manager or immigration agent: "He will do for you all that is right."[141] The measure was mostly moot, since it applied only to officially registered marriages and most Indians weren't legally married.

Although A.H. Alexander maintained that the chief reason was low-class women,[142] even he acknowledged logistical obstacles. Christian marriages were automatically registered, but weddings performed in the colony by Hindu pandits or Muslim maulvis were not recognized by the state. To legitimize such unions, couples had to pay heavy fines, journey to Georgetown, and certify that no impediments, including previous marriages, existed. Fewer than 100 couples a year met the requirements.[143] By 1893, when 110,000 Indians lived in Guiana, only 10,000 Indian couples *ever* had received marriage certificates, and most of those had declared themselves married on landing in the colony.[144] As a result, most Indian children born in the colony were officially bastards;[145] inheritance was a tangled mess; and seducers could rarely be prosecuted.

So, officials fiddled with the marriage laws. They provided a path, in 1894, to legalize Hindu and Muslim marriages, under certain conditions. They also revoked the requirement to travel to Georgetown and lowered fees. But the hurdles were still so great and registered Hindu and Muslim marriages still so few that, as late as 1906, an Indian man wrote to *The Argosy*:

BEAUTIFUL WOMAN WITHOUT A NOSE

When a wife deserts a husband or a husband deserts a wife, we are helpless at law. … I know many of the atrocities for which East Indians are convicted, sent to prison and hanged would be prevented were the law but to recognize the validity of marriage according to the law and custom of East Indians. … If a man or a woman go to the police or the magistrate or the Immigration Department, the first question asked is: 'Were you married by English law?' and if the reply is in the negative, the applicant is told, 'We can do nothing for you.'[146]

From 1887, lawmakers empowered magistrates to divide the property of Indians who separated, whether legally married or not. The attorney general who lobbied for this provision argued that it would remove another motive for the murders: material loss, usually in the form of presents of jewellery, the ornaments that to European eyes defined the exotic allure of Indian women.[147]

But the most significant measure against wife murders—definitely the one most affecting the private lives of the indentured—was one that empowered magistrates to transfer an immigrant from one plantation to another. Enacted in 1864, the provision applied if an immigrant threatened his woman, legal wife or not. At first, managers didn't make much use of it. In five years, they transferred only seventeen immigrants for jealousy.[148] The governor complained that managers hadn't even instructed their drivers to report it whenever a woman left one man for another.[149] He threatened to fine managers for any attack that might have been averted by a transfer.[150] That seemed to do the trick: suddenly, between 1869 and 1870, eighty-eight transfers for jealousy were executed.[151] There was then an official push to intercede in the personal affairs of the indentured. The Colonial Office ordered the governor, if managers failed in this duty, to inform their bosses.[152] And in 1872, the governor overturned a wife killer's death sentence because officials had neglected to transfer him.[153] Still, the government pushed for magistrates to transfer the seducers rather than the cuckolded. It favored keeping couples together, even if that overruled the woman's choice and endangered her.[154] One immigration chief explained: "I have been much distressed to be obliged to separate people who have been living together ten or twelve years and have had children. … The husband was generally the least to blame of the lot."[155] In 1873, the law was amended to clarify that seducers, too, could be removed. After that, transfers for jealousy steadily increased, averaging fifty-six annually until indenture ended.[156] In the system's final two decades, more than 1,100 immigrants were transferred to prevent violence against women.[157] Mostly, it was the men who were moved, but some women were too, for various reasons.[158]

My great-grandmother was one of them. On 17 October 1906, three years after arriving at Enmore, Sujaria was transferred.[159] She was among seventy-one immigrants sent from one plantation to another that year. In two-thirds of the cases, managers said they were intervening before jealousy erupted into murder or maiming. Of the remaining transfers, one was put down to insubordination, one to ill health and seven to misconduct. Eight immigrants changed plantations to rejoin relatives or friends, and seven went at their own request, for unrecorded reasons.[160] Which was my great-grandmother? Was she insubordinate? Did she ask to go? Or was hers a case of management meddling in domestic affairs to prevent tragedy?

Three weeks after the transfer, her legal obligations to labor ended. Starting in 1894, the indenture contract for women bound them to live on their plantation for five years, but to work only for three. It was yet another initiative to lure more women. George Bethune would get no more work out of Sujaria, unless she wanted to give it. That may have prompted the transfer, especially if she wasn't serving the other purpose for which planters wanted coolie women: to be wife to a laborer who didn't already have one. But something else happened in 1906 that could have triggered the move. Sujaria had another baby: this time, a girl. Shewrattan Singh, the married *thakur* who had been her shipmate, was the father. Four of Sujaria's granddaughters tell the same story: She had to leave Enmore because problems arose with Shewrattan's first wife, Munrai.[161]

It could not have been easy to be Munrai. She had sailed from India with Shewrattan, yet had borne him no children. Guianese folk songs point to the bitter lot of childless women, for whom suicide was viewed as valid.[162] In one song, a woman begs a carpenter to carve a child out of wood and promises to love it like a real baby.[163] In another, a woman expresses her profound craving: "Oh, Mother Ganges, my lap is empty./ I cry of the pain of my womb."[164] In the folk traditions inherited from India, barren women were objects of pity and supernatural wonder—capable of dooming others to the same cursed fate with their sight or touch.[165] The songs attest that the status of an issueless woman whose co-wife had children was especially low.[166] In one, a woman laments that a stepson is of no use: "Thirst is not quenched by licking one's lips," she sings. "A co-wife's son, oh brother/ Does not help one along life's path/ And beyond."[167] According to custom, only one's own son could perform last rites. Munrai might have dreaded the thought of Sujaria bearing Shewrattan a son of his own blood, a boy to one day bury him.

It couldn't have helped that Sujaria was an arresting beauty. Her granddaughters remember her as glamorous for her environs: "My Nani* was like a film star," one said.[168] They conjure her with sunglasses and strappy sandals, as she sold milk door-to-door in Cumberland Village. She had light eyes. Its exact tint is a matter of dispute. One granddaughter says blue, one grey. Another swears Sujaria's eyes were cat's eyes. They all agree, however, that her skin was "white like white people." All suggested that she may have been Anglo-Indian—and that perhaps, that was why she had left India, to flee the stigma of mixed blood. Given the odd Indo-Caribbean exaltation, at war with itself, of white skin, given her productive womb, did Sujaria supplant Shewrattan's first wife in his affections? Was theirs an emotional bond of lasting significance? Is that why, when Sujaria arrived at a wedding decades later, the other guests burst out: "*Thakurain* come!"?[169] By then, she had been long married to another, a cowherd by caste, and yet they still thought of her as the *thakur*'s junior wife.

What happened next debunks the theory of discord between Shewrattan's women: there was a child swap, as in folk tales, or Bollywood. The trio arrived at an agreement. Although the archives say that Lal Bahadur was also transferred on 17 October

* Nani means maternal grandmother.

1906, the story handed down in the family says otherwise. It says he stayed with the childless couple, caring for them as their own son would, even doing what a biological son should at their funerals. It says Shewrattan kept the boy, though the girl was his. It says Sujaria left her son born at sea—and they didn't reunite for fourteen years, once the *thakur* and his first wife had died. Sujaria took her newborn daughter Mundi with her as she embarked, in the police custody typical for transfers, on yet another journey: sixty miles east by rail, then by ferry across the undulating brown back of the Berbice River, past a marshy island named after crabs, through the old Dutch town of New Amsterdam, beyond the colony's insane asylum, over to the east bank of Canje Creek, where tucked in a bend in the river sat Rose Hall Plantation. At the time, its manager was George Bethune's brother, Charles, a strict manager but subdued compared to his successor, a cursing man[170] under whose watch one of the deadliest plantation strikes in the Caribbean took place seven years later.[171]

At Rose Hall, Sujaria was called "Mundi Mai": Mundi's mother. Later, when Mundi married, Shewrattan came bearing gifts. But he wouldn't enter the house where Sujaria lived with his stand-in. He waited outside the gate. Sujaria's new man invited him in, but Shewrattan had drawn a boundary line of respect. He had come only to wish Mundi well, he explained. "You are her father," he said. "You have raised her." No cutlass was brandished, and no nose cut off. No jealous rage was displayed. Instead, there was a sense of community and extended family that the newspapers— in their first, sensational draft of the troubled history of coolie intimacy—had missed. The common sense and cooperation went beyond the child swap and the dignified scene outside the wedding house. When Shewrattan and his wife grew sickly, the man who met him at the gate allowed his own daughter—Sujaria's third Guianese child—to take care of them. Belle Pua, as I knew her, did the things expected of a girl, which weren't expected of Lal Bahadur. She cooked, she cleaned, she nursed them. She accommodated their needs.

* * *

If Indian women merely accommodated needs that, given their shortage, couldn't be met except through polyandry or infidelity, then why punish them? What really caused Indian men to commit such chilling crimes against them? Were the attacks a reaction to the power and value the women had gained through scarcity? Did the violence, along with the laws developed to deal with it, end up curtailing the independence of coolie women? And were the men in fact retelling *The Ramayan* in their own lives? Did they see it as their religious duty to maim or kill unchaste women? Were these honor crimes? Or was the overseer's whip as much an influence as Lakshman's sword? Indenture was at least partly to blame.

Indeed, the plantations provided a model for violence more immediate than *The Ramayan*. Managers, overseers and drivers regularly punished their workers by thrashing them. In the West Indies, a cattle whip was the favored weapon.[172] In Fiji, many survivors of indenture reported being beaten.[173] One man said: "We had two alternatives on the cane farm: either finish the task, or get a couple of canes."[174] One woman indicated that beatings were so routine, they occurred on a timetable. "I remember so many cases where immigrants received more than twelve cuts," she said. "Their backs used to swell up, they could not sit down properly and had to be treated at home. Most beatings took place on either Fridays or Saturdays, probably with the intention of enabling the victim to recover from wounds on Sundays."[175] Women were not spared. The overseer in Fiji, the memoirist, admitted using switches from the wild once to flog his weeders, their skirts lifted to expose their naked bottoms.[176] Men were not singled out, but they must have internalized the violence of the plantation in ways that women did not. Their masculinity must have been as battered as their bodies.

It's impossible to know the minds of indentured men without speculating. Thankfully, one written account from Guiana, the only known literary text by an indentured servant in the British Caribbean, has survived to provide some insight.[177] Published in 1916, it's a pamphlet of rhymed verses intended to be sung during the Hindu festival Holi, known in the Caribbean as Phagwah. *Damra Phag Bahar* (Phagwah Songs of Demerara) indicates that indenture both imperiled the faith of the migrants and made it more imperative than ever. The author of the songs, Lal Bihari Sharma, was indentured to Plantation Golden Fleece. Like my great-grandmother, he was from a village in the Bihari district of Chapra. And like her, he was a Brahmin.[178]

Reinforcing how central religion was to its indentured audience, *Damra Phag Bahar* is a devotional book full of tales of Ram and Sita. It borrowed its imagery as well as its archaic dialect from Tulsidas. To describe the moment any man's indenture ends, Sharma used a metaphor from *The Ramcharitmanas*: "The heart," he wrote, "feels as happy as the chakora in the moon finds delight."[179] The chakora, a mythical bird, lives off moonbeams; and Tulsidas compulsively compared Ram's love for Sita to the chakora's need for the moon. Love—specifically, ardor whetted by distance—is the songbook's other preoccupation. It dwells on the torture of separation, a theme that must have been achingly familiar to men and women severed from loved ones by indenture. But Sharma's romantic ballads—"without my beloved, the breeze assails me like iron"[180]—were intended as an allegory for man's pining for God. The indentured man belonged to a long line of Vaishnavite *bhakti* poets,* for whom the divine and desire were fused.[181]

Although his book doesn't mention murder or mutilation, it points to a pervasive demoralization that may have led to both. It suggests that the disappointments of place—rather than race—determined the actions of Indian men. "This country," Sharma wrote:

> is a country of wrongdoing.
> It destroys the wisdom to tell

---

* Sharma was working in a well-established genre. The style, imagery and content of his songs seem to place him in the centuries-old tradition of *viraha*, ballads about unfulfilled desire and the separation of lovers, usually sung in the voices of Radha and Krishna, by sixteenth-century *bhakti* poets.

> good from bad, truth from falsehood.
> It leaves no sense of *dharma*.
>
> I left my land to come to Demerara,
> where they wrote my name as coolie.
> I left behind my hymns and the rest of religion.
> I abandoned the paths of the Vedas
> much to my shame. I degraded my karma
> through immoral acts.[182]

It reads like a confession. To this moral turmoil was added fear, embodied by the overseer:

> Galloping into the fields
> On the heels of the people
> Comes the Sahib
> With a whip in his hand
> The white man's tall hat
> Like a helmet
> High on his head.[183]

He loomed over the landscape, threatening violence, and in his hand, he held another instrument of punishment: the book in which he noted who had failed to complete his task and therefore risked both his day's pay and prison. This hovering prospect of being beaten, jailed or docked wages drove the indentured to doubt. Sharma voiced their crisis of faith:

> On the island of Demerara,
> All around there are police stations,
> All around there are ill consequences.
> Lord, where have you guided us
> Lost, wretched creatures.
> Lord, where have you misled us
> Deceived creatures.[184]

As they awaited indenture's end, some ran "in all directions/impatient, amok," and others coped by viewing the sufferings of the plantation as Maya, mere physical illusion. Sharma urged them all to turn to Ram as refuge: "Without chanting the name of Ram," he preached, "the world is like a beautiful woman with her nose chopped off."[185]

The plantations threw men into the arms of their gods. They were displaced, and Hinduism rooted them. They were brutalized, and it salved their wounds. Indenture drove some to religion and others to madness. Folk songs point to the deranging effect. One lingers on a landscape of incarceration—the court house, the police station, the jail—then bursts into full-throated lament:

> It drives one out of his mind,
> British Guiana drives us out of our minds.

It drives one crazy,
It is British Guiana.[186]

The already precarious sanity of Indian men was further destabilized by anxiety about losing their wives, a point made by an Indian in an 1882 letter to *The Chronicle*. The writer reported that his wife by Hindu rites had recently left him for "a colored man and a so-called Christian," whom she met while working at the city's sea wall. The abandoned husband wrote:

Now, sir, the coolie like every other human being will be glad to live anywhere, providing there is contentment in the bargain; but how can he be expected to rest contented with the continual dread of having his wife taken away from him, with the jewels which he has gone to a considerable expense in adorning her with, besides. If this is not enough to drive a man mad, I don't know what else can, and had I lived in a less civilized community than George-town, one can hardly imagine what would happen.[187]

Insecure about their wives and jewellery, robbed of their liberty, Indian men teetered on the brink.

Madness was alibi for one murderer. In 1906, the indentured man Makundi was sentenced to be hanged for killing a woman who rejected his advances, but was spared by authorities citing his "disordered mind."[188] Within six months of landing in Guiana in 1902, Makundi was jailed for destroying his employer's property at Plantation Wales.[189] While in custody at Georgetown's public hospital, he tried to hang himself with a torn bedsheet. He threw himself on the ground violently and repeatedly. He spat at other patients. A nurse reported that he couldn't sleep and looked agitated and afraid. After two doctors certified Makundi as dangerous and suicidal, he was admit-ted to the colony's lunatic asylum, on Canje Creek.[190] He was released after five months, but soon readmitted after another attempt to hang himself.

Asylum doctors portrayed him as a profoundly disoriented man, unable to come to terms with his new identity and environment. It took Makundi several tries to name his plantation. He insisted that he didn't know how to use a cutlass. One doc-tor remarked that he seemed "unable to grasp or realize his position in this colony as a laborer."[191] When questioned, Makundi refused to answer, repeated himself or enigmatically replied: "You know." If pressed, he looked hounded, on the verge of tears. He seemed nervous and depressed when first admitted, and a doctor warned that he "will likely strike if provoked." Makundi did not, however, enact any suicidal or dangerous tendencies during his year at the asylum. Doctors consistently described him as: dull-witted, silly, namby-pamby, childish. One dismissed him as "another undesirable! Useless for the purposes for which he was brought to this colony." His emigration pass indeed suggests that he was unsuited to field labor: he was a mer-chant by caste, with a weak heart.[192] During neither asylum stay, however, did doc-tors find anything clinically wrong with him. He was a simpleton, they said, but cheerful and amicable. An Indian assistant—probably a fluent Hindi speaker, unlike previous interrogators—found him coherent and rational in conversation. In the end, the doctors concluded: "There is no reason to keep him in an asylum."

He returned to Wales, where twice in 1904 he was convicted of assaulting over-seers and sentenced to a few months of hard labor.[193] Two years later, at another plantation, Makundi offered a woman in his barracks sixpence—not even a day's pay—to live with him. She complained to her husband, who thrashed Makundi. And still, he persisted: a witness said he went to the woman's room and propositioned her again. Makundi blamed her for the beating, she cursed him, and he hit her with his cutlass, fracturing her skull. Twelve days later, she died.[194]

After Makundi was convicted and sentenced to be executed, an immigration agent interviewed personnel at two plantations where he had worked. Their depiction of Makundi, four years into indenture, fit the asylum's profile: he still seemed to be rejecting plantation society. Overseers and drivers reported that he asked for leave often and when refused, wept or threatened to kill himself.[195] He was often in the sick bay. Once, when admitted with a cut on his foot, he tried to smash the hospital windows and break out. Short and squat, with pierced ears and discolored patches on his cheeks, Makundi was physically unimpressive. At thirty, he weighed 109 pounds and was five feet tall.[196] His outburst was so fierce, however, that the estate's strongest man had to be summoned to restrain him. Another time, he refused to work for a week, until his request for a transfer was granted. His unhappiness may have had something to do with a letter he received from India. A sick nurse read it for him. "Because it did not contain the news he expected," the nurse said, "he accused me of reading incorrectly and got into a great rage." By then, Makundi's behavior had become seriously eccentric. He sometimes danced in women's clothes, and other immigrants called him *Bhaujie*, or "brother's wife." When they taunted him, he only laughed. Occasionally, he went to the overseers' yard and yowled like a cat.

Was Makundi acting insane to return to the asylum? He did seem to thrive there: he gained six pounds during his first stay, seven during his second.[197] Or had the plantations driven Makundi mad? If he wasn't crazy to start, indenture made him so. Three years after doctors found nothing fundamentally wrong with him, the asylum superintendent advised that Makundi should not be held responsible for the killing, because he had irresistible morbid impulses.[198] Deeming him criminally insane, the authorities commuted his sentence to life in prison.[199]

Suicide statistics for the indentured point to deep disquiet in the psyches of coolie men. Everywhere in the sugar colonies, the suicide rate outstripped that in India. In Guiana, which had one of the lowest rates, the indentured still killed themselves at twice the rate that Indians in the motherland did.[200] The situation was far bleaker in Fiji. Indentured Indians there killed themselves at twenty times the rate in India.[201] The suicides seemed directly related to the shortage of women; in colonies with less women, men took their lives at a greater rate.[202] Fiji, where the percentage of women among the indentured was the lowest, also had the highest suicide rate.[203]

The correlation seemed to back up the conventional wisdom: that sexual rivalries were to blame. Interviews with ex-indentured men cement the impression. One who landed in Trinidad in 1910 reported many suicides on the plantations and said they hewed to a code of honor: If you saw your wife with another man, you killed yourself.[204] A former coolie in Fiji recalled murder-suicides provoked by empowered women: "When men told something to their women," he said, "the latter replied that, 'I am the King of my mind.' This led to beatings that were sometimes fatal. To escape the law, the men hanged themselves."[205] And indeed, colonial authorities documented cases that fit that pattern. In Guiana in 1914, the year the man who bit his wife's nose committed suicide in custody, another immigrant, failing to win back a woman he believed his, strangled her in the fields and then hanged himself in his room.[206]

But the perception that jealousy motivated most suicides is flawed. In Guiana as elsewhere, many suicides were connected to women, but many more remain mysteries. Eighty-five percent of suicides there in indenture's final years were either unrelated to women or unexplained.[207] In the case of a man who killed himself within a year of landing, no reason could be discovered "beyond the surmise that he was seized with a sudden and intense feeling of homesickness and took his life in a fit of despondency."[208] In 1916, the year Sharma's songbook pointed to abandoned *dharma*, there were sixteen suicides in Guiana, a record for the colony. The authorities couldn't account for five. Two, they attributed to insanity. Two, they blamed on smoking ganja. One victim was an unsuccessful gambler. Another was anguished that he couldn't afford to assist his family in India. Three suicides were ascribed to poor health. Only two were traced to women. Strikingly, all the victims that year were men. Three-quarters were indentured, and half of those were in their first year.[209] By contrast, the suicide rate among free Indians was roughly the same as among Indians in the subcontinent.[210]

The inability to get or keep a woman formed just one part of the despair of indentured men. They had lost more than the hope of stable sexual partners, housekeepers, cooks and companions. It wasn't just marriage and family—but also the support structures of caste, kinship and religion—that indenture had disrupted.[211] These were institutions that gave meaning and sometimes status to Indian men, institutions that might have cushioned them once they realized that recruiter promises of riches and reinvention were largely lies. The fact that so many men who killed themselves did so soon after landing suggests that disillusion and dislocation might have driven them to suicide.

Who *didn't* commit suicide is also revealing. In Fiji, low-caste *chamars*[212] killed themselves less often than the upper-caste.[213] The plantation leveled everyone except drivers to the position of coolie, and drivers were not picked by caste.[214] The plunge in prestige may have been too much for high-caste men to bear while indenture may have buoyed lower-caste men with the sense that, in the words of one historian, it "rewarded individual achievement instead of celebrating divinely preordained social hierarchy."[215] Along similar lines, women in both Guiana and Fiji took their lives at lower rates than men did—overthrowing the norm in India, where women accounted for most suicides.[216]

It begs asking why so few women, in a departure from the trend in India, ended their lives. They had been wrenched out of context, too. Is it possible that the institutions that buttressed men fettered women? Why else might the crumbling of those supports have led men—but not women—to take their lives? And might the same loss also have led them to kill their women?

The semi-forced migration of Indian indentured laborers caused tectonic shifts in power. Men accustomed to authority based on their gender, caste or family position were ousted. On plantations, they confronted a system that flaunted its total control over them. The arsenal of punishment included prison, fines, floggings—and the ability to deprive an immigrant of his woman. A Fijian coolie recalled being told by a driver: "If the company wants to give a woman to a man, or take one from another, it was its business. No man is allowed to beat up his wife as she did not belong to him for the five years of indenture."[217] Two struggles for power unfolded simultaneously: one between indentured men and the system that made such wild claims to ownership—a system that maddened, emasculated and induced suicide—and another between Indian men and their women. As the men lost status and identity, perhaps maintaining patriarchal traditions from India assumed fatal importance. Perhaps they grasped at their faith, with the fundamentalism that displacement can foster. Perhaps they maimed and killed to resist the control of planters as well as to reassert their control over their women.

The word that one ex-indentured woman used to describe these violent consequences is richly, eloquently ambiguous. Half a century after indenture ended, Nanka told an interviewer that if she or others chose more considerate men, when one failed to provide for them and their children, the exercise of this power provoked "lots of *marpeet.*"[218] The Hindi word can mean fights, or beatings. The distinction matters, since the first was waged for women and the second, against them. As this dual meaning suggests, the violence was double-headed: directed at colonial authorities as well as coolie women. After all, could the mutilation of Surpanakha be understood except in the context of Ram's struggle with Ravan, who—like the masters of the indentured—also ruled an empire from a speck of an island?

8

GONE BUT NOT FORGOTTEN

*Is too much tings me eye see, me heart bear in this estate, me picknee!** ... *Overseer, driver all trick me. All take-out me bloomers. All rassle me in canefield. Me was use up like cow-pasture.*

Rooplall Monar, "Immigrant Woman"**

On 7 May 1903, where cane gave way to bush along the Berbice River, two dozen British colonial police formed a wall to block the advance of more than a hundred Indian workers from Plantation Friends. The police bore arms; the laborers carried agricultural implements. With shovels, they met Lee-Enfield rifles fixed with bayonets. The collision lasted about twenty minutes, and at the end of it, two indentured men, shot in the face, were dead. By the next day's dawn, four more Indians had died, and seven lay wounded, including a woman.

An inquest cleared the police of any criminal responsibility. It also concluded that the arrests of four indentured men, escorted away behind the shield of police, had triggered the clash. The trouble had started the previous morning, with a strike. The shovel gang had refused to clear a new field for cane. The workers insisted that, given how tough the task, the wage per row of cane was too low for them to earn their daily shilling. One immigrant complained to plantation manager Alexander McEwan that, at the rate he had set, "belly no full."[1] The overseer in charge of the shovel gang, John Gooding, accused four men of bullying the rest into striking.

The next day, he sought their arrest, on charges of threatening his life. Outside the courthouse in nearby Sisters Village, when Gooding applied there for warrants, a hundred laborers sat on the road, shovels impaled in the ground, unnerving the Brits inside. The Indians were there for immigration agent Henry Taylor, who had prom-

* Picknee means child. Probably from picaninny.
** Epigraph from Rooplall Monar, *Estate People* (Georgetown: Roraima Publishers, 1994), 7.

ised to be at their plantation first thing that morning to resolve the wage dispute. Hours into the workday, however, there had been no sign of their state-designated protector. The courthouse would be on Taylor's way to the Great House. Tired of waiting, the workers aimed to intercept him before he reached the manager. They wanted Taylor to hear them out before the two white men could—they feared—collude.

So it was that the alleged ringleaders were right outside the courthouse when police were told to arrest them. The crowd of immigrants had been calm and orderly until then. When Taylor did eventually stop at the courthouse, to inform Magistrate John Brumell of the strike, the latter placated the workers with a slightly higher wage from McEwan. The immigrants would have accepted the offer and returned to work[2]—but then, four innocent men were seized.

From where he sat inside the courthouse, the magistrate could see the immigrants grow agitated. He sent for backup and ventured out into what looked more and more to him like a mob. Brumell asked the coolies to return to Friends. They refused. Not until their comrades were released would they go. Through an interpreter, Brumell tried to persuade the laborers that the arrests weren't a result of the strike. Overseer Gooding was afraid for his life, the magistrate explained; that's why the men had been arrested. The magistrate, a prominent plantation owner's son, promised a fair trial. Then he read the Riot Act.

An hour later, reinforcements of two dozen constables barricaded the courthouse, their bayonets fixed, as the prisoners were led out in custody. At this, the immigrants rose and, defying a warning to disperse or risk life in prison, walked straight towards the police. Some tried to break through the armed line. Others manoeuvred around it, jumping trenches to join the march to jail. Out front, the indentured man Soobnauth was shouting that the prisoners had done nothing wrong, that if they were punished, all should be. A constable wounded him with a bayonet as police beat the crowd back. The immigrants advanced again, shovels raised. Yet again, the police repulsed them at bayonet point. And still, they pushed forward, this time lobbing missiles—bottles, sticks and half-made bricks, according to British officials. That's when Brumell issued the order to fire, he would later claim; but at the inquest, immigrants testified that they hurled clods of burnt earth and then only when fired upon. The police shot two volleys into the air. Then they aimed lower. As bodies hit the ground, the immigrants finally scattered, wailing.

Taylor had watched the tragedy unfold from the courthouse, for fear of provoking the coolies if he emerged. They clearly blamed him for the arrests. When all was over, and he tried to help, an immigrant warned him to keep his distance. Taylor, who spoke and understood some Hindi, was hurt. "That's wrong for you to say," he said. "I'm your protector." It didn't occur to him that the immigrants might see him in another light: as the brother of an overseer on Friends, which he was.

Also watching, from the gates of the Great House, where bullets whizzed past his head, was McEwan. Rumors were afoot that his coolies would burn down his house, and the factories, that night. A year earlier, after a hundred had fallen grievously ill, the governor had condemned McEwan for neglect. Mutiny may have been simmering ever since. The militia was called in, and McEwan imposed a lockdown in the plantation barracks. At dinnertime, he sent a complimentary bottle of whisky to the courthouse, where Brumell the planter's son and Taylor the overseer's brother were attending to the aftermath. With the aid of two militia officers, they emptied that bottle and three more. That night, Taylor slept curled up, stripped half-naked, on the courthouse floor.

He and the manager weren't the only key players offstage during the incident, which officials deemed a riot. A woman not on the scene, as far as records show, may have ignited it. A placable group waiting to negotiate a better wage had become a force determined, even against guns, to save their comrades from an unjust fate. And in the wings of that metamorphosis, in the wings of the fight, may have been Gooding's kept woman: Cantooh, a free Indian born in the colony. Four years earlier, the pair had left Ogle, a plantation on Georgetown's outskirts where he was an overseer and she an estate laborer's wife. One Sunday in 1899, Ogle's manager had spotted her in Gooding's room. The manager, who disparaged her as a "lewd character," was convinced that she had been to blame. Nonetheless, he immediately fired Gooding. The overseer soon relocated to Berbice and settled Cantooh in a house at Sisters. Everyone there knew that she was his. They called her "Baby Gooding." The couple had even been seen together publicly, as guests at an Indian wedding. A year before the shootings, she had his baby, who died soon after.[3]

What did Cantooh have to do with any threats against Gooding? Did their relationship explain the animosity against him?[4] While hearing Gooding's case for the warrants, the magistrate remarked that he thought the overseer had withheld something. At the inquest, the immigration agent mentioned this remark. Taylor was the scapegoat for the shooting, ultimately forced to retire for failing to arbitrate, promptly, the Friends dispute—and for reclining on the courthouse floor half-naked, drunk and whining of haemorrhoids, while the plantation was in peril. During the inquest, Taylor might have been trying to deflect some blame. Whatever his motive, he opened a line of testimony that was instantly shut down. The attorney general and barrister representing Friends both objected to the detail, and the coroner told Taylor that it was irrelevant.

But it became crucially relevant to the colony's highest official six months later, when one of the men arrested for threats to Gooding's life accused the overseer of assault. Nand Kishore Singh had served two months in prison on the charge that he swore was trumped-up by Gooding. As the indentured man, back from jail, was digging a drain one day, the overseer approached. He ordered the workers to stop as he passed, but Singh did not. His shovelful of mud hit Gooding's face. Infuriated, cursing, the overseer descended into the trench and, Singh said, whacked him. He later complained to the immigration agent, and as he did, he shared a tectonic, incidental detail. He told Taylor's successor: "A *kuli* boy with whose sister Mr Gooding lives came up and caught Mr Gooding by the arm, saying that I did not splash him on purpose and made him desist." None of Singh's witnesses, questioned in front of plantation authorities, would admit to seeing Gooding cuff him. Defeated, the immigrant asked to be transferred, and he was. The immigration agent, meanwhile, had noted the allegation of an affair with a coolie woman. He brought it to McEwan's notice. The manager asked: "What has a woman in Sisters Village got to do with it?"

The agent told him to lean on Gooding if the charge proved true and launched into a lecture about the evils of intimacy with Indian women. It was bad for discipline on plantations, and the government frowned on it, the agent said. McEwan listened but made no comment.

The secret source of disturbances

In 1869, the first year of mass agitation by Indian laborers on Guiana's sugar estates, the government issued a circular, or official memo, to plantation managers. It read: "It appears there are some overseers on estates who, by their intimate relations with the female immigrants, are themselves fostering the laxity of morals which unfortunately obtains to a considerable extent amongst the Indian immigrants." A few cases had been proved beyond a doubt, and the purpose of the circular was to condemn them. It was also to flex the governor's power, under the immigration ordinance, to remove the indentured workers from any estate that neglected or endangered them. That power had never been exercised, but the circular stated firmly that the governor would do what was necessary to force out guilty overseers. Straddling sermon and warning in tone, the proclamation was an extraordinary one for a colony merely three decades removed from the legalized rape of enslaved women.

The circular was issued on 31 August 1869—a month after a shovel gang on Plantation Leonora attacked its deputy manager, in the first major disturbance by indentured laborers in the colony's history. The workers complained that their wages had been unjustly withheld.[5] Over the next few weeks, there were three other serious confrontations between Indian workers and plantation officials across the colony.[6] The circular never mentioned the labor unrest, except obliquely, by declaring: "It is not needful to comment on the pernicious effect such [illicit] behavior on the part of overseers must have amongst the immigrants."[7]

But the following year, a Royal Commission from England commented at length on the pernicious effect, making explicit the link between white plantation officials having sex with Indian women and strikes and uprisings, which intensified over the decades, ending at least nine times in fatal shootings by police. The commission was sparked by former Demerara magistrate G.W. Des Voeux, who had alleged that the incestuous social life of planters, magistrates and immigration agents utterly undermined any safeguards in indenture, allowing for widespread abuse of coolies by their masters. In 1870, an overseer on Canje Creek wrote home to his mother in England:

We are very much annoyed just now by a certain Mr Des Voeux who has written a letter with an hundred and odd clauses in it to the Secretary of State saying that all BG planters are blackguards etc. and bully and cheat their immigrants. It is rather a serious thing for us, as we have to pay a set of commissioners some $80,000 to refute his statements.[8]

And refute they mostly did. However, they did observe: "It is not at all uncommon for overseers, and even managers, to form temporary connections with Coolie women, and in every case with the worst possible consequences to the good order and harmony of the estate."[9] Complaints lodged with immigration agents told them so, as did their own eyes, during visits to half the colony's plantations. A few years later, one commissioner, the abolitionist representative John Edward Jenkins, published a novel set in Guiana. Its heroine, a demure indentured woman preyed upon by a lustful manager, falls in love with a chivalric overseer who tries to save her from both the manager and her increasingly moody husband.[10] In the novel-buying Victorian public's imagination, sexual encounters between colonizing men and colonized women figured either as exploitation or ill-fated romance. The nonfiction account—the commission's report on its findings—made for less sentimental reading. It put the relationships in the context of the woman shortage and plantation realpolitik. The commissioners remarked:

The withdrawal of even a single woman from the coolie dwellings to the overseers' lodge is regarded with jealous eyes by her fellow countrymen; and when it is remembered that any female above childhood is already the actual partner or wife of one of them, it is evident that no surer way could be found of sowing the seeds of discontent and riot. The husband must be considered—he must be made a driver; after a time the woman must be got rid of, someone must be found to take charge of her; in each case it becomes known or is imagined that so-and-so can do anything with such-and-such an overseer, and the abuse of petty authority goes on unchecked. It is our belief, founded on good authority, as well as on incidents which have come to our knowledge, that the recent disturbances have been originally due, in far greater degree than is supposed, to some interference with women on the estate.[11]

Not only did Indian men have to compete with each other for wives, plantation officials, with all the privileges of their race and position, were rivals—when, that is, they bothered with wooing.

The early official warnings about riotous consequences did little to stop the illicit sex. A former chief justice denounced it as "a great grievance to the immigrants" in his exposé on Guianese indenture, titled *The New Slavery*. It couldn't be viewed otherwise, he argued, not with the stark difference in circumstances between coolies and their masters. "The scandalous habit which prevails," Joseph Beaumont wrote, "is by no means to be confounded with the common indulgence of mere vice, but is an evil cognate with and in fact one development of the forcible use of power."[12] Holding physical and economic control over coolie women, overseers often took them as lovers. So common was the practice that the 1896 *Overseer's Manual*, a technical primer on sugar planting, included a cautionary note. In its author's eyes, the women were the ones who abused their power. "Their bright-hued raiment," he warned, "is highly picturesque. Wearing but little clothing, they reveal to the eyes of young and inexperienced overseers more physical charms than young Englishmen and Scotchmen have been accustomed to see, and it is not wonderful that many … of my young confreres have fallen victim to their seductions."[13]

Warnings notwithstanding, the liaisons continued, and so did the agitation on the plantations. In 1890, after receiving reports that several overseers had stolen the wives of indentured men, A.H. Alexander issued another government circular, urging managers to crack down on immorality. It had, the immigration chief said, "proved at times to be the secret source of disaffection and disturbances."[14] The role it played in defiant displays by workers sometimes seemed an open secret. During an 1895 protest in Berbice, the whispers reached a neighboring plantation. At the inquiry into the wounding of twelve protestors, with police bayonets and buck-shot, an Indian from another estate shared what he heard: "The cause of the disturbance among the Skeldon coolies was on account of a driver called Ambah and Mr Phillips the overseer: they interfered with their women and also gave them short pay."[15] Wage grievances often accompanied sexual ones. But the connection may have been, in some cases, mere insinuation. Indian women were so associated with trouble on plantations that a reporter covering one particularly fierce uprising allowed himself to speculate, thrice in one article, that "rebellious spirits were stirred by a far darker passion than a mere desire for increased wages."[16]

Rhetorically speaking, riots to avenge Eastern honor might have seemed a better problem to have than strikes that exposed illegally low wages. That may explain why the distinctly pro-planter Royal Commission highlighted the chaos caused by "immoral relations with coolie women," as the Colonial Office typically put it, as well as why the clearly pro-planter journalist hinted at darker passions. Planters may have welcomed the salacious distraction from charges of economic exploitation. But, dangling the suggestion of illicit sex was different from admitting to it. Being held accountable was even more unthinkable.

After police killed five Indian workers during an 1896 strike on Nonpareil, the plantation's deputy manager evaded a question about his intimacy with the wife of one of the dead men. During the inquest, an attorney for the victims' families tried to ask Gerard Van Nooten about Jamni, describing her as the woman with whom he lived, but the coroner overruled the question. In the witness box at Georgetown's Victoria Law Courts, in the presence of the press, Van Nooten neither confirmed nor denied the relationship. Bantering in the courtroom afterwards, a few men ribbed him about it, and he gave them the impression that the allegation was a fact, but an irrelevant one, because Jamni wasn't indentured.[17] When this got back to A.H. Alexander, the immigration chief started asking his own questions. Two weeks later, the government secretary scribbled a private note to a friend in the Colonial Office about the labor unrest: "That matter," he wrote, "is said to have been the outcome of the acting manager's having taken to himself the wife or woman of one Jungli. As Jungli was shot dead, his resentment for the wrong done him, seems likely to be buried with him."[18]

A twenty-two-year old market gardener by caste, if his emigration pass was accurate, Jungli had arrived in the colony two years earlier, in the midst of a sugar cane industry downturn.[19] The price of cane sugar had fallen in global markets, and Nonpareil, like many plantations, was manipulating wages to compensate, slashing them below the legal minimum by increasing the size of the tasks required to earn a shilling a day. Nonpareil's workers reported earning 2 to 3 shillings for a week's labor.[20] Jungli was one of the leaders of an organized action against the plantation's sleight of hand. For three days in early October, the cane fields burned. The workers asked Van Nooten to raise their pay, and he responded that the plantation was on the brink of financial collapse. He couldn't do anything for them, he said, not unless the Queen intervened with relief for the sugar industry. The workers, pleading that they literally earned starvation wages, asked if the estate could arrange for them to buy rice at cheaper wholesale prices. Van Nooten promised to look into it. Meanwhile, he arranged to have Jungli and three other organizers transferred to another plantation, a convenient move if the overseer did indeed want his wife.[21]

But then, claiming the ringleaders were plotting his murder, Van Nooten instead swore out warrants for their arrests. On 13 October 1896, as hundreds of workers gathered in front of the manager's house to negotiate with him, at a meeting specially arranged by A.H. Alexander, the police executed the warrants, and mayhem broke out. The laborers, throwing stones, rushed the constables and freed the prisoners. They blocked bridges, allegedly cut telephone lines and ran to their barracks for impromptu weapons: cutlasses, sticks, shovels, their tools from the fields. In the ensuing struggle, a man waving a cutlass rigged to the end of a stick knocked the police captain's sword out of his hand, and the captain fired a revolver at him and the friend by his side.[22] Odds are the shots hit Jungli and Kanhai, the only two strikers killed instantly. The coroner found a bullet burrowed in Jungli's back, behind his left shoulder blade.[23] In the end, five workers died, and fifty-nine suffered serious wounds. The coroner concluded that the shooting was justified, and planter arbitrators determined that the wages were fair. But Van Nooten's charges of a murder plot were dropped for lack of evidence.

That's the official account of what happened, the story the archives tell. The unauthorized version, the story the immigrants told, casts Jangli as a career soldier merely passing as market gardener and coolie. According to the grandson of an immigrant who arrived at Nonpareil as a child, the year before the fatal strike, Jungli was its leader, its martyr, its anti-imperial hero.[24] The lore says that he had been a sepoy, one of the native soldiers in the British Indian Army lionized for their fierce valor, ever since the 1857 uprising that the British called the Great Mutiny and the Indians, the First War of Independence.

After that rebellion against British rule, the planters association in London lobbied for the many thousands of defeated sepoys to be sent to the West Indies as convict or exile laborers. Guiana's legislature even drafted proposals to accept 30,000, but sepoys convicted of murder and mutiny were ultimately sentenced to a penal settlement on the Andaman Islands and the rest were disbanded.[25] No soldiers ended up in the Caribbean as part of any organized scheme, but some likely made their way there on their own. They were deprived of career and income, and their families persecuted, creating need enough to leave India. And the region of greatest sepoy unrest was precisely the region that provided the greatest number of recruits for indenture.[26]

Indeed, the first instances of disquiet in Guiana, a decade after the Indian uprising, were blamed on transplanted sepoys.[27] Usually, their presence was raised as a specter, an implied but never proven bogeyman in colonist newspapers; but it was testified to, once. An eyewitness to the first fatal strike, an Indian constable, reported seeing six or seven sepoys in the mix of men and women fighting with hackia sticks and cutlasses on Plantation Devonshire Castle in 1872.[28]

The figure of the sepoy seized the imaginations of both British officials and the indentured, for decades after actual veterans of the Indian rebellion may have arrived on plantations. Jungli was way too young to have been one of them, but gained folk status as a martial hero in the same broad cause. According to the tale handed down to the generations, Van Nooten had tried to rape Jamni, a Brahmin woman who lived on the estate as Jungli's wife and worked as a *khelauni*, or child minder, a privileged position on any plantation because it wasn't hard labor in the fields. As the story goes, when Van Nooten abducted Jamni, she struck the planter in the face with her *berwas*, the heavy silver bangles on her wrists, which a widow ritually breaks when her husband dies. With Van Nooten in pursuit, she fled to the barracks, where Jungli and other men defended her. The clash, in the folk version, was over Jamni rather than plummeting wages. The immigrants demanded that management punish Van Nooten and other sexually exploitative overseers. They did battle in order to protect the chastity of Indian womanhood.

That didn't make their struggle any less an anti-imperial one. In fact, the campaign to end indenture, waged by the nationalists challenging British rule in India, drew heavily on images of the ruined virtue of coolie women. If planters imagined that hinting at affairs with Indian women, then denying or qualifying them, could serve as red herrings, they vastly underestimated the rhetorical significance of a woman's inviolate purity in Indian traditions. After all, weren't armies of monkeys and men dispatched to rescue Sita from the empire-ruling demon who stole her freedom, then made attempts on her honor? In the people's oral history of the Nonpareil uprising, Jungli emerged as epic hero, an incarnation of Ram lunging valiantly forward with his improvised lance to battle the Ravan of British plantocracy.

That plantocracy merely dodged the charge. It feinted. It deflected. It disavowed responsibility. When immigration officials asked about Jamni, Nonpareil's manager declined to answer. It was a private matter, he said, and only Van Nooten could answer.[29] The latter insisted that his reply to the courtroom wags, who asked if the woman was indentured, was purely hypothetical. He claimed to have said: "A man would be a fool to interfere with a bound one." Once again, he neither confirmed nor denied any intimacy. A.H. Alexander alerted Nonpareil's largest stakeholder, the London philanthropist Quintin Hogg, that his employees weren't cooperating. Hogg made them assure him in writing that overseers who stole estate workers' wives were instantly fired. But he told the Colonial Office not to expect his manager "to play the spy on the lives of the white men on the estate." Hogg wrote that a manager should interfere only if an overseer interfered with married coolies, or if he lived "a life of such notorious profligacy as to … render him an improper person to ask a gentleman to associate with."[30] The planter claimed that Van Nooten's woman was neither bound nor married to anyone bound—at least, nobody had proven that she was. Hogg expressed regret that his staff hadn't made that clear to Alexander, whom he knew from youthful days in Demerara. "From what I know of that gentleman," he wrote, "I feel sure he would have pressed the matter no further when he had satisfied himself that the case was not one falling within his duties as protector of the immigrants."

In the end, Alexander issued yet another toothless circular condemning immorality.

Showdown with the government

Eight years later, at Friends, he found himself in the same awkward position, managing the fallout from another strike in which immigrants were shot dead, followed by allegations that an overseer in the eye of the uprising was sleeping with one of their women. Again, he had to confront a manager who winked at decades of government warnings against intimacy with Indian women. As if the official condemnations were mere posturing, all McEwan did to investigate the charge against Gooding was to ask him and accept his denial. Three months later, the immigration office produced proof that the overseer was lying, and McEwan fired him, too late. The manager was judged an "accomplice in an attempt to baffle inquiry" and "mislead and hoodwink … the government."[31] It was hard not to conclude that McEwan was, at the very least, careless. Even before the deadly riot, Alexander had criticized him for "indifference to the welfare of the immigrants under his charge." In 1902, 100 were afflicted with hookworm, anemia, enlarged spleens, scabies and fatal diarrhea; thirteen died on Friends during the outbreak, mainly from intestinal illnesses caused by unclean water. Although declared unfit then, the manager faced no consequences. What finally led Governor James A. Swettenham to call for his dismissal was his breezy attitude to Gooding's indiscretion.

At the time, Swettenham apparently didn't know that McEwan had once kept an Indian mistress at Sisters, too. In the churchyard near the manager's house stood a marble tombstone that was his memorial to the woman.[32] Engraved on it were the words:

I.H.S.
Erected in Loving Memory of Elizabeth Budal
Who Died on 4th December 1898
'Gone But Not Forgotten.'

He called her Elizabeth, had perhaps christened her Elizabeth, but she was born Parbutteah. The daughter of indentured immigrants, she landed in the colony at the age of three, in 1862,[33] the year McEwan was born on Glasgow's outskirts. Theirs was a relationship of long standing. Two of her children were his. Parbutteah was already a wife and mother when he met her at a plantation at the other end of the colony. McEwan took her from an indentured man and, when appointed manager of

Friends, moved her there. His tender epitaph suggests the imponderable: the possibility of a planter's affection, if not love, for a coolie. When the Gooding scandal erupted, their children lived on Friends—whether in the barracks or the Great House is unknown.

McEwan had a wife, whom he described as "very delicate,"[34] and the sight of his illegitimate children could not have helped her health. It's impossible to say whether she knew about them. Had she known, how would she have made sense of her husband? What should posterity make of him? Raised in a two-servant home, the eldest son of a Free Church of Scotland minister, he was a clerk before he ventured to the West Indies at twenty-one.[35] And the fullness of middle age had found him with two half-Indian children and a subaltern lover he valued enough to memorialize. Was Alexander McEwan a sensitive soul who transcended the race and class prejudices of his time, like the heroes of romantic novels about indenture, published during indenture?[36] Would a gallant figure have groused, in the course of denying liability for the illnesses on Friends, that he had to pay the full $55 planter's fee for a new laborer who was pregnant and sick?[37] Was McEwan's tenderness for coolie women confined to the one who shared his bed? And how did she view him?

Ultimately, what mattered wasn't how his wife or mistress viewed him, but how his bosses did. Either they saw him as indispensable, or he benefited from their decision to force a showdown with the government. The New Colonial Company, a titan in the sugar industry, owned Friends. Its chairman, Sir Neville Lubbock, was also chairman of the West India Committee, the moneyed planters lobby in London. Asked on 2 May 1904 to dismiss McEwan, the company stalled. Meanwhile, Alexander advanced another line of attack: How could McEwan not know that Gooding had once been fired for immorality? Didn't he check his references? If the manager claimed ignorance, as he did, ignorance itself would become grounds for censure. New Colonial's attorney, Arthur Summerson, shot back that McEwan hadn't hired the overseer. Robert Duncan, once the company's business representative in Guiana, now a member of its colonial legislature, had. Summerson asked the governor to reconsider.

For his part, Governor Swettenham waited for a reply from Lubbock in London. He waited for two months, and the entire colony waited with him, riveted after Georgetown's *Daily Chronicle* mentioned the standoff, without naming the manager, plantation or charges at bottom. The paper's veiled reference to a scandal in Berbice led to a torrent of anonymous letters to the editor that provided an unprecedented glimpse into the private lives of overseers and revealed just how widespread the taboo practice of keeping Indian women was. The first letter came from Friends. An overseer there wrote: "I think there are few of us who pretend to be moralists, but are there not others in far better positions and perhaps officials themselves who are just as guilty as we are? But money and position cover a multitude of sins in this colony."[38] Events on other estates, earning their own coy mentions in the press, also helped pull back the curtain.

In mid-June, the immigration agent who first asked McEwan to look into Gooding's conduct returned to Friends. McEwan, though embattled, wasn't the reason for the official visit. The manager of a nearby sugar estate was. Five years earlier, when W.E. Warne was head overseer on Providence, he had enticed the wife of an indentured man on Friends. The worker had borrowed money to pay the $70 bride price for Atwaria, born free at Sisters Village. A month after their wedding in 1898, she left to visit her sick mother and never returned. Her husband Bhopat discovered much later that Warne was keeping her and that she had borne him three daughters. One was stillborn; two survived. The Berbice birth register listed their race as mixed and their father as unknown. "I have seen them from afar," Bhopat testified. "They are clear-skinned and do not look like East Indian children but a Sahib's children."[39] Saying that he was a poor and lowly man, a barber by caste, he asked that Warne refund his $70.

Warne denied the relationship, and so did Atwaria. She claimed to have left Bhopat because he "was keeping another woman, and he beat me and drove me away."[40] Summoned to Friends to testify, Atwaria wove a tale of a half-white, half-black lover who fathered her children then disappeared. "I did not ask the mulatto man his name and he did not tell me," she swore. "I do not know what work he did. ... I never spoke much to him." Her mother explained: "It is not the Indian rules to ask names after marriage." But many were the witnesses to her relationship with Warne. They had been seen going to each other at night and walking out together "hundreds of times." The barracks took note when, around the time that Gooding's troubles began, Warne custom-built a house for Atwaria, off the plantation. And his butler testified to being present when Atwaria gave birth to the overseer's stillborn child. This cost the butler his job.

Warne also retaliated against another witness. He ordered her cattle driven off the plantation's pastureland because she told the immigration agent what she knew. The woman was friendly with Atwaria, who had confided why she had actually left Bhopat: Warne had promised to care for her. The confidante also shared a detail that shows the leverage that the kept women of overseers sometimes gained, if they were savvy. And Atwaria was. At the beginning of June, the couple had quarreled. Warne wanted to leave for England for six months, without providing for her and without giving her formal title to the land where her new house stood. Recently, Warne had been made manager, a milestone in an overseer's career that enlarged both his wallet and his chances for a wife: a legally recognized, socially acceptable, white one. Atwaria probably realized this when she threatened to complain at the immigration office. She set down her terms for allowing him to sail unmolested for England: $700, cattle, a donkey and a donkey cart.

Right around then, plantation managers across the colony received another circular from A.H. Alexander. It called attention, without naming names, to recent instances of managers failing to stop illicit sex with Indian women and repeated the threat to seize the indentured from errant estates. When the manager of another New Colonial plantation, Taymouth Manor, shared the circular with his overseers, two fell on their swords. The head overseer and factory overseer both had Indian mistresses. They pleaded ignorance of any disapproving circulars, and they claimed to have banished the women from the county as soon as they learned of Alexander's stern memo. Their boss grudgingly fired them. He gave them two weeks' salary and let them stay in the overseers' quarters until they could auction their furniture. But he grumbled that the government's moralism would lead to the "disjointing [of] the whole immigration system."

Within days, the two overseers petitioned for their jobs back. They promised never to transgress again. And within days, Alexander relented. He accepted their defense that management had never brought the government's repeated warnings to their attention. And he berated New Colonial's attorney for permitting a climate in which the men could plead ignorance. The circulars lacked the force of law. The government had no authority to fire overseers and managers from private estates, and the men hadn't committed any crimes. But Alexander maintained that morality was essential to the rule of planters over their coolies. He wrote: "A manager or overseer who maintains in every way his self-respect and his position of superiority to laborers can and does secure far better results than one who degrades himself." June had fled, and McEwan was still entrenched on Friends. By endorsing the reinstatement of Tay-mouth Manor's overseers, Alexander showed New Colonial how conciliatory he could be, but scolded its directors. Having extended this barbed olive branch, he pointed out that two monthly Royal Mail ships had come and gone with no word from Lubbock.

Glibly, Summerson explained the silence. He said that his bosses believed the governor to be reconsidering his opinion and were merely awaiting his final decision. Alexander replied: "That was His Excellency's final decision, and it stands irrevoca-bly." When, demanded Alexander, will you remove McEwan? The question was met with a flat-out refusal, forcing an ultimatum. Swettenham, already aware that he was being transferred to Jamaica, declared that he would do what no governor in six decades of indenture had ever done. If the company failed to dismiss McEwan within ten days, Swettenham would redistribute the 339 indentured laborers on Friends to other plantations. Days before the deadline, New Colonial tried another delay tactic. Alexander balked. He warned the company that it would forfeit its *entire* order of new coolies for the next season, for *all* its plantations, if it continued to defy the government. And he threatened to lay the sordid details of the dispute, the riot and the illnesses before authorities in India.

Alexander—a Scotsman born in Grenada, a Tory with a passion for yachting, a retired militia officer with four soldier sons—was a conservative and a flexible man. He had to be to fill the oxymoronic role he held for thirty-three years, first in Jamaica, then in Guiana. He was the designated watchdog for the indentured in planter-run colonies where the system for immigrants to get justice was so rigged, they rarely turned to it, preferring strikes and uprisings to resolve labor disputes instead.[41] Indeed, Alexander's department was as much cause for riot as anything awry in overseers' beds or plantation pay lists. At sixty-one, a year from the grave, the immigration agent-general had a well-toned muscle for compromise. New Colonial must have been as perplexed by his stubbornness as he was by its. All the company had to do to stop the impending disaster was get McEwan off Friends. How they did it—whether by leave of absence or ceding him another role in their vast commercial outfit—was their business. Perhaps seeing another barbed olive branch, New Colonial suggested giving McEwan two months of leave—on the condition that he return to managing Friends afterwards. Alexander acidly noted that New Colonial had proposed to reward McEwan with an extended holiday.

In London, the West India Committee became involved—not surprisingly, given that its director was also New Colonial's director. The battle was shaping up to be a strange, internecine one: the planters against their unabashedly pro-planter government. *The Chronicle* laid odds that, in this confrontation, it was the government that "possess[ed] the whip hand." The day after Swettenham issued his ultimatum, the British Guiana Planters Association decided that none of the nine companies that owned the colony's fifty-odd plantations would accept any workers seized from Friends. They would have to be warehoused at Georgetown's Immigration Depot, at taxpayer expense; and a shipping contract would have to be broken and £500 forfeited to cancel New Colonial's order of new coolies. The governor's moral crusade would be costly.

His deadline passed. Nothing happened. Still, New Colonial asked the Supreme Court to stay any removal of immigrants while it sued the government, challenging its right to seize them. Days later, the court denied the injunction, in sympathy with the governor's grave responsibility to prevent another riot on Friends. Yet still, in packed chambers the next day, the legislature entertained a resolution by two planter members to express displeasure with the governor. One was Robert Duncan, the former New Colonial attorney who had hired Gooding.

The governor rose to defend himself. He did have supporters in this fight. By a show of hands one Sunday, the Mission Chapel congregation in New Amsterdam had shown its appreciation for his efforts at "social purity," and all eleven churches in the British Guiana Congregational Union voted to express their approval. A Hindu pandit had praised him as a "strong-handed ruler" standing up for Indians who couldn't, for fear of retaliation, defend themselves. But behind his back, in a flash of raffish schoolboy irony, the planters had christened him "Governor Sweetman." ("Sweet man" is Creolese for ladies man.)[42] In a letter to politicians in London, Lubbock had denounced the governor's actions as misplaced "heroics." Both detractors and backers portrayed him as a "high priest of morality."[43] *The Chronicle* had applauded his earnest attempt to save the colony from becoming "a by-word to civilization and Christianity." And Swettenham did quote the Bible as he confronted planters in the legislature. He said that he "wish[ed] sincerely that the government and the Immigration Department could shut their eyes to the immorality that goes on…, and pass by on the other side like the Levite and say this unfortunate matter was no concern of theirs at all." But he could not. He had an official duty, he said, and the stakes for shirking it were high, for everyone involved, perhaps especially the planters who wished to censure him.

Swettenham argued that the government of India was watching "with jealous care." What, he asked, do you imagine the consequences will be "if you shake their confidence that you will do right and justice and fairness to the people of India who are brought this enormous distance and trusted to your honour"? The planters were imperiling their own labor supply; if they weren't careful, indenture would be abolished, just as slavery had been. He quoted the by-then hoary words of the 1871 Royal Commission, connecting plantation riots to overseers bedding coolie women. Gooding's relationship with Cantooh might have provoked resentment on Friends, the governor said. Her brother held a coveted position there, at the *koker* or sluice gate—a job that, as Swettenham scoffed, involved "raising and lowering the *koker* two or three times a day and sitting on it for the rest of the time to see that it doesn't run away." Didn't the members recall that there had been a riot on Friends?

"About wages," a planter member interjected.

"The honourable member suggests that the riot was about wages," the governor said, then bespoke Nand Kishore Singh's case that false charges by Gooding had been the cause. "It may or not be true, but a man who indulges in the practices of Mr Gooding cannot expect to be treated with the same respect as the man who respects himself would be treated, and hence these troubles."

"He threw mud on Mr Gooding," the member objected.

"Mr Gooding lost his self-respect by keeping a coolie woman," Swettenham shot back, prompting raucous cries of "No! No!" from the legislature.

"I am speaking from the coolies point of view," the governor clarified. "The coolies will say, 'Here is an overseer living with a woman of our country. He is no better than us,' and lose respect for him."

Strikes and uprisings weren't the only signs of this disrespect. In the previous nineteen months, nineteen immigrants had been convicted and sentenced to hard labor for assaulting overseers in the fields.[44] Swettenham knew that it revolted the members to have to deal with this matter, as it did him. It repulsed him especially because McEwan was a friend. "But of course," the governor said, "I have to put my personal feelings aside and do my duty. I have done my duty to the coolies and the country, and I expect the members of the court to do theirs."

And they did: the resolution lost 10–6, although all the planter legislators voted for it. Swettenham seemed to have triumphed. Yet, he took no immediate steps to move the immigrants and softened his stance to transferring only those wanting to go. Removing all would have proved disastrous. Those who grew rice on Friends would have to be compensated for lost crops. And what about those married to the estate's non-indentured workers, who couldn't be moved against their will? They might not take kindly to a forced, mass transfer. Swettenham didn't want to cause a riot, in the attempt to prevent one; but he had prevailed enough not to back down, either.

Just then, the marble tombstone near the Great House made its way into the record. In a memo to Swettenham outlining their case, Alexander disclosed its existence. But no news of it reached the Colonial Office for another half year, well after the dispute had been resolved. Within two weeks of the revelation about McEwan, New Colonial capitulated. Its directors cabled Summerson to drop the suit against the government and send the manager home. Had Swettenham quietly let the company know the dirt he possessed? Was he a gentleman, discreet because the manager had a delicate wife? Or was the official silence part of a backchannel strategy to force New Colonial's hand? The injunction had failed, and so had the planter attempt to censure the governor. Perhaps that alone was enough for the company to end its legal battle.

Show by the government

Ever after, Swettenham's name would be associated with a crackdown on immorality. Those who called him Governor Sweetman blamed him for driving overseers from the sugar industry by introducing "some drastic law debarring [them] of their favorite pastime and hobby."[45] Planters, government officials and the press all agreed that his legacy was to insist on holding managers accountable, after three decades of spasmodic, half-hearted, unheeded warnings about sex with Indian women. "Circulars ad nauseam have already been issued on this subject," *The Chronicle* editorialized. "The documents have been conveniently shelved and forgotten. ... In holding the estates' management to be at fault, His Excellency carried the question into a new phase."[46] The American press even took note. Pointing to Swettenham as paragon, *The Wall Street Journal* urged that New York's financial industry likewise hold managers accountable for employee misdeeds.[47] (That newspaper compared the particular misdeeds in Guiana to "some of the most serious accusations made against overseers in the [American] South fifty years ago.") Yet the facts do not bear out these perceptions of the governor's victory and lasting impact.

Shortly after McEwan was fired, the manager who fired his butler for revealing his affair with a coolie woman evaded serious consequences. Providence Plantation's owner acknowledged that Warne had kept the woman. Writing to Alexander, Sir Henry Davson made rhetorical concessions, declaring his "sympathy with and desire to cooperate ... in raising the moral standard of those employed on the estates." He promised to prevent future misconduct, but not to fire or demote Warne. Alexander quietly thanked Davson for his attention to the matter.

At the same time, at another Davson plantation on the Berbice River, an overseer returned from England to find that the Indian man whose wife he had enticed years earlier had been emboldened to complain, again, to the authorities. When the man had first discovered the affair, he had beaten his wife then informed the local immigration agent. She had promptly left him, and the agent had referred the complaint to the manager. Not only had the manager failed to investigate, he had fired the Indian, an unindentured worker. The coolie had held onto his job by begging for it, and the woman had moved to a neighboring village, where she ultimately gave birth to the overseer's son, christened Adam. The baby was a year old when her ex approached the authorities again. "If she will return to me, I will take her back," he stated.

Nothing had changed since his first petition. The overseer still wanted the woman; he paid her rent, provided her with a washerwoman, sent her letters while on leave in England. Before going, he left her money and instructed a shop to supply her groceries. When her husband sought redress the second time, it was two weeks after McEwan's dismissal, and the Indian may have been testing whether or not the climate had truly changed. Could he finally expect satisfaction for a wrong that, were the seducer a coolie, would undoubtedly have led to transfer? Confronted with the charge, the overseer resigned. Nothing, however, happened to the manager who had treated it as lightly as McEwan had treated the charge against Gooding. The Colonial Office noted the discrepancy, but did not press for accountability. "I don't think we should stir it up anymore," an official there concluded.

Indians weren't the only ones testing the firmness of any new resolve. A week before Swettenham departed his post and the colony, the firm Booker Brothers fired an overseer for seducing a married Indian woman but asked if it could reassign him to another plantation. Alexander objected; the indiscretion occurred right after he had issued his most recent circular condemning immorality. He also refused to be lenient with Nonpareil's head overseer, Charles Barratt. He was to be married and promoted to manager when it resurfaced that he had, for two decades, kept an Indian woman who bore him five children. The relationship was first reported to immigration authorities in 1902, and Barratt had said: "I have nothing whatever to do with Parbuteah and her affairs." Although officials had discovered his name in the birth register as the father of her eldest child, they had let the matter drop. But they had to pursue it when, in the heat of the showdown with New Colonial, more immigrants identified her as "Mr Barratt's girl." The overseer then claimed that the relationship was over. To reports that he stayed with her for a month before a recent England trip, he swore that he only visited for their children's sake. "I was anxious to see everything in order for their welfare before leaving," he said. He acknowledged the children as his, even paying their way at respectable schools in the capital.

Pleading his case was Robert Duncan, the plantation's attorney and one of the legislators who had moved to censure the governor just a few months earlier. He told Alexander that he wouldn't promote Barratt as originally intended, but thought it too harsh to fire him for an intimacy that was a thing of the past, which his engagement to someone else surely indicated it was. How, Duncan asked, would the man support five illegitimate children without a job? Alexander replied: "This case is not different to others and in fairness cannot be treated differently." Duncan pushed back: "My experience has been that in dealing with such cases, no exact line of procedure has been adopted and that each case has been dealt with on its own merits." It didn't help Duncan's case to point out the lack of a consistent policy. Barratt did not get his dispensation. But at least four others had gotten theirs, after promising not to sin again.

Meanwhile, McEwan was the only manager held accountable—but not for long. Two months after being fired, he petitioned the Colonial Office: "If the late governor's harsh decree is allowed to stand, it means my utter ruin." He invoked his "very delicate wife." And he repeated his defense: he didn't know that Gooding kept a coolie woman and, in any case, she was outside his sphere of protection as a free woman born in the colony who neither worked nor lived on his plantation. "I am punished as a scapegoat," McEwan declared, "whilst lately the government has let off several overseers for committing the very offence with which Mr Gooding was charged." The Secretary of State for the Colonies, Alfred Lyttelton, suggested that McEwan be rehired in a few months, with the caveat that it would be "disastrous to permit an impression to get around that the planters were too powerful for the [new] governor." It was then that Swettenham's replacement officially disclosed details of McEwan's own long-term intimacy with a coolie woman. Nonetheless, the Colonial Office permitted his reappointment as a plantation manager in Guiana—on the condition that he withdraw his charge that Alexander was selectively lenient.

In the final analysis, New Colonial won. Swettenham—not McEwan, not the immigrants—was removed, receiving what one critic described as "an Irish promotion" to Jamaica, at the time a lesser colony. By the end of 1905, Alexander was dead of a heart attack. As legacy, he left yet another circular. It asked managers to satisfy themselves of the good moral conduct of overseers before hiring them and to find out, if they were leaving another plantation, why. Like all other circulars, it lacked the clarity and force of a statute. Alexander's own decisions on particular transgressors showed just how open to interpretation the policy was, and the actions of his successors continued to demonstrate how little his circulars mattered.

Three years after his death, his old adversary, the planter legislator Duncan, hired an overseer for Nonpareil who had been dismissed from another plantation over an Indian woman.[48] The manager who fired him promptly informed the immigration office that Duncan hadn't done what the circular suggested he should. He had never inquired into the overseer's character or asked why he was fired. The manager, who had followed the unwritten rules, had lost an overseer with unique technical skills to a rival who didn't follow the rules. How was that just? The manager soon learned what kind of justice he could expect when the overseer sued him for libel—and won. [The judge trusted the overseer's claim that, when the woman stole into his quarters, he was afflicted with venereal disease and thus unable to have sex.] The owners of the plantation held liable for damages begged the Colonial Office for some clarity: If they followed the circulars, would they end up in court again? What was their duty? The answer came, frustratingly, in the form of another circular. Alexander's successor declared that "it would greatly assist this department" if managers informed him when they fired overseers for intrigues with Indian women. "I would be much obliged if you should find it convenient to do so," he wrote.[49]

Ultimately, the public performance over Friends was of little import. Swettenham had far more impact on the lives of Indian women when, in 1904, he exempted Indian parents from compulsory education laws for girls, a policy that stayed in effect for three decades. In the end, the battle between the government and the planters was a kind of Christ-leela, a cathartic morality play with little effect on sex between Indian women and plantation officials. The practice persisted widely for decades, occupying an unstable, disputed borderland between exploitation and sway, as mixed-up and mixed-breed as indenture itself.

A pretty woman's advantage?

Not long after the dispute over Friends, my great-grandmother landed nine miles northeast of the tombstone engraved "Gone But Not Forgotten." In 1906, she and her newborn arrived at Rose Hall Plantation, on Canje Creek. Sujaria's granddaughters all told me that she did no field work there. "Dey send her, and she cyaan make it in the field, because her feet was soft," one said.[50] Instead, Sujaria was assigned to be a child minder. Some plantations provided crèches, at times little more than sacks spread on the ground beneath barracks, where mothers could leave young children to be cared for by *khelaunis*.* (*Khelauna* means plaything and also describes an ecstatic genre of North Indian folk song celebrating births.) Compared to manual labor under a harsh sun, a *khelauni's* job was relatively comfortable, one reserved for the favored or the aged.[51] This was the job that Jamni, the woman at the edges of the Nonpareil uprising, either as kept woman or rape victim, reportedly had. And this was the job that my great-grandmother was given. Perhaps this was because she had a baby to support alone and her caste background had made her useless in the fields. Or, perhaps, she possessed a pretty woman's advantage.

Stories of beauty's sway have survived. Grandchildren heard and passed on tales of how, sometimes, it could be useful in escaping field labor. One Guianese doctor's wife described the protest mounted by her grandmother Phuljharee in Suriname in 1881: "When she was told to go and work in the field and was handed a cutlass, she showed her soft, small hands. She there and then sat down and refused to move, so here there was real trouble. And because she was young, pretty and a fighter, the [planter's] family were very lenient with her."[52] They made her a nurse's assistant in the plantation hospital. Similarly, an upper-caste recruit to Trinidad in the 1890s cried when an overseer showed her the fieldwork she was assigned. "He could see that she was a very delicate person, and he told her that he would assign her to domestic duties," said the granddaughter of the coolie woman and the overseer, eight decades later. "I suppose after that they got friendly, and she had two children for him."[53]

How did my great-grandmother get her coveted job? Did she shed tears? Did she stage her own sit-in? Was there an overseer in the wings, expecting something in return? All I know is that the manager, Charles Bethune, ultimately arranged a match between Sujaria and an immigrant who plied the trade of his *ahir* caste, minding cows and selling milk. This man, Dilchand, noticed her when he delivered milk at her crèche. Sujaria next gave birth eight years after arriving at Rose Hall. The baby, my great-aunt Belle, was strikingly fair, "white like white people white," as the family likes to say. Like my equally light-skinned grandfather Lal Bahadur, she had children and grandchildren who could pass for white and others who couldn't. No one has ever questioned her origins; but they have wondered about his, because of that dash on Sujaria's emigration pass, the emptiness on the line set aside for husband's name.

---

* Although it was illegal for children under ten to labor, the plantations regularly employed them as porters in so-called Creole gangs, carrying manure or water into the fields.

There are two clues to Lal Bahadur's parentage. His shipboard birth certificate listed his father's name and coordinates: Deodhar, in India. And growing up, my father was told that he was a *gosain*, because his father's father was. Originally, *gosains* (meaning "masters of the emotions") were Hindu ascetics. Traditionally, theirs was not a caste to be born into, but a calling: to renounce worldly comforts, such as sex and clothing. In the eighteenth century, however, when naked armies of *gosains* fought first against, and then for, the British East India Company, they embraced identities both martial and marital. These princely monastic soldiers had assets enough for heirs, including biological sons born of prostitutes, concubines and legal spouses.[54] By the late nineteenth century in Bihar, the title had become even more fluid. *Gosains* were celibate—or not. They were married householders with family responsibilities—or unattached, wandering *sadhus*. Sometimes, they were temple priests.[55] Sujaria had said she was on pilgrimage when deceived into indenture, and widows and other outcasts on pilgrimage sometimes gave themselves to temple priests who believed that sex with unmarriageable women was a path to God for the elect.

My grandfather's conception remains an unsettling mystery. Whatever the truth—whether his father was white man or *gosain*, holy man or householder, whether Sujaria was herself Anglo-Indian or simply a fair-skinned Indian—there are no suggestions in the family that the child she had after serving as *khelauni* was anything but the daughter of a driven cow-minder who left India in 1896. There is no inherited innuendo that any plantation official kept my great-grandmother.

Freedom's exercise, or slavery's excesses?

Women who were kept clearly benefited. In addition to easier jobs, they sometimes gained houses of their own in which to live, away from the crowded barracks. At a Berbice plantation in 1908, the manager provided his woman with "a neat little cottage" and $6 a month for their child, and the deputy manager reportedly assigned an indentured man to be butler to his kept woman. The woman's uncle was the plantation's head driver.[56] The records indicate that Indian drivers often arranged women, including their own family members, for plantation officials. Indeed, some drivers may have won or kept their positions that way. Women, too, were promoted as reward. My great-aunt knew one who was made a female driver, or *sardarin*, after bearing an overseer's child. Cumberland Village knew her as "Susie Sardarin."[57] The Colonial Office, meanwhile, was convinced that women kept by planters held the power of blackmail as long as the men could, theoretically, be punished.[58] But did the relationships signal that the women engaged in them were free or, on the contrary, that they wanted to be? Testifying before a Royal Commission, the Enmore house servant Bechu told of a ship brother unable to marry a woman because an overseer desired her. The indentured man couldn't compete. The overseer could—and did—ultimately purchase the woman's freedom.[59] Ironically, her choice only served to underscore her bondage.

The Colonial Office records, unreliable narrators that they are, rarely tell tales of rape and unrecognized children. They leave gaps. Grapple, for instance, with the untold in the report of an unnamed indentured woman found guilty and sentenced to death for killing her newborn on a Berbice plantation on June 19, 1913.[60] She had arrived in the colony sixteen months earlier. No mere single woman, she was a religiously committed celibate, or *sadhin*. The immigration chief wrote of her:

She did little work but her conduct was quite satisfactory and, to use the words of the manager of the estate: 'She was held in very great respect by one and all on the estate', and it came as a very great surprise to all when it was found that she had given birth and [done] away with a child.

Her story begs the question: What circumstances make a baby unwanted enough to prompt infanticide? And how does a *sadhin* come to be with child in the first place? Was her celibacy a guise to resist sexual service, if not indentured service, in the West Indies? Or was she raped? The records do not say. But they do say that the following year, a woman on a Demerara River plantation resisted an overseer's attempt at sexual assault, wounding him with a cutlass.[61] Officials dismissed her accusation and imprisoned her for five years. Clearly, not all sexual encounters between planter and coolie were mutually desired, or mutually beneficial.

In the *Ramayan*, Sita was Ravan's captive and kidnap victim. What coolie women were, precisely, is much harder to define. The archives and oral sources provide competing answers: objects of rape versus concubines with leverage. During the Friends controversy, overseers writing to *The Chronicle* tried to subvert the newspaper's charge that their sexual intrigues recalled the worst excesses of slavery. One ventured that it was actually Swettenham's crusade that led "one to suppose that the days of slavery, though abolished, were in danger of being inaugurated again." In outraged tones, the anonymous letter writers argued that Indian women born in the colony were "free British subjects." Who, they asked, should presume to overrule women who "of their own free will and with their parents' consent form these unions"?

The men claimed consent as a defense, but failed to provide some crucial context. The hidden dynamics behind choices made by the women were laid bare in a barbed exchange between an Indian letter writer identifying himself as DHARMA-CHARI, a name cueing righteousness, and a planter signing off as NOBLESSE OBLIGE. The Indian wrote:

As soon as an overseer eyes a nice looking coolie girl, she must fall a prey to him with the assistance of a *sirdar* or driver, who plays a great figure in it. … If the girl does not consent and exposes the matter, she with her whole family will be turned off the estate. Of course, some fault is found with them as an excuse.

He reported recent retaliations: a family of eight had been ordered off an estate and a woman, locked up by a driver who doubled as constable. In a contemptuous riposte, NOBLESSE OBLIGE blamed Indian men for corrupting overseers and managers by offering up their wives and daughters for sale. DHARMA-CHARI countercharged that if money was ever broached, it was the overseers who introduced it, as "inducement and encouragement." And he insisted that kept women were shunned by their community, including their parents. The women seemed to occupy an uncertain middle ground between slavery and liberty, a kind of demilitarized zone where coercion and incentive intermingled. The consequences, both positive and negative, awaiting them and their families if they refused determined their choices.

Overseers should have sympathized with the argument that exploitative systems led people to do what they otherwise wouldn't. It was, after all, the excuse they advanced for their own lapses. In innumerable letters to the editor during the Friends dispute, they explained that they couldn't marry. The overseers claimed that their paltry salaries left them as "poor as a kirk mouse,"[62] making marriage unrealistic and dooming most "to a life of single cussedness."[63] Many employment contracts in fact required that overseers be single.[64] In 1905, soon after the uproar over McEwan, A.H. Alexander accused New Colonial of "conniving at concubinage." The company had fired a Scottish overseer because he intended to marry a Creole widow.[65] A company official explained: "[Y]oung overseers as a rule are not in receipt of a salary adequate for the support of a wife and family, and we venture to think that improvident early marriages are as prejudicial to the interests of a young overseer as to those of an employer."[66] The company didn't explicitly ban marriage, but it did reserve the right to decide when matrimony was wise for its overseers. Apparently, it wasn't wise if the bride wasn't white.

In this, the company acted oddly like guardian to underage wards. And much like guardians, plantation managers were often placed in charge of the living allowances of their subordinates. Overseers received a generous monthly stipend, equal to their salary, but it usually went directly to managers, to provide room and board. One overseer's wife charged that managers made a profit from this system.[67] Overseers lived in group quarters. They ate what the Great House provided, but weren't always invited to eat it there. Although their backgrounds were often middle-class, even entitled, many managers' wives saw them as unsavory characters unfit to be introduced to their friends. One manager's wife, writing to *The Chronicle* in 1889, summed up the sentiment:

There are, as I suppose every one will admit, men whose overseers may be simply admirable, whom one may respect for their thorough knowledge of their work, whom yet few ladies would care to see at their tables. For whether rightly or not, in the dining room good business ability is quite secondary to such trivial matters as the way of handling one's knife and fork, or even the legitimate use before dinnertime of a nail brush and a clean collar.[68]

The rare overseer who married was expected to continue bunking with bachelor mates, disdained as ever at the manager's table, while his own wife lived separately, in a nearby village. In 1904, any "bold enough to announce his intention of [marrying] would be looked upon as an irresponsible maniac," as one ex-overseer put it.[69] In this context, prohibited and interracial sex was justified as systemic. Or, as the letter writer MAN OF THE WORLD concluded: "It is only like human nature that the men cast around for consolation. While marriage is discouraged, the other thing will have to be tolerated."[70]

But this other thing wasn't just tolerated. It was savored in ways that necessary evils tend not to be, as demonstrated by the reminiscences of one overseer who shared all the details, in smirking, laddish prose in a planters journal in 1961. From the distance of old age, Leslie H.C. Phillips recollected how commonplace it was for overseers to bed Indian women when he arrived in Demerara in 1915, at the age of sixteen. He admitted that:

Besides the occasional assignation a-back, a fellow would sometimes invite a girl to his quarters for an evening of conversation and other pleasantries. Such visits were of necessity made after dusk, for "Krasbi"* took a dim view of things if charges of sexual misconduct between staff members and immigrant women were made and substantiated. ... Looking back on a period that offered maximum temptation and opportunity, one is inclined to exclaim, like Clive of India at his famous impeachment trial, 'My God, Mr Chairman! At this moment, I stand astonished at my own moderation.'

A previous overseer had sawed a trap door into the bedroom floor, in case he was ever caught with an immigrant woman. Phillips rued that the escape route was sealed by the time he inherited the quarters. He recounted an episode that made him wish for the trap door. A woman he described as "a comely but slightly promiscuous young Madrasi" had spent the night with him. When dawn found them still together, her husband came knocking. Phillips panicked and sent another overseer to get the man drunk. After half-emptying a bottle of rum, the husband knocked again. All he wanted was to ask his wife where his clothes were. But then he noticed the overseer's rifle. The coolie, an ex-sepoy, begged to be drilled. Phillips barked a few commands at the former lance corporal, who marched back and forth, fondling the rifle, remembering a higher self. Then he left his wife with the overseer. Phillips recounted giving the man "the assurance that when conniving night again returned to cover such delicate manoeuvres, his property would be returned to him in good order, reasonable wear and tear excepted."

In this winking comedy of errors, the heroic sepoy was reduced to an impotent buffoon who "found more gratification in rum-drinking than in any other pleasure." And the woman confirmed every stereotype of a coolie woman: a *randi*, choosing to be with the overseer, purely for the sake of her libido. Phillips depicted the couple as entirely free agents, although they were bound coolies. "By mutual consent," he wrote, "each permitted the other unquestioned choice of leisure activities. Their ideas of entertainment differed; she being interested in the body, and he in the spirit, so to speak." In his eyes, it was the coolie woman's nature—her intrinsic, unbridled sensuality—that accounted for his good fortune. While failing to rise above the system that employed him, Phillips failed also to see how that system made it hard for

---

* In Guiana, immigration agents were called "krasbi," after the early Immigration Agent-General James Crosby.

Indian women to transcend, too. He didn't understand that indenture enabled his maximum opportunity for assignations in the cane field. Nor did he realize that others might view them as rape and a call to arms, to overthrow the system that corrupted and violated their women.

The arsenal of rhetoric

On 9 September 1913, in the Viceroy's Legislative Council in Delhi, a pioneer in India's nationalist movement spoke aloud the name of my great-grandmother's plantation, uttering into history that remote rectangle of mud, my own. Invoking it in the anti-colonial cause, Surendra Nath Banerjee asked: "Has there recently been a case of collision between the police and some Indian coolies at a sugar plantation, Rose Hall [Canje Creek], Berbice, in British Guiana?" At sixty-four, Banerjee doubted the confrontational tactics that had been so crucial to dismantling indenture in South Africa, two years before. The Brits had nicknamed this elder statesman Surrender Not Banerjee but he had evolved, over time, into a conciliatory figure. He consulted the Viceroy before posing the question: "Is it the case that the police went fully armed and equipped with a Maxim gun to secure the arrest of five Indian coolies, and that resistance being offered, the police fired two volleys upon the coolies, killing sixteen and wounding thirty?"[71]

Six months earlier, on 13 March 1913, Rose Hall had indeed become a scene of carnage. Police killed fifteen workers, including a woman they shot in the stomach, and injured another thirty-nine, seriously enough to warrant amputations. It was perhaps the deadliest suppression of indenture-era unrest throughout the Caribbean.[72]

Sujaria was living on the plantation or right outside it, in Cumberland Village when the colony's police chief, Colonel G.C. de Rinzy, paraded through with a phalanx of men and a Maxim gun. That weapon of war had been credited with swiftly subduing large swathes of Africa for colonial rule in the 1890s, as much because of the panic inspired by its fearsome appearance in battle as the bullets it discharged rapid-fire. Through Cumberland to Rose Hall's Great House, de Rinzy marched with the creature-like machine gun. Leaving it there, he led seventy men into the "nigger yard" where the immigrants lived. In the fusillade that followed, five free and ten bound workers were killed, including some just sitting in their rooms when policemen's bullets, missing their mark or having none, hit them.

The violence was the climax of six weeks of agitation by the plantation's Indian laborers, both the indentured and others who, like my great-grandmother, were by then free. The trouble had started when the manager, James Smith, broke his promise to give the workers four holidays in exchange for forfeiting Sundays off during the sugar-grinding season.[73] His breach of faith infuriated the immigrants. For a day, they defied his order to work. As a result, Smith had seven men criminally prosecuted, for mere labor violations. Hundreds had been absent from work, but only these seven were punished, jailed for six months. The injustice of it roused the indentured to express their grievances. One man accused a driver of assault, but the magistrate threw out the charge. Several women alleged starvation wages and regular beatings by drivers, but the immigration agent dismissed their complaints. "You are strong, healthy women," he told them. "Some of you have healthy-looking babies. You don't look as if you were starved." In the weeks ahead, the shovel gang struck several times to protest against illegally low wages. As usual, manager arbitrators were dispatched, and as usual they determined the wages to be fair.

The wrongs exposed by the immigrants weren't merely economic. There had also been insults to their honor. They claimed that the plantation's head driver Jugmohan reassigned women from one man to another. Any man who wanted to keep his wife had to pay $1. This pimp-like shakedown, as well as the driver's many other sins and extortions, incensed the immigrants. A revered pandit at Cumberland, banned by Jugmohan from performing religious ceremonies at Rose Hall, had fanned their outrage. The immigrants demanded that the driver be fired, but the immigration agent failed to investigate their charges. Indeed, the system did nothing for the workers, except give them the four days off that they had been promised.

In retaliation for the unrest, the manager requested the transfer of five men he deemed ringleaders, and the immigration agent obliged. The five men were called to court, without knowing why. The county police inspector was there, waiting with a car to take them, instantly and forcibly, to five different plantations. The mass of immigrants at the courthouse objected, and the men refused to climb into the car. They said they needed time to gather their property, their wives, their savings. The police promised to send all on later, but the men resisted, asking: "But how will you find what we have buried in the ground?" The crowd grew restive, and the police released the men, for the time being.

But twenty-five armed constables were posted to Rose Hall. The next day, the immigration agent general arrived from the capital to lend authority to the transfer. One of its targets, a Muslim scribe literate in English, a newcomer to the colony and to agricultural labor, waved a soiled copy of the immigration ordinance that he had scavenged in India. Maula Bux knew that its provisions were routinely violated, and he insisted that management lacked legal grounds for a transfer. "They know I can read and suspect me of teaching the people not to go to their work, so they [falsely] put this blame on me," he said. In front of the colony's immigration chief, Bux vowed: "Only my dead body can you remove from this plantation."

In the days ahead, the police ranks grew to forty, and the immigrants kept striking. The indentured urged the unindentured not to work. One day, while escorting free immigrants into the fields to work, the police narrowly escaped a clash with the indentured. Then, a week after the police garrisoned themselves on the estate, they searched the immigrant barracks, fruitlessly, for firearms. The laborers heard rumors that the police had entered their rooms to molest their wives. Sensing the mood, Berbice's police inspector wired Georgetown. "Things are very serious," he alerted his boss. "The coolies are most insolent and overbearing in their manner." The inspector wanted backup.

By special night train, arriving at dawn, came that backup: an added force of fifty under the command of de Rinzy, the very man who shot Jungli in the back seventeen years earlier at Nonpareil. In his self-serving account of the incident, de Rinzy described quelling a murderous riot by coolies. The immigrants described surviving a slaughter by police. The colonel told a reporter that he heard warning whistles as he approached the barracks. "Then," he said, "there was a tremendous roar. It is a noise which some people have never heard. The fierce roar of an angry, infuriated mob."[74] He claimed to see coolies springing "from nowhere and wildly brandishing all kinds of weapons, sticks, cutlasses and spears made from cutlasses mounted on sticks," as if in "a wild, barbarian country." When a corporal tried to arrest one of the wanted men, another indentured man grappled with him, and both the policeman and the immigrant tumbled, wrestling, into a trench. Police fired into it, and neither man emerged alive. That was the testimony of the immigrants, who claimed to be completely unarmed. In de Rinzy's version, the mob pounced on the corporal, beating his brains out in the trench before the police discharged their guns. A bullet definitely pierced the corporal's brain, but whether it—or an attack by the immigrants—killed him was contested. Tellingly, and atypically, the Guianese government decided not to prosecute any immigrants for murder or riot. There was only one legal consequence. Four of the men wanted for transfer were scattered to different plantations. The fifth had been killed in the shooting.

When *The Daily Argosy* splashed the headline "BLOODSHED" across its front page, two special envoys from the British government in India happened to be in Guiana to see it. Their presence made members of the Colonial Office squirm. One worried that the newspaper's language—legacy terms evoking slavery, such as "nigger yard" and "driver"—might disturb the delegation as much as the shooting itself. Indenture was under attack in India, and the men had been delegated by the viceroy to investigate the system in the five colonies where it still existed.

The previous year, the unofficial members of the Viceroy's Legislative Council, who were all Indian, had voted to abolish indenture. In 1910, they had successfully moved to end it in Natal, where Gandhi had been battling laws intended to exclude Indians once their indentures were done. Ex-indentured who failed to return to India, who stayed to compete against white colonists as traders or free workers, had to pay a discriminatory tax. South Africa wanted Indians, but only as cheap, exploitable labor to be repatriated once their contracts in coal mines, on railways or on plantations had been served. The policy made indenture a cause for the nationalists, who saw it as an insult to their dignity and self-respect, an attempt to make Indians permanent coolies in the eyes of the world.

Fresh from their victory over Natal, the nationalists pushed to scrap the system everywhere—even in colonies, such as Guiana and Trinidad, that didn't tax the ex-indentured for the privilege of staying. Indeed, driven by economic calculations, those colonies were doing just the opposite by making it expensive to sail home and offering cash or land to those who ceded their right of return. On 4 March 1912, the man who had introduced the successful Natal resolution did rhetorical combat again in the Viceroy's Council. G.K. Gokhale, Gandhi's political mentor, denounced indenture as "a monstrous system, iniquitous in itself, based on fraud and maintained by force." His resolution failed, but only because none of the official members, none of the British members, voted for it.

Even so, the viceroy, Lord Hardinge, was worried. He sent the envoys to Guiana, the ones who landed in time to read of the carnage at Rose Hall, because he feared that Gokhale would dispatch his own delegation, comprised of less careful men. Hardinge chose as his delegates the senior Bombay tax collector James McNeill, an Ulster Catholic but a conservative, and the Indian businessman Chimman Lal, an honorary magistrate in the United Provinces perceived as a toady. Hardinge's hope was that they would restore confidence in indenture. When his careful men ultimately filed their report, they included, in an appendix, an extract from the government's *Official Gazette* about the Rose Hall shooting. Indeed, the report contained many damning details: statistics on alarming rates of criminal prosecutions for labor violations, allusions to overseers keeping Indian women and the observation that: "There is no doubt that the morality of an estate population compares very unfavorably with that of an Indian village." Nonetheless, the envoys concluded that indenture was, overall, a boon and recommended mending, not ending, it. But their report was embargoed as the rhetoric escalated on the ground, turning Indian public opinion so violently against indenture that British officials in India were forced to turn, too.

By the time that Banerjee posed his question about Rose Hall, Hardinge had already read the transcript of Guiana's inquiry into the shooting. In a dispatch to the Secretary of State for India in London, the viceroy had already criticized government officials as well as the plantation manager. The magistrate shouldn't have convicted the seven men for absence from work, he said, and the immigration agent shouldn't have ignored the charges against Jugmohan. "[W]e are forced," Hardinge wrote, "to the conclusion that the coolies had received considerable provocation and had good reason to complain of unfair treatment."[75] He called for compensation to the wounded and families of the dead—a call that ultimately went nowhere. It was translated—from the viceroy in Delhi to the India Office in London to the Colonial Office to Guiana—into a request that the governor explain what alms houses, widows funds or orphanages were doing for the victims and survivors. And then it was translated into thin air. Still, Hardinge had asked. He understood how emotionally charged the fight against indenture was becoming. Out in the villages and in the cities of India, to the common man, it was emerging as a question of honor.

On 13 August 1913, a few weeks before the official back-and-forth about Rose Hall, a mass-circulation newspaper carried an item, "The Cry of an Indian Woman from Fiji," about the attempted rape of a woman there, named Kunti. The details recited by the paper had already taken on a life of their own, told and retold, after first appearing in a letter to a Calcutta newspaper in the voice of the woman herself. A low-caste cobbler deceived into indenture with her husband, Kunti claimed that she was sent to weed a deserted banana patch, where an overseer and a driver approached and made improper advances.[76] She jumped into a nearby river, preferring to drown rather than lose her honor, when a boy in a dinghy saved her. Kunti closed her letter by urging Indian women to beware the recruiter and by calling for indenture's end.

Gandhi had been key in the struggle against indenture. In 1913, he led thousands of coolies in a march from coal mines to protest against anti-Indian laws and exploitative working conditions in South Africa. It was his biggest campaign yet, one that would end in his imprisonment. By that point in his life, Gandhi had adopted the plain white *dhoti*, which helped define his image, in solidarity with the indentured. He dressed like a coolie. And he resisted indenture like the Guiana coolies colliding with planters and police did; like them, he framed his fight as a defense of Indian womanhood. The difference was this: rhetoric, more raw even than a cutlass rigged to a stick, was his arsenal. And Kunti was part of the rhetorical assault.

The version of her story that most Indians came to know, in 1914, was an account in the polemical autobiography of a Gandhi disciple, the ex-indentured laborer Totaram Sanadhya, ghost-written by another Gandhi disciple. This version cast Kunti's story in overtly religious terms. The former coolie, who consciously framed his own exile in Fiji as "a sorrowful story of Ram,"[77] praised Kunti for resisting four years of attempts on her *satitva*. More than virtue, the word signifies the pious Hindu wife's self-annihilating devotion to her husband, and it conjures Sita.[78] This political evocation of the *Ramayan* wasn't novel. Its potential as anti-colonial metaphor was apparent to many survivors of indenture, who burnt Ravan in effigy at the climax of their Ramleelas and told the generations that "the British people in their oppression ... surpassed even Ravan."[79] Sanadhya's use of a *dharma* text to frame Kunti's story helped ignite the moral campaign against indenture. He chided: "Isn't this a thing of shame for us that our sisters, mothers and daughters across seven seas should suffer these outrages? Isn't there even a particle of self-pride and self-protection in us?"[80]

But Kunti wasn't a rhetorical invention. She was a real woman, with a real complaint, one dismissed by her plantation's manager and Fiji's immigration chief. She claimed that they retaliated against her and smeared her reputation because she complained. They alleged that she slept with a driver who gave her special privileges, that she fabricated her story of a rape when he was fired.[81] They branded her a troublemaker, liar, slut. The Fiji government repeatedly denied a problem with the sexual abuse of indentured women, but India's viceroy kept pressing for a thorough investigation of Kunti's charges. How could Hardinge not when the newspaper *Bharat Mitra* (Friend of India) editorialized in 1914: "We cannot refrain from admiring the patience, bravery and strength of mind shown by Kunti. In spite of being of the cobbler caste, she has surpassed many well-to-do [high-class] ladies by the courage shown by her in jumping into the stream to save her chastity. ... We beg to inform the British government that it would be impossible to get on without putting an end to the indenture system."[82]

By 1914, the First World War intervened, diverting the attention of British officials. But in India, a grassroots effort against indenture was afoot. Sanadhya's autobiography was published. Kunti's story was told and retold. In Calcutta, the Indentured Coolie Protection Society, also known as The Anti-Indentured Emigration League, was founded. It secured permission from magistrates to enter emigrant depots to rescue recruits, on behalf of their families. And in the districts that dispatched the most coolies, it subsidized lectures and leaflets exposing the evils of indenture. In Bihar, a young lawyer and freedom fighter named Puroshottam Das distributed 20,000 pamphlets that raised a cry against recruiters. It read: "ESCAPE FROM DECEIVERS! Beware! Beware! Beware! ... Do not fall into their snare."[83] Das added the postscript that it would be a *yajna*, or a form of service to the gods, to read the warning to illiterate brothers and sisters. Just as the campaign for indenture's abolition had strong religious overtones, its foot soldiers were men who would later be identified with a Hindu vision of the nation. In addition to Das, there was the itinerant sage Swami Satyadev, whose orthodox, exclusionary views on caste and language later caused rifts with Gandhi, but who delivered electric speeches against indenture.

Whatever divisions would later emerge, the nationalists were unified against the system of semi-forced labor. In fact, it was their first major rallying point, as well as the first major issue decided by popular opinion in India, rather than by officials in London.[84] In early 1915, Gandhi returned from South Africa and—remembering the indentured who marched beside him there as well as his late mentor Gokhale, whose cause it was to abolish indenture—joined the campaign. By year's end, the viceroy was reporting to London that indenture had become the central issue of Indian politics, more embittering than any other. "No one who has at heart the interests of British rule in India can neglect it," Hardinge warned in an official dispatch. He explained that indenture offended the pride of Indians by "brand[ing] their whole race in the eyes of the British colonial empire with the stigma of helotry." But this shame over reputations as slaves paled in comparison to their anger over the sullied reputations of their women.[85] As Hardinge told the Secretary of State for India:

It is firmly believed also in this country, and it would appear not without grave reason, that the women emigrants are too often living a life of immorality in which their persons are, by reason of pecuniary temptation or official pressure, at the free disposition of their fellow recruits and even of the subordinate managing staff.

Having scored the viceroy's support, Gandhi continued to press the issue as a moral one. Addressing a packed audience at Bombay's Empire Theatre that included many women, Gandhi called on the viceroy to abolish indenture within a year.[86] At a businessmen's conference presided over by industrialist Dorab Tata, Gandhi argued that India couldn't develop its industries if its population of laborers was lured away and "returned, if it ever did, a broken reed, a moral wreck."[87] In a Gujarati newspaper, he attacked the argument that the indentured benefited economically by emigrating. Even if they did, he wrote, noting the shortage of women, their illegitimate, frail marriages and their ill fame: "Everyone will admit that even though we stand to gain economically by selling our souls, we ought not to do so."[88] On 25 February 1916, Gandhi declared: "This business about the women is the weakest and the irremediable part of the evil."[89]

The strategy seemed to work. On 20 March 1916, an orthodox Brahmin member of the Indian legislative council moved that early steps be taken to abolish indenture.

In calling for its end, Pandit Madan Mohan Malaviya quoted heavily from a report from Fiji by Gandhi's disciple, the Reverend C.F. Andrews, a report redolent with wife murders, suicides, illegitimacy and women changing husbands as they changed their skirts. "My Lord," Malaviya said, "what a horrifying record of shame and crime is unfolded here." The pandit mounted a full critique of indenture, from the deceptions of recruiters to the penal labor laws, but chose for his climax the nationalists' most potent argument, the moral degradation of the indentured: "Of what use," he asked, "can such moral wrecks be to themselves or their fellow men? What shall it profit a man if he gain the whole world but lose his own soul?"[90] Hardinge agreed completely. The British viceroy promised that: "The end of a system which has been productive of so much unhappiness and wickedness and, relatively speaking, of so small advantage to this country, is now in sight."[91]

Despite the assurance, the nationalists were worried. Andrews reported from Fiji that the planters expected five more years of recruitment, after which they still hoped that labor migration would continue in some revised form. The number of recruits had dwindled significantly in recent years, perhaps because of anti-indenture pamphlets and speeches, perhaps because the war competed with the plantations for labor. And it was soon too perilous for ships to cross the Atlantic. On 15 February 1917, the viceroy suspended recruitment until the seas were safe again. The nationalist strategy had by then shifted into its second phase, which deployed Indian women more than it ever had, in two distinct ways.

On the one hand, it enlisted educated, upper-class Indian women as campaigners against indenture. In February 1917, Gandhi reported that Brahmin women planned to meet at a Shiva temple in Ahmedabad to discuss indenture, one of a series of similar meetings held across the country. "Women laborers suffer very much in the colonies, and hence women too should join the protest," Gandhi said.[92] The "ladies branch" of The Home Rule League became involved. According to a British official, "ladies who lived in purdah but read the news" inundated Lady Chelmsford, the new viceroy's wife, with telegrams asking her to use her influence with her husband to halt indenture.[93] One read: "We are confident that as a woman and a mother, Her Excellency will appreciate the deep feelings of Indian women on this subject."[94] A deputation of the wives of magnates and parliamentarians, led by the poet-politician Sarojini Naidu, called on Lord Chelmsford himself to impress upon him "how, as women, we have felt the misery and shame of our sisters in the colonies as if they were our own."[95] It was the first time that Indian women had approached the British government on a matter of public policy. Chelmsford told them that, if a reformed scheme of labor migration took indenture's place: "I can assure you that our first thought and care in that case would be the absolute safeguarding of the honour of the women."[96] Then, after inviting their views in the future on subjects such as education and health, he asked them to take tea with his wife.

The right kind of woman was thus deployed in the name of the wrong kind of woman. The nationalists had so far used the figure of the chaste Hindu woman in peril—Kunti to be saved from her overseer, Sita requiring rescue from Ravan. But they soon shifted to the figure of the harlot, a degraded rather than an elevated image of Indian womanhood, in an aggressive effort to obliterate indenture led by Andrews. The missionary called for its immediate end because "it has been proved to be nothing more nor less, as far as Indian women are concerned, than a legalised form of prostitution."[97] He repeated what an overseer in Fiji had shared: that he allotted unmarried women to men to avoid the chaos of sexual quarrels. Andrews noted that the indentured in Fiji referred to their barracks as *kasbi ghar*, or brothels. And he publicized a Fiji district medical inspector's comment, in a government document, on alarming rates of venereal disease: "When each indentured Indian woman has to serve three indentured Indian men, as well as various outsiders, the results as regards syphilis and gonorrhea cannot be in question."[98]

This assault of indelicate details ultimately proved effective. All the coolie contracts still existing, across the empire, were cancelled at the close of 1919, and no new scheme ever arose to replace indenture. India's freedom fighters had squared off against their British rulers, in moral combat, over the bodies and the honor of indentured women, and they had emerged victorious, unlike generations of coolies mowed down by British colonial police in standoffs driven by similar concerns across the empire. The nationalists had managed to kill off indenture without firing a shot, or taking a single bullet, in the first major success of their anti-imperial struggle.

PART THREE

RETURNING

9

THE DREAM OF RETURN

INDIA, 2008

Our own past was, like our idea of India, a dream.

V.S. Naipaul, "Finding the Center"*

From the beginning, there was a dream of return. In 1838, the year that Indians first arrived in the West Indies, a third of the coolies on Plantation Belle Vue escaped by night. Twenty-two ran. They crossed the broad, silty, shark-filled Demerara by boat and wandered in the woods on the other side, searching for a way back to India. Eventually they were found in a solitary stretch of cane, hungry and exhausted. That year, two escapees from another plantation in Guiana died in the same pursuit. Their corpses were recovered in a swampy wasteland thirty miles away.[1]

Nonetheless, the quest would continue, ill-fated, into the next century. Parties of coolies would occasionally disappear into the wilderness, thinking they could cut an overland path from South America to South Asia. Those disoriented enough to believe they could walk back to India were usually recent immigrants, exploited by unscrupulous old hands such as Lal Singh, who presented himself as guide to successive groups of newcomers in 1884. He told them that after a few days trek in the forest, they would arrive at a mountain. On the other side, he claimed, was a road leading to Calcutta.[2] He promised to escort them for a fee, but abandoned them en route and disappeared with their money. Over the decades, many were similarly misled. As late as 1900, half-starved, nearly naked apparitions were discovered hiding behind tall weeds, trudging through irrigation trenches, camped out under banana

* Epigraph from V.S. Naipaul, *Finding the Center: Two Narratives* (New York: Vintage Books, 1986), p. 49.

163

trees, looking desperately for home.[3] Most ultimately limped back to their plantations—or were hunted down and brought back. But a few died searching, martyrs to
the idea of home.

These men and women were runaways fleeing ill-treatment, and they were also
dupes. But I do not think of them primarily as victims or fools. The con could not
have worked if they hadn't nurtured a determined fantasy of return. More than
anything else, they were exiles—fixated on the moment of repatriation. Wasn't the
divine hero of the epic closest to their hearts, the *Ramayan*, ultimately able to stride
back to his throne in Ayodhya, after beggar-like years in the woods? Couldn't the
forests be for them, as it had been for Ram, the way back to sacred birthplaces?
Huddled outside plantation barracks at sunset, after unending back-break in muddy
fields, they must have considered the parallels. After all, this was the refrain they
constantly recited: ancient verses of exile and its end, the prayerful tale of a trium-
phant return home.

But return wasn't just a story that gave their lives hope. It was a promise, made in
writing. The first indenture contracts guaranteed a free return passage to India after
five years of work. The terms of that promise would change over the decades, as the
colonies wavered between a policy of continually importing temporary laborers and
one of settling permanent workers who would in time, even with scarce wombs, literally reproduce themselves. The planters could not decide whether they wanted their
coolies to return to India, to be replaced by new bond slaves—or stay on unfettered,
to be eventually replaced by their children. By and large, sugar estate owners veered
towards whichever option seemed cheaper at the moment. Their commitment fluctuated, depending on the price for cane in global markets; the size of subsidies to rival
European beet sugar; the expense of shipping coolies across the oceans; and the higher
wages and better working conditions that free, experienced workers demanded.

From the start, the promise seemed capricious. The mistreatment of the first
indentured laborers had been widely publicized in England, as concrete proof of
slavery's revival in all but name. There had been floggings, a child raped, a woman
seduced by an overseer—and a 25 percent death rate. It was thus crucial that the
planters be seen to fulfill the final part of their bargain. The British Colonial Secretary instructed Guiana Governor Henry Light to attend to it himself.[4] In November
1842, two months before the contracts of the coolies were set to expire, Light travelled by steamer to remote Anna Regina Plantation. He assured the Indians there that
they would be shipped home if they wanted to be; but if they didn't seize the chance
at that moment, they would forfeit it forever. Light got the response he expected: a
single-minded determination to return to India. He gave them six hours to reconsider, but none wavered.

Faced with losing his entire workforce, the plantation manager offered to send
them home whenever they wished, should they stay. This tempted three or four,
including a woman Light described as "the wife or mistress of one of the chief or
influential coolies, [who] had played him false and abandoned him," along with her
partner in infidelity. Light speculated that this couple had reason to fear three months

in a ship's belly with her ex. Still, by December, all forty-nine Indians—no matter the intrigues or divisions among them—had agreed to return together.

The sheriff of Berbice found the same resolve among the indentured on plantations there. He advised them to delay leaving for three months to avoid cold weather during the sea voyage but reported that they appeared "so extremely anxious to go, that I do not expect any attention to be paid to my advice." He warned the governor that any delay in dispatching vessels to take them home "will have a bad effect on their mind, will excite their suspicions for want of good faith and will probably lead to their passive resistance, by refusing to work."

The sheriff was prophetic. By the end of January, no ships for India were anywhere in sight, and the coolies struck. Their contracts had expired by then, so they were under no legal obligation to work. Plantation Belle Vue refused to feed them unless they worked. Meanwhile, the legislature warned the planters that they could be prosecuted for breach of contract. Several deputations of coolies, some from the far countryside, called on Governor Light at his house. They pleaded for his intervention. A few from Anna Regina delivered an affidavit to the man who, just two months earlier, had personally assured them of their return to India. Ten men marked X next to their names on the sworn statement, which read: "We want to go back to our own country. Our *matties* all want to go. They tell us to say so. ... We don't want to wait. We want to be sent immediately to our country, according to our agreement when we left home." As a group, the coolies on Anna Regina refused their rations of rice and saltfish. They stopped eating for days. Then, when they could refuse no longer, they insisted on paying for food. Clearly, they feared that accepting rations would leave them in debt and further indentured to the planters.

Governor Light wrote to London:

The one fixed idea 'home' made them wretched at the delay, suspicious of their employer, and for the time unwilling to receive any food. They attribute to me the authority of their own native chiefs: 'There were ships enough in the river; why did I not take one of them and send them back?' It is difficult to reason with these simple people, and still more difficult to persuade them they will not be deceived.

He expressed surprise that the planters, despite knowing that most of the workers had been separated from their wives and families, persisted in "the delusion [that] the coolies [wanted] to remain in this country."

That mad hope by planters lasted throughout the period of indenture. By the end of the nineteenth century, a consensus had emerged against sending coolies back. In 1869, colonial governments across the West Indies offered ten acres in exchange for the free trip home. Some offered a choice of money, land or some combination of both to those who gave up the passage to India.[5] Later, incentives to stay were withdrawn and obstacles to going erected. Coolies were required to pay for part of their return—and to stay in the colony at least ten years before they were even eligible to be sent home. By 1898, ex-indentured men in Guiana had to pay for half their tickets home, and women, one-third. The reluctance and shifting strategies of planters notwithstanding, coolies still possessed a right to return, guaranteed by contract. It was a right that, at least in Guiana, never expired.

So it was that 112 years after the first indentured workers to arrive in the West Indies sailed home, their affidavit and hunger strikes securing for them a return four months later than promised, about 250 ex-coolies and their children climbed aboard a ship in the Demerara River, headed for a landscape they either hadn't seen in four or more decades or had never seen.[6] For the mostly elderly passengers aboard the *MV Resurgent*, memory had remade India, fading details of its map but also intensifying the color of its contours. Their children, also eligible for a subsidized trip, knew India only from the Hindi films screened at Guiana's cinemas—kaleidoscopes of song and sunlight. For both cohorts, India was idea more than physical reality. It was 1955. Indenture was long over. But the first, provisional attempt at self-rule by the colonized in Guiana had been torpedoed two years earlier, when Winston Churchill sent in warships to suspend a government elected and led by the descendants of the enslaved and the indentured. India, by contrast, had ousted its colonizer. Borders had been invented, the lines drawn with blood. Conjoined twins had been separated, the scars of surgery still visible. But India was new and alive, and its twin Pakistan was too. Both were independent nations, not yet a decade old. This all shaped the idea that India had become to the repatriates: it represented freedom.

But this also meant that they would return to shores traumatized by partition. The Indian government, coping with displaced millions, tried to dissuade the returnees. It repeatedly issued press releases advising them not to come. The British government in Guiana conveyed that message but also said that it would honor the promise of return in the indenture contracts. "The decision is yours," it declared, disavowing responsibility for whatever fates the repatriates met in India. Perhaps they had been told the story of how it took petitions and the refusal of food to guarantee the first return, because many mistrusted the warning. The repatriation officer assigned to *The Resurgent*, Chhablal Ramcharan, said that people interpreted the discouraging messages as an old imperialist trick, to keep them from leaving: "Guiana government nah want," they told him. "They tryin' fool us."[7] It was expensive to charter a ship for a return like this; most passengers would be paying just $20 for berths that cost $400. A thousand ex-indentured had initially expressed interest in going, but in the end, fewer than 250 signed up. Trinidad and Jamaica had split the costs of return journeys in the past, but in 1955, no one in either colony was interested. Only one other ship of ex-coolies had sailed from the Caribbean since the Second World War. Weighing the cost against the general dispassion to go, the government announced that *The Resurgent* would be the last ship of former indentured immigrants to return to India, ever.

Its departure was a major event. Indians travelled from across the country to wave goodbye to the few hundred who had claimed the right of return after all these years, seizing the last chance to fulfill a once desperate dream. When the British officer on *The Resurgent* announced, in Hindi, "we are leaving," passengers started to weep. At the last minute, one changed his mind. As the gangplank was being pulled away, an old man cried "Nah me, baiyya!" (Not me, brother!) and jumped off the ship.[8] Among those who sailed were several returning to die, so that their ashes might be scattered in India's sacred rivers. Forty percent aboard were described as invalids, primarily because of their age; about as many suffered from asthma or chronic bronchitis.[9] Several boys born in Guiana, hoping to become playback singers for Bombay's film industry, accompanied their father. "These boys," Ramcharan recalled, "wanted to go to India but all they knew of India was pictures. … Films portrayed India as paradise, as if India was rich. They thought it would be so easy."[10] But at least one man aboard knew how to navigate the terrain: a Muslim fakir, an alms collector who had circled back and forth, whenever ships came and went. He took $4,000 back to India, among the largest remittances by anyone on *The Resurgent*. Three-dozen passengers had paid the full fare to visit India in a form of roots tourism; these included a legislator who had criticized the entire venture as a waste of money. But the vast majority neither had great resources nor were experts at manoeuvering around post-independence India.

This last ship taking ex-coolies back to India differed from the ones that had taken them away from it in one major respect. Just a quarter of the women aboard were travelling without husbands.[11] These fifteen included a family: three generations of women without men, one who remembered India as home, the other two for whom it could only have been a figment. The matriarch, Mahraji, was reversing a journey she had made four decades earlier, as a young woman of twenty, a cow-minder by caste, from a village just north of Ayodhya. I don't know what made her leave India. Nor do I know where exactly she fell on the spectrum of choice in emigrating. But her desire to return was clear, insistent, even obstinate. She had pressured her thirty-three-year old daughter Biphia, born on a plantation in Guiana, and her seventeen-year old granddaughter Jumratan, who went by the name Rosaline, into going with her.[12] Most of the women aboard the ship were domestics or weeders, but Mahraji was a fruit vendor, a small businesswoman. She had moved up in the world, from coolitude in the far countryside to an address in the capital, from indenture to independent wealth enough to buy her granddaughter—ineligible for the cheap subsidized fare—a $400 ticket on *The Resurgent*. And yet she wanted to leave the country where she had been upwardly mobile. Something potent must have been luring her back to India.

Few scholars of indenture have tried to determine whether women were less likely than men to repatriate. Their findings, limited to particular colonies at particular times, suggest that a slightly smaller percentage of the women who left India returned to it, compared to men. One historian has used statistics on return journeys from Suriname as one pylon to hold up his argument that indenture amounted to a "great escape" for women.[13] They were less likely to return than men, he has asserted, because emigrating emancipated them from illiberal social and religious customs in India. Undermining his thesis, ships leaving India around when my great-grandmother sailed ferried the same percentage of women as ships returning to India did.[14]

However softly the data speaks, it is reasonable to conclude that women had more reasons to be anxious about returning. Many could not return to their homes, having once left them. Due to transgressions or widowhood or injustice, some had already lost their homes before leaving India. And women who had formed relationships with men in the colonies couldn't count on being accepted into any homes in India that those men tried to reclaim. In 1962, the novelist V.S. Naipaul found a woman with milky eyes and cracked skin in the house in India belonging to the family of his pandit grandfather Capildeo.[15] She spoke Caribbean English. The old woman was Capildeo's "outside woman," or mistress, in Trinidad. In 1926, when the old man returned to India, he took her with him. Capildeo died on the train before making it back to his village of white shrines, flat fields and immense skies. But the woman made it back—and was accepted there. She seems to have been the exception that proved the rule.

Not only was a woman married in the colonies unlikely to be welcomed into her husband's Indian home, where a first wife may or may not have been waiting. She also made it harder for that husband to be reclaimed himself. One ex-coolie, on arriving in Calcutta with his wife from Guiana, only took her as far as Howrah railway station. Surgeon-Major D.W.D. Comins, the government-appointed protector of indentured emigrants, reported what happened next: "He told her and his child to sit while he got tickets, and heartlessly deserted her."[16] The man and woman were of different castes. She was proof, in the flesh, that he had been polluted. To be readmitted, he felt he had to abandon her. Among coolies, there was a sense that once men or women married outside India, especially if they also married outside caste, there was no going back. The belief ran so deep that some men deferred marriages to preserve the hope of someday returning to India. "Plenty of them didn't want to marry on the estate," one ex-coolie said, seven decades after leaving his child bride behind in India.[17] He ultimately remarried in Trinidad, to a woman who bore him a son and a daughter. "If I was to go back to India," he said, "I would have had to leave the woman somewhere."[18] The fear of being discarded kept one Trinidadian from going back to India when her husband and in-laws did. "They all wanted to take me, my husband, my wedded husband," she recalled, when she was eighty. "But my brother said, 'You can't take her. If you take her to India, who knows where you will leave her, who knows what you will do.'"[19] She had migrated as a small child and had met and married her husband in Trinidad, thousands of miles from his kin and hers, well outside the scope of their matchmaking and approval.

The prospect of being rejected caused trepidation for many returnees, both men and women, over the decades. The mood on *The Resurgent* reflected that. The repatriation officer Ramcharan set up stations on deck for the returnees to pray, Hindus in one section, Muslims in another. He tried to distract them from their distress and lift their spirits. To that end, the passengers played Indian records. They told 'nansi stories, tall tales from West Africa about the spider Anansi, a souvenir of their time in the West Indies. And they read from the *Ramayana*. When they rounded the southern tip of Africa, the tables and chairs on deck had to be nailed down. Perhaps they relived the terror of when they first hit those mad seas, decades before. Even those not on that first journey imagined it. Ramcharan, born in Guiana, described it thus: "We could see the water crashing against the ship and feel the tremors, as if the ship was a calabash. ... It was terrible because when you go around the Cape both the Atlantic Ocean and the Indian Ocean are coming at you and all you can think about are those early bamboo ships—How did they survive?"[20]

In this retrospective mood, the returnees pulled into the Hooghly, past the depots where they had said their goodbyes to India, some ceding sacred threads to the river. Most likely, they hadn't imagined then that it would take half a century to lay eyes on this landscape again. It had changed beyond recognition. Makeshift camps for refugees from East Bengal, suddenly part of Pakistan, scarred the river banks. On previous return journeys, as Calcutta's cremation ghats came into view, the men aboard had shaved their heads, leaving only a tuft at the top called a *churki*, as Hindu men do to perform funeral rites for their parents.[21] Evidently, the shearing had also become part of a rite of return, forcing the question: Was returning an occasion for mourning? Did the shaved heads signify that the repatriates felt the need to prostrate themselves before the gods? A woman was dying aboard *The Resurgent* as it pulled into Calcutta, but there is no record of any of its passengers shaving their heads, for any reason. Mahraji wouldn't have, in any case. Neither for rituals of mourning nor return do women shave their heads. But she and the others did mark their homecoming; two days before the ship docked, they threw a party. Ramcharan gave a speech, thanking the returnees for the chance to visit India. He also gave them some advice: "Do your best to adjust and resettle," he said. "Keep an open mind. Do not worry about Guiana. Try to adapt."[22] Tears formed. They cried, and he cried. When the ship docked, Prime Minister Jawarharlal Nehru announced its arrival. Back in Guiana, people listening to All India Radio heard him say: "*Thetar log agaye.*" The stubborn people have come.

Already overwhelmed by partition's uprooted millions, Nehru sounded irked by the prospect of any more displaced people—even just 243 more. But he had legitimate reasons to fear that the returnees might become burdens. Earlier waves had failed to find their way back into the fold of their villages. In some cases, they literally couldn't find the villages; floods along the Ganges had washed them away.[23] A few couldn't remember the way back to their villages. Others, outcast before leaving India, effectively had no homes to try to reclaim. Even if returnees located their villages, and even if they paid priests the extravagant sums demanded to restore them to caste, they still faced rejection by their clans and their kin. Hundreds reported that they could not touch the village well, or share in smoking a hookah, or consider marrying their sons and daughters to anyone without the specter of pollution being raised.[24] Their time overseas had turned them into a people apart, branded *tapuhas* or islanders. It had transformed them into a social problem.

The plight of ex-coolies and their children had attracted the attention of no less a figure than the future father of the future nation. In 1926, writing in the newspaper *The Young India*, Gandhi described them as "social lepers, not even knowing the language of the people."[25] Those born and raised in India were lost in Calcutta, where Bengali was spoken, rather than their own dialects—primarily Bhojpuri and Awadhi.

And their overseas-born children, although conversant in what Gandhi called "kitchen Hindustani," were far from fluent in any of the subcontinent's languages. Its customs and taboos were even more indecipherable to them. Benarsidas Chaturvedi, a Gandhi disciple dedicated to the cause of repatriates, concluded that: "Having been accustomed to life in the socially free atmosphere of the colonies … these colonial born children chafe at the caste-ridden atmosphere all around."[26] Chaturvedi offered the example of a Brahmin priest's son from Guiana. The relocation to India had debased him from a decently-dressed, English-speaking schoolboy with "a colonial air about him" to "a mere skeleton of his former self," a child laborer in dirty rags, packing matchboxes in a Calcutta factory for a few annas a day. "Gone for him," Chaturvedi lamented, "are the days when he could go to school and move freely."[27]

For the most part, returnees had not belonged to the vast, kinetic, uncertain middle in the sugar colonies but were the wealthy or the abject—lepers, certified lunatics, paupers.[28] But these gradations frequently disappeared back in India. Thieves targeted those with money, who were also sapped by an unexpectedly high cost of living and fleeced by everyone from railway clerks to Brahmin priests. Like their destitute fellow *tapuhas*, some ended up in squatter settlements along the Hooghly, working—if they were lucky—at Calcutta's docks or jute mills. In the 1920s, thousands of malaria-ridden, jobless and hungry returnees huddled in the muddy slums of Metiabruz on the city's outskirts. Less than five miles away were the old indenture depots at Garden Reach, the nearness of which must have taunted returnees, reminding them constantly that they should have treated it as a point of no return. The Calcutta YMCA's secretary said: "All of them, disillusioned on their return to India, had come to the riverside with the vague hope that a ship might somehow and sometime take them back to the colony they had left."[29] C.F. Andrews compared them to spirits thronging at the edge of the River Styx, which divides the living from the dead, "stretching forth their hands in sick longing for the other shore."[30]

Returning to India had been a dream not only because of the desire running through the scenes of imagined homecoming, but also because of the quality of fantasy. Ultimately, returnees had to wake up to a reality that rebuffed their longing. Chaturvedi, looking back over two decades of experience with repatriates, saw not the dream but "the blunder of returning to India."[31]

Crowds of people greeted *The Resurgent* when it docked in Calcutta. In past decades, those crowds had included hundreds of repatriates clamoring to be taken back to the colonies.[32] No such scene unfolded in 1955. Perhaps too much time had passed for a display on that scale. But there was still a makeshift settlement along the Hooghly where returnees lived, a place called Baboo Ghat, just a few miles from the substandard sheds where indenture recruits had waited on the threshold of a new world. Ramcharan asked the people who had come to meet *The Resurgent* if they knew an old schoolmate of his, a man who had returned from Guiana by an earlier ship. To his surprise, they brought his friend to him the next morning. "He was no longer the man I knew," Ramcharan recalled—he was mentally broken, unable to remember Ramcharan's name, asking for clothes to put on his back.[33] Ramcharan gave him a shirt. The man, born in Guiana, had returned with his mother to India but when they awoke to its realities, their family could beg and borrow only enough money to send his mother home. He had been forgotten and forsaken.

Did the phantom of this man give Ramcharan pause as he sent *The Resurgent*'s returnees off into India's hinterlands? A process had been set up to smooth their way: train tickets purchased for them, buses arranged to take them to Howrah railway station, their savings handed right over in rupees or forwarded to a post office near their village, whichever they preferred. Had Mahraji spent all her savings on her granddaughter Rosaline's fare, or was there enough left for them to resettle? Did she try to make it back to the Hindu heartland around Ayodhya? Did she remember the way? Did her village still exist? Whom did she find there, and how did they greet her? Did *pujaris* extort money to restore her caste? Would it have meant anything to Biphia and Rosaline to be accepted as *ahir*, members of the caste of cow-minders linked with the mischievous god Krishna, or did they revolt against the whole concept of caste? What place could rural India have made for this trio of women without men? Little of their trajectory is known. Whether it meandered or was purposeful, whether Mahraji caught strains of familiar folk tunes along the way or tasted remembered fruit, whether that fired synapses, stirring regions of her head and her heart in strange, aching ways—none of that is known.

What is known is that she and her family ended up in Calcutta in The Refuge, a shelter for "the homeless, helpless and the hapless." A newspaper reported, in an article on the returnees, that Rosaline and Biphia fretted that they had no place to settle in India, that the old woman had made them accompany her despite this. The emigration authorities tried to find jobs for them as nannies for European families, but nothing came of it. Ramcharan may have found the shelter for them. Soon after sending his charges out into India, to confront their pasts, he saw forty of them again. They turned up in the lobby of his hotel in Calcutta. They had made the trek back to their villages but, he said, "they no longer fit in."[34] They didn't know where to go. They had nobody, they said. They clung to Ramcharan for ten days, weeping and begging his help, but there was little he could do. A passenger liner sailed to Trinidad a few times a year; the protector of emigrants in Calcutta suggested the returnees get word to their friends and family in Guiana to send passage money. From Trinidad, they could take a schooner home. Ramcharan placed the ten people with no kin to contact in a refuge he described as being in "regrettable" condition.

The clamor to leave India, once again, continued long after Ramcharan departed. Within six months of arriving, more than eighty-four repatriates showed up at British consulates in Calcutta, Bombay and Madras agitating to go. "Their mood was at times ugly; threats of violence were made," the British High Commissioner in New Delhi reported.[35] Officials in India sent frantic missives, trying to locate relatives in Guiana willing to rescue the returnees. A year after *The Resurgent* landed, the officials sent out an all-points bulletin for two women believed to be living in the same bend in the Canje River as my family. Hindel and Lachmanen were wanted because their husbands, cane-cutters who had left them to return to India, were stranded and

171

needed their help.[36] Meanwhile, a professional boxer named Balgobin tried to earn the return fare one fight at a time, bloodying so many noses that the state was forced to ship him back.[37] In the end, only about twenty-five—or 10 percent of *The Resurgent*'s passengers—returned to Guiana.[38]

Rosaline was one of them. Her will to leave India was so fierce that she apparently suggested, in petitions to government officials, that her mother was missing and her grandmother dead.[39] Two men aboard *The Resurgent*—the ship's surgeon and the legislator who had argued that return journeys were a waste—solicited donations from the public to save stranded returnees. But Rosaline was afraid that her benefactors hadn't raised enough to extricate all three of them. She returned alone to Guiana, where, a newspaper reported, she was "very lonely without her mother and grandmother."[40] It took two years of appeals to the charity of wealthy Guianese, but Rosaline managed to bring them home, too. Their return to India had been a colossal mistake.

In total, only about one quarter of indentured servants taken to the West Indies ever returned to India. Of those, a significant number didn't remain there but headed again to the sugar colonies. Some paid their own passage but, more often, they signed new contracts as bound coolies. Only one of my indentured ancestors—my great-great-grandfather Bindesri—returned to India. In 1891, he took advantage of the free passage back to India, shortly after becoming eligible for it. Before the year was out, however, he quit India again, this time unindentured and paying his own way. On the ship back to Guiana, he met the woman he would soon marry—a woman alone, from the caste of palanquin-bearers.[41] Her name was Ramdulari, and she was a force to be contended with, a savvy entrepreneur who ran their rice mill when Bindesri died. She built a successful business in Cumberland, where she crossed paths with the other matriarch with an independent spirit, the one who led me to India. Sujaria, by then a village milk-seller's wife, no doubt drove her herd of cows past Ramdulari's rice mill, just up the road. She bought goods from the shop that Ramdulari and her son, in time, started. Whenever she went, she lingered for a *gyaff*—the kind of chat that stretches well beyond the requirements of business, roaming along dirt roads for an unhurried visit, losing itself in the expanse of cane beyond. I am told Sujaria loved to *gyaff*, so much so that her husband would cut her short with a peremptory "Chup." ("Quiet.")[42] I wonder whether these two women talked about "home"; they had come from the same district in Bihar. Did their talk ever meander to the subject of going back? Perhaps Ramdulari confided what had happened to Bindesri on his return.

In any case, Sujaria never returned to India. One of her granddaughters remembers that she used to cry bitterly to see it again.[43] But she never did. She may have accepted money or land in exchange for relinquishing her right of return. Perhaps she knew that India was best kept in the past—that it would stay sweet as long as she shed tears for it, and desired it, but never actually held and beheld it. Perhaps she was wise enough to know the subtle tricks that nostalgia plays. Or, perhaps she had the good sense to realize that she had acquired things outside India that would irrevocably estrange her from it—Guiana-born children, a husband not of her caste. Neither fabulously rich nor crushingly poor, she belonged to the vast majority who stayed in the West Indies to build a future, in her case a humble empire of cows along Canje Creek. Who knows if she was tempted when news of the last ship to India reached that backcountry bend. Who knows if she wanted to die in the spot where her navel string was buried. She was about eighty when *The Resurgent* sailed—just seven years from her grave. By then, she was a matriarch with grandchildren and great-grand-children. Her desire to see India would be ours to inherit. It would fall to us to realize the return that she never did.

I can't help but imagine this return that never happened. Immigrants might be predisposed to see the world as an ongoing exercise in speculation. We are primed to brood on what might have been, had we never left. And in that alternate universe unfolding in our heads, other adventures are chosen, other selves explored. I couldn't help but play out the possibilities. How might it have gone for Sujaria had she returned to India? Would she have found her way to Bhurahupur, as I did in the winter of 2008, for my second visit in two years? Would scam artists have targeted her on her way there, or while she was there? Would there have been relatives to greet her? Would they have received her the way their descendants received me, feeding me grapes by hand in the family's courtyard? What questions would they have had for her? Or about her? Would they have wondered about her character, or considered her tainted? How much money would they have demanded to remove the taint? What was the price of readmission?

As I was being fed grapes, the villagers from Dubey Tola, the hamlet in Bhurahu-pur where everyone is a Dubey, fired questions at my driver about me: "Who's that man with her?" "What's their relationship?" "How much is she paying him?" "And what does she want—does she want the land?" No, I did not want their acre in India's hardscrabble Cow Belt. Little seemed to grow there but stalks of flowering mustard and—understandably for a state as corrupt and lawless as Bihar—fields of mistrust. Of course, they doubted my motives, as I doubted theirs. And we both doubted our middleman. He called himself "Roots Man." Dr Tiwary, a PhD in philosophy, had stumbled into the business of tracking ancestors a decade earlier. As credentials of a kind, he carried a letter testifying that he was instrumental in reunit-ing the Trinidadian Prime Minister Basdeo Pandey with his "long-lost loved ones."

The testimonial bore a stamp from the Ministry of Overseas Indian Affairs. Tiwary claimed to have escorted dozens of Indo-Caribbeans through the hinterlands of their foreign motherland, in search of their origins. Given an emigration pass, he would try to locate an ancestral village and any relatives living there now. The quest usually failed if the indentured laborer had been a woman; he found the female histories harder to unravel. Still, clean-shaven and briefcase-in-hand, Tiwary had travelled all the way from Delhi to be my guide. I was denying him his accustomed role. I had already followed the paper trail to my great-grandmother's village on my own. What I needed was an interpreter, and he was fluent in Bhojpuri. Tiwary had picked up the idiosyncratic dialect as a child, because his civil servant father had been posted near

Bihar. Bhojpuri, oddly for the patriarchal terrain where it is spoken, breaks standard rules about gender. The verbs don't change endings based on whether the subject is masculine or feminine. Tiwary, exceptionally for an outsider, could handle this eunuch of an idiom.

As such, he felt he knew his way around the task at hand. Whenever I contradicted his methods, or tried to seize control of the expedition into my own history, he addressed me as "Raaaaani," the "a" infinitely stretchable, as bubblegum in a mocking, flirtatious mouth. It was the equivalent of calling me "Your Highness." As we hurtled along the highway from the capital, past thatched huts with cow-dung patties drying on their sides, he made snide comments about controlling American women. When we stopped overnight at a hotel, he seemed to enjoy hinting at the salacious conclusions that the waiters bringing our dinner would draw when they found us huddled in his room, conferring.

He used the same tone to inform me that there had once been a settlement of *tawaifs* not far from my great-grandmother's village. *Tawaifs* are courtesans who sang and danced for princely landowners in another era. The women once practiced the high art of pleasure, but now are viewed as mere prostitutes. In fact, not seventy miles away sits Muzzafarpur, a town with an infamous red light district that has been home to *tawaifs* for generations. The town has an established connection to the great sugar migration. Every single emigrant registered as a coolie there from 1877 to 1879 was a woman. George Grierson, the British civil servant sent to investigate abuses in the recruitment of indentured servants, had tried to track down relatives of those women. "I found that the names of some of them, and the fact of their having emigrated, were still remembered," he wrote in his diary. "They were said to have all been unsuccessful prostitutes, and hence they left no relations behind, and there was no one who took any interest in, or knew anything about, their subsequent career."[44]

Tiwary's innuendoes only sharpened my anxieties about meeting my own long-lost relatives again. I didn't know how to behave in their presence. I also didn't know how to feel about their claiming my great-grandmother, given that their ancestors might once have cast her out. I approached Bhurahupur slowly and cautiously on my second visit, leaving time enough for the taking of many teas with countless strangers along the way. A mile outside Sujaria's village, we stopped in a railway town. A newspaperman there had assembled a dozen people to meet me. There was a folk singer and a college principal, a merchant and a schoolteacher. This impromptu gathering didn't shed much light on the history of migration, but the people were warm and welcoming. The afternoon had almost evaporated by the time we finally managed to climb into our Ambassador, headed for Bhurahupur. The car stopped at a railway crossing.

The train chugged slowly past, leading to a question: "Well, Raaani?" Tiwary asked. Push ahead, or retreat? My lips had already run dry from telling and retelling Sujaria's story. My hair had come undone. The scarf of my *salwar kamiz* had slipped immodestly from my shoulders. It had taken us more than an hour on Bihar's pot-holed roads to reach the town, but I couldn't go on. I wasn't up to the emotions it would summon or the feats of protocol it would require. I wasn't ready to be scrutinized or judged. We turned around.

But the next day, we made it past the roadblock of returns past, their fantasy and their failure, the sad record of those that happened and the unfulfilled ache of those that never did. The patriarch of the family that had claimed me two years earlier greeted us. Bijender Dubey peered into my face before breaking into a broad smile. He pointed at me and said something with hilarity. It sounded as though it might have been, "You again!" Bijender escorted us to the family home and seated us at a table in its courtyard. People from the village piled in. One pushed to the front of the crowd, snapped a photograph of me with a cell phone and disappeared. Chai, water and sweets were presented. Bijender's wife Manju, her sari pulled over her head, fed me grapes.

With Bijender's help, Tiwary sketched a family tree that linked us as fourth cousins. This time, a slightly different story emerged: Sujaria's father, Mukhlal, had taken his family to Burma, where he was a sepoy. An unknown tragedy occurred there. "Something happened to the daughters," Tiwary told me. "What happened, they don't know." According to the tale, Mukhlal's daughters both disappeared, and the ensuing shame made it impossible for him to stay in Burma. He deserted the army. This account of a disgraced exit varies considerably from what I had heard in the village in 2005: that my great-grandmother died there, against the evidence of a tombstone in a Guyanese cemetery. Other details clash, too. In the new story, Mukhlal dies almost two decades earlier, and Sujaria has a sister rather than a brother. The discrepancies call for an explanation. Perhaps my interpreters on the first trip understood Bhojpuri poorly. Maybe Bijender was inventing the story. Or, it could just be that facts get compromised with time, and family lore becomes its own shifting truth, with competing and evolving details. A century is a long time to stay consistent, if the facts were ever known to begin with.

The sudden intimation of scandal surprised me, because Tiwary the interpreter had also served as Tiwary the censor. As we told Sujaria's story, he skipped the fact that she gave birth mid-ocean to my grandfather, despite listing no husband on her emigration pass. I understood why I couldn't tell the family *that*. But he censored other things, too. He refused to tell them that Sujaria worked on a plantation. I thought I had already shared that two years earlier, but I was never really sure what Abhijit had conveyed. The family is Brahmin. The Dubeys were poor but caste-proud. It would have damaged their prestige to disclose that Sujaria was a common laborer. We were in the family's private courtyard, but it was mobbed with people from the hamlet eager to see an American, and Tiwary said nothing when I asked him to translate.

"Tell them," I insisted.

"It is not always necessary that all the things I must explain to them," he replied, in his soft, circumventing way.

"No, *tell* them," I ordered.

He remained silent.

The tension between us could be attributed to Bihar's indigenous crop: doubt about the motives of others, which I had inherited in good measure as a true daughter of the land. I had agreed to pay Tiwary $50 daily plus all his expenses on the road. He pushed instead for a flat fee of $100 a day. This seemed a bit much, but gender got in our way much more than money did. I bristled against Tiwary's control. I didn't want this man—or any, for that matter—telling me what to say. That has always been my instinct, but it was even more acute in Bihar because of the century-old story written under it. The details of Sujaria's exit from India had been erased by time, but the impression of her rebellion was still strong and clear. In retrospect, I realize Tiwary was probably right to censor me, to keep me within the boundaries of custom and shame.

In the moment, however, all I knew was anger and the dissonance of rejecting shame, when the situation seemed to require that I touch its feet. I have never felt anything but pride in my great-grandmother, for her honest if menial toil and for her bravery in crossing borders. My Bihari fourth cousins thought I might covet their land. I did covet something, to be honest. The riches I was after were stories: theirs, my great-grandmother's, my own. Call it a quest for identity, or an exploration for narrative gold. Even use the awful word "roots." It may be clichéd, but it's raw and nervy and real nonetheless. Many Indo-Caribbeans I know suffer from a kind of phantom leg syndrome. Dismembered from our imaginary homeland, we have felt the absence of the severed limb of India for generations. And if that meant that I had to bend at the waist, like an obedient great-granddaughter seeking blessings, then I would have to do so, suspending doubt.

The next day, I asked to be alone with the Dubey women. I thought I might learn more if they had a chance to speak, and they wouldn't in the presence of their men. The women invited me into a bedroom decorated with Technicolor posters of Hindu gods and goddesses. Manju and her sister-in-laws sat cross-legged on the bed, and they invited me to do the same. I gave them sweets, and they gave me bolts of blue-and-white cloth for a *salwar kamiz*. They fed me potato curry, and they complained about their men. One of them sang a Bhojpuri folk song for me. Her voice was husky, and her hymn to the goddess Durga full of heartbreak. Then, the women confided that Sujaria's name had not been lost to them. They didn't grow up knowing it, because they had married into the family from surrounding villages, but they recited her name at every family wedding. According to custom, the songs that women sing on the eve of a wedding list all ancestors for five generations back, in homage. Even if Sujaria had been a source of shame to her father, she had apparently not been cut out of that tradition.

At that point, Bijender barged into the room, telling Tiwary he had something to say. He must have been curious to know why I wanted to be alone with the women. His wife had already shooed him out several times, and he had sent his son in to make a phone call just as I gave the women money. Bijender wanted me to contribute cash for a *puja* at the shrine to the village's founder. "They are considering you as one of the daughters who has come back to the village, kind of a homecoming," Tiwary told me. "Take whatever you think and give it to the family, and they will do this *puja*, maybe tomorrow, maybe next day, whenever they find a suitable time."

THE DREAM OF RETURN

I gave Bijender a few thousand rupees. Somewhere in a house nearby, someone played a scratchy record loudly, and the lyrics of a Hindi film song filled the awkward silence. I returned to the subject of my great-grandmother.

"It's nice to know that her name is spoken here," I said. "Can you tell them, Tiwary?"

"Name will keep going," he said, interpreting the women's words.

I was touched by the thought of that, although I wasn't sure about the Dubeys. The Dubey matriarch sang a hymn for me in honor of Durga, the mother goddess whose name suggests protection. She has a dark aspect, however. She can become Kali. In that incarnation, she is usually portrayed dancing on the god Shiva, grinding his chest underfoot like the malevolent goddess she is. Kali, with her charcoal face, necklace of skeletons and darting serpent tongue, personifies woman's wrath. Worship of her, through unorthodox rituals of spirit possession and fire walking, was popular among Indians in the West Indies during indenture. It's no wonder, given the dangers attributed to coolie women and their sexuality on the plantations.

The goddess who mattered to me, growing up, was a feminist icon in an entirely different style: Saraswati. Associated with knowledge and purity, she is the only major goddess unaffiliated with a god. She is no one's consort. According to Hindu lore, Saraswati gave birth to the Vedas, the four revealed holy books at the religion's heart and its oldest sacred texts. Stories were her children. I went to India as Saraswati's devotee, in search of buried narrative, and I had failed to find it. I had not managed to excavate my great-grandmother's story. I knew my father would be disappointed. He wanted to know who his father's father was. I wish I could have brought back the answer, but I have since decided that it doesn't matter. It doesn't even matter if I have, in fact, found the right family or the right village. Sujaria may have lied about her origins to cover up the tracks to a disapproving husband or father. The Dubeys may also have lied, or been mistaken, when they called me one of their own. None of this matters because, along the way, I discovered the story of what happened to the many other women like my great-grandmother, from the moment they left their villages, through their middle passages, to their reinvention and struggle in a new world. And as solace against the silence wrought by history and its asymmetries—between men and women, colonizer and colonized—I have the voices of women from a remote village near the Ganges telling me a story. Believe, don't believe, but they say they still speak her name, four generations later.

10

EVERY ANCESTOR

SCOTLAND, 2009

Maturity is the assimilation of the features of every ancestor.
Derek Walcott, "The Muse of History"*

Along the River Cassley, on the sheep-grazed face of the Highlands, in Scotland's once nearly unpeopled north sits the Rosehall estate. For over a century, it has been a holiday hunting ground for the rich, with thousands of acres of game encircling a Georgian mansion set in "very fine wooded scenery."[1] In 2009, the year the Scottish government declared an official year of homecoming to attract roots tourism, I made my own pilgrimage to that picturesque corner, in the county of Sutherland. The mansion still stood, though uninhabited for forty years. Cracks grew from its roof, and red vines of neglect from its high, stone walls.

I am not, as far as I know, descended from any emigrant Scots. I venture to call it fatherland because many of Berbice's earliest plantation speculators were gentry and minor peers from the grouse moors and deer forests around Inverness.[2] And it had been a Scotsman who conceived the plan to replace slaves with indentured Indians in the Caribbean. The politician John Gladstone was born just north of Edinburgh. Profits from his Guiana sugar estates bought the Aberdeenshire castle where his son the future prime minister spent his childhood. There are some who share my history who could literally trace their bloodlines to the Highlands. For them, I imagine, going there might be like finding a father who had failed to acknowledge them. For me, the visit was far less charged, but no less surreal.

* Epigraph from Derek Walcott, "The Muse of History," in *The Routledge Reader in Caribbean Literature* (New York and London: Routledge, 1996), p. 353.

179

The plantation where three generations of my family, beginning with Sujaria, had worked was owned in the nineteenth century by a succession of Highland Scots: a Fraser, a Cameron, a Davidson. But none of these men had ever owned the Scottish Rosehall. Its eighteenth-century laird was William Baillie, who let the land in a semi-feudal manner to small-scale tenant farmers. Although he didn't invest in the West Indies himself, marriage and blood linked him to many others who did. An inter-locking, intermarrying network of families from the Inverness area—all members of the same few clans—were among the first to build Berbice's plantations. Baillie was related to three families that partnered with Lord Seaforth, the Highlands nobleman who governed Barbados, to purchase and develop 3,000 acres near the Berbice River around 1800.

Baillie's son George, one of the biggest slave traders of his day, a London-based cotton merchant and plantation owner, was in the thick of West Indies commerce. When he went bankrupt in 1806, he sold two plantations in Guiana: one named Inverness, just west of the Berbice River, and an unnamed one on Canje Creek.[3] This may have been Rose Hall. It's possible that, just before selling the unchristened lot of land, George Baillie named it after his family's Highlands estate. It's hard to be sure; Colonial Office land records exist only from 1815, once Berbice had become British. That year, the owner of Rose Hall Plantation was James Fraser of Belladrum, a Baillie relative.[4] And in 1817, its owners also owned the Baillie plantation Inverness. Did Rose Hall Plantation owe its name to the pastoral stretch along the River Cassley, where tumult to come was hidden in the hills, like so many shaggy Cheviot sheep?

Any definitive answer lies in the fog beyond memory and record-keeping. But all around the Scottish Rosehall, the road signs pointed to places I knew from Berbice's Atlantic coast: Tain, Tarlogie, Fyrish, Ross, Belladrum, Foulis, Alness, Kildonian, Nigg, Cromarty, Dunrobin, Golspie, Dingwall. All were once plantations in Guiana, and the towns that replaced them still bear those names. At least thirty places in the Highlands gave their names to Berbice plantations, hinting at their Scottish parent-age. Proof of the ties can be found imprinted in the landscape around Inverness, too. There's a house there called Berbice Cottage, and money made in the colony paid for footbridges across the River Ness, a hospital and two elite academies.

The familiar names in that unfamiliar landscape, its evident reproduction half a world away, disoriented me. The curve of coast near Inverness, strung with inlets the color of lapis lazuli, is like a necklace of blue: pretty and cool to the touch. Despite the chill, tourism anchors the local economy. The climate and terrain did not remind me of Guyana, where women require umbrellas to shield them from the fierceness of the sun and the Atlantic touches Berbice in silty, brown embraces that don't attract sunbathers. Few tourists tread its marshy coast. Still, the two landscapes share a sense of being stranded at the earth's end. Maybe, when fortune-seeking sons from the best families in that stretch of the Highlands first went to Guiana two centuries ago, they saw something in Berbice, the backwaters of a backwater, that struck a chord.

During an 1813 jaunt in the Highlands, one planter blended the disparate land-scapes. He observed in his diary that the climate "put me more in mind of a fine dewy morning in the dry weather season in Berbice, and I could not help reflecting on my life there and its various quiet pleasures." The diarist was James Baillie Fraser, whose family—the Frasers of Reelig—were Baillie relatives heavily invested in Lord Seaforth's Berbice planting ventures. Fraser was on his way to India and Persia—and to modest renown as a producer of watercolors, sketches and travel and adventure books that evoked "The East," after first failing as a Guiana planter.

In India, he would join his brother William, a beef-and-pork-abstaining East India Company official once described as being "as much Hindoo as Christian."[5] William belonged to a set of British civil servants and soldiers who, in the late eighteenth and early nineteenth centuries, took fiercely to the dress, habits and women of the subcontinent. Their relationships with Indian mistresses and their Anglo-Indian children reflected a relative openness to cultural crossover and interracial unions that would recede during the Victorian era.[6] Many of these "white Mughals" provided for their mixed-race children in their wills and sometimes saw that they received British educations. During the same period, the Caribbean witnessed a similar phenomenon, with instances of miscegenation frequently acknowledged in Wills, a legal recognition striking for societies yet to emerge from slavery. Some of the many planters who took free black or mulatto "housekeepers" bequeathed the women money and property, including slaves in some cases.

That was the pragmatic and permissive culture in which James had foundered in Berbice. His little brother Edward, who followed him out in 1803, found him moody and misanthropic and the "tone of society" low, marked by too much drunken carousing and too few women.[7] In letters home, Edward reported that James no longer cared for smartness, or even neatness, in dress. He disliked being at home, and Edward saw little of him. He fretted that James had "got too much into the ways and manners of this country."[8] Edward depicted an uncouth frontier "almost entirely without the society of women, which acts as a check on liberties which men would otherwise take."[9] At the Governor's Ball that James attended, there were only fifteen women to dance with seventy men.

The shortage of British women in the colony was also evident in the power of the few willing to live there to reject suitors. In 1807, James appears to have suffered a broken engagement at the hands of one such woman. Edward returned from a trip home to Scotland bearing a ring and alluding to a "great calamity" connected with it, a calamity he avoided discussing with James. When Edward presented the ring to his brother, James sullenly accepted it and withdrew to his room. The following month, the daughter of a Demerara official from Inverness married another Demerara official from Inverness, and Edward remarked in a letter to his mother that it would be "enough to prejudice you against" anyone, if he or she merely visited the bride's family. In 1808, he wrote: "I hear that Alex Fraser ... is quite mad about Miss Heywood's marriage. He was to have been married to her—she must be a curious sort of girl on the whole, I think. She has jilted two or three gentlemen in this country and left one or two broken hearts by marrying."[10] As for James, he didn't marry until forty, right after retiring to Scotland. In 1813, while remembering dewy

Berbice days on his way to a new life in India, James counted, among the Guiana pleasures he would miss: "none more than the good creature who lived with me and made my life comfortable in the colony."[11] Who that was is unknown.

One of James Fraser's contemporaries—possibly the same jilted planter "mad about Miss Heywood's marriage"—found solace with a free black woman. In his will, drawn up when he was thirty, this Alex Fraser identified "my housekeeper Peggy" as the mother of his five "colored" children in Guiana, as well as a sixth on the way.[12] He left her his furniture, horses, cattle, clothes and slaves. The children inherited £10,000, to be kept in the Royal Bank of Scotland, with the interest to be paid yearly "to educate and support the said children with their mother in a decent and genteel manner." He also instructed that, should any of the children be in Guiana when he died, "it is my earnest wish and desire that they and their mother should be sent immediately to Scotland and that none of them ever return to this colony or the West Indies." Such a move wasn't unprecedented. Mixed-race children of Berbice planters did live in Britain. Several were enrolled at elite schools in the Inverness area in the early nineteenth century.[13] In the end, three of Alexander Fraser's children fulfilled his wish. Hannah Fraser, Marjory Fraser and Alexander Fraser Jr all ultimately made it to the United Kingdom.[14]

And this was how the Highlands imprinted itself far from its moors, giving names to plantations and progeny misbegotten when its men were on youthful adventures abroad. At least six different Frasers from the Inverness area made Berbice their planter's playground, and the slaves they owned and the children they fathered passed on the surname to their descendants. Countless black and brown Frasers live in Guyana today. And there still stands, in a desolate coastal stretch called East Lothian, a landmark known as the House of Fraser. Once, it hosted balls with the colonial governor as guest of honor. Light and airy, with 101 windows, the house is nothing like the stone-solid Rosehall mansion in Scotland, except for an aura of decayed elegance. And it, too, is uninhabited, its stairs too rotten to climb. Its caretaker David Fraser— the white descendant of Scots who, atypically, stayed beyond independence—lives in an adjoining cottage with his Indian wife. His walls provide a view of Scotland. There hang oil paintings of the Highlands—grazing cattle, babbling brooks, receding mountains—and a red crown, a symbol from the ancestral Fraser coat of arms. But from his verandah, the eye scans coconut palms, pink lotus ponds and the cane harvesters who daily cut across the lonely handsomeness of his savannah, its tall grass swaying as they make their way to and from Rose Hall and Albion, the sugar estates that border his land. (Albion alludes to Scotland, known as *Alba* in Gaelic.)

* * *

Beginning in the late eighteenth century, Highlanders of all classes had reasons to leave Scotland. Two interconnected forces drove them away. First, those who fought to overthrow the throne with Bonnie Prince Charlie, in the Jacobite uprising, were repressed. Under the command of Lord Lovat, the hereditary chief of the Fraser clan, thousands of rebels were slaughtered in 1746 on Culloden Moor on the outskirts of Inverness, in the last pitched battle on British soil. The Crown punished the rebels for their disloyalty by emasculating the clan system. The chiefs were stripped of their military and political authority; their private armies were dissolved, their judicial powers abruptly ended, their lands effectively wrested from them. Even the symbols of clan identity were targeted; tartan and bagpipes were banned. Thus disarmed, dekilted and dispossessed, the sons of lairds had to go elsewhere to make their fortune.

To seek it, they had access to the Empire. Hundreds of Jacobite prisoners of war were banished to the West Indies and sold into indentured servitude.[15] One rebel transported to Barbados escaped and became a successful planter in Jamaica. (His son later expanded their business to Guiana.)[16] Many more Scots Highlanders ended up in the West Indies of their own volition and on their own enterprise, becoming speculators in cotton, sugar and slaves in the destructive aftermath of the Jacobite defeat. One of Demerara's founding fathers, the planter Thomas Cuming, was the orphan of a rebel who survived the Battle of Culloden Moor only to die in a British prison.[17] But both Jacobites and loyalists and their sons and grandsons emigrated, pulled by the chance to make money and pushed by an economic and social climate that had been transformed for everyone, rebel or not, when the British Crown sought to castrate the clans.

Perhaps the most far-reaching change was in the relationship between clan chiefs and their clansmen, an upheaval that forced many who weren't gentry or aristocracy also to strike out for Empire's edges. When the British disbanded the armies of the chiefs, their clansmen no longer served a purpose as soldiers; seen in the most ruthless light, they no longer justified their existence. Especially as the population exploded, landowners saw their tenants more and more as an uneconomical use of their acres. Thus began the Clearances, the forced evictions from the Highlands of those who cultivated the land to make way for more profitable sheep, introduced by the hundreds of thousands. Families with centuries-old links to the land were relocated to tiny plots on coastal fringes, called crofts. In some cases, they were literally homeless. Beginning in the late eighteenth century, the process unfolded in brutal fits and starts, affecting generations and lasting nearly a century. Along with a cholera epidemic and famine caused by the failure of Ireland's potato crop, the Clearances ignited the wide-scale and typically permanent emigration of tenants and their families, especially to Canada and America.

By the time the Frasers of Reelig struck out for Berbice, around 1800, factories near Inverness were shipping hemp cloth and linen to the West Indies for sacks and slave clothing, but the chief export of the Highlands was its people. The epicenter of all the leaving and churning, ground zero for the Clearances, was the Sutherland estate. It spanned more than a million acres immediately north, east and west of Rosehall, all owned by the Countess of Sutherland, who was notoriously cruel in removing tenants. Her agents turned people out of their homes by burning them down. After an elderly woman died in one fire in 1814, Sutherland's estate manager was tried for murder but acquitted by a jury of landowners. Not all tenants fled flames. Faced with rising rents and the prospect of eviction, many left voluntarily as New World emigrants.

The patriarch of the Frasers of Reelig disapproved of the exodus. Edward Satchwell Fraser—who was related to the Lord Lovat who was arguably responsible for the emigration, by leading the rebels to death and defeat at Culloden Moor—rued the loss of so many clansmen. In 1803, as his sons were contending with cotton and the low tone of society in Berbice, he wrote: "It is to be regretted that every soul who contemplates emigration is not encouraged to remain by being placed in a situation in which he can benefit his country, his landlord and himself."[18] He did his part to place a few in such situations, which called for leaving Scotland, but not forever. In 1806, his wife wrote to a son in India: "Your nurse's son, David Shaw, got out to Berbice and found James, who took him into his service ... so that James now has a good overseer."[19] The role that the Clearances played in staffing West Indian plantations was sometimes direct and obvious. In 1811, in the eye of the evictions on the Sutherland estate, its administrator reported to the Countess that "a native of Sutherland in Demerara ... is remitting small sums of money to his mother in Golspy," a fishing community where some of the evicted had been resettled.[20]

Overseers and managers with the name Sutherland show up repeatedly in the archives. In 1819, the manager on Rose Hall, my Rose Hall, was a Mr Sutherland. Seven slaves complained that he hired them to gin cotton on Sundays—a free day when they could hire themselves out for wages—but failed to pay them. When they exposed the broken promise, that Mr Sutherland summoned a driver to whip them.[21] And in 1823, a Major Fraser from the Inverness area used his family connections to negotiate a free steerage passage to a Guiana plantation and a three-year contract, with medical benefits and annual pay raises, for "the young man Sutherland."[22] It sometimes seemed like a few intimately interconnected shires in the Highlands had been lifted across the Atlantic and dumped in the same swampy, feverish corner of Guiana. Writing from Canje Creek in 1809, a Roderick Macdonell reported to his father, an Inverness lawyer, that he had run into "both Shaw the carrier's sons" working as overseers for the Frasers of Reelig, who had also employed him, to repair dams destroyed by the rains on their plantation.[23]

By providing jobs to peasants and professionals in their orbit, the Frasers and other gentry with business ventures in the West Indies helped set up a circular migration, with bachelors embarking in their youth but returning to Scotland to marry, retire and hand off to a new generation to continue the circle.[24] It was a novel twist on noblesse oblige, a different expression of their duty as lairds and a sign that the traditional clan structure had not completely outlived its meaning. Planters throughout the West Indies recruited workers by relying on ties to kin and to particular local geographies in Scotland.[25] They hired relatives and young men they knew, whose parents may have been tenants or servants or other associates. They also attracted capital and forged trading and planting partnerships in a similar way. As they deployed their networks transatlantically, in order to succeed in business on distant shores, Scottish planters set up a pipeline from their estates in the Highlands to their estates across the West Indies.[26]

EVERY ANCESTOR

These men laid the foundations of the place I once called home, a century before my family landed there. Their history subtly haunts mine, even though they were long gone when Sujaria arrived in Berbice. I don't know which faction, Jacobite or loyalist, claimed the founders and namers of Rose Hall Plantation as partisans. But I do know this: the village near the sugar estate, my village, is called Cumberland, and the man who slaughtered the rebels outside Inverness was the Duke of Cumberland, known ever after to Highlanders as "The Butcher of Culloden Moor." The influence of the early Scots speculators in Guiana extended well beyond the strange wonder of mimic names. As I was to discover, both the pipeline and the pattern of sleeping with subaltern women that they established lasted for more than a century.

* * *

I went to Scotland hoping to learn more about an overseer on Rose Hall Plantation whose indiscretions were catalogued in a declassified dossier, marked "confidential," in the Colonial Office archives.[27] The history it revealed spanned fourteen years and four Indian women. The overseer bought one a house in Cumberland, and she bore him two children: a daughter she named Dukhni (Hindi for "suffering") and a son she named after him. George William Sutherland Jr lived and died in my village, and my family knew him. He ran a rum shop on Canje Road, which led to the sugar estate. My family remembers him as tall, thin, light-skinned—a brawler. The nearness to me of this man—whose father's misdeeds were filed away in London, under the heading "immoral relations with coolie women," a case study in hypocrisy like so many others—was downright exhilarating. He walked the same roads that my parents did—that, in fact, I did, at the same time I did. Grandma's brother wrestled him once; I am told that everyone but Grandma's brother feared George. The image of two grown men, constables both, grappling in the streets for some unknown reason cuts the whiff of crumbling sepia from the whole enterprise.

On arriving in Scotland, I probably knew more about the grappler's father, George William Sutherland Sr, than the overseer's own people had, thanks to that file in London. I did not, however, know where exactly he was from. Transatlantic ship manifests and census records in Inverness led me to the remarkable answer: he was born in a modest stone farmhouse at the top of the valley where the Rosehall mansion sits. And in the end, he went home to the Rosehall district to settle down, becoming a butcher's vanman and, at the age of fifty-one, marrying a Scottish domestic servant, a cattleman's daughter. An elderly woman in the village where he wed and worked told me: "He was slim, tallish, a nice looking man."

George W. Sutherland Sr was a shepherd's son. The Clearances were not quite over, and tenants were still susceptible, during his parents' youth. But they had adapted, seizing the chances that existed, farming sheep and sending a son to the West Indies. The arc of his life, the fact that he started and ended it in the district where William Baillie was once laird, suggests that his Rosehall was tied to mine for more than a century. The connection wasn't exactly umbilical. It was a link to fathers and a fatherland, not mothers and a motherland; and the nourishment flowed as much from child to parent as the opposite, with plantation profits paying for Scottish bridges, schools and manses. But it was as bloody, as primal, a supply line as an umbilical cord.

Sutherland's affairs came to light because there was unrest at Rose Hall. It was 1920, seven years after the fatal shooting by colonial police that had alarmed the Indian nationalists and a few months after all coolie contracts across the British Empire were voided. Indenture was done, but the complaints of abuse continued. The government received a signed petition alleging inconsistent wages and trumped-up court cases against workers at Rose Hall; in keeping with the pattern during indenture, economic grievances accompanied accusations of illicit relationships with Indian women. An Indian immigrant charged that Sutherland kept a woman in Cumberland and that the manager dismissed repeated complaints about it. He was James Smith, the same man in charge during the deadly suppression of strikes in 1913. Then, when they rose up over wages, working conditions and the honor of their women, Smith had cursed the workers in Hindi. He had said: "Let a pig f*** the mother of any immigrant who strikes." In 1920, he ignored their complaints entirely. The immigration chief received anonymous letters alleging that Sutherland had stolen Sukhri, a woman born in Guiana, from her high-caste husband. One read: "Joe Joe gets driver work by taking a Maharaj's wife to the acting deputy's house, which causes a separation between the two parties, and now the deputy buy a house for she in Cumberland Village."

When the immigration authorities tried to investigate, Smith ignored them too. For months, he said and did nothing. Only when the immigration chief involved his bosses did they finally receive an answer to their queries. To Booker Brothers, McConnell & Co., the conglomerate that owned the plantation and many others in the colony, Smith explained that he had asked Sutherland about Sukhri and the overseer had denied their affair. Booker Brothers took each man at his word. Their representative forwarded a letter from Smith: "I can find no trace of Mr Sutherland carrying on what is termed WHOLESALE ILLICIT TRADE with East Indian girls on or about the estate," it read. "As a British subject, I have always been proud of British justice but begin to wonder whether the British flag still flys [sic] over us when such a thing could be written about anyone in the position of … deputy manager. Mr Sutherland is not now nor has he at any time openly or otherwise cohabited with Sukhri nor does he visit her house in Cumberland Village."

Much later, Sutherland and Sukhri both acknowledged that he had kept her since 1916, when she was eighteen, and continued to keep her for four years after denying it. In 1921, Dukhni was born. And in 1923, George William Sutherland Jr was. Their relationship ended that year, but Sutherland still supported the children. He gave them clothes and 10 shillings a week, or £26 pounds a year, at the time about 5 percent of an experienced overseer's salary.

The truth finally came out in 1930, after a Hindu pandit's son was punished with hard tasks and then fired by Smith, who accused him of being a troublemaker "at the bottom of a lot of lawlessness amongst the estate Creole young men." Sutherland had cursed the boy, who then journeyed to Georgetown to inform on his persecutors. He named four estate wives who slept with Sutherland, each younger than the next. The overseer challenged anyone to prove that he interfered with the wives of workers, and the pandit's son was cleared off Rose Hall. Smith threatened to evict his entire family, unless the manager "got peace and quietness."

Meanwhile, the immigration chief took statements from the women. One, Nelly, swore that Sutherland had kept her for five years, then discarded her after she gave birth to his daughter, a girl he neither acknowledged nor supported. The baby was dark-skinned. Then there was a woman nicknamed Gold Bead, who admitted going twice to Sutherland's quarters but only to plead for money that he had withheld from her husband's wages. The fourth woman, Edith, the one he was allegedly seeing at the time, denied any intimacy. But her husband said he saw Sutherland fetch her to his quarters to stay the night.

The immigration authorities forwarded the statements to Smith, who replied: "I really cannot find anything there that I can call upon him for a defense." The manager disparaged Edith's husband and the pandit's son. Sutherland acknowledged Sukhri's children as his own. She said they were, and their skin color made them difficult to disavow. As the immigration chief observed: "It is apparent that her children's father is a white man." But Sutherland denied paternity of Nelly's brown child. In the birth register, no father was listed. That raised suspicions because, as the immigration chief noted, "On sugar estates, the sick nurse has strict instructions to record the father's names of all East Indians on the estate unless paternity is disputed." Nonetheless, the official decided not to take Nelly's word. "The child does not appear as though its father was a European," he explained. The immigration chief concluded that there was no proof of intimacy with Gold Bead and "no positive proof" of intimacy with Edith. Unless a white man, or white skin, testified otherwise, each allegation was discounted.

Presented with these findings, the managing director of Booker Brothers, Frank Mackey, had to admit that Sutherland and Sukhri had been intimate for many years. But he was mollified by the fact that the relationship was over and Sukhri was living with an Indian man in Cumberland. Mackey lobbied for Sutherland to be warned rather than dismissed and argued that the other three affairs were fabrications. "It seems there is truth only in so far as Sookari is concerned, and as this is now a matter of the past, ... we consider that more harm than good would be done should any further notice be taken of it," Mackey wrote. Smith had resigned, and the mood on the estate had settled. Why provoke it by firing Sutherland, Mackey reasoned.

The Colonial Office accepted the firm's logic. It did as it had almost always done in such cases. It made the right noises, deprecating Sutherland's case as "an unsavory business" and warning of dire consequences if he ever repeated the offence, but forgave him. The practice of imperial policymakers had been to treat the affairs of white plantation officials with indentured women as peccadilloes and look the other way, if they could. And since indenture was over, they argued that Indians could no longer claim any special privileges. Even if there was still a shortage of women on the plantations, even if half of estate workers were still immigrants and thus theoretically protected by laws punishing seducers, the government no longer had any power to compel an overseer's dismissal by threatening to remove immigrant workers from an estate. Colonial Office Undersecretary George Grindle observed:

There is no more justification for punishing cohabitation with an Indian woman than there would be if she were a Negress or a Portuguese. But I doubt whether we ought to be strictly logical in this matter. For some generations, Indians will in fact be on a different footing, and interference with their women will be especially dangerous to peace and order.

Still, he echoed generations of bureaucrats who had distrusted and discounted the word of coolies: "Indians are past masters at false charges," he said.

Sutherland kept his job for another decade. He returned home by 1944, when he married Jane Jack, the cattleman's daughter, in the Highland district where he was born. Did he ever talk to Sukhri about that Rosehall or the oppression by land-masters in its orbit that had led him half a world away, to a sugar estate bearing its name? By the time he left Rose Hall Plantation, his own namesake would have been a young man and, by all accounts, just like him: lanky, fair-skinned and a bit of a bully. Did the overseer regret this mirror image of himself? Or did he regret leaving him behind? Sutherland died in 1952 at Inverness Northern Infirmary, a hospital built with contributions from planters in Berbice. He left a widow twelve years younger than he was. He and Jane Jack never had any children.

* * *

The house in Cumberland that George Sutherland Sr bought for Sukhri, rescuing her from the squalor of the coolie barracks, did not last. But ninety years later, on the same spot, stands one with a black placard that reads: GEORGE W. SUTHERLAND, LICENCE, LIQUOR RESTAURANT. The year before I was born, Sutherland the son opened his rumshop, "The Canje Pheasant," downstairs. Upstairs, he lived with his family. His own son Sean, the last of his children, lives there now and runs the business, selling liquor and poultry on the road to the Rose Hall Sugar Estate. He told me that when George Jr was a small boy, he used to go to the plantation to spend time with his overseer father, who had baptized him at its Anglican church. But when George Sr returned to Scotland during the Second World War, he disappeared from their lives. His grandson does not view him with bitterness. "If a man love a woman, and he buy a property for her, he living with her, he got kids with her, I ain't see no wrong with that," Sean told me. "The only thing was, he was like a playboy." His father, however, is a tougher figure for him to contend with. Sean shared photographs with me, and when I remarked that his father was a good-looking man, he said: "Good-looking and hard-hitting. He used to hit a lot of people real hard."

George Jr had three wives. Sean's mother was the third. The second was an Indian named Bhanmat, who, on 3 September 1968, was cooking Sunday dinner on the very plot of land that the overseer had bought all those decades ago. With her were her one-year old and her five-year old. Her older children were in the backyard, playing. Murenia Sutherland, who was five at the time, remembers what happened when her father came home. "He was drunk, and everytime he came home drunk, my mother used to be so afraid of him," she told me. He used to beat Bhanmat regularly. When she heard him crashing in, shouting her name, she fled to the neighbor's house. George Jr followed. The neighbors denied she was there, but he bellowed, begging her to come, promising he wouldn't hurt her. Bhanmat, the baby in her arms and Murenia at her side, descended the stairs. George yanked at her, and she came tumbling down, shielding the baby as best she could, and fractured her skull on the Bottom House concrete. She died at the hospital the next day. George W. Sutherland Jr was convicted of manslaughter and spent six years in prison.

Murenia Sutherland knows what everyone else knew about her father: that he was fierce, a fighting man ready to take anyone on at any provocation. "He was so angry," she said. "When we were little, I didn't think about that, that maybe he was angry." Where his anger came from, is a question that still preoccupies her. After he was released from prison, he brought the children back to the house in Cumberland that held such traumatic memories. Many years later, when she was an adult, she visited him there, and he told her how sorry he was, how much he wished that he could retract that day. And Murenia forgave him.

SURVIVING HISTORY

GUYANA, 2010

... pirates in search of El Dorado
Masked and machete bearing
Kidnapped me.
Holding me to ransom,
They took my jewels and my secrets
And dismembered me.

Mahadai Das, "Beast"*

The sun stood up, stiff-backed, looking directly at the things I preferred not to see. I was on a verandah around the corner from the plot of land where I grew up. A mile to the southeast sat the factories of the Rose Hall Sugar Estate, sinking slowly into the mudbanks of the Canje River, if Bottom House gossip was right. A few yards away, a hand-painted sign at the village's edge read: "Leaving Cumberland." Thirty years before, we had done exactly that: moved, run, rejected inertia. But the process of leaving Cumberland, psychologically, had never really ended. And so, here I was again, doing what I know seemed like turning back, sinking into the mudbanks of the past. I had returned to Cumberland for one long summer. For the first time since I was six, I was living in the village where I was conceived and half raised, where my great-grandmother had ultimately settled, where for a century Bahadurs have known home. As the sun stared down at its stagnant waters, I rang a number that I had coaxed from the village clerk minutes before.

"May I speak to Mrs Richmond, please?"

* Epigraph from *Bones*, Peepal Tree Press, 1998. Used by courtesy of Peepal Tree Press, Ltd.

There was silence. Then Mrs Richmond said: "Wha' yuh mean pullin' all da fancy Yankee taak pon me?"

She must know that I'm looking for her father, I thought. I had asked for him everywhere, from the live poultry shop to the internet cafe. I thought perhaps she had heard—the village does not keep secrets—and wanted to give the American a hard time, for whatever reason. I tried to sound helpless and lost, which, largely, I was. I explained that I was in Guyana to help untangle the affairs of my Nana, who had died the previous year in New Jersey. Mostly, this involved the house he left behind, on a street with no name. It had once been a respectable house, with an indoor toilet and a grandfather clock, about ten miles from Cumberland. From its ground floor, my maternal grandparents had run a provisions shop and snackette. In 1983, armed men broke into the house in a racially targeted attack, and my teenaged aunt hid in a wardrobe with her earrings stuffed in her mouth until the robbers fled. The shots they fired—which hit Nana in the back and killed his sister—ultimately sent my grandparents running to America.

Ever since then, their house had been let to one tenant after another. Each had allowed my grandparents to stay occasionally, as refuge from East Coast winters. Nani and Nana would spend their month "back home" fixing gutters, tenderly applying fresh paint and intently renovating their hope of return. When Nana passed away, the tenants stopped paying rent. The situation, if it lasted, could give them squatters' claims to the house under Guyanese law. That's why I needed to find Mrs Richmond's father. Rumor was, he had died overseas recently. And without him—the witness to Nana's decades-old, undated, easily-challenged will—my grandmother could lose her house in Guyana.

As soon as I explained all this to Mrs Richmond, she apologized. My well-ironed English had thrown her. She thought it was a prank-call. That's why she had answered so cuttingly, severing me—the fancy Yankee—from the place where I was born and had come again, searching. Mrs Richmond had good news: her father was alive. The bad news, however, was that she didn't know how to reach him. He had emigrated, and she hadn't heard from him in years.

I was staying in a house in Cumberland that belonged to Nana's sister, now a New Yorker. Hers was an old-fashioned country house, an airy, wooden bungalow with a zinc roof that made it oppressively hot when the sun was high, and it was barely furnished. There were two beds, a rocking chair, a kitchen table. On otherwise empty shelves sat a faded picture, entitled "Exile of Rama," in a broken frame. I spent as much time as I could out on the verandah, watching the perpetual traffic of cows, sugar estate lorries, hire *cyars*, donkey *cyarts*, couples sharing bicycles built for one. I looked out onto the scene of my childhood: a succession of bungalows on stilts, with gangplanks leading over trenches into front yards with miniature *mandirs* and back-yards with trees that gave up, as largesse or loot, their star-apples, mangos and coconuts to boys who could climb for them.

Somewhere in the middle of the sameness and natural plenty, the slowness and human poverty, my six-year old self had belonged. I tried to locate myself in the landscape, to remember who that little girl was. Did she talk that cracked-saucer

English that makes small children in rural Guyana sound so jagged? I know she didn't talk any fancy Yankee taak. She used to live nearby, in the house that Lal Bahadur had built. Thirty years later, the house was gone, but nothing had arisen in its place. We could still call the land ours. To see it, all I had to do was walk up the road towards Rose Hall Sugar Estate and—before I hit the village temple that Lal Bahadur helped found, before I reached the cemetery where he and his mother lay buried, right after I passed the house belonging to his grandson and namesake, the second Lal Bahadur, our only relative left in Cumberland—all I had to do was turn right onto Main Street.

But I couldn't bring myself to do it more than once. Soon after arriving, I had visited the land with my parents, who were in Guyana with me for the start of my sojourn. I knew what to expect. In my late twenties, while flipping through albums in a cousin's attic, I stumbled across a photograph of our Cumberland house being taken apart, plank by plank. No one had bothered to tell me that an uncle, on a trip back, had disassembled it. I discovered through the photograph. Beginning in the 1970s, our epic-sized extended family had emigrated in waves. The house had been handed down until it finally ended up with squatters who didn't care. My uncle had found it in such ruin, the timbers literally rotting, that he had no choice but to break it down. The image of its dismantling, branded into my brain, flickered like a flash card whenever I experienced a certain kind of loss: the inarticulate, irreparable kind. Lal Bahadur's legacy to his eight children, made with his own hands, from heartwood he had thought impervious to time, no longer stood, and I was in mourning for it. By 2010, when I returned with my parents, there was no structure left for us to invest with nostalgia, not even our concrete temple.

A brown cow sat placidly in the tall grass, looking languorously on as my father mustered some men to chop back the bush. Gone were the stickers on my Color-forms map of the past, the flat but vivid images from my childhood: the mandir, the garden, my cousin Brudda's blue taxi. How could I play my game of Memory without them? But as we pushed back into the area where the outhouse had been, I spotted a rusty sheet of metal, with flecks of blue paint, poking out from the weeds. It was scrap from Brudda's car, somehow still there, confirming that once this had been our home, that somewhere on that overgrown lot, my umbilical cord was buried. That custom should have connected me to the land in some cosmic way. And yet, I didn't feel that. What I did feel was elusive, unsettling. It kept me away from the land, once my parents had gone. Our abandoned plot of earth had become one of many things in Guyana that I preferred not to see. I couldn't confront it. I don't know why. Nothing bad had happened, not there.

The house next door looked tumble-down on its stilts, like an old man on last legs. Our bend in the Canje River, like so many bends in Guyana, was dotted with ageing wooden bungalows left behind by owners who had migrated. Elderly Guyanese living abroad sometimes spent their winters back home; but for most of the year, they shut up the houses, paying caretakers to air and clean them occasionally. The house where I was staying was a well-tended house like that. But many others lay rotting, a toll of the emigration that has drained the country for decades.

193

In the local idiom, emigration has become a matter of leaving house. When men in hammocks, *gyaffing*, wander to the subject of old friends and absent family, they will frequently add: "She gone outside." She emigrated. A process requiring excruciating waits for visas, and sometimes illegal border crossings, becomes as casual as the hammock's sway, as easy as: "She went for a walk. She'll be back by dinner." Maybe this language helps. Maybe it softens the blow to compare leaving the country to leaving the house. Domesticating emigration in this way might make it seem less final to those left behind. Only 750,000 people live in Guyana. A quarter of its native-born now live in Britain, Canada or the United States. In 2011, Guyana ranked among the top five countries worldwide in its net outmigration rate. Only three small island nations in the South Pacific lost a greater share of their populations through emigration.[1] Guyanese have gone "outside" on an outsized scale, and its landscape is defined by houses entrusted to the care or neglect of squatters, relatives or tenants. The emigrants—we emigrants—have become like absentee landlords in our own past, trying to maintain ties from afar.

From a distance, over the decades, I had turned the land where Lal Bahadur's house once stood into almost sacred ground. In my imagination, it was the place where once we were whole: a parallel world where we continued to live as if we had never left. Perhaps this was too much to expect of one plot of land. And perhaps what I felt in avoiding it was the fear of accepting what it had become: an empty lot bisected by foul trenches and claimed by weeds and a cow. Perhaps it was the fear of feeling that the cow could have it, if it wanted it. Had I simply come to the ready-made realization that I couldn't go home again? Or was there something far more traumatic from which to avert my eyes? I tried to imagine the alternate reality in which we had never migrated, and the Cumberland house still stood, and I grew into a Guyanese woman, pure and simple, no hyphens. Through that looking-glass, who would I be? Who might I have become, and where would I fit, in a society that offered not wholeness but dismemberment—still—for some women? I merely had to come to terms with the fact that I couldn't reclaim the past. But these women had met an opposite and far worse fate: they had failed to escape history.

They suffered what their female forebears had. In 2010, the year I returned, at least eighteen women died, allegedly at the hands of intimate partners, in Guyana.[2] Every month from 2007 to 2010, on average, a woman was killed, and her husband or boyfriend implicated.[3] That translates into an alarming rate of intimate partner homicide: 4.07 per 100,000 women, four times the rate in the United States in 2007 and thirteen times the rates in the United Kingdom and Canada that year.[4] Half the victims were Indian. In covering the murders, whatever the victim's ethnicity, the press resurrected the indenture-era stereotypes of jealous husband and naughty wife. Infidelity by promiscuous women, or the fear of it in possessive men, frames the narrative now as then. Nor has the method changed. Most households in Guyana's villages possess a cutlass. It's still the tool to chop cane, and it's still an instrument to dismember women.

* * *

SURVIVING HISTORY

A few months before I arrived, a pretty, baby-faced woman was chopped to death by her common-law husband in Glasgow, a Canje Creek village much like my own. Pinky Seeram was roughly my age. She had attended high school, but never graduated. Pinky was a mother, and she was a wife. For happiness, she had her children, and she had her house: a modest bungalow along an unpaved road, bounded by swamp. Her husband, Kelly Boodhoo, a cane cutter with the Rose Hall Sugar Estate, paid the mortgage. When the fight that ended in Pinky's death erupted, her mother was living with them.[5]

Cheryl Inderdeo was there to see Pinky cower behind her bed and Kelly jump onto it, cutlass raised, ready to strike. The children were away that night. Nicholas, ten, was not there to see the cutlass bust the back of his mother's head. Nerisa, thirteen, was not there to see her father hack off her mother's fingers. Cheryl, an evangelical Christian, thanks Jesus for the small mercy that her grandchildren weren't there to witness the scene on constant playback in her own brain.

She can't forget that day. Kelly had come home exhausted, but still he went out drinking. With her grandchildren at her ex-husband's, the afternoon was quiet. Cheryl was unwell, so she rested in bed. From the backyard, where her daughter was working in the garden, came the strains of a hymn: "All of my help, all of my help comes from the Lord." Pinky was singing: "My help, my help comes from the Lord. He is my help." Cheryl forced herself to get up, and together the women planted two beds of yard-long snake beans. Kelly wasn't back yet, so they ate dinner without him. Then they passed the time rocking in hammocks, *gyaffing* until the mosquitoes began to bite. And still there was no Kelly. They took two tall glasses of steaming tea up to the verandah, from where Pinky kept a lookout for her husband.

The couple fought often, about his drinking and about her brother Mahendra, who repaired TVs in New Jersey and regularly wired money back home. He had sent boots once, and Kelly had turned the gift into a weapon, pelting Pinky with them. He resented the help from outside and the interference in their affairs that came with it. Once, Mahendra had asked a policeman friend to warn Kelly about the beatings. The sugar estates in Guyana pay by kilograms of cane cut, not hours worked, as during indenture, and Kelly was a top earner. He was a small man who couldn't read or write, but he was agile and muscular. From the start, Kelly had used his strength against his wife. In their first year of marriage, Cheryl said, "she been pregnant, and he climb top her and beat her like a donkey." Once, Pinky called the police. At the time, the couple was living with her father, Ramnarine Seeram, who told the police that her bruises were self-inflicted.

Ramnarine saw Kelly hit his daughter repeatedly, yet it was Pinky whom he counseled to change. He told her: "Baby, you must look after him. Daddy and you modder get wrong, and me na want to know that you and he get separated like dat. Try to treat him good." It was Ramnarine who usually went from rumshop to rumshop searching for Kelly, to pluck him with the gentle reprimand: "It's enough. You had enough." The old man witnessed other cruelties, like when Kelly withheld his pay or spent it on liquor, leaving Pinky without grocery money. Still, Ramnarine pampered his son-in-law, buying Kelly the occasional bottle of stout, cooking for him when Pinky couldn't or wouldn't, even delivering roti lunches to him in the fields. And when the boy cut his feet while working, Ramnarine tenderly applied turmeric and snake leaf to the wounds. "I could do anything for him," Ramnarine said, between sobs. "Me like he bad, because he does work." Whenever Pinky wanted to report Kelly to the police, Ramnarine stopped her. He explained: "Me does say: 'No, baby. Na do him da. Na do him da. Na do him da.' … Me na want me pickne [child] lock him up. Me feel fah say, he go change. One day, he go change."

Pinky clung to that hope, too. Their marriage wasn't arranged; she had fallen in love with Kelly, at eighteen. Also, she had Nicholas and Nerisa to consider. Pinky relied on her husband financially, and if she left him, how would she buy school supplies and uniforms for the children? How would they pay for "hire *cyars*" to shuttle them to school, along Glasgow's back roads, past the Bible-toting young men, the gangly white boys who seemed always to be walking through the landscape of rumshops and Bottom Houses? Pinky had heeded their crusade years earlier. A Christian convert, she had confided in her pastor about Kelly's alcoholism and abuse, and the pastor had tried to make peace between them. One Christmas Eve, after threatening Pinky with a cutlass, Kelly was prostrate with regret. To please her, he agreed to be baptized. He even stayed away from rumshops, but that didn't last long. As she scanned the road for him on her final night, did Pinky allow herself to believe that he might someday stop drinking for good? At 10 p.m., she gave up her vigil, and the two women went to bed.

The next thing Cheryl was conscious of, at 1:30 a.m., was a raised voice coming from Pinky's room. It was Kelly, yelling: *I get a mind to beat you and you modder in dis house.* Instinctively, Cheryl began praying. Through the open door of her bedroom, she saw Pinky run down the stairs and Kelly throw a pair of boots at her, the same boots that her brother had sent. Cheryl got up to plead with him. "Man, you all nah fight," she begged. "Try and make peace." As Cheryl tried to appease Kelly, Pinky slipped back into their bedroom. Kelly followed, raging: *Did Pinky think her brother was a millionaire?* Kelly cursed Mahendra and the barrel of swag from Outside that he had promised to send. *Don't bad talk my brother*, Pinky said. Kelly knocked the television set over. Then he reached under their bed and pulled out a cutlass. Pinky darted behind the bed, but Kelly struck too swiftly for her to escape. The cutlass landed on her head.

"Ow Mommy," Pinky screamed, "me dead."

Neighbors heard her cries, but dismissed them as the white noise of the couple's usual row. Cheryl ran to Pinky, and Kelly turned the cutlass on his mother-in-law, chopping her right shoulder and left hand. Cheryl was stunned. She thought: "How dis bhai can lash me like dis? Me nah do dis bhai nothing." She looked at her palm. It looked like sliced bread. Kelly returned to his wife. He broadsided her with the cutlass, leaving her black-and-blue and dismembered. He chopped three fingers off her left hand, wrapped white-knuckle tight around the bed. Then, there was silence. Pinky crumpled, like the bloody mosquito net lying on the floor, and Cheryl fled the house. When Kelly caught up with her at the gate, she begged for her life, and he relented. "Look after my children," Kelly told her. Vowing suicide, armed with the cutlass and a length of rope, he disappeared into the maze of cane. The police, who have issued a warrant for his arrest, have not found him yet. Pinky's family believe that the police were bribed to ignore the case.

Cheryl had wanted a life for her daughter different from her own. Instead, Pinky depended on an abusive husband, as several other women in their family had. Decades earlier, an aunt had run as far as England to flee a husband who beat her. That aunt commented online on an article reporting Pinky's death: "Since I came to the UK, I realize that women do have rights and fight for them."[6] Cheryl had imagined that Pinky's escape might come through emigration, too. "I always feel dat when she finish high school, she gon get to go to America, and she gon live a better life there. You know, get better opportunity. But de dream didn't come to pass."

* * *

Feminism is still an emerging value, often discredited as a foreign influence in Guyana. Many women think collectively, putting family before individual rights. Masculinity often shows itself in public spaces as threat. At Georgetown's main department store, titles such as *Guns & Ammo*, *Muscle* and *Handguns* dominate the magazine racks. Women walk down the streets pursued by the rude compliment of susurrant cheeps, the bird-like equivalent of kissing noises. When I asked a stranger how to get to Austin's Bookstore, she gave directions that doubled as warning: "Walk to Bourda Market, then *ask any female*." But the spaces that have proven the most dangerous to Guyanese women are the private spaces inside the home, where the family stands on pillars.

The murders are the most extreme manifestation of a pervasive, persistent problem. Year after year, the US State Department consistently cites domestic violence among Guyana's most serious human rights violations. Spousal abuse disfigures the lives of many Guyanese women, of all ethnicities. Many suffer assaults serious enough to require medical treatment. The July I spent in Guyana, one in six of the women in the Georgetown Public Hospital's trauma unit divulged that an intimate partner had inflicted their injuries.[7] The hospital's emergency room director suspects abuse in many more cases than the women will acknowledge. "It's not culturally the thing for them to tell you that," he said. Despite taboos against speaking out, surveys of women in Georgetown and its outskirts have found disturbing levels of conjugal violence. In 1988, two in three women reported being hit at least once by a husband or boyfriend.[8] A decade later, 37 percent reported physical abuse and 46 percent reported physical, sexual or psychological abuse by a partner.[9] And neither study ventured into Berbice, into the more isolated countryside where wife beating is perceived to be more entrenched than in the capital and its orbit. Meanwhile, a 1988 review of complaints to police and social welfare agencies led sociologists to conclude that domestic violence was the most common form of violence in Guyana.[10]

In large-scale surveys conducted in other countries, smaller proportions of women reported physical abuse, from 10 percent in Paraguay and the Phillipines to 34 percent in Egypt.[11] There are places in the developing world with rates of physical abuse by intimate partners as high or higher than Guyana's: the cities of Peru and Bangladesh and the Ethiopian and Tanzanian countryside, for example.[12] And 45 percent of men in Uttar Pradesh, the province in India whence most of the indentured had come, acknowledged beating their wives in 1996.[13] Still, the reported abuse in Guyana falls at the higher end of the world range. In its immediate Caribbean neighborhood, the statistics are slightly better. In Barbados and Trinidad, about 30 percent of women surveyed in the 1990s reported being battered.[14]

What might make Guyana a more menacing place for women? It makes sense to seek answers in factors that make the country distinct, beginning with its poverty. Guyana is among the five least developed nations in the Western Hemisphere, more destitute than any country in South America or the Caribbean, except Haiti.[15] The rural communities along Guyana's coast, the scene of most of the fatal violence, are particularly depressed. Their major employer, the government company that runs the country's sugar estates, is almost bankrupt. Gold from the interior currently brings in four times more foreign currency than sugar does.[16] But that matters little to the coastal poor, who rely on the other major foreign currency source: remittances from relatives overseas. They account for 12.5 percent of Guyana's GDP, a greater percentage than in nine-tenths of the world.[17]

The money transfers point to the other factor that sets Guyana apart: its colossal emigration rate. At first glance, this seems to have resulted in economic benefit: $216 million in remittances, in the first half of 2011.[18] But emigration has profound social costs, which are harder to tally. Some advocates believe that it has contributed to violence against women. A founder of the group Help & Shelter, for one, has observed that abused Guyanese women often lack family support, because their closest relatives are abroad.[19] Emigration has also created a complex, self-contradictory psychology of dependency: an over-reliance on gifts and money from outside alongside its opposite, a brooding resentment like Kelly's.[20] Remittances may contribute to a sense of impotence among Guyanese men; and in the Caribbean, male insecurity over their role as financial provider often motivates conjugal violence. Those who work to end the violence say that the country's profound loss of human capital has also had a significant impact. The exodus of Guyana's best and brightest makes justice more elusive, because police and magistrates fail to enforce laws that protect women or to investigate and prosecute assaults and killings effectively.

Across Guyana, there is an expectation of impunity. And indeed, Kelly isn't the only suspect who hasn't faced any legal consequences. No one was held responsible in more than half the cases in which women were killed in 2010 and their partners credibly implicated. Of eighteen cases, four ended with suspects eluding police and five with the partners arrested but released without charge. Another case was dismissed for lack of evidence, and one ended in the suspect's suicide. In only seven cases were suspects charged or indicted. All were in custody, awaiting trial, two years after the crimes were committed.[21]

In one case, a senior police official explained that his department didn't pursue charges, despite evidence against the victim's ex, because the coroner's report was inconclusive.[22] The victim was forty-three-year old Jairool Ruhomon, a weeder on the Rose Hall Sugar Estate. On 9 March 2010, her hog-tied body was found floating in Canje Creek. There were signs of violence: on her chin, a cutlass chop and on her back and hands, burn marks. Her long hair had been shaved off and used, along with the canvas sling of a hammock, to bind her hands and feet together. On her death certificate, the government pathologist indicated that the cause of her death was "unascertainable." Jairool's brother, Asim Ruhomon, contends that her death was clearly a homicide, inconclusive post-mortem or not: Had she chopped her own chin, burnt her own back, hog-tied herself and jumped into the river? Why did the police end their investigation? Asim is convinced that her common-law husband killed her.[23]

Jairool was a young widow with two small children when she met Megnauth Shivkumar, a security guard at Rose Hall. He used to watch her come and go from the sugar estate, where she had worked since she was thirteen. The couple made a home together in Gangaram, a village up the sugar estate road from Cumberland, and they had children together. Then, about three years ago, the abuse started. He used to chase her with a cutlass, and he beat her so badly, she suffered blackouts.[24] After the fights, she would flee to her brother's for a week at a time. Shivkumar always begged her to return, and she always did. Three months before her death, however, Jairool left for good. She still occasionally cooked and cleaned for Shivkumar, but had moved into an empty house near her brother. She also took a new man. One day, Shivkumar stopped by and found them rocking in a hammock together. He threatened to kill her. Asim overheard the threat.

The last time he saw his sister, she was on her way to cook for Shivkumar. Neighbors saw her enter his house, but no one saw her emerge. Asim believes that his sister was killed there. He claims that the investigating officers found incriminating evidence in Shivkumar's house: the acid-wash jeans that Jairool was wearing when last seen, a hammock sling that matched the one hog-tying her and blood-stained clothes belonging to Shivkumar. Then that evidence apparently disappeared, Asim said. He also claims that the pathologist told him that a blow to the back of the head killed his sister, but withheld that finding from his official report. The relatives of several women killed in 2010 have impugned the integrity of government post-mortems; Asim is just one.[25] In the village, he heard that Shivkumar's relatives outside had sent $US 5,000 to bribe the pathologist and the police: "Who ge' money, ge' free," Asim told me. "Who nah ge', gah suffer. The law is there, but ah money wha' buy law."*

Transparency International ranks Guyana among the fifty most corrupt countries, in the bottom third of the world.[26] But Guyanese do not need outsiders to tell them

---

* "Who has money, goes free. Who doesn't have, must suffer. The law is there, but it's money that buys the law."

that their officials can be bought. They expect it, and this only feeds the violence. Bribery is an issue, both because it's common and because people believe it's common. As one judge explained: "A perp will figure to himself: the police may not bother with this, so I can get away with it."[27] Assailants are emboldened, and victims are discouraged from seeking help or justice.[28] In small, close-knit communities like those along Guyana's coast, corruption also works in a more subtle way: "Quite often, the police or somebody at the station knows the perpetrator and therefore doesn't necessarily even need to be bribed," said Help & Shelter co-founder Josephine Whitehead. Indeed, a recent report to the government noted that there were many accounts of police failing to serve protection orders because officers were friendly with the abusive husbands.[29]

Competence is as much a concern as corruption. A magistrate and a judge told me that the police often emerge from crime scenes without photographs or fingerprints and fail to note relevant details such as smashed furniture or broken plates.[30] In one case, the crucial evidence allegedly missed were spots of blood on a shirt belonging to the suspect.[31] Police lack basic forensic abilities and investigative skills, due to Guyana's brain drain and meager coffers. But the dearth of ability and integrity doesn't entirely explain the impunity. For those who confront it, there's a nagging sense that something even more entrenched is at work.

The sister of a woman who died, after her husband was seen thrashing her, continues to ask, insistently: Why isn't he being held accountable? Indramattie Boladass died of a heart attack in a hospital thirteen days after her husband Rampertab allegedly broke her hip and four ribs. Their neighbors in Cane Grove witnessed the fight. One intervened to peel him off her.[32] The villagers said that Rampertab regularly beat Indramattie, especially when he drank. They said that he sometimes starved her. Indramattie, who was diabetic, turned to neighbors for food. That is allegedly what sparked the assault on 2 March 2010. A neighbor had provoked Rampertab by chiding: "I can't feed your wife and feed me own, too."[33] Rampertab denied that there ever was an assault. He claimed that Indramattie fell twice in one day, in precisely the same spot, hitting herself on a small metal cylinder in their backyard. He also said that he took her to the closest medical facility, a rural hospital that treated and released her that same day.[34]

Four days later, her sister heard about the assault and, rushing over, found Indramattie on the floor, lying in her own excrement, a bowl of dry biscuit and a cup of water near her. She couldn't talk or move, and her face was swollen. The sister, Hamawattie Singh, contacted the police, then took Indramattie to the hospital, where she was admitted with bruises covering her arms, legs, breast, hip and head. Singh photographed the bruises and waited for police to come interview her sister. They never did, she said.[35] Meanwhile, Rampertab was taken into custody, questioned and released.[36] Indramattie's condition worsened, and she was transferred to the hospital in the capital, where the staff saw her nod yes when asked whether her husband had beaten her. The next morning, she died. Police took a statement from Rampertab, but didn't arrest him. Indignant, Singh asked: "So the post-mortem show that my sister die because she heart stop working, but why did this happen? Is not because he beat she?"[37] She pressed the police to investigate Indramattie's death as a homicide. Guyana's crime chief, Seelall Persaud, responded with a question of his own: "She died of a natural cause, so what is there to investigate?"[38]

Its brazen insensitivity aside, the crime chief's reply was fairly representative, reflecting a deep-seated acceptance of domestic violence among police. Many officers view it as a private affair rather than a matter for their intervention, although domestic violence has violated civil law in Guyana since 1996. Legislation that year gave women the right to apply for court-ordered protection, by themselves or through the police, social workers or lawyers. Even before that, the police had the ability to charge abusers with criminal assault. In practice, however, conjugal violence rarely was and often still isn't treated as illegal by police. A 1988 study showed that, unless someone was killed, police rarely pursued complaints of intimate partner abuse.[39] The officers interviewed expressed widespread tolerance for it: 68 percent believed that men have a right to hit unfaithful, lying or thriftless women, and more than half reported hitting their own wives.[40] In the quarter century since then, Guyana's police college has integrated sensitivity training into its curriculum; many, though not all, stations have an officer designated to handle complaints; and some have separate areas where women can make complaints privately.[41]

But the machismo remains high-proof in the police department. Its ranks still include many perpetrators, says Justice Roxanne George-Wiltshire, an architect of the country's domestic violence law. During sensitivity sessions, police have told her: "The Bible says a man can beat his wife." According to Help & Shelter counselors, women who report abuse still receive hostile, unsympathetic treatment from police, who fail to respond to calls for help or just warn abusers or refer couples to counselors.[42] Officers usually don't assist women in applying for protection orders, although the law says they should.[43] In 2000 and 2005, the United Nations expressed concern that Guyana's domestic violence law wasn't being widely or consistently enforced.[44] The police, who reflect the attitudes of society as a whole, are not solely to blame. Magistrates and court clerks also fail to implement the law.

The lack of aggressive governance—the practice of not interfering in intimate partner violence, whatever the law might say—marks a definitive break with the past. During the indenture era, the colony hanged or imprisoned men who killed their wives, and plantation managers actively meddled in the private lives of immigrants and their descendants. Indeed, unofficial courts where managers or their deputies presided, settling marital disputes and handling complaints of assault, persisted in Guyana through at least the 1950s.[45] Each plantation was its own country, and the manager imposed his own law and order. Of course, the colonial planters' state intervened for different reasons: to control its laborers, not to represent citizens, the presumed goal of the independent nation that replaced it. Nor was British colonial governance of "wife murders" effective. Death sentences did not deter, and the plantocracy did not address the underlying causes of the violence: the shortage of women, the deprivations and dislocation of indenture and the psychological effects of both.

But, there was punishment. There wasn't a culture of impunity, at least not for the literal perpetrators, the men who wielded the cutlasses.

* * *

In a sense, other men, the colonizers, were also responsible for the dismembering. The British had severed the indentured from their country, their caste, their kin. And imperial officials had created the conditions for violence against women through unnatural gender ratios. From this angle, colonialism rather than physical chopping was the crime, and colonial policy and practice, the perpetrator. There was certainly precedent in more symbolic actions by European colonizers. They had maimed ancient statues found in Indian caves; offended by the sexuality manifested in the stone, they had cut off noses and breasts. Could those mutilations be seen as a metaphor for real and lasting disfigurements to the people who would become Indo-Caribbeans? Does history gather a momentum of inevitable loss, following the physics tending to chaos, entropically devoid of blame? Or can history be held to account for current intimate partner violence in Guyana?

At the entrance to the Rose Hall Sugar Estate, a billboard looks out over ageing factories and the guardhouse that workers file past every morning and every afternoon, carrying their sheathed cutlasses. It reads: "Too Many Families, Too Many Lives Lost or Destroyed. ALCOHOL ABUSE DESTROYS LIVES!" There is bitter poetry in the placement of the public service announcement at that precise spot, staring out over the fields of sugar, valleys of ash when the black dust from burnt cane settles. Rum comes from cane. It's a by-product of sugar, made by fermenting molasses or cane juice. And the dependence on rum in many Indo-Caribbean men, what one anti-violence advocate calls "the ugly legacy of our alcohol heritage,"[46] is a by-product of indenture.

The spirit was introduced to coolies at the outset of their journeys west. At the emigration depots in Calcutta, the British issued recruits rum as medicine.[47] Visitors and officials in colonies as scattered as Reunion, Mauritius and Guiana noted the weakness for alcohol among indentured men.[48] British civil servant D.W.D. Comins, travelling through Demerara on official duty in the early 1890s, described drink and cricket as the chief pastimes of Indian men there. He observed coolies spending days off huddled in plantation rum shops. With rue rare for one so given to describing indenture as morally and physically uplifting, Comins remarked that it was, to him:

a novel experience, and one giving food for reflection, to see coolies from the north-west, who had never tasted liquor in their own country, boozing in the verandah of a rum shop, and resisting with angry vehemence the entreaties of their children to come home. No doubt both they and their mothers know from painful experience what to expect when they do eventually make their appearance in the domestic circle.

Comins guessed at heartbreak. In this, he was both clairvoyant and prophetic. Children and mothers for generations to come would know that sorrow. The correlation between drinking and the recent violence against women in Guyana has been well documented.[49] One magistrate in Berbice went so far as to blame alcohol for all the spousal abuse cases in his court.

In a jeremiad from the bench in 2010, Magistrate Tejnarine Ramroop called for a crackdown on rumshops, an institution in Guyana's countryside.[50] Tucked away in Bottom Houses and backyards, enlivened by chutney-soca music and the cheapest, hardest liquor, they are often dingy masculine dugouts. Women seen there instantly earn reputations. When the human services ministry decided to take its public awareness campaign against domestic violence directly to men, it took it first to a village rumshop in Berbice. "I wasn't there," explained then-minister Priya Manickchand, "because I'm female."[51] Ramroop described a crisis across the length and breadth of rural Guyana, where regulations restricting the number of rumshops per capita are flouted; liquor stores operate as rumshops though they merely have off-licenses; and both sell to minors.[52]

In the past, indentured men drank as a strategy for survival, to make bearable the harsh conditions on plantations.[53] Alcohol, consumed in the company of mates, downed with the equally downtrodden, became their escape when the promises of recruiters proved illusory.

For the solace of forgetting, Indians had initially preferred ganja, which they had brought with them from the subcontinent. But with the help of missionaries and colonial officials, Caribbean planters engineered a shift to rum.[54] While Indians could and did profit from growing and selling marijuana, it was British planters who controlled rum-making, an intensive process requiring labor, machinery and capital. The colonial authorities were as interested in capturing consumers as in keeping the grievances of their coolies safely drowned. Rum gradually gained over its rival as the government imposed heavy license fees for growing and selling ganja, as missionaries were enlisted to crusade against it and as the plantations became aggressive distribution points for cheap and potent rum.[55] The "company stores" where coolies bought their rations sold it, even after closing hours, and rum shops were located right on the plantations or at their very edges. Unsubstantiated reports suggest that coolies were sometimes even paid in rum.[56]

In the end, innumerable indentured men became indebted to the company store and wasted money on rum that might have been saved or invested. Their survival strategy proved self-destructive in the long term, trapping them in multigenerational cycles of poverty and heavy drinking from which many of their descendants are still struggling to emerge. Alcoholism is just one disfigurement of indenture that contributes to the current violence against women in Guyana.

The economic inequality that makes it hard for them to walk away from abuse is another. Around 1900, with the sugar industry too beset to bear the expense of perpetually shipping in new workers, planters shifted strategy. It was time to settle, permanently, the Indian workers they already had and to encourage the birth, locally, of the next generation of workers. For this to happen, Indian women had to return to traditional roles as housewives. The government of Guiana lowered the number of years indentured women had to work from five to three. As in other colonies, the land it granted to immigrants who relinquished return passages to India was difficult to husband and doomed to failure. Other, better land was available for purchase only in unattainably large parcels. Eventually, the colonies offered for sale acres small enough to be within the reach of Indians, but the terms were such that, even if the land could be husbanded, it needed a wife, too. As a result, Indian women across the West Indies were pushed out of the paid workforce, into the home and greater financial dependence on their men.

In Guiana, Indian girls were further hindered because, in 1904, Governor Swettenham officially sanctioned denying them an education. At the time, the vast majority of Indians sent their children to the fields rather than to school.[57] Parents needed the extra money, planters wanted the extra labor and Hindus and Muslims were wary of schools run by Christian missionaries, as most were.[58] But children's rights advocates and indenture critics in Britain—as well as some Indians in Guiana—were alarmed at the widespread flouting of compulsory education laws. Aiming to appease, Swettenham implemented a grace period that applied to boys. For their first ten years in the colony, Indian immigrants who kept their boys out of school would be spared fines for breaking the law. But no Indian, immigrant or native-born, no matter their tenure in the colony, would ever incur penalties for keeping their girl children home. The edict stayed in effect for three decades, and Indian girls suffered the consequences of illiteracy and limited opportunity for far longer, lagging significantly behind their counterparts in other sugar colonies for generations.[59]

Today, Guyana ranks in the bottom half of the world, much lower than Trinidad or Jamaica, in indexes measuring how women fare socioeconomically, compared to men.[60] Among CARICOM nations, only Haiti ranks lower. In 2011, fewer than half of Guyanese women earned wages in the formal economy, compared to 85 percent of men, and those women who do participate in the official workforce make less than half as much as men.[61] It's not surprising, then, that many women in Guyana say they don't leave abusive relationships for fear they won't be able to support themselves and their children.[62]

An even bolder line has been drawn between indenture and conjugal violence than alcoholism and gender inequality trace. In the late 1980s, sociologists at the University of Guyana argued that both systems of coerced labor that mar the country's past explain how domestic abuse came to be accepted as normal behavior. "Violence," they wrote, "was intimate to social relations for most of the history of Guyana."[63] It characterized the relationship between master and slave as well as that between master and coolie. Overseers flogged laborers instead of providing incentives to work. Planters used physical punishment to extract work, and they used it as a form of control, to suppress unruly or challenging behavior, including strikes and uprisings. Did slaves and coolies internalize that sometimes fatal violence as the way to flex power, obtain respect and resolve disputes? Did they take it into their homes and treat women as their chattel, to be managed through physical might? The sociologists concluded that it was the plantation, as an institution built on the backs of a whipped workforce, that created "a culture of violence" in Guyana, and the country's most basic social institutions, marriage and the family, still bear the scars.

Women's organizations note with alarm that reports of gender-related killings, sexual offences, rapes and assaults have increased in the Caribbean and worldwide.[64] Feminists have pointed to one possible explanation in developing countries: economic policies pursued to meet conditions attached to loans from the World Bank and International Monetary Fund. They argue that cuts in social spending, spiraling costs of living and greater unemployment have resulted from those policies, creating a climate of insecurity for the poor.[65] In the mid-1990s, a decade after such "structural adjustment" was introduced, an activist in Trinidad made her case against it: "Violence against women increases. Men are being fired in the thousands, and their frustration contributes to this. It is a very unfortunate, natural human response to take out your frustration on somebody who is perceived as weaker."[66]

Historically, the murders of Indian women by partners or would-be partners peaked during the sugar crisis, the era of greatest economic uncertainty for the indentured. Declining prices for cane on the global market meant they earned less money for more work, when there was work to be had.[67] In Guiana, the murders declined in the early twentieth century, during indenture's final years.[68] But a century later intimate partner homicides are occurring at troubling rates there,[69] as in other ex-colonies where indenture-era "wife murders" had caused alarm. In Fiji, almost all the twenty-five victims in the 1980s were housewives, financially dependent on husbands in a culture that restricted women's work outside the home, and a significantly disproportionate number were Indian.[70] Accusations of infidelity prompted half the cases and most of the Indian ones. Most commonly, the victims were chopped with a cutlass or stabbed with a kitchen knife. In Trinidad and Tobago, at least 150 men of all ethnicities killed their intimate partners between 1990 and 2006, and the statistics indicate a steady increase over that period.[71] Jealousy, as well as failed attempts to reconcile with women, figured in many of the killings.

In Guyana and elsewhere, it's difficult to know definitively whether the violence itself has risen, or merely the reports of it, as a result of consciousness-raising, a boom in media and legislation specifically addressing domestic abuse.[72] It's difficult to know whether the violence has continued steadily since indenture, or reemerged with force in the past three decades. The literature on domestic murders in the intervening decades is dark.

* * *

In the intervening dark, the institution of family was reconstructed from the ruins it was in during indenture. The rebuilding happened slowly, on humble plots like the one in Cumberland that I was avoiding, as Indians moved from plantation barracks into surrounding villages. That shift was far from easy, especially if those villages had to be built from the ground up, on swampy land requiring resources to be reclaimed, by people indebted to planters and the company store when their indentures ended.

For the impoverished majority, leaving the plantation was a feat. It took years, even generations, to accomplish. My paternal grandmother, never indentured, was born on the same plantation as her mother, also never indentured, had been. As late as 1950, 44 percent of Indians in Guyana still lived on plantations.[73] The situation was far better in Trinidad, where half had moved off them by 1890.

But in neither place could the move have been accomplished without the retreat of women into the domestic sphere. This was done for survival's sake: the family was a collective economic unit, based on a division of labor by sex, with women working unpaid at home. While modest bungalows with Bottom Houses were being constructed in villages reminiscent of North India, the family was likewise rebuilt, on concrete pillars of custom, religion and strictly defined gender roles. The structure raised up was tight, watchful and rigid. As V.S. Naipaul wrote of the Indian family in the West Indies: "It protected and imprisoned, a static world, awaiting decay."[74] The patriarchal institutions restored with the shift from the plantation included child and arranged marriages; the joint family, with daughters-in-law the lowest in the hierarchy of extended relatives living together; temples and mosques; and the *panchayat* or council of (male) village elders. One Indo-Caribbean sociologist, whose interviews with ex-indentured women in Trinidad documented the re-establishment of this order, has described their acceptance of it as "the collusions of women with Indian tradition to ensure the survival of the community."[75] For these women, and many others like them in my family and native country, independent, individual incomes were less important than salvaging the community's traditional identity—its honor—as well as contributing to the economic chances of the whole family.

That is not, at all, to say that they didn't work. As a Guyanese woman born in plantation barracks during indenture told me:

No, me nah work ah backdam [the cane fields]. Me work home. More hard. More than backdam. I fork. I dig drain. I do all kind a ting. Cut grass. Mind cow. Mind donkey. Mind children. Plant garden. Mind cow and sell de milk. Feh get ting feh buy for dem picknee.*
… Me work more hard home. More than backdam. Mmmhmm. Me work hard.[76]

Indian women who withdrew from plantation labor carried colossal burdens. In addition to cooking, cleaning, washing and raising children, they reared cattle, grew rice on family farms and tended vegetable plots in family gardens, to sell the produce at market or feed their own. Some even continued to labor on the plantations off-and-on, as necessary, but to a large extent, they left the paid labor force to contribute to their family's livelihood. In this, the planters' wishes appear to have coincided with those of Indians, both male and female.

Wasn't it, after all, Sita's sacrifice to serve husband and kin before self? And didn't every Indian woman of a certain generation have a reminder of Sita's duties branded into her skin? Many elderly Guyanese women have an intricate tattoo, its tendrils climbing up their inner arms, that dates back to their weddings. The woman

* children.

who told me that family work was harder than plantation work explained her tattoo this way:

> Dis a when you married.
> *Sita ka rasai.*
> Dah di kitchen.
> You gah feh cook.
> *Sita ke rasai.*
> Da mean, dey give you feh cook
> In di kitchen.
> Food me modder-in-law gi' me.

Sita ki rasoi, or "Sita's Kitchen," is a shrine in Faizabad, near Ayodhya, with the image of a rolling pin carved above the entrance. Sita was supposed to have cooked the first meal for Ram there, after their marriage. Tradition in northeastern India once dictated that brides couldn't cook for their in-laws until inked with a symbol representing Sita's kitchen.[77] My great-grandmother Sujaria, registered for indenture in the same city where that shrine was located, possessed that tattoo. For coolie women, many of their daughters and some of their granddaughters, their vow of housewifely devotion was written on their very bodies.

When Sujaria arrived at Rose Hall in 1906, the milkseller she would legally marry a dozen years later still lived on the plantation, although he was no longer indentured. Together, at some unknown point, they moved from the plantation to Cumberland, one of the colony's oldest established villages. She and her milkseller settled on a plot adjoining the very one where, generations later, my cousin and I would circle imagined fires in our improvised saris seven times, to become playtime wives. Whether the plantation granted or rented them the land to keep their labor close at hand, whether they ceded their right of return to India in exchange for it or whether they managed to buy it, is unknown.

What is known is that Sujaria, a paid *khelauni* on the plantation, became an unpaid milkseller's wife in the village. Every morning, she boiled a pot of fresh cow's milk and went door to door with a tin can and pine cup, peddling. Every evening, she boiled another pot and set it to curdle in chamber pots, purchased from fine shops in town and repurposed to make yoghurt for sale. Her husband was a hard, ambitious man, a moneylender as well as a milkseller. One granddaughter distinctly remembers how, once, he thrashed a constable who tried to impound his cows. She recalls his violence towards Sujaria as well: "He used to take a *dandta*, a big walking stick and maul her behind. He used to beat her bad."[78]

The sole photograph of Sujaria that survives is a family portrait, taken three decades after her arrival in Guiana. She sits on a chair in front of a rough-hewn house, an *urni* properly draped over her silver hair, bangles stretching up her arms, her collar covering her throat, her brow high and proud. She looks every bit the matriarch, with a grandson cradled expertly on her lap and another by her side, clutching her sari. Although thin and taut, a centerpiece of composure and respect,

Sujaria doesn't look severe. The corners of her mouth hint, ever so slightly, at a mother's satisfaction. Flanking her, her son born at sea and her daughter born in Berbice both rest a hand on her shoulder. Having likely relinquished parents, siblings, children—and possibly a husband—in Bihar, Sujaria succeeded in recreating family in Berbice. She instilled in her son and her son's sons a sense of duty to family religious in its fervor and commitment. They labored as a unit, with children working too, because they had to—to feed each hungering body and also each starving sense of self, to eke out peasant existences away from the exploitation and indignity of the plantation, in villages where they might nourish themselves with institutions remembered from India and seek the consolations of religion, kin and identity.

This feat of survival and, in slow time, progress was not without costs. When she endured her husband's beatings and his silencing cries of "Chup," his attempts to control her charisma and sparking will, perhaps she contemplated the tattooed reminder of Sita's devotion on her arm. Did she ever doubt whether it was worth it to suffer dutifully like that remote goddess, to preserve family in a form of self-sacrifice? Much as I had as an immigrant child, Sujaria had to tread between inside and outside. She had receded from the public sphere of the plantation to the more private sphere of the home and the village. Each delivered its own set of licks, and each required its own brand of forbearance. As much as religion or culture, imperial policy had nudged her inside. For this, too, had been a disfigurement of indenture: the complicity of women in their own fates, the tortured attachment—the tenderness—they felt and continue to feel in the cave of their hearts for their own men, who had also been disfigured by planters and the colonial state.

* * *

From behind the rust-red walls of the New Amsterdam Prison, a cane-cutter who stabbed his common-law wife to death on 23 July 2010 told me the old indenture-era story, a tired plot about provocation and punishment, set in motion once a woman leaves. The mother of his three children, his partner for twenty-five years, had left him. She had moved back to her mother's house, a few lanes away in the same village, many months before he slashed her throat and stabbed her in the chest and back. Kumar Ranjisingh wanted very badly to avert his eyes from what he had done. He kept denying that he had killed her, and he swore that he wasn't a heavy drinker. His father had been an alcoholic, and he knew intimately the dissonance of loving someone who harmed him. In his own eyes, he was striving to transcend that background.

Kumar acknowledged that his wife left when he came home drunk one day, but said that he only started drinking because she spurned him. He denied reports that he used to hit her. A soft-spoken man in his mid-forties, thin, with jaundiced eyes, scars on his brow and ears that stick out, he saw himself as a victim, made an object of ridicule by a misbehaving wife. For years, he said, Sunita had been horning him.

"Everybody know that," he told me. "The village knows that, how she running around. The people dem watchin' me and laugh."

Kumar reacted by becoming possessive and controlling. When they quarreled, she would leave for her mother's house for weeks at a time. The suspicion that she was sleeping around would keep him up nights, crying. The last time she left, her relatives said, he stalked her and smashed her cell phone. Magistrate Ramroop ordered that he replace the phone and stay away from the house where Sunita and the children were staying. Her mother says that Kumar violated the order. He jumped their fence with a saw-toothed Rambo knife, threatening to kill her shortly before he actually did. Kumar denied that but conceded going to her mother's house, to confront Sunita about driving away with a man one evening and staying out until 3:30 a.m.

"Wha' she go tell me?" he said. "[That] she been go fuck, [because] me na able fuck she."

Kumar contended with sources of male insecurity both new and old in Guyana's cane country: cell phones, which provide a degree of privacy and freedom to communicate to village women whose physical movements might be curtailed, and the low-tech, immemorial problem of impotence, both literal and figurative. Disputes caused by seeing cell phones as accessories to flirtation, and alcohol-related sexual dysfunction, frequently play a role in domestic cases handled by social workers and magistrates in Guyana.[79] Kumar couldn't perform, he said, because he was working too hard. He had to take side jobs to supplement his ever-shrinking pay from the Albion Sugar Estate. He complained that Sunita made demands on his small savings, and he was upset that she had opened her own bank account. Shortly before she was killed, she had started working at a campus canteen. Before that, she had earned petty cash selling snacks at a roadside stand. Sunita had $US 30 saved, money she could call her own, money to aggravate his insecurities.

Kumar told me that he had tried to deal with them, without harming Sunita. He sought his pastor's counsel, visited a psychiatrist—and attempted suicide by ingesting pesticide used in the cane fields. Nothing ended his pain. On the verge of sobs, he asked:

Why did she have to go and sex out? Why? Why? Me nah do fuh she. My wife gone three days, somebody must deh top em. How can a man live like that? Working all 'e life, sleeping in de bed now, thinking: 'Oh, wife gone out, another man top em.' Me nah eat food. Me nah sleep at night. It make me turn mental.

The day he knifed her in a village shop, with their seven-year old daughter watching, he fled and tried to hang himself from the rafters of their house. The police cut him down. He was put on suicide watch at the New Amsterdam Jail.

Kumar failed at the highest freedom, the ability to rise above environment and background. But seeing him as bound to history, as the indentured were to penal plantations, is less crucial than understanding why he might be. Studies in the Caribbean and elsewhere have concluded that boys who witness violence against women in their families are more likely to deploy it as grown men, just as abused boys are also more likely to grow up to abuse their wives.[80] The past perpetuates itself through children's eyes; history becomes hard to escape, when they see.

A local newspaper asked twelve-year old Trevor Albert what he saw when he came home on 1 March 2010. He told the reporter:

Me see Mummy lie down on a ground. She head full a blood, she face full a blood, all she mouth swell up and full a blood. She eye been shut, and she nah been talking. She just groaning all the time and lie down on the floor. All me Daddy deh doing is cussing she out.[81]

It was Phagwah, the springtime festival about love and longing and mischief. Trevor's parents had been celebrating at a relative's house. His father was upset that his mother had danced at the party. The old man kept tongue-lashing her, after inflicting more than enough literal licks. Trevor wiped his mother's brow with a tissue: "Me deh wiping the blood to see if she gwine start to talk again and feel better, but it nah wuk, she still deh ah groan," he said.

The boy wanted to get help, but his father wouldn't let him. When the old man went to bed, Trevor kept dabbing his mother's face with a tissue, "trying fuh fix she." He was still by her side when his father woke up and threatened to hit Trevor, if he didn't go to bed at once. The boy did as he was told. The next morning, he awoke to find his mother stretched out in bed. She was still alive, he thought. His father sent him to fetch some Limacol to revive her. Trevor obeyed. He watched as his father rubbed his mother's face with it, but it was too late for mentholated spirits. Kamla Albert was already dead.

The day before she was beaten—and strangled, the coroner concluded[82]—Trevor's mother had burned his school clothes and locked him outside. She often pulled him out of school to work in the field. If he protested, she hit him, once with a wire that cut his face. Even so, Trevor missed his mother: "Me want she come back now," he said, "but she got to send me to school fuh larn education."[83] What in fact he has learned, by witnessing, is unsettling to imagine. He and his brother now live with their grandmother. Their father ran. Daveanand Albert said he was going to inform the police about his wife's death, but disappeared instead.

* * *

My interview with Berbice's police commander lasted no more than five minutes. It ended with the commander accusing me of an attitude problem. "Dat's why you come back he'," he declared. "Because de white maaaan don't tek attitude like dat."

During the economic downturn, quite a few overseas-based Guyanese had returned. The perception was that they were back because they had failed to make it outside, or worse. A disbarred lawyer, convicted of mortgage fraud abroad, had just set up practice right over the Canje Creek Bridge, in New Amsterdam. Then there were the deportees, convicted felons sent back from America and blamed for rising levels of drug-related crime in Guyana. I suppose the police commander was justified in wondering where I fit in that spectrum. What was I doing back in Guyana? If nothing else, I was there to deal with my grandfather's estate. With Nana's passing, and Nani too ill for winter visits back alone, we had to decide what to do about their house. Should we sell it or maintain absentee rights? Should we let go of our last, concrete claim to the country, or hold on? Either way, we had to oust the squatters.

I found Mr Gobardhan hunched, shirtless, in the shadows of my grandparents' house, a wound on his exposed back. The shutters were drawn, leaving the house in a strange noonday gloom. He sat rooted to the spot downstairs where my grandparents' shop had been. Graffiti defaced the walls. Outside, the gutters were broken. Upstairs, a plastic bag plugged a gaping hole in the ceiling. More than a dozen people lived in the house, and mattresses everywhere on the floor made it seem like a flophouse. Gobardhan stared me down with disconcerting hazel eyes, red-rimmed and bristling: "My lawyer," he told me, "has advised me not to pay the rent."

We had served the Gobardhans with notice to vacate by summer's end, but they refused. Ever since my grandfather died, they hadn't paid the token amount we asked in rent; and anyone living rent-free for twelve years in a house could legally claim it as their own. The courts were full of such cases, brought by the caretakers of houses owned by emigrants, often relatives, to wrest the properties from those who had left them behind. Naipaul had been wrong about the Indian family in the West Indies in one important respect. It wasn't static. After colonial rule ended, it suffered major disruptions again, as it had through indenture. Families were severed as hundreds of thousands crossed borders, leaving mothers, fathers, siblings and children behind in another mass emigration. And the very land that had been key to rebuilding family after indenture became contested ground that drove families apart. But Gobardhan, thankfully, wasn't family.

"Any magistrate will tell you: you have to pay," I told him, as firmly as I could. "I just saw the magistrate this morning. I can have him down here in five minutes to tell you that."

Where had that sudden boast of influence come from? I told myself that I had to brandish something, to deal with the man in front of me, his eyes lightning-like with threat and entitlement, his paunch appropriating. In the past, Gobardhan had been nearly impossible to dislodge from other people's property. His game was to sow confusion about who owned the land.

"You move in high places, eh?" he sneered. "I move in high places too. It nah matter wha' de magistrate tell me here in dis house. He got to tell me in court."

"He'll tell you that in court, too."

"We nah even know who own dis place. Who own dis place really?"

"This house is in my grandfather's name, and soon it will be in my grandmother's. Don't try that nonsense with me," I answered, atremble.

I had done my duty, and it had exacted a price. It made me want to avert my eyes. I had wanted to know who I was and where I came from, and here, certainly, was an answer. Guyana exposed to me the thing I least wanted to see. With its undercurrent of violence, its brutality beside storefront godliness, it bared to me a bully within. When pushed, by the brute logic of how things get done, I pushed back. So it was that my own foreign homeland accused me. It suspected my motives: Was I failure, or wrongdoer? What did I want coming back here? In gesture after gesture, in countless tiny interactions, the country shoved me outside, saying it wasn't my house anymore. Despite its blaze of beauty, its sheer physical wonder, despite sunlit kiskadees and birds of paradise lining fields of cane, I didn't want to see an inch more of it. To a country falling down, a shack of state on rotting stilts of everyday corruption, who even wanted to be an absentee owner? In that moment, I couldn't help but think that we should sell the house and the land in Cumberland, too, whatever foothold to dignity they had been to my family, however much generations of women might have sacrificed or colluded in their own harm to sustain it.

I felt horror and shame at my own apparent capacity to posture with irascible force, to brandish a connection I had made as a journalist from overseas. Guyana had brought out the worst in me, and I couldn't help but feel that letting go was best. If this was how houses ended up when their owners lived outside, if they decayed the way Lal Bahadur's had and the way Nana's soon would, wasn't it better to divest? Wasn't nostalgia, in a sense, unethical? If we held onto our Cumberland plot out of sentiment, to return every few years to pay property taxes and cut back weeds, wasn't that a wrong to the neighbors? Wouldn't it be more responsible to leave Guyana to the people who actually lived there, to tend as their property, not as squatters or caretakers or token renters but as owners with a stake? For the first time, it occurred to me that clinging to the past might weigh down not just us, but also the people we had left behind.

Emigration provided an escape for me and many others. But leaving the country cannot be the only way to transcend a history of exploitation, degradation and violence. The immigrant women who lived it directly managed to build homes, families, even small businesses. They managed to salvage stories and song, faith and culture for the generations to come. As testament to that feat of community survival, some of their descendants have been strong enough to elude indenture's legacies without having to cross borders. Meanwhile, some who crossed them have not escaped. It would be false to assert that violence against women ceases with emigration. It doesn't, and it hasn't. Indo-Caribbean women in Canada, the United States and Britain continue to be victims of domestic abuse; the stresses of reinvention in first world addresses sometimes increase the odds. In a few cases in New York City, which seized tabloid attention there, possessive men went so far as to murder their immigrant partners. But for the most part, leaving for countries with better-rooted traditions of feminism and greater opportunities for education and economic independence has meant that women in the second diaspora are transcending their history. At the same time, through brain drain and even remittances, relied upon while resented, our emigration has made things worse for those who didn't leave.

* * *

Latchmin Mohabir, the wife of a Demerara poultry farmer who chopped her eight times on 10 August 2010, didn't escape history. But she has survived it. The doctors had to amputate the index and middle fingers of her left hand. She had raised her hands to shield herself from her husband's blows, and the cutlass opened up great gashes across her arms, leaving scars raised like features on the topographical map of a country, ridges that point to extensive traumatic injuries and intensive surgical repair. The doctors fixed her fractures with metal wires, screws, a steel plate.[84] Latchmin is permanently disfigured, but she carries on. Her husband Subhash couldn't. He drank pesticide moments after attacking her.[85]

Half a year after the assault, she was in physical therapy, determined to master again tasks such as bathing and dressing herself, combing her hair, washing dishes.[86] For a few hours each week, she worked at her exercises at the Georgetown Public Hospital. She squeezed a ball in her left claw, an effort; she still had trouble grasping things. She yanked a pulley up and down to retrain her elbow and shoulder muscles. Supine, she moved a soda can back and forth in an arc over her head. Focusing on the rhythm and repetition, Latchmin tried not to brood about the things her fingers likely won't do again: braid hair, cut vegetables, peel potatoes. Instead, she concentrated on a simple goal: "to [be able to] do things for myself and for my children."

For the sake of her daughters, Latchmin couldn't dwell on what happened, or what might have happened. She couldn't think about the life she almost had, foiled when her fiancé in America broke off their engagement and her chance to emigrate fifteen years earlier. And she couldn't obsess about what had possessed her husband, who had suddenly become paranoid about her separate bank account and convinced that she was having an affair. The trigger was tragic in its banality. Latchmin rarely ventured out alone, but she did that summer—to fix two front teeth that stuck out. She had been saving for ages, and her mother in Canada had recently sent some cash to make up the difference. For this one vanity, Latchmin made half-day long visits every week to a dentist, and her husband started asking odd, accusing questions: What was the dentist's name? When did she start seeing him? Exactly what was going on between them?

Their marriage had not been perfect. Over their twelve years together, Subhash had denigrated her frequently, calling her backward, reminding her that she never went to high school. But he wasn't a regular drinker, and he had hit her only once, in the beginning of their marriage, leaving a welt on her back. She thought that, his unpredictable moods and verbal abuse aside, he was a good husband and father. He did his duty, and she did hers, helping him to build up their chicken farm, a few miles from Enmore. Latchmin had never thought of leaving Subhash. She did what was necessary to placate him and agreed to close her bank account. Even when he hit her a second time, cuffing her when she couldn't remember the dentist's name, she hesitated to leave. "Me say: me married, me married for life," she explained.[87] After he hit her, she ran to her brother's house, but returned a few days later, worried that she couldn't afford to educate two children by herself. The day she went home was the day he chopped her and committed suicide, leaving her to the fate that she had feared: she was alone, with two daughters to support.

Latchmin wasn't always able to subdue her memories of the violence. "I try," she told me, in 2011. "Sometimes, I'm not strong. Sometimes, I think about it a lot."[88] In her weakest moments, she would stew about how unjust the attack was, how she had done nothing wrong, how her children didn't deserve such hardship. Then, she would get angry with her husband. "Everybody saying just forgive, [that] if you don't forgive, you can never forget," she said. "What he do me, I can't forget." Latchmin would cry often, too, though never in front of her daughters. She had stopped taking the sleeping pills that the psychiatrists had prescribed, and she had stopped going to monthly appointments with them. What good did it do for them to ask whether she was having flashbacks? She was. The past was baggage that she had to heft, somehow, with disfigured arms, as generations of coolie women before her had done. To survive her history, she did as they had. She thought of her family, and she carried on.

NOTES

PREFACE

1. Poem cited in "Note on emigration from India to British Guiana," Major D.W.D. Comins to India Office, 12 September 1893. India Office Records, The British Library.
2. Tinker, Hugh, *A New System of Slavery*, London: Hansib Publishing, 1993, p. 42.
3. At the time my great-grandmother arrived in British Guiana, more Indians lived there than anywhere else in the entire world, except for India.
4. Vatuk, Ved Prakash, "Protest Songs of British Guiana," *The Journal of American Folklore*, 77, 305 (1964), p. 226.
5. The speaker declares that Guiana is the coolie girl's to inherit: "The Carib, Negro, Portuguese,/ They have all tried their hands, and now/ They leave it mostly to yourself." By using "they," the speaker positions himself outside each of the groups he names. He also describes the customs of the coolie girl as strange, suggesting that he isn't Indian. While it's possible that the poet created a speaker who did not share his identity, it's unlikely. The poem was discovered by the British colonial administrator D.W.D. Comins in a newspaper while in British Guiana on official duty, and he probably read *The Argosy* or *The Demerara Daily Chronicle*, organs of the planter class and the planter-dominated government. My guess on authorship is based on the rhetoric of the poem, the identity of the man who discovered it and the outlet in which he likely discovered it.
6. Singh, Rajkumari, "I am a coolie," *They Came in Ships: An Anthology of Indo-Guyanese Prose and Poetry*, McDonald, Ian (ed.), Leeds: Peepal Tree Press, 1998, pp. 85–7.
7. Carter, Marina and Khal Torabully, *Coolitude: An Anthology of the Indian Labour Diaspora*, London: Anthem Press, 2002, p. 11.

1. THE MAGICIAN'S BOX

1. Fanon, Frantz, *Black Skin, White Masks*, New York, Grove Press, 1967, p. 18.

2. ANCESTRAL MEMORY

1. Das, Arvind N., *The Republic of Bihar*, New Delhi: Penguin Books, 1992, p. 6.
2. Mahendra Bahadur, in conversation with the author, 2010, New Jersey.

215

3. THE WOMEN'S QUARTERS

1. Carter, Marina and Khal Torabully, *Coolitude: An Anthology of the Indian Labour Diaspora*, London: Anthem Press, 2002, p. 27. The authors cite the work of A.A. Yang, published as "Peasants on the Move: A Study of Internal Migration in India" in *The Journal of Interdisciplinary History* in 1979, on the recruitment of marginal peasants for armies. By the mid-nineteenth century, 10,000 sepoys had been recruited for the British Army in Saran, the district in Bihar embracing Bhurahupur.
2. Banerjee, Sumanta, *Under the Raj: Prostitution in Colonial Bengal*, New York: Monthly Review Press, 1998, p. 93.
3. Lal, Brij V., "Veil of Dishonour," *The Journal of Pacific History*, 20, 3 (1985), p. 140. Women made up 56 percent of migrants in Bengal from the eastern United Provinces, according to the 1901 Census of India.
4. Pitcher, Major D.G., Report on the System of Recruiting Labourers for the Colonies [17 June 1882], P/2057, Government of India Proceedings on Emigration, India Office Records, The British Library.
5. Report of the Committee on Emigration from India to the Crown Colonies and Protectorates [1910], XXVII (Cd. 5192–94), British Parliamentary Papers, The British Library. Testimony before the British Parliament's Lord Sanderson Commission indicated that there were 9,789 indentured immigrants in British Guiana in 1907–1908, and employers brought 3,385 criminal complaints against them, resulting in 2,019 convictions.
6. Robert Mitchell to the Undersecretary of State for the Colonies, 9 November 1904, Colonial Office Correspondence, Public Record Office, The National Archives of the UK, Kew.
7. Robert Mitchell to Governor of British Guiana, 3 September 1903, File No. 40336, CO 111/538, Colonial Office Correspondence, Public Record Office, The National Archives of the UK, Kew.
8. Robert Mitchell, Report on the Past Emigration Season [17 March 1904], File No. 14515, CO 111/543, Colonial Office Correspondence, Public Record Office, The National Archives of the UK, Kew.
9. Seecharan, Clem, "Guyana," *The Encyclopedia of Indians Overseas*, Lal, Brij (ed.), Honolulu: University of Hawaii Press, 2006, p. 288.
10. Hill, Arthur Harvey, "Emigration from India," *Timehri*, 6 (1919), p. 48.
11. Robert Mitchell to Magistrate at Raipur, 18 June1903, File No. 40337, CO 111/538, Colonial Office Correspondence, Public Record Office, The National Archives of the UK, Kew.
12. Pitcher, Major D.G., Report on System of Recruiting Labourers for the Colonies [17 June 1882], Diary entry dated 25 April 1882 in Appendix, P/2057, Government of India Proceedings on Emigration, India Office Records, The British Library.
13. Pitcher Report, 17 June 1882, India Office Records.
14. Dimock Jr, Edward C., *The Place of the Hidden Moon: Erotic Mysticism in the Vaisnava-Sahijaya Cult of Bengal*, Chicago: University of Chicago Press, 1966, pp. 5–13, 211–3.
15. Ibid., p. 72.
16. Bhattacharya, Malini, "The Hidden Violence of Faith: The Widows of Vrindaban," *Social Scientist* 29, 1/2 (2001), p. 81.
17. Dimock Jr, *The Place of the Hidden Moon*, pp. 234–5.
18. "In the face of this increasing scrutiny and criticism, as Stewart agues, the Sahajiya schools

were progressively forced deeper into the underground realms of secrecy and silence." Urban, Hugh, *The Economics of Ecstasy: Tantra, Secrecy and Power in Colonial Bengal*, New York: Oxford University Press, 2001, p. 167.

19. "The holy precincts of Brajadham are also the hotbed of sexual exploitation of destitute women who come here though direct or indirect religious connections." Bhattacharya, "The Hidden Violence of Faith: The Widows of Vrindaban," p. 81.

20. Rai, Usha, *Spirituality, Poverty, Charity Brings Widows to Vrindaban*, New Delhi: Guild of Service, 2006, p. 11.

21. Bhattacharya, "The Hidden Violence of Faith: The Widows of Vrindaban," pp. 79–80.

22. Narasimhan, Sakuntala, *Sati: Widow Burning in India*, New York: Doubleday, 1992, p. 115. Between 1813 and 1828, the Bengal Presidency recorded the burning of 7,941 widows.

23. Rai, *Spirituality, Poverty, Charity Brings Widows to Vrindaban*, p. 9.

24. Grierson, George Abraham, Report on Colonial Emigration [25 February 1883], Diary entry dated 13 January 1883 in Appendix, P/2058, Government of India Proceedings on Emigration, India Office Records, The British Library.

25. Grierson Report, 13 January 1883 Diary Entry, India Office Records.

26. Grierson Report, 17 March 1882 Diary Entry, India Office Records.

27. Grierson Report, 6 January 1883 Diary Entry, India Office Records.

28. Grierson Report, 23 December 1882 Diary Entry, India Office Records.

29. Grierson Report, 27 January 1883 Diary Entry, India Office Records.

30. Pitcher Report, Subsection 77, India Office Records.

31. Pitcher Report, Subsection 36, India Office Records.

32. Pitcher Report, Subsection 75, India Office Records.

33. Pitcher Report, 2 April 1882 Diary Entry, India Office Records.

34. Banerjee, *Under the Raj*, p. 77.

35. Ibid., p. 22.

36. Hyam, Ronald, *Empire and Sexuality: The British Experience*, Manchester: Manchester University Press, 1990, p. 64.

37. Tambe, Ashwini, *Codes of Misconduct: Regulating Prostitution in Late Colonial Bombay*, Minneapolis: University of Minnesota Press, 2009, pp. 39–43.

38. Ibid., p. 41.

39. Thanks to Ashwini Tambe for this insight.

40. Carter, Marina, *Lakshmi's Legacy*, Mauritius: Editions de L'Ocean Indien, 1994, p. 27. The quote comes from a June 1869 letter by Madras agent Charles Doorly.

41. Ibid., p. 27.

42. McNeill, James and Chimman Lal, Report on the Condition of Indian Immigrants in the Four British Colonies: Trinidad, British Guiana or Demerara, Jamaica and Fiji and in the Dutch Colony of Surinam or Dutch Guiana [1915], Part II, Section 60, XLVII (Cd. 7744), British Parliamentary Papers, The British Library.

43. Kelly, John, *A Politics of Virtue: Hinduism, Sexuality and Countercolonial Discourse*, Chicago: University of Chicago Press, 1991, p. 58.

44. Banerjee, *Under the Raj*, p. 78. The interviews appeared in the 1 May 1851 edition of *Sangbad Bhaskar*.

45. Grierson, George Abraham, *Bihar Peasant Life, Being a Discursive Catalogue of the Surroundings of the People of That Province*, Calcutta: The Bengal Secretariat Press, 1885, pp. 358–9.

46. Banerjee, *Under the Raj*, p. 78.
47. Ibid., p. 116. The letter appeared in the journal *Vidyadarshan* in 1842.
48. "The notion of male breadwinner became entrenched through laws limiting women's employability, such as the Factory Acts." Tambe, *Codes of Misconduct*, p. 11.
49. Banerjee, *Under the Raj*, p. 116.
50. Grierson Report, Chapter 8, India Office Records.
51. Jha, J.C., "The Background of the Legalisation of Non-Christian Marriages in Trinidad and Tobago," *East Indians in the Caribbean: Colonialism and the Struggle for Identity*, Brereton, Bridget and Winston Dookeran (eds), New York: Kraus International, 1982, p. 117.
52. Pitcher Report, 8 April 1882 Diary Entry, India Office Records.
53. Pitcher Report, Subsection 67(3), India Office Records.
54. Ibid.
55. Pitcher Report, 25 April 1882 Diary Entry, India Office Records.
56. Grierson Report, Chapter 8, India Office Records.
57. Grierson Report, Chapter 5, India Office Records.
58. Vatuk, Ved Prakash, "Protest Songs of British Guiana," *The Journal of American Folklore*, 77, 305 (1964), p. 224.
59. Ibid., p. 224. The pamphlet was *Ishvar ki Santan ko hai Varsa ka Nark aur Sitaharan*, by Chandra Shekhar Sharma, published in Berbice in 1930.
60. The widow's daughter-in-law Ramnanee Maharaj, interview by Peggy Mohan, 1978, transcript, OP55, Oral and Pictorial Records Programme, The University of the West Indies, St. Augustine, Trinidad.
61. Fazal Ali, interview by Noor Kumar Mahabir, 18 September 1982, transcript, OP13, Oral and Pictorial Records Programme, University of the West Indies, St. Augustine, Trinidad.
62. Singh, Alice Bhagwandy, "The Autobiography of Alice Bhagwandai Sital Persaud, 1892–1958," (unpublished manuscript, last modified April 1962), Microsoft Word file of this autobiography by Phuljharee's granddaughter, edited by Moses Seenarine and provided by The Rajkumari Singh Cultural Center in New York City.
63. Banks, C., Report of the Protector of Emigrants on Emigration from the Port of Calcutta [30 April 1904], P/6830, Government of India Proceedings on Emigration, India Office Records, The British Library.
64. Pitcher Report, 16 March 1882 Entry, India Office Records.
65. McNeill and Lal Report, Part II, Section 60, British Parliamentary Papers.
66. Protector of Emigrants Report, 30 April 1904, India Office Records. Of the 2,509 women who sailed, only 598 were accompanied by husbands, according to this report.

4. INTO DARK WATERS

1. Richmond, Theophilus, *The First Crossing: Journal of Theophilus Richmond*, Dabydeen, David and Ian McDonald (eds), Georgetown: The Caribbean Press for the Government of Guyana, 2010, p. 55.
2. Ibid., p. 54.
3. Ibid., pp. 91–2.
4. Kelly, John, *A Politics of Virtue: Hinduism, Sexuality and Countercolonial Discourse in Fiji*, Chicago: University of Chicago Press, 1991, p. 29.
5. Hill, Arthur H., "Emigration from India," *Timehri*, VI (1919), pp. 43–52. Hill was an

immigration agent in British Guiana who later retired as head of the colony's immigration agency.

6. Robert Mitchell to the Government Secretary of British Guiana, 17 March 1904, File No. 14515, CO 111/543, Colonial Office Correspondence, Public Record Office, The National Archives of the UK, Kew.

7. Hill, "Emigration from India," pp. 43–52.

8. Khan, Munshi Rahman, *Jeevan Prakash: The Autobiography of an Indian Indentured Labourer*, Delhi: Shipra Publications, 2005, p. 77.

9. Memorandum by A.C. Stuart, Emigration Agent for Jamaica, 6 January 1891, enclosed in File No. 15947, CO 384/190, Colonial Office Correspondence, Public Record Office, The National Archives of the UK, Kew.

10. Tinker, Hugh, *A New System of Slavery: The Export of Indian Labour Overseas, 1830–1920*, Oxford: Oxford University Press, 1974; London: Hansib, 1993, p. 140. Citations refer to Hansib edition.

11. See, for instance: Report on the arrival of *The Jura* by Immigration Agent General of British Guiana, 9 December 1897, File No. 26300, CO 111/497, Colonial Office Correspondence, Public Record Office, The National Archives of the UK, Kew. Some of the clothes provided to the immigrants aboard were rotten.

12. Sanadhya, Totaram, *My Twenty-One Years in the Fiji Islands*, Suva, Fiji: The Fiji Museum, 1991, p. 39. He migrated to Fiji in 1893.

13. Vatuk, Ved Prakash, "Protest Songs of British Guiana," *The Journal of American Folklore*, 77, 305 (1964), p. 224.

14. Ibid., p. 255. *Sala* is an insult on par with motherfucker.

15. Civil Surgeon in Benares to the Inspector General of Civil Hospital, North-Western Provinces and Oudh, 19 May 1894, enclosed in File No. 15947, CO 384/190, Colonial Office Correspondence, Public Record Office, The National Archives of the UK, Kew.

16. Moolian, interview by Noor Kumar Mahabir, *The Still Cry*, Tacarigua, Trinidad: Calaloux Publications, 1985, p. 69.

17. Pahalad, interview by Ahmed Ali, "The Indenture Experience in Fiji," *Bulletin of the Fiji Museum*, 5 (1979), p. 36.

18. Khan, *Jeevan Prakash*, p. 80.

19. *The Laws of Manu* 3: 150–158. Available online at http://www.sacred-texts.com/hin/manu.htm

20. Arp, Susmita, *Kalapani*, Stuttgart: Franz Steiner Verlag, 2000, pp. 254–8. My thanks to Sonam Kachru for bringing this University of Hamburg dissertation to my attention and for raising important questions about place, caste and identity.

21. Bhagmanti "Bebi" Ramanan (Sujaria's granddaughter), interview by author, New Jersey, Summer 2011.

22. Ship manifest for *The Clyde*, 1903, The Walter Rodney Archives, Georgetown, Guyana.

23. Bernadette Persaud (Mahadai Singh's great-granddaughter), e-mail message to author, 22 July 2011. Reuben Lachmansingh (Mahadai Singh's grandson), interview by author, 25 October 2011.

24. Annetta Seecharan (Manakia's great-granddaughter) and Kamla and Daro (Manakia's granddaughters), interview by author, August 2011.

25. Maharani, interview by Patricia Mohammed, 1990, tape 33, OP62, Oral and Pictorial Records Programme, Alma Jordan Library, University of the West Indies, St. Augustine,

Trinidad. Maharani, interview by Noor Kumar Mahabir, *The Still Cry*, Trinidad: Calaloux Publications, 1988, pp. 79–88.

26. Maharani, interview by Noor Kumar Mahabir, *The Still Cry*, Trinidad: Calaloux Publications, 1988, p. 79.

27. Maharani, interview by Patricia Mohammed, 1990, tape 33, OP62, Oral and Pictorial Records Programme, Alma Jordan Library, University of the West Indies, St. Augustine, Trinidad.

28. Maharani, interview by Noor Kumar Mahabir, *The Still Cry*, Trinidad: Calaloux Publications, 1988, p. 80.

29. Lakhpat, interview by Ahmed Ali, "The Indenture Experience in Fiji," *Bulletin of the Fiji Museum*, 5 (1979), p. 28. Lakhpat left India in 1911.

30. Sanadhya, *My Twenty-One Years in the Fiji Islands*, p. 40.

31. Vatuk, "Protest Songs of British Guiana," p. 255.

32. Maharani, interview by Noor Kumar Mahabir, *The Still Cry*, Trinidad: Calaloux Publications, 1988, p. 81.

5. HER MIDDLE PASSAGE

1. This narrative is based on testimony and correspondence about *The Main*'s 1902 journey in The British Library's India Office Records and Colonial Office Correspondence at National Archives of the UK at Kew. See primarily Report on the Voyage of the Ship *Main*, 10 May 1902, File No. 928, L/PJ/6/600, Public and Judicial Departmental Papers, India Office Records, The British Library.

2. A copy of the contract is enclosed in "Mutiny on *The Main*," 29 August 1902, File No. 34612, CO 111/535, Colonial Office Correspondence, Public Record Office, The National Archives of the UK, Kew.

3. Laing, James M., "Handbook for Surgeons Superintendent of the Coolie Emigration Service," London: Colonial Office, 1889, enclosed in File No. 565, L/PJ/6/249, Public and Judicial Departmental Papers, India Office Records, The British Library.

4. Tinker, Hugh, *A New System of Slavery: The Export of Indian Labour Overseas, 1830–1920*, Oxford: Oxford University Press, 1974; London: Hansib, 1993, p. 157. Citations refer to Hansib edition.

5. Report on the arrival of *The Brenda* in British Guiana, 11 January 1894, CO 384/186, Colonial Office Correspondence, Public Record Office, The National Archives of the UK, Kew.

6. Ireland, John, "Journal of Surgeon Superintendant aboard *The Brenda* in 1893," enclosed in 'The Employment of Negro Sailors,' 17 July 1894, File No. 12444, CO 384/190, Colonial Office Correspondence, Public Record Office, The National Archives of the UK, Kew.

7. Report on the arrival of the Coolie Ship *Main* in British Guiana, enclosing medical inspector's report, 24 April 1902, File No. 15784, CO 111/532, Colonial Office Correspondence, Public Record Office, The National Archives of the UK, Kew.

8. Report on the arrival of *The Bann* in British Guiana, 17 May 1894, File No. 8520, CO 384/189, Colonial Office Correspondence, Public Record Office, The National Archives of the UK, Kew.

9. Report on the arrival of *The Moy* in Jamaica, 16 July 1891, File No. 14342, CO 384/181, Colonial Office Correspondence, Public Record Office, The National Archives of the UK, Kew.

10. "Employment of Negro Sailors on Ships Conveying Coolies Between India and the Colonies," 30 July 1894, File No. 1333, L/PJ/6/378, Public and Judicial Departmental Papers, India Office Records, The British Library.

11. "Employment of Negroes and Mulattoes on Emigrant Vessels and the Discharge of Refractory Sailors at Ports of Call," 6 March 1895, File No. 465, L/PJ/6/393, Public and Judicial Departmental Papers, India Office Records, The British Library.

12. Letter enclosed in "Voyage of the Emigrant Ship *Main*: Question of Employing Black or Coloured Crew," 26 March 1903, File No. 737, L/PJ/6/632, Public and Judicial Departmental Papers, India Office Records, The British Library.

13. "Employment of Lascars on Coolie Ships to Fiji and the West Indies," 12 February 1884, File No. 424, L/PJ/6/119, Public and Judicial Departmental Papers, India Office Records, The British Library.

14. Report on the arrival of *The Avoca* in British Guiana, 8 March 1894, File No. 4159, CO 384/189, Colonial Office Correspondence, Public Record Office, The National Archives of the UK, Kew.

15. Laing, "Handbook for Surgeons Superintendent," 46, India Office Records.

16. Ibid., 44, India Office Records.

17. Tinker, *A New System of Slavery*, p. 148.

18. Report on the arrival of *The Mersey* in British Guiana, 7 December 1898, File No. 25575, CO 111/506, Colonial Office Correspondence, Public Record Office, The National Archives of the UK, Kew.

19. The details and testimony pertaining to the mutiny aboard *The Ailsa* come primarily from: Report of the Commissioners Appointed to Inquire into the Treatment of Immigrants from India on Board the Immigrant Ship *Ailsa*, enclosed in "Voyage of *The Ailsa* from Calcutta to British Guiana, October 1876," P/932, Government of India Proceedings on Emigration, India Office Records, The British Library.

20. Death announcement for William Holman, 15 April 1895, *The Times of London*, accessed online at http://www.rootsweb.ancestry.com/~nyggbs/VitalRecords/DeathsHtoL.pdf

21. Tinker, *A New System of Slavery*, p. 161.

22. "Conduct of the Crew of *The Hesperides* during a Voyage from Calcutta to Trinidad," 16 August 1884, File No. 1694, L/PJ/6/133, Public and Judicial Departmental Papers, India Office Records, The British Library.

23. Lt. Colonel B. Fischer, MCS, British Consular Agent in Karikal to the Chief Secretary of the Government of Madras, 21 December 1883, enclosed in Ibid.

24. William Holman to J. Grant, Protector of Emigrants at Calcutta, 28 November 1883, enclosed in "Conduct of the Crew of *The Hesperides*…," 16 August 1884, India Office Records.

25. "Conduct of the Crew of *The Hesperides*…," 16 August 1884, India Office Records.

26. William Holman to Grant, 28 November 1883, in Ibid.

27. Report on the arrival of *The Ganges* in British Guiana, 19 April 1895, File No. 6800, CO 384/191, Colonial Office Correspondence, Public Record Office, The National Archives of the UK, Kew. Holman's death on that vessel is described in his assistant's logbook.

28. "Conduct of the Crew of *The Hesperides*…," 16 August 1884, India Office Records.

29. G. Stewart, Esq, MD to Grant, 3 December 1883, enclosed in Ibid.

30. J.G. Winstone, Esq, MD, late SS of *The Plassey* (51st voyage) to Grant, 13 December 1883, enclosed in "Conduct of the Crew of *The Hesperides*…," 16 August 1884, Ibid.

31. Laing, "Handbook for Surgeons Superintendent…," p. 40, India Office Records.

32. Report on the arrival of *The Ems*, 27 December 1895, File No. 22979, CO 384/191, Colonial Office Correspondence, Public Record Office, The National Archives of the UK, Kew.

33. "White people call these biscuits 'dog biscuits' and feed them to dogs. Oh dear God. Are we Indians equal to dogs?" Sanadhya, Totaram, *My Twenty-One Years in the Fiji Islands*, Suva, Fiji: The Fiji Museum, 1991, pp. 33–43.

34. *Census of India*, 1901, accessed through Google Books.

35. Bhagmania Seekumar, interview by linguist Peggy Mohan, 1978, OP 55, Oral and Pictorial Records Programme, The Alma Jordan Library, University of the West Indies, St. Augustine, Trinidad.

36. Rabe, Elizabeth, "A Social History of Indentured Indian Immigration to British Guiana and Trinidad, 1854–1884," unpublished master's thesis, University of the West Indies, 2006, Alma Jordan Library, University of the West Indies, St. Augustine, Trinidad.

37. Ibid.

38. Report by the Immigration Agent General of British Guiana to the Secretary of State for the Colonies [1903–1904], SEV+, British Guiana Administration Reports, The New York Public Library.

39. Journal by Surgeon Superintendent Richard Fonseca, enclosed in the Report by the Immigration Agent General on the Arrival of *The Clyde* in 1900, 16 May 1900, File No. 17888, CO 111/519, Colonial Office Correspondence, Public Record Office, The National Archives of the UK, Kew.

40. Report on the arrival of *The Jura* in British Guiana, 29 December 1892, File No. 24868, CO 384/184, Colonial Office Correspondence, Public Record Office, The National Archives of the UK, Kew.

41. Report on the arrival of *The Jura* in British Guiana, 10 December 1898, File No. 27797, CO 111/507, Colonial Office Correspondence, Public Record Office, The National Archives of the UK, Kew.

42. Report on the arrival of *The Rohilla* in British Guiana, 12 April 1883, File No. 6112, CO 384/144, Colonial Office Correspondence, Public Record Office, The National Archives of the UK, Kew.

43. Report on the arrival of *The Jura* in British Guiana, 25 February 1892, File No. 3744, CO 384/184, Colonial Office Correspondence, Public Record Office, The National Archives of the UK, Kew.

44. Report on the arrival of *The Main* in British Guiana, 8 February 1894, File No. 2431, CO 384/189, Colonial Office Correspondence, Public Record Office, The National Archives of the UK, Kew.

45. Report on the arrival of *The Jura* in British Guiana, 25 February 1892, Public Record Office.

46. Report on the arrival of *The Avoca* in British Guiana, 8 March 1894, Public Record Office.

47. Report on the arrival of *The Avon* in British Guiana, 8 March 1893, File No. 3917, CO 384/189, Colonial Office Correspondence, Public Record Office, The National Archives of the UK, Kew.

48. Report on the arrival of *The Rohilla* in British Guiana, 22 May 1875, File No. 1241, CO 384/106, Colonial Office Correspondence, Public Record Office, The National Archives of the UK, Kew.

49. Report on the arrival of *The Foyle* in British Guiana, 15 February 1900, File No. 5347,

CO 111/517, Colonial Office Correspondence, Public Record Office, The National Archives of the UK, Kew.

50. Report on the arrival of *The Bann* in British Guiana, 17 May 1894, Public Record Office.

51. Moses Seenarine notes that suicide constituted one form of resistance by enslaved African women in the Caribbean, raising the possibility that Indian women on indenture ships might also have killed themselves to resist. See Seenarine, Moses, "Indentured Indian Women in Colonial Guyana: Recruitment, Migration, Labour and Caste," *Sojourners to Settlers: The Indian Migrants in the Caribbean and the Americas*, Gosine, Mahin and Dhanpaul Narine (eds), New York: Windsor Press, 1999.

52. Report on the arrival of *The Brenda* in British Guiana, 28 November 1894, File No. 20736, CO 384/189, Colonial Office Correspondence, Public Record Office, The National Archives of the UK, Kew.

53. Report on the arrival of *The Volga* in British Guiana, 29 December 1892, File No. 24867, CO 384/184, Colonial Office Correspondence, Public Record Office, The National Archives of the UK, Kew.

54. Report on the arrival of *The Atalanta* in British Guiana, 20 May 1875, File No. 1225, CO 384/106, Colonial Office Correspondence, Public Record Office, The National Archives of the UK, Kew.

55. Report on the arrival of *The Linguist* in British Guiana, 22 November 1875, File No. 14130, CO 384/106, Colonial Office Correspondence, Public Record Office, The National Archives of the UK, Kew.

56. "Outrage on the *SS Avon*," 7 May 1907, File No. 16200, CO 111/559, Colonial Office Correspondence, Public Record Office, The National Archives of the UK, Kew.

57. Report on the arrival of *The Lena* in British Guiana, 23 November 1899, File No. 32512, CO 111/514, Colonial Office Correspondence, Public Record Office, The National Archives of the UK, Kew.

58. This figure is based on my analysis of data in the fifty-six surviving British Guiana indenture ship reports from 1890 to 1902 and found in Colonial Office Correspondence, Public Record Office, The National Archives of the UK, Kew.

59. Angel, Capt. W.H., *The Clipper Ship 'Sheila'*, London: Heath Cranton Limited, 1921, p. 185.

60. Bronkhurst, Rev. H.V.P., *The Colony of British Guiana and its Labouring Population*, London: published for the author by T. Woolmer, 1883, p. 148.

61. Report on the arrival of *The Silhet* in British Guiana, 31 March 1883, File No. 5432, CO 384/144, Colonial Office Correspondence, Public Record Office, The National Archives of the UK, Kew.

62. Report on the arrival of *The Elbe* in British Guiana, 23 March 1893, File No. 4775, CO 384/186, Colonial Office Correspondence, Public Record Office, The National Archives of the UK, Kew.

63. Report on the arrival of *The Foyle* in British Guiana, 17 February 1900, Public Record Office.

64. "Arrival of *Erne*," 15 February 1892, File No. 3009, CO 384/185, Colonial Office Correspondence, Public Record Office, The National Archives of the UK, Kew.

65. Francis Mewa to Crown Agents, 18 March 1892, enclosed in "Conduct of Dr Cecil," File No. 5729, CO 384/184, Colonial Office Correspondence, Public Record Office, The National Archives of the UK, Kew.

66. John Morton, Missionary to Indian Immigrants, to the Secretary of State for the Colo-

nies, 21 June 1893, enclosed in "Francis Mewa," File No. 11814, CO 384/187, Colonial Office Correspondence, Public Record Office, The National Archives of the UK, Kew. Testimonial by John Morton, 19 May 1892 and Minute from Protector of Immigrants Charles Mitchell, 12 July 1892, both enclosed in "Mr F. Mewa," 28 July 1892, File No. 15128, CO 384/184, Colonial Office Correspondence, Public Record Office, The National Archives of the UK, Kew.

67. Janky's emigration pass, Ship manifest for *The Silhet*, 1883, The Walter Rodney Archives, Georgetown, Guyana. Marriage certificate of Janky and T.D. Atkins, St. Andrew's Kirk, Georgetown, British Guiana. The marriage certificate identifies her as a widow and identifies her father as a clerk named Bhagwanpersad.

68. Report on the arrival of *The Silhet* in British Guiana, 31 March 1883, Public Record Office.

69. Marriage certificate of Janky and T.D. Atkins, St. Andrew's Kirk, Georgetown, Guyana.

70. *The British Medical Directory* and *Australasian Medical Directory*, 1875–1895.

71. Birth, death, baptismal and burial notices, India Office Family Records, The British Library.

72. Cable, K.J., "Atkins, Thomas (1808–1860)," in *Australian Dictionary of Biography*, accessed online at http://adb.anu.edu.au/biography/atkins-thomas-1724

73. Atkins, Thomas, *The Wanderings of the Clerical Eulysses*, self-published: Greenwich, 1859.

74. "Marriage of Dr Atkins with Coolie Immigrant Janky," 15 March 1883, File No. 4560, CO 384/144, Colonial Office Correspondence, Public Record Office, The National Archives of the UK, Kew. Shepherd, Verene, *Maharani's Misery*, Kingston: University of the West Indies Press, 2002, p. 30.

75. Report on the arrival of *The Foyle* in British Guiana, 17 February 1899, Public Record Office.

76. Report on the arrival of *The Foyle* in British Guiana, 17 February 1899, Public Record Office.

77. My analysis of data provided in indenture ship reports filed between 1883 and 1908 and found in Colonial Office Correspondence, Public Record Office, The National Archives of the UK, Kew.

78. Chanansingh, interview by Noor Kumar Mahabir, 18 September 1982, OP13, Oral and Pictorial Records Programme, The Alma Jordan Library, University of the West Indies, St. Augustine, Trinidad.

79. Report on the arrival of *The Foyle* in British Guiana, 17 February 1899, Public Record Office.

6. A NEW WORLD

1. Raleigh, Sir Walter, "The Discoverie of Guiana," *Voyages and Travels, Ancient and Modern: The Harvard Classics, Volume 33*, New York: P.F. Collier and Son Company, 1910, p. 321.

2. Copley, Ian Alfred, *Down in Demerara: A Student Song Set for S.A. Bar, Choir and Unison Chorus*, London: Alfred Lengnick & Co., 1964.

3. Rodney, Walter, *A History of the Guyanese Working People*, Baltimore: The Johns Hopkins University Press, 1981, pp. 35–6.

4. Report of the Comptroller of Customs on the Customs Revenue and the Trade and Navigation of the Colony for the Year 1899–1900, British Guiana Administration Reports, Georgetown: C.K. Jardine, Printer to the Government of British Guiana, 1900, p. 11.

5. British Guiana Directory, Georgetown: *The Daily Chronicle*, 1904, transcription of entries accessed through ancestry.com at http://www.rootsweb.ancestry.com/~nyggbs/Transcriptions/1904Directory/ One solicitor and one reporter of Indian origin, E.A. Luckhoo and Joseph Ruhomon respectively, were listed as living in the colony but both were based in New Amsterdam, the capital of the outlying province of Berbice.

6. *The Demerara Daily Chronicle*, 5–18 November 1903, British Library Newspapers Collection, Colindale.

7. "Notes by the way," *The Sunday Chronicle*, 18 October 1903, British Library Newspapers Collection, Colindale.

8. Robert Mitchell to Governor of British Guiana, 3 September 1903, enclosed in File No. 40336, CO 111/538, Colonial Office Correspondence, Public Record Office, The National Archives of the UK, Kew.

9. Circular from Immigration Agent-General A.H. Alexander, 15 September 1903, enclosed in File No. 40336, CO 111/538, Colonial Office Correspondence, Public Record Office, The National Archives of the UK, Kew.

10. *The Argosy*, 11 May 1904, as cited in Mangru, Basdeo, "The Sex Ratio Disparity and its Consequences Under Indenture in British Guiana," *India in the Caribbean*, Dabydeen, David and Brinsley Samaroo (eds), London: Hansib Publishing Ltd., 1987, p. 225.

11. Higman, B.W., *Slave Populations of the British Caribbean*, 2nd edn., Baltimore: Johns Hopkins University Press, 1984; Kingston: University of the West Indies Press, 1995, p. 116. Citations refer to the UWI edition.

12. Ibid., p. 117. This applied to the entire Anglophone Caribbean, except Trinidad and the provinces making up British Guiana, where the ratios were still slightly skewed. At Emancipation, there were 110 male to 100 female slaves in Demerara and Essequibo, and 114 male to 100 female slaves in Demerara.

13. Checkland, S.G., *The Gladstones: A Family History*, Cambridge University Press, 1971, p. 320. He received £84,718.

14. John Gladstone to Gillanders, Arbuthnot & Co., March 10, 1837, as cited in Scoble, John, *A Brief Exposure of the Deplorable Conditions of the Hill Coolies in British Guiana and Mauritius and the Nefarious Means by Which They Were Induced to Resort to These Colonies*, London: Harvey & Darton, 1840, p. 6.

15. Scoble, *A Brief Exposure of the Deplorable Conditions of the Hill Coolies*, p. 27.

16. *Royal Gazette*, 8 May 1838, as quoted in Ruhomon, Peter, *Centenary History of East Indians in Guiana*, Georgetown: *Daily Chronicle* Reprints, 1947, p. 26.

17. Deposition by Plantation Belle Vue manager John Russell to W.B. Wolseley, Report on living conditions of coolies at Belle Vue, 11 March 1839, enclosed in Governor Henry Light to the Marquess of Normanby, 13 April 1839, File No. 8, CO 111/163, Colonial Office Correspondence, Public Record Office, The National Archives of the UK, Kew.

18. Wolseley, W.B., Report on living conditions of coolies at Belle Vue, 11 March 1839, enclosed in Governor Henry Light to the Marquess of Normanby, 13 April 1839, File No. 8, CO 111/163, Colonial Office Correspondence, Public Record Office, The National Archives of the UK, Kew.

19. Erickson, Edgar L., "The Introduction of East Indian Coolies into the British West Indies," *The Journal of Modern History*, 6, 2 (1934), pp. 127–46.

20. *The British Emancipator*, 9 January 1839, enclosed in Governor Henry Light to the Marquess of Normanby, 13 April 1839, File No. 8, CO 111/163, Colonial Office Correspondence, Public Record Office, The National Archives of the UK, Kew.

21. Tinker, Hugh, *A New System of Slavery: The Export of Indian Labour Overseas, 1830–1920*, Oxford: Oxford University Press, 1974; London: Hansib, 1993, p. 60. Citations refer to Hansib edition.

22. Reddock, Rhoda, "Freedom Denied: Indian Women and Indentureship in Trinidad and Tobago, 1845–1917," *Economic and Political Weekly*, 20, 43 (1985), p. WS-80.

23. Governor Longden to Earl of Carnarvon, 28 October 1875, File No. 218, CO 384/106, Colonial Office Correspondence, Public Record Office, The National Archives of the UK, Kew.

24. Mangru, Basdeo, "The Sex Ratio Disparity and its Consequences," pp. 211–2. In 1868, the quota became forty to 100.

25. These details come from advertisements and the weather report in *The Demerara Daily Chronicle*, 6 November 1903, The British Library Newspaper Collections, Colindale.

26. I base these figures on: Immigration Agent General A.H. Alexander, Half-yearly Report on the Immigrant Population, September 1903, P/7136, Government of India Proceedings on Emigration, India Office Records, The British Library.

27. *Guyanese Sugar Plantations in the Late 19th Century: A Contemporary Description from the Argosy, 1882*, Walter Rodney (ed.), Georgetown: Release Publishers, 1979. When Enmore's 709 slaves were emancipated, its owners received roughly $4.3 million in current US dollars, one of the six largest compensation awards worldwide, according to the Register of Claims T71/885 British Guiana, Records Created and Inherited by HM Treasury Office of Registry of Colonial Slavery and Slave Compensation Commission Records, The National Archives of the UK, Kew.

28. Charles Bethune (G.M. Bethune's grandson), in e-mail to author, 29 December 2011.

29. Charles Bethune (G.M. Bethune's grandson), in e-mail to author, 24 January 2012.

30. Platt, John, "Enmore and its Devon Links," unpublished paper, presented at the Woodbury Historical Society, September 2009, courtesy of its author. Platt, who worked in the 1960s for the multinational Booker Brothers, which ultimately bought Enmore, interviewed the descendants of the estate's three managers from the 1870s-1890s. A granddaughter of one of the couples pictured gave the Enmore photograph to Platt.

31. Kirke, Henry, *Twenty-Five Years in British Guiana*, London: Sampson Low, Marston & Company Limited, 1898, p. 45.

32. Ibid., p. 46.

33. Comins, Surgeon-Major D.W.D., Note on Emigration from India to British Guiana, 12 September 1893, p. 17, File Nos. 1902 & 1903, L/PJ/6/357, Public and Judicial Departmental Papers, India Office Records, The British Library.

34. Vatuk, Ved Prakash, "Protest Songs of British Guiana," *The Journal of American Folklore*, 77, 305 (1964), pp. 220–235.

35. Tinker, *A New System of Slavery*, p. 194. See also p. 56 of Report of the Committee on Emigration from India to the Crown Colonies and Protectorates, known as the Lord Sanderson Commission [1910], XXVII (Cd. 5192–94), British Parliamentary Papers, The British Library.

36. Seecharan, Clem, *Bechu: Bound Coolie Radical in British Guiana, 1894–1901*, Kingston: University of the West Indies Press, 1999, pp. 3–4. The biographical details about Bechu emerged during his testimony before the West India Royal Commission in 1897.

37. Memorandum by Bechu to the West India Royal Commission, as reproduced in Seecharan, *Bechu: Bound Coolie Radical*, p. 120.

38. Bechu to *The Daily Chronicle*, 8 July 1898, as reproduced in Seecharan, *Bechu: Bound Coolie Radical*, p. 68.

39. A.H. Alexander's Half-yearly Report on the Immigrant Population, September 1903, India Office Records.

40. As quoted in Mohapatra, Prabhu P., "Wife Murders and the Making of a Sexual Contract for Indian Immigrant Labour in the British Caribbean Colonies," *Studies in History*, 11, 2 (1995). These comments by planter Robert Guppy appeared in an official report to an 1888 Royal Commission on the franchise and electoral districts in Trinidad.

41. Vatuk, "Protest Songs of British Guiana," p. 226.

42. Andrews, C.F., *Impressions of British Guiana*, Mangru, Basdeo (ed.), Chicago: Adams Press, 2007, pp. 69, 94.

43. Excerpt from the 8 July 1899 *Argosy* quoted in Bechu to the Immigration Agent General, enclosed in File No. 1535, L/PJ/6/226/1535, Public and Judicial Departmental Papers, India Office Records, The British Library.

44. Bethune to Immigration Agent General, enclosed in File No. 1535, L/PJ/6/226/1535, Public and Judicial Departmental Papers, India Office Records, The British Library.

45. An indentured immigrant in Suriname, for example, described the procedure thus: "You were allotted a room. Everybody also received a woman to share the room with. If there were no women left, you got a man. I got a woman, but didn't want her. A week later a man came who wanted a woman but hadn't received one. I gave her away. I didn't ask anything for her." Hoefte, Rosemarijn, *In Place of Slavery*, Gainsburg: University of Florida Press, 1998, p. 110.

46. Faizal Ali, interview by Noor Kumar Mahabir, 18 September 1982, OP13, Oral and Pictorial Records Programme, Alma Jordan Library, University of the West Indies, St. Augustine, Trinidad.

47. This story is reconstructed from: Maharani and her daughter Mahadaye Ramsewak, interviews by Patricia Mohammed, 1990, tape 33, OP62, Oral and Pictorial Records Programme, Alma Jordan Library, University of the West Indies, St. Augustine, Trinidad as well as Maharani, interview by Noor Kumar Mahabir, *The Still Cry*, Trinidad: Calaloux Publications, 1988, pp. 79–88.

48. Khan, Munshi Rahman, *Jeevan Prakash: The Autobiography of an Indian Indentured Labourer*, Delhi: Shipra Publications, 2005, p. 91.

49. Ibid.

50. Ibid.

51. Ibid., p. 96.

52. Ibid.

53. Tinker, *A New System of Slavery*, pp. 201–2, 206.

54. Hoefte, *In Place of Slavery*, pp. 75–76.

55. Ibid.

56. Lakhpat, indentured immigrant, interviewed by Ahmed Ali, "The Indenture Experience in Fiji," *Bulletin of the Fiji Museum*, 5 (1979), p. 28.

57. Comins, Surgeon-Major D.W.D., *Note on Emigration from India to Trinidad*, 1893, as cited in Reddock, Rhoda, "The Indentureship Experience: Women in Trinidad and Tobago, 1845–1917," *Women Plantation Workers: International Experiences*, Jain, Shobita and Rhoda Reddock (eds), Berg: Oxford, 1998, p. 35.

58. Hoefte, *In Place of Slavery*, pp. 75–76.

59. Shepherd, Verene, "Constructing Visibility: Indian Women in the Jamaican Segment of

the Indian diaspora," *Gendered Realities: Essays in Caribbean Feminist Thought*, Moham-med, Patricia (ed.), Kingston: University of the West Indies Press, 2002, p. 112.

60. Mohapatra, Prabhu P., "Restoring the Family: Wife Murders and the Making of a Sex-ual Contract for Indian Immigrant Labour in the British Caribbean Colonies, 1860–1920," *Studies in History* 11, no. 2 (1995): pp. 227–260.

61. *The Law Reports of British Guiana*, 1919, The Law Offices of Cameron & Shepherd, Georgetown, British Guiana.

62. Naidu, Vijay, *The Violence of Indenture in Fiji*, Suva: World University Service, in associ-ation with the University of the South Pacific, 1980, p. 38. Naidu interviewed three women and twelve men who had been indentured in Fiji.

63. Duff, Rev. Robert, *British Guiana*, Glasgow: Murray, 1866, p. 319.

64. Ibid.

65. Report on the arrival of *The Brenda* in British Guiana, 26 January 1893, File No. 1311, CO 384/186, Colonial Office Correspondence, Public Record Office, The National Archives of the UK, Kew.

66. Hyam, Ronald, *Empire and Sexuality: The British Experience*, Manchester: Manchester University Press, 1990, pp. 128–9.

67. See Dalrymple, William, *White Mughals: Love and Betrayal in 18th-Century India*, Lon-don: Penguin Books, 2004.

68. Governor Henry Light to Lord Glenelg, 11 January 1839, File No. 7, CO 111/162, Colo-nial Office Correspondence, Public Record Office, The National Archives of the UK, Kew.

69. Correspondence Relating to the Return of Coolies from British Guiana to India [3 July 1843], pp. 14 and 31, XXXV, no. 404, Parliamentary Papers, The British Library.

70. Kirke, *Twenty-Five Years in British Guiana*, p. 263.

71. This account is reconstructed from correspondence, newspaper clippings, sworn state-ments and trial transcripts to be found in 22 March 1906, File No. 9983, CO 111/549; 2 April 1906, File No. 11533, CO 111/550; 16 April 1906, File Nos. 13396 & 13397, CO 111/550; 30 April 1906, File No. 15249, CO 111/550; 5 June 1906, File No. 20143, CO 111/550; 14 August 1906, File No. 29963, CO 111/551; 19 March 1906, File No. 9570, CO 111/554; and 4 July 1906, File No. 24054, CO 111/554, Colonial Office Correspondence, Public Record Office, The National Archives of the UK, Kew.

72. Diptee, Audra, "Cultural Transfer and Transformation: Revisiting Indo-Afro Sexual Rela-tionships in Trinidad and British Guiana in the Late 19th Century," *The Society for Carib-bean Studies Annual Conference Papers*, 4 (2003), p. 9.

73. These observers included Methodist missionary H.V.P Bronkhurst and the sheriff Henry Kirke, both authors of travelogues about British Guiana in the late nineteenth century.

74. Bronkhurst, H.V.P., *The Colony of British Guiana and its Labouring Population*, London: published for the author by T. Woolmer, 1883, p. 390.

75. Diptee, "Cultural Transfer and Transformation," p. 12.

76. Ibid.

77. Rodney, *A History of the Guyanese Working People*, p. 180.

78. Diptee, "Cultural Transfer and Transformation," pp. 9–11.

79. Jenkins, John Edward, *The Coolie: His Rights and His Wrongs*, New York: George Rout-ledge and Sons, 1871, p. 213.

80. Kirke, *Twenty-Five Years in British Guiana*, pp. 188–9.

81. Governor Scott to Kimberley, 15 August 1870, CO 111/376, Colonial Office Corre-

spondence, Public Record Office, The National Archives of the UK, Kew, as quoted in Mangru, "The Sex Ratio Disparity."

82. Josa, Archdeacon, "The Hindus in the West Indies," *Timehri: The Journal of the Royal Agricultural and Commercial Society*, 3 (1913), pp. 27–8.

83. Morton, Sarah Etter Silver, *John Morton of Trinidad: Pioneer Missionary of the Presbyterian Church in Canada to the East Indians in the British West Indies*, Toronto: Westminster Co., 1916, p. 342–3. As quoted in Niranjana, Tejaswini, *Mobilizing India: Women, Music and Migration Between India and Trinidad*, Durham and London: Duke University Press, 2006, p. 65.

84. Niranjana, *Mobilizing India*, p. 66.

85. "The coolie in Guiana," *The Daily Chronicle*, 24 September 1899, as excerpted in Seecharan, *Bechu: Bound Coolie Radical*, pp. 189–190.

86. Reddock, "The Indentureship Experience: Women in Trinidad and Tobago," p. 35. For British Guiana, see Diptee, "Cultural Transfer and Transformation," p. 7. Shameen, Shaista, "Migration, Labour and Plantation Women in Fiji," *Women Plantation Workers: International Experiences*, Jain, Shobita and Rhoda Reddock (eds), Berg: London, 1998, p. 57. Hoefte, *In Place of Slavery*, pp. 118, 122, 147.

87. Reddock, Rhoda, "The Search for Origins: Women and Division of Labour During Slavery and Indentureship," *Women, Labour and Politics in Trinidad and Tobago*, London: Zed Books, 1994.

88. Reddock, "The Indentureship Experience," p. 38. Shameen, "Migration, Labour and Plantation Women in Fiji," p. 58.

89. Carter, Marina, *Lakshmi's Legacy*, Stanley, Rose Hill, Mauritius: Editions de L'Ocean Indien, 1994, p. 115.

90. Ibid., p. 121.

91. Ibid., p. 119.

92. Ibid., p. 126.

93. Josa, "The Hindus in the West Indies," p. 27.

94. Annual Report of Emigration from the Port of Calcutta to British and Foreign Colonies, 21 August 1899, File No. 22154, CO 111/515, Colonial Office Correspondence, Public Record Office, The National Archives of the UK, Kew.

95. Reddock, "The Search for Origins," p. 30.

96. Governor Henry Irving to the Earl of Derby, 5 December 1883, File No. 21925, CO 384/144, Colonial Office Correspondence, Public Record Office, The National Archives of the UK, Kew.

97. Register of Births in Demerara, February to April 1878, transcription accessed online at: http://www.rootsweb.ancestry.com/~nyggbs/Transcriptions/RegistrarsLogBooks/1878_Pg162.pdf The logbook shows mothers and fathers arriving in the same year in twelve cases, mothers arriving after the fathers in fourteen cases and fathers arriving after the mothers in five cases. In one case, the father was in India.

98. Tinker, *A New System of Slavery*, p. 203.

99. Kirke, *Twenty-Five Years in British Guiana*, pp. 240–2. He tells the story of a teenaged girl married off for $50 and a cow by her father, who later reneged on his agreement, and gave her away in marriage to another man for a higher bride price.

100. Josa, "The Hindus in the West Indies," p. 27.

101. Baby's story is reconstructed from correspondence, petitions and hearing and trial transcripts found in: "Petition of Soomereah, Indian Immigrant Woman," 25 November

1896, File No. 24320, CO 111/488; "Suspension of G.H. Alexander," 1 October 1896, File No. 20373, CO 111/487; "G.H. Alexander Asks for Clemency," 1 October 1896, File No. 20376, CO 111/487; "Resignation of G.H. Alexander," 11 November 1896, File No. 23422, CO 111/488; "A.H. Alexander Applies for Appointment for Son," 25 January 1894, File No. 1505, CO 111/471; "A.H. Alexander Asks For a Cross to be Erected in Son's Honour in Lagos," 31 August 1898, File No. 19670, CO 111/505; "A.H. Alexander Must Pay For Son's Cross Himself," 27 September 1899, File No. 26106, CO 111/514, Colonial Office Correspondence, Public Record Office, The National Archives of the UK, Kew.

102. "Application from Mr Solomon for Release of Female Emigrant, Sukdai," 5 July 1894, File Nos. 1325 & 1348, L/PJ/6/378, Public and Judicial Departmental Papers, India Office Records, The British Library.

103. Bronkhurst, *The Colony of British Guiana*, p. 355.

7. BEAUTIFUL WOMAN WITHOUT A NOSE

1. For details from the coroner's report, see: "A horrible death," *The Daily Chronicle*, 13 October 1903, British Library Newspapers Collection, Colindale.

2. "Brutal assault by a coolie: woman shockingly mutilated," *The Daily Chronicle*, 23 June 1903, British Library Newspapers Collection, Colindale.

3. For more on colonial attitudes and laws regulating unions among Indian immigrants in British Guiana, see the works by Prabhu P. Mohapatra, Brian Moore, Basdeo Mangru and Dwarka Nath cited in this chapter.

4. Mangru, Basdeo, "The Sex Ratio Disparity and its Consequences," *India in the Caribbean*, Dabydeen, David and Brinsley Samaroo (eds), London: Hansib, 1987, p. 213.

5. Nath, Dwarka, *A History of Indians in Guyana*, Georgetown, Guyana: The Government of British Guiana, 1970, pp. 225–7. See statistical table listing annual figures for marriages among Indians from 1860 to 1969.

6. Report by the Immigration Agent General of British Guiana to the Secretary of State for the Colonies [1903–1904], SEV+, British Guiana Administration Reports, The New York Public Library.

7. See Kelly, John, "Fiji Indians and the Law," introduction to Sanadhya, Totaram, *My Twenty-One Years in the Fiji Islands*, Suva, Fiji: The Fiji Museum, 1991, p. 168. Kelly, a scholar of indenture in Fiji, notes that many of the murder cases there involved food: women refusing to cook, or cooking for someone else.

8. "A horrible death." *The Daily Chronicle*, 13 October 1903.

9. Ibid.

10. "Brutal assault by a coolie: woman shockingly murdered," *The Daily Chronicle*, 23 June 1903.

11. "The Plantation Vriesland murder," *The Daily Chronicle*, 14 October 1903, British Library Newspapers Collection, Colindale.

12. Ibid.

13. Ibid.

14. Reports by the Immigration Agent General of British Guiana to the Secretary of State for the Colonies [1903–1905], New York Public Library. The murders took place from May 1903 to July 1904.

15. "Execution at Georgetown: Vriesland murderer hanged," *The Daily Chronicle*, 1 November 1903, British Library Newspapers Collection, Colindale.
16. Sen, Nabaneeta Dev, "When Women Retell the *Ramayan*," *Manushi*, 108 (1998), p. 18.
17. Das, Tulsi, *Sri Ramacaritmanasa: The Manasa Lake Brimming Over With the Exploits of Sri Rama*, Gorakhpur, India: Gita Press, 2004, p. 725. All quotes are from the Gita Press edition.
18. Manuel, Peter, *East Indian Music in the West Indies*, Philadelphia: Temple University Press, 2000, p. 27. Manuel, an ethnomusicologist, describes the use of the dholak drum in plantation song sessions.
19. Ibid., p. 9. Manuel has traced the evolution of folk and religious songs brought to the Caribbean by indentured immigrants. Among the forms that survived was the chanting of verses from *the Ramayan* by male choruses "in a vigorous antiphonal style."
20. Tewari, Laxmi Ganesh, "Singing the Glory of Ram: The *Ramayan* Among Trinidad Indians," paper presented at ISER-NCIC Conference on Challenge and Change: The Indian Diaspora in its Historical Contexts, University of the West Indies, St. Augustine, Trinidad, August 1995. Tewari describes the *Ramcaritmanas* as "the most important document of the bhakti tradition."
21. Das, Tulsi, *Sri Ramacaritmanasa*, p. 689.
22. Erndl, Kathleen M., "The Mutilation of Surpanakha," *Many Ramayanas: The Diversity of a Narrative Tradition*, Berkeley: University of California Press, 1991, p. 82.
23. Doniger, Wendy, *The Hindus: An Alternative History*, New York: Penguin Books, 2009, p. 233.
24. Erndl, "The Mutilation of Surpanakha," p. 82.
25. Ibid., p. 72.
26. Das, Tulsi, *Sri Ramacaritmanasa*, p 707.
27. Ibid., p. 794.
28. Ibid., p. 948.
29. Tewari, "Singing the Glory of Ram."
30. Prasad, Shiu, *Indian Indentured Workers in Fiji*, Suva: The South Pacific Social Sciences Association, 1974, p. 29.
31. Manuel, *East Indian Music in the West Indies*, p. 17.
32. Maharaji Bahoori, interview with author, New York, August 2011. Bahoori, born during indenture, was raised in plantation barracks in Demerara.
33. "In those days, there were frequent recitals of the katha. One's jahajis from another estate often sent invitations for such occasions but one had to be back at one's own estate by 5:30 p.m. on Sunday. If one failed to return in time, one could be fined as much as 15/- or in lieu given two weeks jail. Then this fortnight was added to one's contract." Lakphat, interview by Ahmed Ali, "The Indenture Experience in Fiji," *Bulletin of the Fiji Museum*, 5 (1979), p. 28.
34. Nasaloo Ramaya, interview by Rosabelle Seesaran, 19 February 1991, tape 9, OP60, Oral and Pictorial Records Programme, Alma Jordan Library, University of the West Indies, St. Augustine, Trinidad.
35. Bronkhurst, H.V.P., *The Colony of British Guiana and its Labouring Population*, London: published for the author by T. Woolmer, 1883, p. 389. Bronkhurst refers to plantation theatrical exhibitions, dramatizing stories from the life of Ram, that continued well into the night.
36. Several scholars, including Patricia Mohammed for Trinidad and John Kelly for Fiji, have

noted the all-pervasive importance of the *Ramayan* to indentured immigrants in their attempts to make sense of their lives.

37. This cumulative figure is based on data compiled by the historians David Dodd, Basdeo Mangru and Brian L. Moore, the literary scholar Jeremy Poynting, and my own analysis of Immigration Agent General reports from 1906–1917. It covers forty-seven years, from 1859 to 1917, excluding two years for which statistics were not available.

38. Laurence, K.O., *A Question of Labour*, Kingston: Ian Randle Publishers, 1992, p. 238.

39. Mangru, "The Sex Ratio Disparity and its Consequences," p. 219.

40. Henry Bullock to his brother Fred, 5 December 1864, Letters and Photos from Berbice, Guyana by Henry Bullock, D/DVv 74, Essex Record Office, Chelmsford, England.

41. Mohapatra, Prabhu P., "Restoring the Family: Wife Murders and the Making of a Sexual Contract for Indian Immigrant Labour in the British Caribbean Colonies, 1860–1920," *Studies in History* 11, 2 (1995), pp. 227–260.

42. Bronkhurst, *The Colony of British Guiana*, p. 403.

43. Memorandum by Smith, W.H., "Defects and Abuses in the Immigration Department of British Guiana," 28 June 1883, P/2058, Government of India Proceedings on Emigration, India Office Records, The British Library.

44. Andrews, C.F. and W.W. Pearson, *Report on Indentured Labour in Fiji*, Allahabad: The Leader Press, February 1916, in P/V 160, Official Publications Series, India Office Records, The British Library.

45. Tinker, Hugh, *A New System of Slavery: The Export of Indian Labour Overseas, 1830–1920*, Oxford: Oxford University Press, 1974; London: Hansib, 1993, p. 204. Citations refer to Hansib edition.

46. Tinker, *A New System of Slavery*, p. 204.

47. Reddock, Rhoda, "The Search for Origins: Women and Division of Labour During Slavery and Indentureship," *Women, Politics and Labour in Trinidad and Tobago*, London: Zed Books, 1994, p. 29.

48. Comins, Surgeon-Major D.W.D., Note on Emigration from India to British Guiana, 12 September 1893, Section 45, File Nos. 1902 & 1903, L/PJ/6/357, Public and Judicial Departmental Papers, India Office Records, The British Library. See also Mangru, "The Sex Ratio Disparity and its Consequences," p. 217.

49. Report by the Immigration Agent General of British Guiana to the Secretary of State for the Colonies [1914–1915], New York Public Library.

50. Doolarie, interview by Noor Kumar Mahabir, 19 July 1982, OP13, Oral and Pictorial Records Programme, The Alma Jordan Library, University of the West Indies, St. Augustine, Trinidad.

51. Bronkhurst, *The Colony of British Guiana*, p. 247.

52. In British Guiana between 1886 and 1890, thirty-one of the thirty-seven Indian murder victims were women. Meanwhile, women accounted for sixty-eight of the ninety-six murder victims among the indentured in Fiji from 1890 to 1919.

53. Reports by the Immigration Agent General of British Guiana to the Secretary of State for the Colonies [1897–1917], New York Public Library. In the twenty years before the last indenture ships arrived, forty-one women were killed by men who were intimate partners or wanted to be. In the same period, only four male rivals were. See also Moore, *Cultural Power, Resistance and Pluralism*, p. 173.

54. Mohapatra, "Restoring the Family." The first murder of a male rival in Trinidad was in 1885, and the first in British Guiana was in 1889.

55. Report by the Immigration Agent General of British Guiana to the Secretary of State for the Colonies [1914–1915], New York Public Library.

56. Naidu, Vijay, *The Violence of Indenture in Fiji*, Suva: World University Service, in association with the University of the South Pacific, 1980, p. 71.

57. Mangru, "The Sex Ratio Disparity and its Consequences," p. 221.

58. "The Execution of Ramotar," with notes on his trial by Judge Hewick, 2 November 1904, File No. 39298, CO 111/542, Colonial Office Correspondence, Public Record Office, The National Archives of the UK, Kew.

59. Ibid.

60. "The job of randi-wallah died with the ending of the indenture system. The name was the local idiom for the cane estate junior in charge of the Indian women's gang." Gill, Walter, *Turn North-East at the Tombstone*, London: Robert Hale Ltd., 1969, p. 33.

61. "Shocking tragedy at Plantation Nonpareil: woman brutally murdered," *The Daily Chronicle*, 13 July 1904, British Library Newspapers Collection, Colindale.

62. "The Execution of Ramotar," 2 November 1904, Colonial Office Correspondence. The plantation manager, H.L. Humphreys, testified to this at Ramautar's trial.

63. Ibid.

64. Ibid.

65. "District news: Enmore," *The Daily Chronicle*, 11 November 1903, British Library Newspapers Collection, Colindale.

66. "A light sentence," *The Daily Chronicle*, 15 January 1904, British Library Newspapers Collection, Colindale.

67. Ibid.

68. "A wounding case at Canje," *The Daily Chronicle*, 16 December 1903, British Library Newspapers Collection, Colindale.

69. "A woman cruelly disfigured," *The Daily Chronicle*, 13 January 1904, British Library Newspapers Collection, Colindale.

70. *The Daily Chronicle*, 14 January 1904, British Library Newspapers Collection, Colindale.

71. Report by the Immigration Agent General of British Guiana to the Secretary of State for the Colonies [1903–1904], New York Public Library.

72. "Brutal coolie murder at Kitty Village," *The Daily Chronicle*, 23 May 1903, British Library Newspapers Collection, Colindale.

73. "Kitty murder continued," *The Daily Chronicle*, 15 October 1903, British Library Newspapers Collection, Colindale.

74. "The Kitty murder," *The Daily Chronicle*, 16 October 1903, British Library Newspapers Collection, Colindale.

75. "Brutal coolie murder at Kitty Village," *The Daily Chronicle*, 23 May 1903.

76. "Kitty murder continued," *The Daily Chronicle*, 15 October 1903.

77. "The Kitty murder," *The Daily Chronicle*, 14 October 1903.

78. Ibid.

79. "Kitty murder continued," *The Daily Chronicle*, 15 October 1903.

80. "The Kitty murder," *The Daily Chronicle*, 14 October, 1903.

81. "Kitty murder continued," *The Daily Chronicle*, 15 October, 1903.

82. "Brutal murder on the East Bank: a jealous coolie's shocking crime," *The Daily Chronicle*, 27 January 1904, British Library Newspapers Collection, Colindale.

83. "The Herstelling murder case," *The Daily Chronicle*, 12 April 1904, British Library Newspapers Collection, Colindale.

84. Report by the Immigration Agent General of British Guiana to the Secretary of State for the Colonies [1903–1904], New York Public Library.

85. "Wounding case at Plantation Enmore," *The Daily Chronicle*, 4 May 1904, British Library Newspapers Collection, Colindale.

86. *The Daily Chronicle*, 13 May 1904, British Library Newspapers Collection, Colindale.

87. "Barbarous attack by a jealous coolie," *The Daily Chronicle*, 12 May 1904, British Library Newspapers Collection, Colindale.

88. "A jealous husband and a naughty wife," *The Daily Chronicle*, 8 June 1904, British Library Newspapers Collection, Colindale.

89. Report by the Immigration Agent General of British Guiana to the Secretary of State for the Colonies [1904–1905], New York Public Library.

90. "Jealous man's shocking barbarity," *The Daily Chronicle*, 21 August 1904, British Library Newspapers Collection, Colindale.

91. Mohapatra, "Restoring the family," p. 239.

92. Faruqee, Ashrufa, "Conceiving the Coolie Woman: Indentured Labour, Indian Women and Colonial Discourse," *South Asia Research*, 16, 1 (1996), pp. 61–76.

93. Report of the Royal Commissioners to British Guiana [1871], pp. 187–191, XX (393), British Parliamentary Papers, The British Library.

94. Report on the Past Emigration Season by the British Guiana Emigration Agency, 30 January 1892, File No. 4142, CO 384/185, Colonial Office Correspondence, Public Record Office, The National Archives of the UK, Kew.

95. Persad, Basmat Shiv and George K. Danns, *Domestic Violence in the Caribbean: A Guyana Case Study*, Georgetown, Guyana: University of Guyana, 1989, p. 16. In 1891, there were forty-three Chinese women for every 100 Chinese men in British Guiana, compared to sixty-three Indian women for every 100 Indian men.

96. As quoted in Sue-a-Quan, Trev, *Cane Reapers: Chinese Indentured Immigrants in Guyana*, Vancouver: Cane Press, 2003, p. 150.

97. *The Royal Gazette*, 8 May 1866, as quoted in Sue-a-Quan, *Cane Reapers*, p. 151. The woman, Wong Shee, was stabbed in fourteen places with a knife.

98. From 1853 to 1879, 13,541 Chinese were introduced to Guiana as labourers, compared to 238,979 Indians.

99. See, for instance, the 19 August 2010 issue of "History This Week" column in *The Stabroek News*. No one has tested this perception to see if it stands up under rigorous statistical analysis. The population statistics suggest that fewer than ten murders of Chinese women in half a century would equal the rate of intimate partner killings by Indians in the same time period.

100. As quoted in Report by the Immigration Agent General of British Guiana, 1881, in appendix for P/2057, February 1883, Government of India Proceedings on Emigration, India Office Records, The British Library.

101. Kirke, Henry, *Twenty-Five Years in British Guiana*, London: Sampson Low, Marston & Company Limited, 1898, p. 219.

102. Ibid., p. 325.

103. Jayawardena, Chandra, "Religious Belief and Social Change," *Comparative Studies in Society and History*, 8, 2 (1966), pp. 211–240.

104. Henry Irving, British Guiana's governor, wrote: "The crime is almost in every instance committed by coolies under indenture and generally in the earlier period of it, [usually] … provoked by the seduction of the women by coolies who have been longer in the

country and are consequently better off and in a position to be more lavish in presents of jewellery or other articles of personal adornment." Governor Irving to the Earl of Derby, 5 December 1883, File No. 21925, CO 384/144, Colonial Office Correspondence, Public Record Office, The National Archives of the UK, Kew. See also Mangru, "The Sex Ratio Disparity and its Consequences," p. 223 and Moore, Brian L., *Cultural Power, Resistance and Pluralism in Colonial Guyana, 1838–1900*, Montreal: McGill-Queens University Press, 1995, p. 172.

105. Chief Justice of British Guiana to Governor, 3 August 1882, File No. 320, CO 384/139, as quoted in Mohapatra, "Restoring the Family," p. 234.

106. Kirke, *Twenty-Five Years in British Guiana*, p. 217.

107. "History This Week," 19 August 2010, *The Stabroek News*.

108. Beaumont, Joseph, *The New Slavery: An Account of the Indian and Chinese Immigrants in British Guiana*, London: self-published, 1871, p. 53.

109. "The source from which the women were mostly obtained in previous years is now dried up: in plain language, the feuds which rendered large numbers of women destitute widows are at an end." Sue-a-Quan, *Cane Reapers*, p. 99.

110. Surgeon Superintendent Dr T.A. Chaldecott to Colonial Office, 13 August 1861, as quoted in Sue-a-Quan, *Cane Reapers*, p. 88.

111. Andrews and Pearson, *Report on Indentured Labour in Fiji*, p. 18.

112. Mohapatra, "Restoring the Family," pp. 227–260.

113. "The cooly wife murder on the west coast," *The Daily Chronicle*, 24 July 1882, appended in Smith, "Defects and Abuses in the Immigration Department of British Guiana," 28 June 1883.

114. Minute by Sir Thomas William Clinton Murdoch, head of the Colonial Land and Emigration Commission, "Execution for Murder," 18 April 1873, File No. 174, CO 386/97, Colonial Office Correspondence, Public Record Office, The National Archives of the UK, Kew.

115. Naidu, *The Violence of Indenture in Fiji*, p. 38.

116. Gill, *Turn North-East at the Tombstone*, p. 71.

117. Ibid., p. 77.

118. Lal, Brij V., "Veil of Dishonour: Sexual Jealousy and Suicide on Fiji Plantations," *The Journal of Pacific History*, 20, 3 (1985), p. 139.

119. Bronkhurst, *The Colony of British Guiana*, p. 244.

120. Jenkins, John Edward, *The Coolie: His Rights and His Wrongs*, New York: George Routledge and Sons, 1871, p. 450.

121. "The existing social evils amongst these people unquestionably have their root in the disproportion of sexes. It is only by abating that disproportion that the polyandrous habits of the immigrants, with their demoralizing consequences, can be checked or eradicated." Governor Henry Irving to Secretary of State for the Colonies, 16 October 1885, enclosed in Minute on Marriage Law, 28 December 1885, File No. 2392, L/PJ/166, Public and Judicial Departmental Papers, India Office Records, The British Library.

122. A.H. Alexander, 23 February 1885 letter, as quoted in Comins, Note on Emigration from India to British Guiana, 12 September 1893.

123. Mangru, "The Sex Ratio Disparity and its Consequences," p. 219.

124. Reddock explores the quantity versus quality dimension of the debate on increasing the gender ratio in Trinidad in "The Search for Origins: Women and Division of Labour

During Slavery and Indentureship," *Women, Labour and Politics in Trinidad and Tobago*, London: Zed Books, 1994.

125. Kirkpatrick, Margery, *From the Middle Kingdom to the New World: Aspects of the Chinese Experience in Migration to British Guiana*, Georgetown, Guyana: self-published, 1993, pp. 72–91. This story is told by Margery Kirkpatrick in a self-published oral history of Chinese women in British Guiana, obtained from the author.

126. Kirkpatrick, *From the Middle Kingdom to the New World*, p. 155.

127. The child was William Adrian Lee.

128. Report by the Immigration Agent General of British Guiana to the Secretary of State for the Colonies [1908–1909], New York Public Library.

129. Reports by the Immigration Agent General of British Guiana to the Secretary of State for the Colonies [1897–1917], New York Public Library.

130. Report by the Immigration Agent General of British Guiana to the Secretary of State for the Colonies [1897–1898], New York Public Library.

131. Report by the Immigration Agent General of British Guiana to the Secretary of State for the Colonies [1914–1915], New York Public Library.

132. Report by the Immigration Agent General of British Guiana to the Secretary of State for the Colonies [1917], New York Public Library.

133. Report by the Immigration Agent General of British Guiana to the Secretary of State for the Colonies [1902–1903], New York Public Library.

134. Mangru, "The Sex Ratio Disparity and its Consequences," p. 212.

135. Ibid., p. 223.

136. Robert W.S. Mitchell, Report by the Immigration Agent General of British Guiana, 1881, in P/2057, February 1883, India Office Records.

137. Three instances were found in The Report of the Immigration Agent General of British Guiana, 1917. See also Kirke, *Twenty-Five Years in British Guiana*, p. 325.

138. Bronkhurst, *The Colony of British Guiana*, p. 399.

139. Ibid., p. 251.

140. Mohapatra, "Restoring the Family," pp. 227–60.

141. Ordinance 10 of 1860, Section 2, enclosed in Smith, "Defects and Abuses in the Immigration Department of British Guiana," 28 June 1883.

142. A.H. Alexander, 23 February 1885 letter, as quoted in Comins, Note on Emigration from India to British Guiana, 12 September 1893.

143. Nath, *A History of Indians in Guyana*, pp. 224–8. Tables show registered marriages by year.

144. Ibid. Between 1860 and 1893, 1,900 Indian couples legally married in the colony; another 8,100 were issued marriage certificates by the immigration agent general on landing.

145. Persad and Danns, *Domestic Violence in the Caribbean: A Guyana Case Study*, Chapter 2. In 1903, only 17 percent of children born to Indians in British Guiana were legitimate.

146. Baksh, S. Mohamed, "An East Indian Grievance," *The Argosy*, 30 June 1906, as quoted in Mangru, "The Sex Ratio Disparity and its Consequences," pp 214–5.

147. Attorney General W.F. Haynes Smith, 16 October 1885 letter, enclosed in Minute on Marriage Law, 28 December 1885, File No. 2392, L/PJ/166, Public and Judicial Departmental Papers, India Office Records, The British Library.

148. Mangru, "The Sex Ratio Disparity and its Consequences," p. 222.

149. Ibid., p. 220.

150. Ibid. p. 220.

151. Ibid., p. 222.

152. Ibid., p. 220.

153. Ibid.

154. Faruqee, "Conceiving the Coolie Woman."

155. Mohapatra, "Restoring the Family," pp. 227–60.

156. Reports by the Immigration Agent General of British Guiana to the Secretary of State for the Colonies [1897–1917], New York Public Library. See also: Mohapatra, who says transfers averaged sixty-five a year during the 1890s and fifty-seven a year during the 1880s.

157. Reports by the Immigration Agent General of British Guiana to the Secretary of State for the Colonies [1897–1917], New York Public Library. More than a third of transfers during these two decades were so-called jealousy cases.

158. "The Rose Hall wounding case," *The Daily Chronicle*, 4 May 1909, British Library Newspapers Collection, Colindale. The woman Chunkey, the victim of a cutlass attack by her husband, had been transferred from Plantation Rose Hall because they quarreled frequently but returned at her own request.

159. Register of immigrants arriving on *The Clyde*, 1903, General Register Office, Georgetown, Guyana.

160. Report by the Immigration Agent General of British Guiana to the Secretary of State for the Colonies [1906–1907], New York Public Library.

161. Somewati Persaud, Bhagmanti Ramanan, Edna and Sarojini Baisakhu, interviews by author, 2011.

162. Vatuk, Ved Prakash, "Craving for a Child in the Folk Songs of East Indians in British Guiana," *The Journal of the Folklore Institute* 2, (1965), p. 63.

163. Ibid., p. 62.

164. Ibid.

165. Ibid., p. 63.

166. Ibid., p. 68.

167. Ibid.

168. Edna Baisakhu, phone interview by author, October 2011.

169. Sarojini Baisakhu, phone interview by author, October 2011. She is Sujaria's grandson's wife.

170. Testimony of Deputy Manager Robert Hunter, Rosehall Riot Enquiry, 5 July 1913, File No. 25266, CO 111/589, Colonial Office Correspondence, Public Record Office, The National Archives of the UK, Kew.

171. Tinker, pp 228–9.

172. Ibid., p. 192.

173. Prasad, *Indian Indentured Workers in Fiji*, p. 21.

174. Ibid.

175. Ibid.

176. Gill, *Turn North-East at the Tombstone*, p. 37.

177. Prabhu Mohapatra discusses the text in the monograph "The Politics of Representation in the Indian Labour Diaspora: West Indies, 1880–1920," Delhi: V.V. Giri National Labour Institute, 2004, http://www.indialabourarchives.org/publications/prabhu2.htm, last accessed 2011.

178. Sharma, Lal Bihari, *Damra Phag Bahar*, Demerara: published by the author, 1916, 4 in B.424/4, Hindi Pamphlets Collection, India Office Records, The British Library. The sections of the text quoted throughout were translated by Shashwata Sinha, with input and collaborative writing by Gaiutra Bahadur.

179. Ibid., p. 6.

180. Ibid., p. 14.

181. For more on *bhakti* poets in the Vaishnavite tradition, see Edward Dimock's introduction to *In Praise of Krishna: Songs from the Bengali*, translated by Edward C. Dimock Jr and Denise Levertov, Chicago: University of Chicago Press, 1981.

182. Sharma, *Damra Phag Bahar*, p. 4.

183. Ibid., p. 5. The author uses the word *topi*. I have rendered it as: "the white man's tall hat/ like a helmet/ high on his head".

184. Ibid., p. 6.

185. Ibid., p. 31.

186. Vatuk, Ved Prakash, "Protest Songs of British Guiana," *The Journal of American Folklore* 77, 305 (1964), p. 227.

187. The letter is quoted in Bronkhurst, *The Colony of British Guiana*, pp. 404–405.

188. "Commutation of Death Sentence," 14 May 1906, File No. 18938, CO 111/550, Colonial Office Correspondence, Public Record Office, The National Archives of the UK, Kew.

189. Extract from register of Georgetown Prison, July 1902, in "Convict Makundi," 8 August 1906, File No. 29160, CO 111/551, Colonial Office Correspondence, Public Record Office, The National Archives of the UK, Kew.

190. Public insane asylum admission report for Mokundi, 28 July 1902, enclosed in "Convict Makundi," 8 August 1906, Public Record Office.

191. The details and quotes in this paragraph are from the notes of various doctors who examined him during his two stays at the asylum, found in "Convict Makundi," 8 August 1906, Public Record Office.

192. Makundi's emigration pass, Ship manifest for *The Main*, 1902, Walter Rodney Archives, Georgetown, Guyana.

193. Governor James A. Swettenham to Colonial Office, "Assaults by Coolies on Superior Officers," 8 September 1904, File No. 31478, CO 111/541, Colonial Office Correspondence, Public Record Office, The National Archives of the UK, Kew. Makandi's assaults were among twenty-nine recorded between November 1902 and July 1904.

194. The details of the murder and trial are in the Report by the Immigration Agent General of British Guiana to the Secretary of State for the Colonies [1905–1906], New York Public Library and in "Communication of Death Sentence," 14 May 1906, Public Record Office.

195. Unless otherwise noted, the details and the quotes in this paragraph are to be found in a report by the Immigration Agent General on visits to Plantations Diamond and Providence, enclosed in "Convict Makundi," 8 August 1906, Public Record Office.

196. The doctors at the asylum provided this physical description of Makundi in their notes on his two admissions. To be found in "Convict Makundi," 8 August 1906, Public Record Office.

197. The insane asylum admission reports are in "Convict Makundi," 8 August 1906, Public Record Office.

198. Report by P.M. Earle, Medical Superintendant of Public Insane Asylum, in "Convict Makundi," 8 August 1906, Public Record Office.
199. "Commutation of Death Sentence," 14 May 1906, Public Record Office.
200. Nath, *A History of Indians in Guyana*, p. 143.
201. Ibid. p. 143. In the decade ending in 1912, the proportion of women was 39.6 percent in British Guiana, with a suicide rate of 100 million; 35 percent in Trinidad, with a suicide rate of 406 per million; 30.4 percent in Fiji, with a suicide rate of 926 per million.
202. Ibid. 143. An Australian missionary to Fiji, Florence Garnham, observed this in 1918.
203. Ibid.
204. Dharam Phal, interview by Noor Kumar Mahabir, 18 September 1982, transcript, OP13, Oral and Pictorial Records Programme, University of the West Indies, St. Augustine, Trinidad.
205. Naidu, *The Violence of Indenture*, p. 38.
206. Reports by the Immigration Agent General of British Guiana to the Secretary of State for the Colonies [1897–1917], New York Public Library. In British Guiana, between 1897 and 1917, two men killed themselves after murdering their wives.
207. Reports by the Immigration Agent General of British Guiana to the Secretary of State for the Colonies [1910–1917], New York Public Library. Of sixty-three suicides among Indians in British Guiana from 1910 to 1917, seven men killed themselves after being deserted by romantic partners. One hanged himself after the parents of the girl he wanted chose another husband for her. And in one case, the victim married an underage girl, with the proviso that she would stay with her mother until puberty—yet hanged himself when denied visits before then.
208. Report by the Immigration Agent General of British Guiana to the Secretary of State for the Colonies [1914–1915], New York Public Library.
209. Report by the Immigration Agent General of British Guiana to the Secretary of State for the Colonies [1916], New York Public Library.
210. "Miss Florence Garnham's Report, 1918," *Indians Outside India*, New Delhi: All India Congress Committee, 1951, p. 565.
211. Lal, "Veil of Dishonour," p. 138.
212. Leather-workers, among the lowest in the caste hierarchy.
213. Lal, "Veil of Dishonour," p. 150.
214. IAG Robert Mitchell to Governor Henry Light, 14 March 1883, in Smith, 28 June 1883, "Defects and Abuses in the Immigration Department of British Guiana." The caste background of drivers on ninety-five plantations in British Guiana was: 120 Brahmin and high-caste, 110 middle and agricultural castes, 118 low-caste and ninety-five Muslim.
215. Lal, "Veil of Dishonour," p. 150.
216. Ibid., pp. 136–7, 148. During the four decades of indenture in Fiji, 291 men committed suicide, while only thirty-two women did. Men committed 90 percent of suicides in Fiji in that time period. Meanwhile in British Guiana, of sixty-three suicides in the final seven years of indenture, only three victims were women, and of twenty-eight suicides there between 1886 and 1890, only one victim was a woman.
217. Naidu, *The Violence of Indenture in Fiji*, p. 46.
218. Nanka, interview by Naidu, Ibid., p. 38.

8. GONE BUT NOT FORGOTTEN

1. Testimony of Alexander McEwan at coroner's inquest. The account that follows is based on a transcript of the inquest, as well as newspaper accounts and correspondence between the governor and the Colonial Office to be found in two dozen files, dated May 1903 to January 1904, in CO 111/537–538; CO 111/540–542, Colonial Office Correspondence, Public Record Office, The National Archives of the UK, Kew.

2. Testimony of Mohamed Umar: "If [the four] were released, then we would have all returned to the estate, and we would have gone to work the next day, and would have been content with the five shillings offered." "Coolie Riots on Friends Estate," 4 June 1903, File No. 20580, CO 111/538, Public Record Office.

3. Immigration agent Joseph King to IAG A.H. Alexander, letter reprinted in *The Daily Chronicle*, 29 July 1904, British Library Newspapers Collection, Colindale.

4. The historian Hugh Tinker concluded that there was a hard connection between the two: "On Plantation Friends," he wrote, "a serious strike stemmed from the major grievance of the manager and overseers having 'immoral relations' with coolie women." (Tinker, *A New Form of Slavery*, p. 222.) But the official sources never identify the relationship as the cause of the strike. In a report on major uprisings on West Indian plantations from 1881 to1903, a footnote stated that it "was not shown, however, that [this] conduct had any immediate connection with the causes of the outbreak." ("Notes on West Indian Riots: 1881–1903," March 1905, CO 884/9, Colonial Office Correspondence, Public Record Office, The National Archives of the UK, Kew.)

5. Seecharan, Clem, "Guyana," *The Encyclopedia of Indians Overseas*, Lal, Brij (ed.), Honolulu: University of Hawaii Press, 2006, pp. 288–90.

6. Ramnarine, Tyran, "One Hundred Years of Disturbances on the Sugar Estates of Guyana, 1869–1978: A Historical Overview," *India in the Caribbean*, Dabydeen, David and Brinsley Samaroo (eds), London: Hansib Publishing Ltd., 1987, p. 120.

7. 1869 Circular in "Assaults by Coolies on Superior Officers," 8 September 1904, File No. 31478, CO 111/541, Colonial Office Correspondence, Public Record Office, The National Archives of the UK, Kew.

8. Henry Bullock to his mother, 18 August 1870, Letters and Photos from Berbice, Guyana by Henry Bullock, D/DVv 74, Essex Record Office, Chelmsford, England.

9. Report of the Royal Commissioners to British Guiana [1871], paragraph 308, XX (393), British Parliamentary Papers, The British Library.

10. Jenkins, John Edward, *Lutchmee and Dilloo*, London: William Mullan & Son, 1877.

11. Report of the Royal Commissioners to British Guiana [1871], paragraph 309, XX (393), British Parliamentary Papers, The British Library.

12. Beaumont, Joseph, *The New Slavery: An Account of the Indian and Chinese Immigrants in British Guiana*, London: self-published, 1871, p. 74.

13. Thompson, J., *The Overseer's Manual, or a Guide to the Cane Field and Sugar Factory*, Georgetown, Guyana: Argosy Press, 1896, p. 80.

14. 1890 Circular in "Assaults by Coolies on Superior Officers," 8 September 1904, Public Record Office.

15. Sampath, ex-driver on Plantation Eliza and Mary, in "Coolie Disturbances at Skeldon," 16 May 1895, File No., CO 384/191, Colonial Office Correspondence, Public Record Office, The National Archives of the UK, Kew.

16. "The coolie rising at Leguan," *The Daily Chronicle*, 9 February 1895, in "Coolie Riot at

Plantation Success," 12 March 1895, File No. 4471, CO 384/192, Colonial Office Correspondence, Public Record Office, The National Archives of the UK, Kew.

17. Immigration agent Sealy to IAG A.H. Alexander, 21 December 1896 in "Immoral Relations between Van Nooten and Coolie Girl Jamni," 22 January 1897, File No. 1621, CO 111/492, Colonial Office Correspondence, Public Record Office, The National Archives of the UK, Kew.

18. N. Darnell Davis letter, 10 November 1896 in "Immoral Relations between Van Nooten and Coolie Girl Jamni," 22 January 1897, Public Record Office.

19. Jungli's emigration pass, Ship manifest for *The Ganges*, 1894, Walter Rodney Archives, Georgetown, Guyana.

20. Riot at Nonpareil, Report by Sgt. Seeraj, 14 October 1896, File No. 6460, Walter Rodney Archives, Georgetown, Guyana.

21. Seecharan, Clem, *Bechu: Bound Coolie Radical in British Guiana, 1894–1901*, Kingston: University of the West Indies Press, 1999, p. 7. Seecharan suggests this as a possible motive by Van Nooten. It was the Nonpareil uprising that prompted the first letter to the newspapers by the indentured man Bechu.

22. Confidential dispatches on "Nonpareil Riot," Capt. G.C. de Rinzy's Report, 13 October 1896, File No. 6457, Walter Rodney Archives, Georgetown, Guyana.

23. Confidential dispatches on "Nonpareil Riot," Identification of Dead Bodies, Report by Lt. H.W. Cobb, 14 October 1896, File No. 6457, Walter Rodney Archives. Georgetown, Guyana.

24. Rampersaud Tiwari, interview by author, Toronto, Summer 2011. A former civil servant in Guyana, Tiwari was born in a village near Nonpareil, thirty-six years after the uprising. His great-grandparents, who arrived in the colony in 1895 and were indentured on Nonpareil, participated in the strike. His grandfather, nine years old on arrival, told him the stories that had been passed down about Jungli and Jamni.

25. Alapatt, George K., "The Sepoy Mutiny of 1857: Indian Indentured Labour and Plantation Politics in British Guiana," *Journal of Indian History*, 59 (1981), pp. 295–314.

26. Carter, Marina and Crispin Bates, "Empire and Locality: A Global Dimension to the 1857 Indian Uprising," *Journal of Global History* 5 (2010), 68.

27. Alapatt, "The Sepoy Mutiny of 1857," pp. 295–314.

28. "They were all the fighting men. Some sepoys were amongst them; some had cutlasses. … There were six or seven sepoys amongst them to the best of my knowledge." Testimony of Lutchman, Report on The Coolie Riots in Essequibo [1873], The Caribbean Research Library, University of Guyana, Georgetown, Guyana.

29. Mr Ebbels, Nonpareil's manager, to IAG A.H. Alexander, 15 December 1896, in "Immoral Relations between Van Nooten and Coolie Girl Jamni," 22 January 1897, Public Record Office.

30. Quintin Hogg to Undersecretary of State for the Colonies, 1 February 1897, File No. 2467, CO 111/492, Colonial Office Correspondence, Public Record Office, The National Archives of the UK, Kew.

31. A.H. Alexander to Summerson, 2 May 1904, in "On Mr A.W.L. McEwan," 19 May 1904, File No. 17711, CO 111/540, Colonial Office Correspondence, Public Record Office, The National Archives of the UK, Kew.

32. Memo by A.H. Alexander, 5 August 1904 in "Case of Mr McEwan," 12 January 1905, File No. 1065, CO 111/542, Colonial Office Correspondence, Public Record Office, The National Archives of the UK, Kew.

33. Register of immigrants arriving on *The Collingwood*, 1862, General Register Office, Georgetown, Guyana.

34. Petition by A.L.W. McEwan, 27 October 1904, in "Case of Mr McEwan," 29 October 1904, File No. 37095, CO 111/543, Colonial Office Correspondence, Public Record Office, The National Archives of the UK, Kew.

35. 1881 Census and Birth Records, Scotland, accessed with help of researchers at Inverness Public Library and ancestry.co.uk. McEwan was born on 27 July 1862 to Margaret Low and John McEwan in Roseneath, Dunbarton, Scotland.

36. In addition to Jenkins's *Lutchmee and Dilloo*, there's the 1917 novel *Those That Be in Bondage*, by A.R.F. Weber, a politician and newspaper editor in British Guiana.

37. Medical Inspector's report on condition of new immigrants at Friends, 14 April 1902, enclosure in 12 August 1903, File No. 30047, CO 111/538, Colonial Office Correspondence, Public Record Office, The National Archives of the UK, Kew.

38. "The overseers and the government," Letter to the Editor, *The Daily Chronicle*, 3 July 1904, British Library Newspapers Collection, Colindale.

39. "On Charges Against Mr Warne," 7 October 1904, File No. 34730, CO 111/541, Colonial Office Correspondence, Public Record Office, The National Archives of the UK, Kew.

40. Ibid.

41. Ramnarine, "Over a Hundred Years of East Indian Disturbances," p. 123.

42. In a book of reminiscences and tall tales by an overseer, a sugar planter turned gold digger vilified "a Governor Sweetman whom he said was the cause of all good planters leaving sugar estates, by his introduction of some drastic law debarring overseers of their favourite pastime and hobby." Oswald, Archibald, *It Happened in British Guiana*, Ifracombe, Devon: AH Stockwell, 1955, p. 22.

43. Letter to the Editor by NOBLESSE OBLIGE, *The Daily Chronicle*, 8 July 1904, British Library Newspapers Collection, Colindale.

44. "Assaults by Coolies on Superior Officers," 8 September 1904, Public Record Office.

45. Oswald, *It Happened in British Guiana*, pp. 22–3.

46. *The Daily Chronicle*, 16 July 1904, British Library Newspapers Collection, Colindale.

47. *The Wall Street Journal*, 11 August 1904, as excerpted in *The Daily Chronicle*, 27 August 1904, British Library Newspapers Collection, Colindale.

48. "The Horsfall-Fleming suit," *The Daily Chronicle*, 1 July 1909, British Library Newspapers Collection, Colindale.

49. Horsfall v Fleming, 19 August 2009, File No. 27734, CO 111/569, Colonial Office Correspondence, Public Record Office, The National Archives of the UK, Kew.

50. Somewati Persaud, interview by author, Jersey City, New Jersey, 2010.

51. A woman who migrated to Trinidad as a coolie said: "Well to mind the children, there's a baby sitter, mhmmmn, there is, one old woman, she was there to look after the small children with her and we would leave them and go to work, and she would mind them, she would feed them their milk, she would mind them, bathe them, and then the mother would come and she'll take her own home. ... Yes you call it a kilomni some. You can also call it a di." Achama, interview by Peggy Mohan, 1978, transcript, OP55, Oral and Pictorial Records Programme, University of the West Indies, St. Augustine, Trinidad.

52. Singh, Alice Bhagwandy, "The Autobiography of Alice Bhagwandai Sital Persaud, 1892–1958," unpublished manuscript, last modified April 1962, Microsoft Word file of this autobiography by Phuljharee's granddaughter, edited by Moses Seenarine and provided

by The Rajkumari Singh Cultural Center in New York City. Excerpts are also available at: http://mosessite.blogspot.com/2011/05/autobiography-of-alice-bhagwandy-sital.html

53. Rosabelle Seesaran, interview by Patricia Mohammed, October 1991, tape 33, OP62, Oral and Pictorial Records Programme, Alma Jordan Library, University of the West Indies, St. Augustine, Trinidad.

54. Pinch, Vijay, "Gosain tawaif: Slaves, Sex and Ascetics in Rasdhan, 1800–1857," *Modern Asian Studies* 38, 3 (2004), pp. 559–97.

55. Pinch, William R., *Peasants and Monks in British India*, Berkeley: University of California Press, 1996, p. 43.

56. Immoral Relations with Female Immigrants, 15 September 1908, File No. 3633, CO 111/562, Colonial Office Correspondence, Public Record Office, The National Archives of the UK, Kew. The report was prepared by George Bethune, in his capacity as planting attorney for Port Mourant, where three overseers, the manager and the deputy manager were all accused of interfering with Indian women.

57. Maharani Persaud, interview by author, Toronto, July 2011.

58. Particularly telling is one note in a Colonial Office file involving a woman who complained when a plantation official tried to drop her: "This occurrence shows that once a man has got into the toils of an unscrupulous woman, the connection must be maintained. Any attempt on the part of the man to break it is likely to result in denunciation by the woman and consequent ruin." Illicit Connections Between Estate Employees and Indentured E. Indian Women, 3 August 1917, File No. 38883, CO 571/5, Colonial Office Correspondence, Public Record Office, The National Archives of the UK, Kew.

59. Testimony of Bechu, *Report of the West India Royal Commission*, Appendix C, Volume II [1897], p. 131.

60. Report by the Immigration Agent General of British Guiana to the Secretary of State for the Colonies [1913–1914], SEV+, British Guiana Administration Reports, The New York Public Library.

61. Report by the Immigration Agent General of British Guiana to the Secretary of State for the Colonies [1914–1915], New York Public Library.

62. Letter to the Editor by an overseer, *The Daily Chronicle*, 8 July 1904, British Library Newspapers Collection, Colindale.

63. "The government and its overseers," Letter to the Editor by MAN OF THE WORLD, *The Daily Chronicle*, 6 July 1904, British Library Newspapers Collection, Colindale.

64. Letter to the Editor by KING OF SIAM, *The Daily Chronicle*, 17 July 1904, British Library Newspapers Collection, Colindale.

65. The overseer did marry the woman and was sacked. Another plantation hired him. *The People*, a New Amsterdam newspaper, editorialized: "If this young man had been content to prostitute his manhood by living in open adultery, nothing would have been said, for under the same manager that kind of bestial existence is pursued without rebuke; but because he chooses to retain self-respect and decency, to be a man rather than a town bull or stallion, he is discharged." In Dismissal of Overseer from Mara, 10 August 1905, File No. 28478, CO 111/546, Colonial Office Correspondence, Public Record Office, The National Archives of the UK, Kew.

66. New Colonial on "Scandalous and False Charges Made by Mr Alexander," 18 August 1905, File No. 29679, CO 111/548, Colonial Office Correspondence, Public Record Office, The National Archives of the UK, Kew.

67. Notes by the Way, *The Daily Chronicle*, 10 July 1904, British Library Newspapers Collection, Colindale.

68. Notes by the Way, *The Daily Chronicle*, 10 July 1904.

69. Letter to the Editor from EX-PBO AND MANAGER, *The Daily Chronicle*, 14 July 1904, British Library Newspapers Collection, Colindale.

70. "The government and its overseers," *The Daily Chronicle*, 6 July 1904.

71. "Disturbances on Rosehall," 13 August 1913, File No. 28162, CO 111/592, Colonial Office Correspondence, Public Record Office, The National Archives of the UK, Kew.

72. "… the last and perhaps the gravest plantation revolt in the Caribbean." Tinker, *A New Form of Slavery*, p. 229.

73. The account that follows is based on testimony at the inquest, newspaper clippings and confidential dispatches in six files in CO 111/588 and CO 111/589, Colonial Office Correspondence, Public Record Office, The National Archives of the UK, Kew.

74. *The Daily Argosy*, 16 March 1913 in 1 April 1913, File No. 10833, CO 111/588, Colonial Office Correspondence, Public Record Office, The National Archives of the UK, Kew.

75. L&P 3371, No. 54 of 1915, India Office Records, The British Library.

76. Lal, Brij V., "Kunti's Cry: Indentured Women on Fiji's Plantations," *The Indian Economic and Social History Review*, 22, 1 (1985).

77. Sanadhya, Totaram, *My Twenty-One Years in the Fiji Islands*, Suva, Fiji: The Fiji Museum, 1991, p. 32.

78. Ibid., p. 43.

79. The author of a 1948 Hindi-language manifesto said: "Those who passed through this ordeal and are still living tell us that the British people in their oppression of the Indians during the indenture period surpassed even Ravan." Kelly, John, *A Politics of Virtue: Hinduism, Sexuality and Countercolonial Discourse*, Chicago: University of Chicago Press, 1991, pp. 44–5.

80. Sanadhya, *My Twenty-One Years in the Fiji Islands*, p. 60.

81. Kelly, *A Politics of Virtue*, p. 49.

82. *Bharat Mitra*, 8 May 1914, as quoted in Ibid., p. 51.

83. Translation of pamphlet in Secretary to the Government of Bihar and Orissa to the Secretary to the Government of India, 13 September 1915 in J&P 5279, No. 52 of 1915, India Office Records, The British Library.

84. Tinker, *A New System of Slavery*, p. 288.

85. Kelly has described this as a fear by Indians of being seen as "the helots and harlots of Empire." Kelly, *Politics of Virtue*, p. 33.

86. "Speech on indentured labour at Bombay," *The Collected Works of Mahatma Gandhi*, (Electronic Book, Vol. 15), Delhi: Publications Division, Government of India, 1999, pp. 55–8.

87. "Speech at Industrial Conference, Bombay," *The Collected Works of Mahatma Gandhi* (Electronic Book, Vol. 15), Delhi: Publications Division, Government of India, 1999, p. 87.

88. "Indenture or slavery," *The Collected Works of Mahatma Gandhi* (Electronic Book, Vol. 15), Delhi: Publications Division, Government of India, 1999, pp. 74–5.

89. "Indentured Labour," *The Collected Works of Mahatma Gandhi* (Electronic Book, Vol. 15), Delhi: Publications Division, Government of India, 1999, p. 190.

90. Resolution in Viceroy's Council by Pandit Madan Mohan Malaviya, 20 March 1916,

enclosed in File No. 6552, CO 323/717, Colonial Office Correspondence, Public Record Office, The National Archives of the UK, Kew.

91. "Indian Indentured Labour; Abolition Decided Upon; Rejoicings in India," *The Times of London*, 22 March 1916, enclosed in File No. 6552, CO 323/717, Public Record Office.

92. "Speech at Anti-Indenture Meeting, Ahmedabad," *The Collected Works of Mahatma Gandhi* (Electronic Book, Vol. 15), Delhi: Publications Division, Government of India, 1999, p. 304.

93. Tinker, *A New System of Slavery*, p. 353.

94. Reddock, Rhoda, "Freedom denied: Indian Women and Indentureship in Trinidad and Tobago, 1845–1917," *Economic and Political Weekly*, 20, 43 (1985), p. WS–86.

95. Article on ladies deputation to Lord Chelmsford, *Civil and Military Gazette*, 27 March 1917, enclosed in IWSA 3/118, Clips on Prostitution from International Women's Suffrage Alliance, John Rylands Library, Manchester University, Manchester, England.

96. Article on ladies deputation to Lord Chelmsford, *The Tribune*, 28 March 1917, enclosed in IWSA 3/118, Clips on Prostitution from International Women's Suffrage Alliance, John Rylands Library, Manchester University, Manchester, England.

97. "The Indentured System: A Legalised Form of Prostitution," Letter from C.F. Andrews to *The Tribune*, 16 January 1917, enclosed in IWSA 3/118, Clips on Prostitution from International Women's Suffrage Alliance, John Rylands Library, Manchester University, Manchester, England.

98. Kelly, *The Politics of Virtue*, p. 56.

9. THE DREAM OF RETURN

1. "Horrible treatment of the hill coolies," *The Lancet*, 24 August 1839.

2. Surgeon-Major D.W.D. Comins, Note on Emigration from India to British Guiana, 12 September 1893, page 17, File Nos. 1902 & 1903, L/PJ/6/357, Public and Judicial Departmental Papers, India Office Records, The British Library.

3. Other instances can be found in: Comins, Note on Emigration from India to British Guiana, India Office Records; *The Demerara Daily Chronicle*, 29 May 1900 (as cited in Seecharan, Clem, *Bechu: Bound Coolie Radical*, p. 92); *The Demarara Daily Chronicle*, 10 January 1900 and 19 July 1900; and in the testimony of Robert Duff, British Guiana's Immigration Agent General in Report of the Committee on Emigration from India to the Crown Colonies and Protectorates, known as the Lord Sanderson Commission [1910], XXVII (Cd. 5192–94), British Parliamentary Papers, The British Library.

4. The account in the following paragraphs is based on forty-three pages of letters and statistical returns in: Correspondence Relating to the Return of Coolies from British Guiana to India [3 July 1843], XXXV, no. 404, Parliamentary Papers, The British Library.

5. Samaroo, Brinsley, "Homeward Bound: The Last Return Ship to India in 1955," Introduction to *The First Crossing*, Coventry: The Derek Walcott Press, 2007, pp. xlvii–lxi.

6. Mohabir, Nalini, "Women and Return Journeys: from Guyana to India and Back," *MaComère*, 12, 2 (2010), pp. 166–189. Mohabir, Nalini and Hyacinth Simpson, "*Resurgent* (Rise Again)," *Interventions: the International Journal of Postcolonial Studies*, 8, 3 (2006), pp. 487–506.

7. Mohabir, "*Resurgent* (Rise Again)," p. 498.

8. Ibid., p. 500.

9. Samaroo, "Homeward Bound," p. lvii.
10. Mohabir, "*Resurgent* (Rise Again)," p. 501.
11. Mohabir, "Women and Return Journeys," p. 179. Sixty-six women and girls sailed.
12. "The daughter and the granddaughter of another old woman were fretting that they had no place to settle in India, but they had to accompany the old woman at her insistence. The emigration authorities are now trying to obtain employment for them as *ayahs* with European families." *The Statesman* (Calcutta), 13 October 1955, as cited in Ibid., p. 183.
13. Emmer, Pieter, "The Great Escape," *Abolition and its Aftermath*, Richardson, David (ed.), London: Frank Cass, 1985, pp. 257–8. In Suriname, 23 percent of returnees from 1878–1890 were women and 28 percent from 1891–1931 were.
14. Appendix, Lord Sanderson Commission [1910], British Parliamentary Papers. About 31 percent of coolies going to Guiana, Trinidad and Fiji between 1899 and 1907 were women; and about 31 percent of ex-coolies going back to India from those colonies, in the same years, were women.
15. Naipail, V.S., *Finding the Centre*, London: Penguin, 1984, pp. 51–8.
16. Tinker, Hugh, *A New System of Slavery*, London: Hansib, 1993, p. 175.
17. Dharam Phal, interview by Noor Kumar Mahabir, 18 September 1982, transcript, OP13, Oral and Pictorial Records Programme, University of the West Indies, St. Augustine, Trinidad.
18. Dharam Phal, interview by Mahabir, 18 September 1892.
19. Bhagmania Seekumar, interview by Peggy Mohan, 1978, OP 55, Oral and Pictorial Records Programme, The Alma Jordan Library, University of the West Indies, St. Augustine, Trinidad.
20. Mohabir, "*Resurgent* (Rise Again)," p. 495.
21. Linton Gibbon, sailor on *The Forth*, from Trinidad to Calcutta in 1902, interview by Lucila Gibbon, 1976, OP70, Oral and Pictorial Records Programme, The Alma Jordan Library, University of the West Indies, St. Augustine, Trinidad. The ship carried fifty razors for just that purpose, suggesting that it was common practice.
22. Mohabir, "*Resurgent* (Rise Again)," p. 502.
23. Samaroo, "Homeward Bound," p. lviii.
24. Andrews, C.F., *The Indian Review*, July 1922, as excerpted in Chaturvedi, Benarsidas, "A Report on the Problem of Returned Emigrants from All Colonies," Sasaram, India: B.D. Sannyasi, 1931, pp. 2–4.
25. As cited in Chaturvedi, "A Report on the Problem of Returned Emigrants from All Colonies," p. 9.
26. Ibid., p. 18.
27. Ibid., p. 19.
28. Tinker, *A New System of Slavery*, p. 174.
29. Chaturvedi, "A Report on the Problem of Returned Emigrants from All Colonies," p. 2.
30. Andrews, C.F., *The Indian Review*, July 1922, as excerpted in Ibid., p. 3.
31. Chaturvedi, "A Report on the Problem of Returned Emigrants from All Colonies," p. 19.
32. Naipaul, *Finding the Centre*, pp. 51–8. Naipaul notes one such scene in 1932, when hundreds of derelicts who had returned the year before on the same ship stormed it, begging to be taken back to Trinidad.
33. Mohabir, "*Resurgent* (Rise Again)," p. 503.
34. Ibid., p. 504.
35. Samaroo, "Homeward Bound."

36. Ibid., p. lix.
37. Ibid., p. lix.
38. Mohabir, "*Resurgent* (Rise Again)," p. 504.
39. Mohabir, "Women and Return Journeys," p. 184.
40. Stanley, Clifford, "Tales from way back when: Rosaline will get her Mama and Granny," *The Guyana Chronicle*, 27 December 2009. (Reprinted from *The Guiana Graphic*, 6 September 1958.)
41. Casual Register, 1892, Walter Rodney Archives, Georgetown, Guyana. The Register of the Bann, 1892, Walter Rodney Archives, Georgetown, Guyana.
42. Maharanee Persaud, Ramdulari's granddaughter, interview by author, Toronto, Summer 2011.
43. Bhagmanti Ramanan, interview by author, New Jersey, 2011.
44. George Abraham Grierson, Report on Colonial Emigration [25 February 1883], Diary entry dated Muzzafarpur, 27 January 1883 in Appendix, P/2058, Government of India Proceedings on Emigration, India Office Records, The British Library.

10. EVERY ANCESTOR

1. Hall, Robert, *The Highland Sportsman*, Edinburgh: John Menzies & Co., 1882, p. 587.
2. The website "Slaves and Highlanders," http://www.spanglefish.com/slavesandhighlanders/, last accessed 2012. I am indebted to historian David Alston, who has documented the links between plantations in Berbice and investors from the Inverness area and other parts of the Highlands and who presents his findings at this site.
3. Bankruptcy Notice of George Baillie, *Bristol Journal*, 17 January 1807, excerpted, Bristol Libraries Flickr Page, http://www.flickr.com/photos/bristol-libraries/3327536871/, last accessed August 2012.
4. Bulloch, M.D., Joseph Gaston Baillie, *A History and Genealogy of the Baillie Family of Dunain*, Green Bay, Wisconsin: The Gazette Print, 1898, p. 36.
5. Dalrymple, William, *White Mughals*, New York: Penguin Books, 2004, p. 42.
6. Ibid. tells this story in detail.
7. Edward S. Fraser to his mother, 1 November 1803, Bundle 27, Fraser of Reelig Papers, Reelig House, Kirkhill, Scotland.
8. Edward S. Fraser to his mother, 22 March 1808, Bundle 8, Fraser of Reelig Papers, Reelig House, Kirkhill, Scotland.
9. Ibid.
10. Edward S. Fraser to his mother, 6 April 1808, Bundle 8, Fraser of Reelig Papers, Reelig House, Kirkhill, Scotland.
11. Diary of James Baillie Fraser, 24 February 1813 Entry, Bundle 397, Fraser of Reelig Papers, Reelig House, Kirkhill, Scotland.
12. Last Will and Testament of Alexander Fraser, of the Colony of Essequibo, GD23/10/694, National Archives of Scotland, Edinburgh, Scotland.
13. "Hugh Miller sat next to a 'mulatto' pupil in Cromarty in the 1810s and, shortly before, there were three 'coloured' pupils at Inverness Royal Academy, all brothers named Macrae." David Alston, "Very Rapid and Splendid Fortunes? Highland Scots in Berbice in the Early Nineteenth Century," *Gaelic Society of Inverness*, LXIII (2006), pp. 208–36.
14. Petition to the Commissioners of HM Treasury by Marjory Fraser, residing at Frome, Somerset, Alexander Fraser, residing in Whitechapel, London, Isobel Fraser, spouse of

Angus Fraser of the Colony of Demerara and Elizabeth Fraser, spouse of Edward Thorpe of Demerara, natural children of deceased Alexander Fraser of Ballindown, Inverness, and the said Colony of Demerara, for the gift of the estate of their sister, the deceased Hannah Fraser, 1839, GD23/10/732, National Archives of Scotland, Edinburgh, Scotland. Burial registers for St. Mary's Islington, cited on http://www.british-genealogy.com, indicate that Hannah Fraser died in England.

15. Of 143 Scots who left London indentured between 1682 and 1755, half went to Jamaica. Dobson, David, *Scottish Emigration to Colonial America, 1607–1785*, Athens, Georgia: University of Georgia Press, 1994, p. 123.

16. Alston, David, "Mackay (McCay) Macdonald," "Slaves and Highlanders," http://www.spanglefish.com/slavesandhighlanders, last accessed August 2012. The Jacobite transported to Barbados was Donald Mackay, and his son was John Mackay MacDonald, who owned Bloomfield Plantation in Berbice.

17. Alston, David, "Cumingsburg," "Slaves and Highlanders," http://www.spanglefish.com/slavesandhighlanders, last accessed August 2012.

18. Exhibit on emigration at The National Library of Scotland, Edinburgh, Scotland, 2009.

19. Mrs Fraser to Alexander Fraser, 15 September 1806, Bundle 28, Fraser of Reelig Papers, Reelig House, Kirkhill, Scotland.

20. William Young to Lady Sutherland, 1 July 1811, Dep313/1574.no16, Sutherland Papers, The National Archives of Scotland, Edinburgh, Scotland.

21. Rose Hall Fiscals Report, 27 May 1819, in Further Papers Relating to Slaves in the West Indies (Demerara and Berbice) [13 April 1824], p. 15, XXVI, no. 401, Parliamentary Papers, The British Library.

22. Major Fraser of Newburn Cottage, near Inverness, to his brother, 16 August 1823, GD23/10/712, National Archives of Scotland, Edinburgh, Scotland.

23. Roderick Macdonell to his father, 4 February 1809, Macdonell of Milnfield Papers, NAS D128/9/2, National Archives of Scotland, Edinburgh, Scotland.

24. Dobson, *Scottish Emigration to Colonial America*, p. 124.

25. "This practice of employing relatives or associates from the same part of Scotland as overseers or managers was widespread throughout the later part of the century. It was done in a manner that suggests the adaptation of some traditional forms of clan trusteeship to a more entrepreneurial imperial setting." Hamilton, Douglas, *Scotland, The Caribbean and The Atlantic World, 1750–1820*, Manchester: Manchester University Press, 2005, p. 55.

26. Ibid.

27. Sugar Plantations: Alleged Immoral Conduct of Overseers, 19 May 1930, File No. 75101, CO 111/688/5, Colonial Office Correspondence, Public Record Office, The National Archives of the UK, Kew.

11. SURVIVING HISTORY

1. The CIA World Factbook, 2011.

2. News clips, Gender Documentation Centre, The Ministry of Social Services, Georgetown, Guyana.

3. Ibid. The newspaper accounts indicate that fifty-five women were killed, allegedly by intimate partners, between 2007 and 2010.

4. According to the US Bureau of Justice Statistics, the rate of intimate partner murder in

the USA was 1.07 per 100,000 female residents. In both Canada and the UK, the rate of intimate partner murder for women was about 0.3 per 100,000 women, according to Home Office Statistics and Canadian police.

5. This account is based on author interviews with Cheryl Inderdeo, Ramnarine Seeram, Pastor Lucius Bruyning of the Rhema World Harvest Mission and e-mail, text and telephone conversations with Mahendra Seeram.

6. Ullah, Shabna, "Man hacks wife to death, wounds mother-in-law at Glasgow, Berbice," *The Stabroek News*, 28 March 2010. See online comments by Lizo Inderdeo, available at http://www.stabroeknews.com/2010/archives/03/28/man-hacks-wife-to-death-wounds-mother-in-law-at-glasgow-berbice/ and confirmed by the author in a telephone interview.

7. "Battered lives: domestic violence sends many to hospital," *Stabroek News*, 29 November 2010. Vanderbilt University researchers interviewed 180 female patients admitted to the trauma unit over two weeks in July 2010.

8. Persad, Basmat Shiv and George K. Danns, *Domestic Violence in the Caribbean: A Guyana Case Study*, Georgetown, Guyana: University of Guyana, 1989. The authors surveyed 110 women in Georgetown and its outskirts.

9. The Georgetown-based women's group Red Thread surveyed 360 women; 184 were abused.

10. Persad and Danns, *Domestic Violence in the Caribbean: A Guyana Case Study*.

11. "Intimate Partner Violence: Facts," World Health Organization, 2002, http://www.who.int/violence_injury_prevention/violence/world_report/factsheets/en/ipvfacts.pdf

12. "WHO Multi-Country Study on Women's Health and Domestic Violence Against Women," 2005, http://www.who.int/gender/violence/who_multicountry_study/Appendix-Index.pdf, last accessed 2012. The figure for physical abuse in urban Bangladesh is 37 percent and urban Peru 49 percent. For provincial Tanzania, it's 45 percent and provincial Ethiopia, 49 percent.

13. "Domestic Violence Against Women and Girls," Florence: Innocenti Research Center, UNICEF, 2000.

14. For the Barbados figure, see Clarke, Roberta, *Violence Against Women in the Caribbean: State and Non-State Responses*, UNIFEM, 1998, p. 10. The Trinidad figure comes from a randomized 1998 survey of 200 women by CAFRA, the Caribbean Association for Feminist Research and Action.

15. It ranks 117th of 187 nations in the UN Development Programme's Human Development Index. In the Western Hemisphere, only Haiti and Guatemala, Honduras and Nicaragua—in Central America—rank lower.

16. In the first half of 2011, gold exports brought $229 million in foreign currency into Guyana's coffers, while sugar exports brought in about $50 million. Gold and remittances were the top two sources of foreign currency.

17. UNDP Human Development Report, 2011, Statistical Tables.

18. The Bank of Guyana, Half-Year Report, 2011.

19. Help & Shelter founder Josephine Whitehead, interview by author, Georgetown, March 2011.

20. Lucas, Rawle, "Milking the cash cow," *The Stabroek News*, 18 September 2009. He argues that remittances contribute to declining productivity and income, because workers subsist on cash from relatives overseas.

21. Based on my review of newspaper clips at the Gender Documentation Centre of Guy-

ana's Ministry of Health and Human Services, twenty-one women died and allegations were made against intimate partners, eighteen credibly.

22. "Inconclusive autopsy thwarts charges in brutal death of Canje woman," *The Stabroek News*, 7 May 7 2010.

23. Asim Ruhomon, interview by author at his home in Canje, Guyana, March 2011.

24. "Canje woman found floating in canal with feet tied," *The Stabroek News*, 10 March 2010.

25. See "Inconclusive: justice delayed in suspicious deaths of four Women," *The Stabroek News*, 5 September 2010.

26. Guyana was ranked 134th of 183 countries on Transparency International's Corruption Index in 2011. Its score reflects high susceptibility to bribes, embezzlement of funds, kickbacks in public procurement.

27. Justice Roxanne George, interview by author, Georgetown, Guyana, August 2010.

28. "Campaign Against Sexual Violence," Guyana Human Rights Association leaflet, as cited in Insanally, Sarah, "The Response to Domestic Violence in Guyana," submitted to the National Task Force on Domestic Violence, January 2007. The leaflet declared that women were "repelled by the legal process" because they believe witnesses, court officials and police will be bribed and witnesses intimidated.

29. Insanally, "The Response to Domestic Violence in Guyana," accessed at the Guyana Ministry of Labour, Human Services and Social Security's Gender Documentation Centre in Georgetown.

30. "I can see the guilt [in many cases] but the police didn't handle the scene right. They don't know what to look for. A lot of times people get off because police haven't investigated properly. We do not have intelligent young men and young women." Tejnarine Ramroop, interview by author, Blairmont, Berbice, August 2010.

31. "Inconclusive: justice delayed in suspicious deaths of four women," *The Stabroek News*, 5 September 2010.

32. Bharrat, Sara, "Relatives say Cane Grove woman died from beating," *The Stabroek News*, 17 March 2010.

33. Ibid.

34. "Cane Grove woman died of a heart attack," *The Stabroek News*, 18 March 2010.

35. "Family of dead Cane Grove woman file complaint over police investigation," *The Stabroek News*, 24 April 2010.

36. "Boladass's relatives determined to secure justice," *The Stabroek News*, 26 March 2010.

37. "Case closed, crime chief says of cane grove woman's death," *The Stabroek News*, 19 March 2010.

38. Ibid.

39. Persad and Danns, *Domestic Violence in the Caribbean: A Guyana Case Study*, p. 126. The sociologists analyzed how police across Guyana treated reports of abuse. Police failed to detain, charge or prosecute perpetrators in 86 percent of cases. In only 7 percent of cases did the women themselves ask police not to take any action.

40. Ibid., p. 128.

41. Insanally, "Response to Domestic Violence," p. 24.

42. Ibid., p. 22.

43. Ibid.

44. Ibid., p. 19. Guyana is a signatory to the Convention on the Elimination of Discrimination Against Women.

45. Jayawardena, Chandra, "Interim Report on a Study of Social Structure and Processes of

Social Control Amongst East Indian Sugar Workers in British Guiana," unpublished paper, Instititute of Social and Economic Research, University College of the West Indies, 1957, p. 11.

46. Kissoon, Vidyaratha, Letter to the Editor, *The Stabroek News*, 5 August 2010.

47. "The Surgeon-General repeat[ed] that he does not agree with the practice of giving medicated rum to the emigrants." Register of Colonial Office Correspondence, 1905–1908, CO 345/18, Colonial Office Correspondence, Public Record Office, The National Archives of the UK, Kew.

48. Tinker, *A New System*, pp. 212–13. The governor of Mauritius observed: "I have seen, since I came to Mauritius, more instances of drunkenness among Indians than I witnessed during the whole period of my service in India."

49. Half the women counselled by Help & Shelter for spousal abuse said their husbands were under the influence at the time, the group's intake statistics indicate. In the Persad and Danns study, 88 percent of battered women reported that their partners had been drinking when they attacked, and 95 percent of women married to regular drinkers reported being hit by their spouses. Two more recent studies also point to a strong correlation between alcohol use and domestic abuse: an unpublished 1996 paper by Josephine Whitehead, cited in Insanally, and "Final Draft Survey Research on Gender-Based Violence in Guyana: The Incidences and Drivers," 2010, commissioned by UNFPA and Guyana's Ministry of Labour, Human Services and Social Security.

50. "Magistrate blames alcohol for spiralling domestic violence in Berbice," *Kaieteur News*, 28 July 2010.

51. Priya Manickchand, interview by author, Georgetown, March 2011.

52. Tejnarine Ramroop, interview by author, Blairmont, Berbice, Guyana. August 2010.

53. Mahabir, Joy, "Poetics of Space in the Works of Mahadai Das and Adesh Samaroo," *Anthurium: A Caribbean Studies Journal*, 7, 1, article 11 (2010), p. 7.

54. Angrosino, Michael V., "Rum and Ganja: Indenture, Drug Foods, Labor Motivation and the Evolution of the Modern Sugar Industry in Trinidad," *Drugs, Labor and Colonial Expansion*, Phoenix, Arizona: University of Arizona Press, 2003, pp. 101–16.

55. Alleged Instances of Intemperance Among Indians, 19 April 1883, File No. 8145, CO 384/144, Colonial Office Correspondence, Public Record Office, The National Archives of the UK, Kew. Trinidad's governor argued that any restrictions on rum or increase in licence fees would be useless, while ganja was the greater evil and needed to be regulated.

56. Angrosino, "Rum and Ganja," p. 107.

57. Ramnarine, Tyran, "The Growth of the East Indian Community in British Guiana, 1880–1920," unpublished doctoral thesis, University of Sussex, 1977. In 1901, 20 percent of Indian children were in school. Two decades later, 29 percent were, while the vast majority of black, Portuguese and Chinese children were enrolled.

58. Ibid. In 1898, 210 of 223 schools in the colony were church-run. Plantations ran the remaining thirteen. The first state-sponsored school was built in 1926.

59. Poynting, Jeremy, "East Indian Women in the Caribbean: Experience and Voice," *India in the Caribbean*, Dabydeen, David and Brinsley Samaroo (eds), London: Hansib Publishing Ltd., 1987, p. 236. In 1925, only 25 percent of the Indian children in primary schools were girls. Of Indians who could read and write in English in 1931, only 30 percent were female. As late as 1947, only 6 percent of Indians who had property and income enough to entitle them to the vote were women.

60. UNDP Human Development Report, 2011, Statistical Tables. Guyana ranked 106 out of 187 countries, Trinidad 53 and Jamaica 81.

61. The World Economic Forum Global Gender Gap Report, 2011.

62. It ranked as a top reason that women stayed with abusers in the Guyana Ministry of Labour, Human Services and Social Security and UNFPA report, the 1998 Red Thread survey and the Persad and Danns report. My interviews with stakeholders—social workers, magistrates, victims and others—indicate that as well.

63. Persad and Danns, *Domestic Violence in the Caribbean: A Guyana Case Study*, p. 15.

64. A 23 May 2012 report to the UN General Assembly by the UN Special Rapporteur on Violence Against Women noted an increase in gender-related killings worldwide. A December 2005 UNIFEM/ECLAC report on the Caribbean, "Eliminating Gender-Based Violence, Ensuring Equality," cited studies suggesting an increase in rapes and sexual offences as well as a widespread perception that domestic violence is on the rise in the region.

65. Trotz, Alissa, "Stop the Slaughter," *The Stabroek News*, 10 August 2009.

66. *Fifty Years is Enough: The Case Against the World Bank and the International Monetary Fund*, Cambridge, Massachusetts: South End Press, 1994, p. 124.

67. Rodney, Walter, *A History of the Guyanese Working People*, Baltimore: Johns Hopkins University Press, 1981, p. 36.

68. Mohapatra, Prabhu P., "Wife Murders and the Making of a Sexual Contract for Indian Immigrant Labour in the British Caribbean Colonies," *Studies in History*, 11, 2 (1995).

69. A social worker, a High Court judge and a pastor in charge of the newly created Men's Affairs Bureau in Guyana's government all told me that intimate partner murders seemed to be increasing.

70. Adinkrah, Mensah, "Spousal Homicides in Fiji," *Homicide Studies*, 3, 3 (August 1999), pp. 215–40. From 1982–1992, Indians were 43 percent of the population but 66 percent of killers and 62 percent of victims.

71. From 1990—1994, 26 women were killed by intimate partners, according a 1999 report by UNDP's Inter-Agency Campaign on Violence Against Women and Girls. From 1995—2006, 124 women were killed by intimate partners, according to a CARICOM-funded study of cases in Trinidad's Homicide Bureau of Investigation files.

72. Clarke, Roberta and Jackie Sealy-Burke, "Eliminating Gender-Based Violence, Ensuring Equality," Barbados: United Nations Development Fund for Women and Economic Commission for Latin America and the Caribbean, December 2005.

73. Poynting, "East Indian Women in the Caribbean," p. 234.

74. Naipaul, V.S., *The Middle Passage*, London: Picador, 1996, p. 96.

75. Mohammed, Patricia, *Gender Negotiations Among Indians in Trinidad, 1917–1945*, Palgrave, 2002, p. 167.

76. Maharaji Bahoori, born on Plantation Lusignan in 1915, interview by author, Long Island, Summer 2010.

77. Crooke, William, *The Popular Religion and Folk-Lore of Northern India*, Volume 2, London: Archibald Constable & Co., 1896, p. 32.

78. Edna Baisakhu, phone interview by author, October 2011.

79. Social worker Reubena Marshall, interview by author, New Amsterdam, March 2011. Tejnarine Ramroop, interview by author, Blairmont, Berbice, August 2010.

80. Persad and Danns, *Domestic Violence in the Caribbean: A Guyana Case Study*, p. 57. The study found that 71 percent of men who witnessed men in their family beat women

became wife beaters; 48 percent who never witnessed such behaviour did; and 97 percent of men beaten as children did. UNIFEM's Regional Assessment to End Violence Against Women in the Caribbean (2005) cites studies across the Caribbean with similar findings.

81. "No new leads in Crabwood Creek murders," *Kaieteur News*, 15 March 2010.

82. "Crabwood Creek woman was strangled," *Kaieteur News*, 4 March 2010.

83. "Son grieves for abusive mother," *Kaieteur News*, 22 March 2010.

84. Notes on medical referral sheet to physical therapist, Donna Bovell-Sinclair, Georgetown Public Hospital.

85. "Mon Repos businessman dead, wife in serious condition," *The Guyana Chronicle*, 11 August 2010.

86. Latchmin Mohabir, interview by author, Georgetown Public Hospital, 27 January 2011.

87. Latchmin Mohabir, interview by author, Triumph, Demerara, 23 August 2010.

88. Latchmin Mohabir, interview by author, Georgetown, Guyana, March, 2011.

BIBLIOGRAPHY

1. MANUSCRIPT SOURCES

Essex Record Office, Essex, England

Henry Bullock Papers, Letters and Photos from Berbice, Guyana, D/DVv 74.

Public Record Office, The (UK) National Archives, Kew

Colonial Office Documents

CO 111/161–166, Original Correspondence on Gladstone Coolies, 1838–1839.

CO 111/404–405, Despatches and Ship Reports, 1875.

CO 111/487–562, Despatches between the Colonial Office and the Governor, Crown Agents, Board of Trade, Individuals, Admiralty and India Office, 1896–1908.

CO 111/588–592, Despatches relating to the "Rose Hall Riot", 1913.

CO 571/3, Emigration Letter Books for the West Indies and Fiji, 1915.

CO 571/5, Emigration Letter Books for the West Indies and Fiji, 1917.

CO 384/180–192, Emigration Despatches, West Indies, 1891–1896.

CO 384/144, Arrival of the Ship Silhet, Case of Dr Atkins and Janky, 1883.

CO 386/97, Land and Emigration Commission Despatches, 1869–1873.

CO 111/688/5, Confidential Papers on Alleged Immoral Conduct of Overseer, 1930.

India Office Records, The British Library, St. Pancras

Government of India Proceedings on Emigration:

1876, Report of the Commissioners Appointed to Inquire into the Treatment of Immigrants from India on Board the Immigrant Ship Ailsa, P/932.

1882, Report on System of Recruiting Labourers for the Colonies, (Major D.G. Pitcher's Report), P/2057.

1883, Report on Colonial Emigration (George Grierson's Report), P/2058.

1883, Memo by W.H. Smith on Defects and Abuses in Immigration Department, British Guiana, P/2058.

1903, Report of the Protector of Emigrants on Emigration from the Port of Calcutta, P/6830.

BIBLIOGRAPHY

Public and Judicial Departmental Papers, Annual Files:

1884, "Conduct of the Crew of the Hesperides to Trinidad," L/PJ/6/133.

1884, "Emigration to Fiji and WI: Question of Employing Lascar Crews on Vessels," L/PJ/6/119.

1885, "Bill to Amend the Immigration Ordinance in British Guiana; Memo by Attorney General W.F. Haynes Smith on Treatment of Women, Crime and Divorce," L/PJ/166.

1888, "New Marriage Ordinance for British Guiana," L/PJ/6/219.

1889, "Handbook for Surgeons Superintendent of the Coolie Emigration Service" (James Laing), in L/PJ/6/249.

1889, "Emigrant Ships; Resolutions of Surgeons Superintendent of Coolie Emigrant Vessels," L/PJ/6/252.

1893, Comins, Major D.W.D., "Note on Emigration from India to British Guiana," in L/PJ/6/357.

1894, "Application from Mr Solomon for Release of the Female Emigrant Sukdai," L/PJ/6/378.

1894, "Employment of Negro Sailors on Ships Conveying Coolies Between India and the Colonies," L/PJ/6/378.

1895, "Emigration to Surinam; Application for Release from Contract by Sukdai, a Female Immigrant," L/PJ/6/391.

1895, "Surinam Emigration: Case of Woman Sukdai," L/PJ/6/398.

1895, "Employment of Negroes and Mulattoes … and the Discharge of Refactory Sailors at Ports of Call," L/PJ/6/393.

1899, "Misconduct of an Overseer in British Guiana" (Complaint by Bechu), L/PJ/6/226.

1902, "Voyage of the Ship Main from Calcutta to British Guiana," L/PJ/6/621.

1902, "Emigration to British Guiana: Report on the Voyage of the Ship Main," L/PJ/6/600.

1903, "Voyage of the Emigrant Ship Main…; Question of Employing Black or Coloured Crew Members," L/PJ/6/632.

1906, "Notification Under the Emigration Act Regarding the Separation of the Crew from Female Emigrants on Emigrant Vessels," L/PJ/6/787.

India Office Family History Records:

Birth and Baptism Records for Thomas Dealtry Atkins, N/1/68 f.30.

Burial Record for Olivia Harrison Atkins, N/1/289 f.23.

Birth and Baptism Records for Olivia Harrison, N/1/10 f.117.

Marriage Record in Calcutta for Reverend T. Atkins of Allipore and Miss Harrison, East India Register, 1840.

Parliamentary Papers, The British Library, St. Pancras

1843, Correspondence Relating to the Return of Coolies from British Guiana to India, British Parliamentary Papers, XXV (404).

1874, Report on Emigration from India (J. Geoghegan), British Parliamentary Papers (annual series), XLVII (314).

1910, Report of the Committee on Emigration from India to the Crown Colonies and Protectorates (Lord Sanderson Commission), British Parliamentary Papers, XXVII (Cd. 5192–94).

BIBLIOGRAPHY

1915, Report on the Condition of Indian Immigrants in Four British Colonies Trinidad, British Guiana or Demerara, Jamaica and Fiji and in the Dutch Colony of Surinam or Dutch Guiana (James McNeill and Chimman Lal Report), British Parliamentary Papers (annual series), XLVII (Cd. 7744).

Asia, Pacific and Africa Printed Books and Serials, The British Library, St. Pancras

Andrews, C.F. and W.W. Pearson, Report on Indentured Labour in Fiji, Allahabad: The Leader Press, 1916, P/V 160.
Sharma, Lalbihari, *Damra Phag Bahar: Holi Songs of Demerara*, 1916, Hin.B.424/4.

Newspaper Collection, The British Library, Colindale

The Demerara Daily Chronicle, 1903–1904.

Map Collection, The British Library, St. Pancras

A sketch map of the coast of British Guiana. Edward Stanford Ltd., 1900. Maps x.7046.
Sketch map of New Amsterdam, British Guiana. Great Britain, General Staff, Geographical Section, 1910. Maps MOD GSGS 2545.

Manchester University, John Rylands Library

Clips from International Women's Suffrage Alliance.
IWSA 3/105, India, 1915–1919.
IWSA 3/118, Prostitution, 1916–1919.

The National Archives of Scotland, Edinburgh

1782, Last Will and Testament of William Steele, Planter, Demerara, GD1/470/1.
1809, Last Will and Testament of Peter Gordon, of Berbice, GD23/7/39.
1818, Last Will and Testament of Alexander Fraser, of the Colony of Essequibo, GD23/10/694.
1823, Letter from Major Fraser of Inverness to his brother, GD23/10/712.
1839, Petition to the Commissioners of HM Treasury by Marjory Fraser et al, GD23/10/732.
1888, Last Will and Testament of Peter McClaren, Plantation Zeeburg, CS46/11/31.
1874, Journal of Plantation De Willem, GD314/54.

New York Public Library

Annual Reports of the Immigration Agent-General of British Guiana, 1897–1917, SEV+.

Walter Rodney Archives, Georgetown

Confidential Report from Inspector General of Police on Nonpareil Riot, No. 6457, 14 October 1896.
The Ship Manifest of *The Clyde*, 1903.

BIBLIOGRAPHY

The Ship Manifest of *The Silhet*, 1883.
The Ship Manifest of *The Main*, 1902.
The Ship Manifest of *The Ganges*, 1893.
The Ship Manifest of *The Forth*, 1899.
The Ship Manifest of *The Bann*, 1892.
The Ship Manifest of *The Malabar*, 1880.
The Casual Register, 1892.

Caribbean Collection, University of Guyana Library, Georgetown

"The coolie riots in Essequibo," Pamphlet printed in Georgetown: The Colonist Office, 1873.

Private Archives

Fraser of Reelig Papers, Inverness.
British Guiana Law Reports, Law Offices of Cameron & Shepherd, Georgetown.

2. UNPUBLISHED PAPERS AND DISSERTATIONS

Platt, John, "Enmore and its Devon links." Paper presented at the Woodbury Historical Society, Devon, England, 2009.
Rabe, Elizabeth R, "A Social History of Indentured Indian Immigration to British Guiana and Trinidad, 1854–1884," PhD dissertation, University of the West Indies, St. Augustine, 2006.
Ramachandran, Tanisha, "Three Tellings, Four Models and Different Perceptions: The Construction of Female Sexuality in the *Ramayana*," PhD dissertation, Concordia University, 2000.
Ramnarine, Tyran, "The Growth of the East Indian Community in British Guiana, 1880–1920," PhD dissertation, University of Sussex, 1977.
Seenarine, Moses, "Recasting Indian Women," *Colonial Guyana: Gender, Labour and Caste in the Lives of Indentured and Free Labourers*, Saxakali Web Publications, 1996. Made available by the author.
Singh, Alice Bhagwandy, "Autobiography of Alice Bhagwandy Sital Persaud, 1892–1958." Unpublished manuscript held in Special Collections, University of Guyana Library.
Tiwari, Rampersaud, "My Elders and the Nonpareil Uprising of Oct. 13, 1896." Paper presented at 2011 South Asian Diaspora Conference, University of the West Indies, St. Augustine, Trinidad and Tobago.

3. NEWSPAPERS

The Demerara Daily Chronicle, 1903–1904. Newspaper Collection, Colindale, The British Library.
The Stabroek News, Georgetown, Guyana, 2007–2010. Online archives accessed at http://www.stabroeknews.com
Clippings on wife murders from *The Guyana Chronicle*, *Kaietur News* and *The Stabroek News*, 2007–2011. Gender Documentation Centre, Ministry of Human Services, Georgetown, Guyana.

BIBLIOGRAPHY

4. BOOKS AND PERIODICAL ARTICLES: PRIMARY SOURCE

Andrews, C.F., *Impressions of British Guiana, 1930*, Chicago: Adams Press, 2007.

Angel, Captain W.H., *The Clipper Ship Sheila*, London: Heath Cranton Limited, 1921.

Bayley, George D., (ed.), *Handbook of British Guiana*, Georgetown: The Argosy Company, Ltd., 1909.

Beaumont, Joseph, *The New Slavery: An Account of the Indian and Chinese Immigrants in British Guiana*, London: self-published, 1871.

Bronkhurst, H.V.P., *The Colony of British Guiana and its Labouring Population*, London: published for the author by T. Woolmer, 1883.

———. *Among the Hindus and Creoles of British Guiana*, London: published for the author by T. Woolmer, 1888.

Burton, Rev. John Wear, *The Fiji of Today*, London: Charles H. Kelley, 1910.

Des Voeux, George William, *Experiences of a Demerara Magistrate, 1863–1869*, Reprint Georgetown: Daily Chronicle, 1948.

Duff, Rev. Robert, *British Guiana*, Glasgow: Thomas Murray & Son, 1866.

Gandhi, Mohandas K., *The Collected Works of Mahatma Gandhi* (Electronic Book, Volume 15), Delhi: Publications Division, Government of India, 1999.

Gill, Walter, *Turn North-East at the Tombstone*, London: Robert Hale Ltd., 1969.

Grierson, George Abraham, *Bihar Peasant Life, Being a Discursive Catalogue of the Surroundings of the People of that Province*, Calcutta: The Bengal Secretariat Press, 1885.

Hill, Arthur Harvey, "Emigration from India," *Timehri*, 6 (1919), pp. 43–52.

Jenkins, John Edward, *The Coolie: His Rights and His Wrongs*, New York: George Routledge & Sons, 1871.

Josa, Archdeacon Fortunato, "The Hindus in the West Indies," *Timehri*, 3 (1913), pp. 25–31.

Khan, Munshi Rahman, *Jeevan Prakash: Autobiography of an Indian Indentured Labourer*, Delhi: Shipra Publications, 2005.

Kirke, Henry, "Our Criminal Classes," *Timehri*, II (New Series, 1888), pp. 3–15.

———. *Twenty-Five Years in British Guiana*, London: Sampson Low, Marston & Company Limited, 1898.

Kirkpatrick, Margery, *From the Middle Kingdom to the New World: Aspects of the Chinese Experience in Migration to British Guiana*, Georgetown: self-published, 1993.

Lubbock, Alfred Basil, *Coolie Ships and Oil Sailers*, Glasgow: Brown, Son and Ferguson, Ltd., 1935.

Naipaul, V.S., *Finding the Centre*, London: Penguin, 1985.

Phillips, Leslie H.C., "Single Men in Barracks: Some Memories of Sugar Plantation Life," *Timehri*, 40 (1961), pp. 23–34.

Richmond, Theophilus, *The First Crossing*, Dabydeen, David and Ian McDonald (eds), Georgetown: The Government of Guyana, 2010.

Rodney, Walter, (ed.), *Guyanese Sugar Plantations in the Late 19th Century: A Contemporary Description from the Argosy, 1882*, Georgetown: Release Publishers, 1979.

Ruhomon, Peter, *Centenary History of East Indians in British Guiana, 1838–1938*, Georgetown: The Daily Chronicle, 1947.

Sanadhya, Totaram, *My Twenty-One Years in the Fiji Islands*, Suva: The Fiji Museum, 1991.

Sannyasi, Bhawani Dayal and Benarsidas Chaturvedi, *A Report on the Emigrants Repatriated to India under the Assisted Emigration Scheme and On the Problem of Returned Emigrants from All Colonies*, Calcutta, India: self-published pamphlet, 1931.

BIBLIOGRAPHY

Scoble, John, *Hill Coolies: A Brief Exposure of the Deplorable Conditions of the Hill Coolies in British Guiana and Mauritius and of the Nefarious Means by Which They Were Induced to Resort to These Colonies*, London: Harvey and Darton, 1840.

Thorpe, F.C., *The Overseer's Manual, or a Guide to the Canefield and the Sugar Factory*, 3rd edition. Georgetown: Argosy Press, 1896.

Vatuk, Ved Prakash, "Protest Songs of British Guiana," *The Journal of American Folklore*, 77, 305 (1964), pp. 220–35.

5. BOOKS AND PERIODICAL ARTICLES: SECONDARY SOURCE

Adrinkah, Mensah, "Spousal Homicides in Fiji," *Homicide Studies*, 3, (1999), pp. 215–40.

Ali, Ahmed, *Plantation to Politics: Studies on Fiji Indians*, Suva: University of the South Pacific and The Fiji Times & Herald Limited, 1980.

Alston, David, "Very Rapid and Splendid Fortunes? Highland Scots in Berbice in the Early 19th Century," *Transactions of the Gaelic Society of Inverness*, 63, (2006), pp. 208–31.

Angrosino, Michael V., "Rum and Ganja: Indenture, Drug Foods, Labor Motivation and the Evolution of the Modern Sugar Industry in Trinidad," *Drugs, Labor and Colonial Expansion*, Phoenix: University of Arizona Press, 2003, pp. 101–16.

Banerjee, Sumanta, *Under the Raj: Prostitution in Colonial Bengal*, Calcutta: Seagull Books, 1998.

Bhardwaj, Surinder Mohan, *Hindu Places of Pilgrimage in India: A Study in Cultural Geography*, Berkeley: University of California Press, 1973.

Bhattacharya, Malini, "The Hidden Violence of Faith: The Widows of Vrindaban," *Social Scientist*, 29, 1–2 (2001), pp. 75–83.

Carter, Marina and Khal Torabully, *Coolitude: An Anthology of the Indian Labour Diaspora*, London: Anthem Press, 2002.

Carter, Marina, *Lakshmi's Legacy: The Testimonies of Women in 19th Century Mauritius*, Mauritius: Editions de L'Ocean Indien, 1994.

Dalrymple, William, *White Mughals: Love and Betrayal in 18th Century India*, London: Penguin Books, 2004.

Das, Arvind, *The Republic of Bihar*, New Delhi: Penguin Books, 1992.

Dimock Jr, Edward C., *The Place of the Hidden Moon: Erotic Mysticism in the Vaisnava-Sahijaya Cult of Bengal*, Chicago: University of Chicago Press, 1966.

Diptee, Audra, "Cultural Transfer and Transformation: Revisiting Indo-Afro Sexual Relationships in Trinidad and British Guiana in the Late 19th Century," *The Society for Caribbean Studies Annual Conference Papers*, 4 (2003), pp. 1–19.

Dobson, David, *Scottish Emigration to Colonial America, 1607–1785*, Athens, Georgia: University of Georgia Press, 1994.

Doniger, Wendy, *The Hindus: An Alternative History*, New York: Penguin, 2009.

Emmer, P.C., "The Great Escape: The Migration of Female Indentured Servants from British India to Surinam: 1873–1916," *Abolition and its Aftermath*, David Richardson, (ed.), London: Frank Cass & Company Limited, 1985, pp. 245–66.

Faruqee, Ashrufa, "Conceiving the Coolie Woman: Indentured Labour, Indian Women and Colonial Discourse," *South Asia Research*, 16, 1 (1996), pp. 61–76.

Ferguson, Niall, *Empire: The Rise and Demise of the British World Order And The Lessons for Global Power*, New York: Basic Books, 2004.

BIBLIOGRAPHY

Hamilton, Douglas J., *Scotland, the Caribbean and the Atlantic World, 1750–1820*, Manchester: Manchester University Press, 2005.

Hochschild, Adam, *Bury the Chains: Prophets and Rebels in the Fight to Free an Empire's Slaves*, New York: Houghton Mifflin, 2005.

Hoefte, Rosemarijn, *In Place of Slavery*, Gainesville: University of Florida Press, 1998.

Hyam, Ronald, *Empire and Sexuality: The British Experience*, Manchester: Manchester University Press, 1990.

Jayawardena, Chandra, "Religious Belief and Social Change: Aspects of the Development of Hinduism in British Guiana," *Comparative Studies in Society and History*, 8, 2 (1966), pp. 211–40.

Kelly, John, *A Politics of Virtue: Hinduism, Sexuality and Countercultural Discourse in Fiji*, Chicago: University of Chicago Press, 1992.

Lal, Brij V., "Kunti's Cry: Indentured Women on Fiji Plantations," *Indian Economic and Social History Review*, 22, 1 (1985), pp. 55–72.

———. "Veil of Dishonour: Sexual Jealousy and Suicide on Fiji plantations," *The Journal of Pacific History*, 20, 3 (1985), pp. 135–55.

Laurence, K.O., *A Question of Labour: Indentured Immigration into Trinidad and British Guiana, 1875–1917*, Kingston: Ian Randle Publishers, 1994.

Lazarus-Black, Mindie, *Everyday Harm: Domestic Violence, Court Rites and Cultures of Reconciliation*, Chicago: University of Illinois Press, 2007.

Look Lai, Walton, *Indentured Labor, Caribbean Sugar: Chinese and Indian Migrants to the British West Indies, 1838–1918*, Baltimore: Johns Hopkins University Press, 1993.

Mahabir, Joy, "The Poetics of Space in the Works of Mahadai Das and Adesh Samaroo," *Anthurium: A Caribbean Studies Journal*, 7, 1 (2010), Article 11, pp. 1–18.

Mangru, Basdeo, "The Sex Ratio Disparity and its Consequences Under Indenture in British Guiana," *India in the Caribbean*, Dabydeen, David and Brinsley Samaroo (eds), London: Hansib, 1987, pp. 211–30.

Manuel, Peter, *East Indian Music in the West Indies: Tan Singing, Chutney and the Making of Indo-Caribbean Culture*, Philadelphia: Temple University Press, 2000.

Mohammed, Patricia, *Gender Negotiations Among Indians in Trinidad, 1917–1945*, New York: Institute of Social Studies in association with Palgrave, 2002.

Mohapatra, Prabhu P., "Following Custom? Representations of Community Among Indian Immigrant Labour in the West Indies, 1880–1920," *Coolies, Capital and Colonialism: Studies in Indian Labour History*, Behal, Rana P. and Marcel van der Linden (eds), Cambridge: The Press Syndicate of the University of Cambridge, 2004, pp. 173–202.

———. "Longing and Belonging: The Dilemma of Return Among Indian Immigrants in the West Indies, 1850–1950," *Research in Progress Series, History and Society*, Third Series. New Delhi: Centre for Contemporary Studies, Nehru Memorial Museum and Library, 1998.

———. "Wife Murders and the Making of a Sexual Contract for Indian Immigrant Labour in the British Caribbean Colonies,' *Studies in History*, 11, 2 (1995), pp. 227–60.

Moore, Brian L., *Cultural Power, Resistance and Pluralism in Colonial Guyana, 1838–1900*, Montreal: McGill-Queens University Press, 1995.

Naidu, Vijay, *The Violence of Indenture in Fiji*, Suva: World University Service, in association with the University of the South Pacific, 1980.

Nath, Dwarka, *A History of Indians in Guyana*, Georgetown: The Government of British Guiana, 1950.

BIBLIOGRAPHY

Niranjana, Tejaswini, *Mobilizing India: Women, Music, and Migration Between India and Trinidad*, Durham: Duke University Press, 2006.

Pinch, Vijay, "Gosain Tawaif: Slaves, Sex and Ascetics in Rasdhan, 1800–1857," *Modern Asian Studies*, 38, 3 (2004), pp. 559–97.

Poynting, Jeremy, "East Indian Women in the Caribbean: Experience and Voice," *India in the Caribbean*, Dabydeen, David and Brinsley Samaroo, (eds), London: Hansib, 1987, pp. 231–263.

Ramdin, Ron, *The Other Middle Passage: Journal of a Voyage from Calcutta to Trinidad, 1858*, London: Hansib, 1994.

Ramesar, Marianne Soares, "The Repatriates," *Across the Dark Waters: Ethnicity and Indian Identity in the Caribbean*, Dabydeen, David and Brinsley Samaroo (eds), London: Macmillan Education Ltd., 1996, pp. 175–200.

Ramnarine, Tyran, "One Hundred Years of Disturbances on the Sugar Estates of Guyana, 1869–1978: A Historical Overview," *India in the Caribbean*, Dabydeen, David and Brinsley Samaroo, (eds), London: Hansib, 1987, pp. 119–144.

Reddock, Rhoda, "Freedom Denied: Indian Women and Indentureship in Trinidad and Tobago, 1845–1917," *Economic and Political Weekly*, XX, 43 (1985), pp. 79–87.

———. "The Search for Origins, Women and Division of Labour During Slavery and Indentureship," *Women, Labour and Politics in Trinidad and Tobago*, London: Zed Books, 1994.

Rodney, Walter, *A History of the Guyanese Working People, 1881–1905*, Baltimore: The Johns Hopkins University Press, 1981.

Samaroo, Brinsley, "Homeward Bound: The Last Return Ship to India in 1955," Introduction to *The First Crossing*, Coventry: The Derek Walcott Press, 2007, pp. xlvii-lxi.

Seecharan, Clem, *Bechu: Bound Coolie Radical in British Guiana, 1894–1901*, Kingston: University of the West Indies Press, 1999.

———. "Guyana," *The Encyclopedia of the Indian Diaspora*, Lal, Brij, Reeves, Peter and Rajesh Rai (eds), Honolulu: University of Hawaii Press, 2006, pp. 287–97.

Sen, Nabaneeta Dev, "When Women Retell the *Ramayan*," *Manushi*, 108, (1998), pp. 18–27.

Shameen, Shaista, "Migration, Labour and Plantation Women in Fiji," *Women Plantation Workers: International Experiences*, Jain, Shobita and Rhoda Reddock (eds), Oxford: Berg, 1998.

Shepherd, Verene, "Constructing Visibility: Indian Women in the Jamaican Segment of the Indian Diaspora," *Gendered Realities: Essays in Caribbean Feminist Thought*, Mohammed, Patricia (ed.), Kingston: University of the West Indies Press, 2002.

———. "Sex in the tropics," *I Want to Disturb My Neighbour: Lectures on Slavery, Emancipation and Postcolonial Jamaica*, Kingston: Ian Randle, 2007.

———. *Maharani's Misery*, Kingston: University of the West Indies Press, 2002.

Sue-A-Quan, Trev, *Cane Reapers: Chinese Indentured Immigrants in Guyana*, Vancouver: Cane Press, 1999.

Tambe, Ashwini, *Codes of Misconduct: Regulating Prostitution in Late Colonial Bombay*, Minneapolis: University of Minnesota Press, 2009.

Tinker, Hugh Russell, *A New System of Slavery: The Export of Indian Labour Overseas, 1830–1920*, London: Hansib, 1993.

Urban, Hugh, *The Economics of Ecstasy: Tantra, Secrecy and Power in Colonial Bengal*, New York: Oxford University Press, 2001.

BIBLIOGRAPHY

6. ORAL SOURCES (Other than interviews by the author)

Oral and Pictorial Records Programme, Alma Jordan Library, University of the West Indies, St. Augustine

Trinidad Bhojpuri Speakers, Interviews by Peggy Mohan, 1978, OP55.

East Indian Family and Gender Relations, Interviews by Patricia Mohammed, 1990–1991, OP62.

East Indian Immigration, Interviews by Noor Kumar Mahabir, 1982, OP13.

Linton Gibbon, Interview by his granddaughter Lucila Gibbon, 1976, OP70. As part of the crew of *The Forth*, Gibbon sailed with returnees to India in 1902.

East Indians in Trinidad, Interviews by Rosabelle Seesaran, 1990–1991, OP60.

Transcripts of Interviews with Ex-Indentured and Others

"The Indenture Experience in Fiji," *Bulletin of the Fiji Museum*, 5 (1979). Transcripts of interviews conducted in Hindi by Ahmed Ali with two dozen ex-indentured labourers at The Old People's Home in Suva, in Lautoka and in Labasa.

Mahabir, Noor Kumar, *The Still Cry*, Tacarigua, Trinidad: Calaloux Publications, 1985.

Mohabir, Nalini and Hyacinth Simpson, "*Resurgent* (Rise Again)," *Interventions* 8, 3 (2011), pp. 487–505. Interview between Chablall Ramcharan, officer on the last immigrant ship back to India, and his grand-niece.

Naidu, Vijay, *The Violence of Indenture in Fiji*, Suva: World University Service, in association with the University of the South Pacific, 1980. Including transcripts of interviews with fifteen ex-indentured men and women.

Prasad, Shiu, *Indian Indentured Workers in Fiji*, Suva: The South Pacific Social Sciences Association, 1974. Pamphlet including transcripts of interviews with more than twenty elderly ex-indentured.

7. FICTION AND POETRY

Buck, William, *Ramayana*, Berkeley: University of California Press, 1976.

Das, Mahadai, *Bones*, Leeds: Peepal Tree Press, 1988.

They Came In Ships: An Anthology of Indo-Guyanese Prose and Poetry, Edited by Joel Benjamin, Lakshmi Kallicharan, Ian McDonald and Lloyd Searwar, Leeds: Peepal Tree Press, 1998.

Espinet, Ramabai, *The Swinging Bridge*, Toronto: HarperCollins, 2003.

Ghosh, Amitav, *Sea of Poppies*, New York: Farrar, Straus & Giroux, 2008.

Jenkins, John Edward, *Lutchmee and Dilloo*, London: William Mullan & Son, 1877.

Ladoo, Harold Sonny, *No Pain Like This Body*, Toronto: House of Anansi Press, Ltd., 2003.

Menon, Ramesh, *The Ramayana: The Great Indian Epic Rendered in Modern Prose*, New York: Farrar, Straus and Giroux, 2003.

Mohan, Peggy, *Jahajin*, New Delhi: HarperCollins, 2007.

Narayan, R.K., *The Ramayana*, New York: Penguin Books USA, 1977.

Tulsidas, *Sri Ramacaritmanasa: The Manasa Lake Brimming Over With the Exploits of Sri Rama*, Gorakhpur, India: Gita Press, 2004.

Webber, A.R.F., *Those That Be in Bondage*, Georgetown: The Daily Chronicle Printing Press, 1917, Reprinted Wellesley: Callaloux Publications, 1988.

INDEX